Sufism, Culture, and Politics

'...[T]he study brings to light new evidence, as it is meticulously researched and grounded on a sturdy bedrock of original Persian sources...Secondly, the book makes a significant contribution to our understanding of the place of the Afghans in India's medieval history...'
—Richard M. Eaton, Professor of History,
University of Arizona

'The value of this book is in its careful reappraisal of the well-known Persian sources and presentation of a thorough overview of an often ignored era...a useful addition to the study of the Afghan period in medieval India and...on the social roles and personalities of the Sufis in the period.'
—David W. Damrel, *Journal of Islamic Studies*

'Aquil's book...attempts a refreshingly nuanced approach to the emerging history of the period, using current research and primary Persian sources to produce a book of astonishing detail on the political influences that the Afghan rulers had...in medieval times.'
—Serene Kasim, *South Asia Research*

'Raziuddin Aquil...makes a laudable attempt to strike a balance by focusing on important themes of religion and politics in [a] crucial but neglected period.'
—Harbans Singh, *The Tribune*

'There is no better book on the reign of Sher Shah. With its accessible style, it is a work that also deserves to reach wide general readership...'
—Nile Green, *The Book Review*

Sufism, Culture, and Politics
Afghans and Islam in Medieval North India

RAZIUDDIN AQUIL

OXFORD
UNIVERSITY PRESS

OXFORD
UNIVERSITY PRESS

Oxford University Press is a department of the University of Oxford.
It furthers the University's objective of excellence in research, scholarship,
and education by publishing worldwide. Oxford is a registered trademark of
Oxford University Press in the UK and in certain other countries

Published in India by
Oxford University Press

© Oxford University Press 2007
22 Workspace, 2nd Floor, 1/22 Asaf Ali Road, New Delhi 110002, India

The moral rights of the author have been asserted

First Edition published in 2007
Oxford India Paperbacks 2012
17th impression 2022
Digitally Printed in 2025

ISBN-13 (print edition): 978-0-19-806915-7
ISBN-10 (print edition): 0-19-806915-4

ISBN-13 (eBook): 978-0-19-908784-6
ISBN-10 (eBook): 0-19-908784-9

Typeset in Minion 10.5/12.7
by Excellent Laser Typesetters, Pitampura Delhi 110034
Printed in India by Manipal Technologies Limited, Manipal

To
Professor Narayani Gupta

Contents

Preface to the Paperback Edition

IT IS A MATTER OF some satisfaction that Oxford University Press is bringing out a paperback edition of my book, *Sufism, Culture, and Politics*. The book was out of print soon after its first edition appeared in hardcover in 2007. A small reprint in 2009 ran a similar course. Thus, the book has been out of stock for the major part of its history of being in the public domain. An indication of the demand for the book may be seen in many friends and well-wishers inquiring from the author about its availability and the grateful author parting with his last two-three copies as *nazranas* to the discerning and in the process remaining, for the most part, without a copy for himself!

There is a need for scholarly work on religion and politics in medieval India, especially on the extremely crucial period of late fifteenth and early sixteenth century, and I think the printing of a paperback edition of this book is a welcome endeavour. I have continued to work on related themes over these past few years and have published my current research. However, I do not think any of it substantially alters my arguments in the book, nor has any new research by other scholars made me think that a revision of the book is needed at this stage. Hence, the text of the book in the paperback remains unaltered from what it was in the 2007 hardcover edition.

Meanwhile, some reviews of the book have appeared, ranging from the hostile to the appreciative. In either case, I am convinced that the book has something to offer that disturbs existing historiography, both on the period as also on medieval India generally. Thus, primarily as a work of comparative historiography, I think the book has done its job. I do not claim to have written a path-breaking treatise of lasting value; new questions in the future will mean historians will look at the period and the issues differently. For now, I am happy to share with new readers of the book what I think is the state of the art.

I hope readers will realize that I have sincerely tried to express what I have comprehended from literary, religious, and historical texts relating to Afghans, Mughals, Sufis, and other men of religion as well as those of the pen. This is certainly not the final word on the Afghan rule, spanning the period of the later Delhi Sultanate and the early struggles of the Mughals for carving out an empire for themselves; a period generally neglected by the historians. I shall be happy if other scholars work in the field and contribute to a better understanding of the peculiarities of the time.

The book was completed when I was on a comfortable research position at the prestigious Centre for Studies in Social Sciences, in Kolkata, from where I moved to a teaching position at a vibrant history department of Delhi University late in 2009. I miss the animated academic environment of Kolkata, and I am happy to be able to continue my association with some of the colleagues there. I especially thank Anuradha Chanda, Partha Chatterjee, Amit Dey, Tilottama Mukherjee, and Kaushik Roy for their kind appreciation of my humble research efforts and their continuing interest in my work.

Delhi is a difficult place to be in, especially when one is not politically sophisticated enough. I am glad to be able to get the support of friends and colleagues, including Saifuddin Ahmad, Anirudh Deshpande, Shonaleeka Kaul, Anshu Malhotra, Biswamoy Pati, R.P. Rana, R.C. Thakran, and David Zou, and thankful to them for making me realize that the Sufi way of simultaneously being here and not being here in the world is the best strategy to survive with minimum damage!

Meanwhile, I have lost a number of friends and colleagues. Especially, two of my windows to the world outside medieval Indian history, Satish Saberwal and Anjan Ghosh, left us in quick succession, leaving me with fewer dedicated readers.

Narayani Gupta continues to remain an important pillar of support and the book remains dedicated to her. I take this opportunity to also note that it has been a privilege to work with an extremely efficient team of editors at Oxford University Press. The usual disclaimers apply.

RAZIUDDIN AQUIL
University of Delhi

Preface to the First Edition

THIS BOOK EXAMINES THE PROBLEM of sovereignty and governance under the Lodi and Sur Afghan rulers in North India in the late fifteenth and early sixteenth centuries. In doing so, it takes note of the significant linkages between religion and politics in the period. For this purpose, I have focused on the valuable role played by the Sufis in shaping the politics and culture of the age. A related aspect explored here is the contribution of the Mahdawi and Raushaniyya movements to this process. The work is almost entirely based on medieval Persian sources, though the significance of the emergence of a large corpus of vernacular literature and the Sufis' contributions to it has been highlighted.

The study is divided into three sections of two chapters each. The first section explores the Afghan attempt at empire-building under the leadership of Sher Shah Sur. The second refers to the incorporation of the Rajputs in the Afghan imperial project and more generally to the ideals and institutions of governance. The third section investigates the social and political role of the Sufis. These chapters are prefaced by a comprehensive introduction, which locates this work in the broader framework of the study of medieval Indian history and issues related to it. Following an older and marginal tradition of scholarship represented by the likes of Abdul Halim, K.R. Qanungo, S.M. Imamuddin and I.H. Siddiqui, this work is an attempt to rectify the imbalance in the existing historiography, even as many established propositions are reconsidered and revised.

In transliterating the Persian terms, Perso-Arabic names and titles of books I have followed, with some modifications, F. Steingass, *A Comprehensive Persian-English Dictionary*. For calenderical equivalents, I have consulted Abdul Quddus Hashimi's *Taqwim-i-Tarikhi*. When taken from primary sources, the *Hijri* date is given first, followed by a slash and the Christian era date; dates taken from secondary literature are given only in the Christian era.

An earlier version of this work was submitted as a doctoral thesis in Jawaharlal Nehru University, New Delhi, in the year 2000. I am grateful to the Jamila Brijbhusan Memorial Trust, New Delhi, for a studentship in 1996–7. I thank the Charles Wallace India Trust for a research grant in 2001–2, which enabled me to consult valuable Persian sources in British Library, London, during the preparation of this work. Thanks are also due to the Royal Asiatic Society, London, for providing microfilm copies of some rare Persian manuscripts in its collection. I have profited immensely from the excellent infrastructure available at the Centre for Studies in Social Sciences, Calcutta, and I thank Prabir Basu and his administrative staff for facilitating my work smoothly.

My teacher Narayani Gupta has been a constant source of encouragement for many years now, and our relationship is marked by her critical appreciation of my training as a researcher. I wish to dedicate this humble effort of mine to Professor Gupta as an expression of my deep sense of gratitude for her active interest in my research endeavours. I take this opportunity to express my gratitude to *ustad-i-muhtaram* Muzaffar Alam for his guidance and support, which has sustained my interest in research. The work has benefited greatly from his learned comments during the course of our discussions over an extended period.

I am also grateful to my teachers Kunal Chakrabarti, Rajat Datta, Refaqat Ali Khan, Harbans Mukhia, Satish Saberwal, Yogesh Sharma, Dilbagh Singh, K.K. Trivedi and I.A. Zilli for supporting the project from their diverse perspectives. My colleagues at the Centre for Studies in Social Sciences, Calcutta, especially Gautam Bhadra, Partha Chatterjee, Anjan Ghosh, Susanta Ghosh, Tapati Guha-Thakurta, Janaki Nair and Lakshmi Subramanian have helped me in more ways than they are aware of.

Acknowledgement is also due to the librarians and staff of JNU Library, NMML (Teen Murti, New Delhi), Dr Zakir Husain Library (Jamia Millia Islamia, New Delhi), Khuda Bakhsh Library, Patna, British Library, London, and the National Library, Kolkata, for their help in collection of material. Abhijit Bhattacharya, Prabir Mukherjee,

Kali Babu and S.S. Ray of CSSSC Library and Archive have been extremely helpful. Shabbir Ahmad and Reyaz Ahmad of the Asiatic Society, Kolkata, have been very cooperative in their assistance. I must also thank P.N. Sahay, Nardev Sharma, M.D. Joshi, and Krishna Devi of the ICHR Library, New Delhi; and Shanti Sarkar of the National Archives Library, New Delhi, for their kind support.

Several relatives and friends have consistently provided moral support and encouragement over many difficult years during my growth as a fledgling researcher. I would especially like to thank Shakil Ahmad, Jamil Akhtar, Gita Arya, Deeksha Bhardwaj, Rimi Chatterjee, Rosinka Chaudhuri, Sohel Firdos, Mazhar Hussain, Bharati Jagannathan, Sanal Mohan, Tilottama Mukherjee, Kashifa Rizvi, Md. Sajid, Dhruba Sharma, Anup Taneja and Asim Tripathi.

The work would not have taken its current shape without the keen interest of the editors at the Oxford University Press. But for their timely intervention, I might possibly have dumped the manuscript to move on in life. That would conform to the fate of a typical 'Afghan' historian, struggling against many an academic mogul since the time of Akbar.

Lastly, I submit that I alone am responsible for the shortcomings and limitations of my research.

RAZIUDDIN AQUIL
Centre for Studies in Social Sciences, Calcutta

Introduction
The Study of Medieval Indian History

THE STUDY OF MEDIEVAL INDIAN history suffers from what is characterized as Mughal centrism.[1] Even within Mughal studies, scholars have noted a 'play of light and shade'. While the so-called period of decline after 1707 has got much-needed attention in recent times, the first half of the seventeenth century remains neglected. There has been an over emphasis on Jalal-ud-Din Muhammad Akbar (ruled 1556–1605) who is hailed as a 'hero' for his 'religious tolerance' and for providing a 'centralized', 'secular', and 'national' government.[2] Conversely, Aurangzeb (ruled 1658–1707) is condemned as a 'villain' for his alleged 'bigotry', which destroyed the 'Mughal system' he had inherited.[3] As Muzaffar Alam and Sanjay Subrahmanyam have pointed out, to talk of a uniform and centralized system of Mughal empire perfected by Akbar is misleading. According to them, the Mughal system was not

[1] The word 'medieval' is being used here in the broader, conventional sense of the period covering thirteenth-eighteenth century. Though scholars like Sanjay Subrahmanyam have argued in favour of the use of the term 'early-modern' for even the fifteenth century, it will be avoided here. Cf. Sanjay Subrahmanyam, *Penumbral Visions: Making Polities in Early Modern South India* (Delhi, 2001), pp. 253–65.

[2] Ironically, a good synthesis of the material on the emperor is still awaited, though articles galore. For recent examples, see Irfan Habib, ed., *Akbar and His India* (Delhi, 1997). For the suggestion that Akbar contributed to the making of the Indian nation, see Irfan Habib's introductory note in Iqtidar Alam Khan, ed., *Akbar and his Age* (Delhi, 1999).

[3] For the controversial reign of the emperor, one may consult the voluminous writings of Jadunath Sarkar and S.R. Sharma on the one hand, and later researches by M. Athar Ali and Satish Chandra on the other.

born in 'adult form'. It grew and evolved both before and after Akbar's reign in quite significant ways. The incorporation of new regions into the dominion had necessitated adjustments to local conditions. Therefore, the state eventually resembled a 'patchwork quilt' rather than a 'wall-to-wall carpet'. Also, political decentralization or Mughal decline in the eighteenth century, often misconstrued and confused with a generalized social and economic dislocation, ignores the vast variety of regional experiences, particularly a vigorous process of economic reorientation in the period.[4]

However, a rather narrow framework of economic history, caught in the dichotomy of economic decline and prosperity, continues to dominate eighteenth century studies. Those looking for a discussion on religion, culture, literature, architecture, and paintings, among other topics, in secondary works will be disappointed. The period is significant for the history of Islam in India. Sufis and scholars not only tried to stem the tide of Mughal decline, but also contributed to the consolidation of Muslim power in the regions through their writings and active involvement in political matters. The period is marked by rapid growth in urban centres and diffusion of a refined Indo-Muslim culture in the regions where 'successor states' emerged. The ceremonials of the resplendent courts with conspicuous consumption were tempered with the presence of mosques and shrines. Immense progress was made in the field of Islamic religious and political thought during the period. Significant advances were made in the development and growth of vernacular literature even as Persian dominated as the language of elite intellectual discourse. The process of identity formation along religious and ethnic lines took divergent trajectories. The varying indigenous responses to the impact of the colonial encounter may also be taken into account. Conversely, the diverse images of Indian society in early British and European writings need to be examined closely. Recognizing the challenges involved in a broad sweep of comparative history, some efforts at delineating the common pattern of decline and fall of the contemporary Safavid, Ottoman, and Uzbek empires will be valuable for explaining the 'culture-lag' in the East.[5]

[4] Muzaffar Alam and Sanjay Subrahmanyam, 'Introduction', in their edited volume, *The Mughal State, 1526–1750* (Delhi, 1998).

[5] For recent collections of representative writings on the eighteenth century, see Seema Alavi, ed., *The Eighteenth Century in India* (Delhi, 2002); P.J. Marshall,

Thus, apart from chronological imbalance and sweeping generalizations, the scope of Mughal history is further limited to counting of nobles of various stocks and ranks and the revenue-figures they were expected to know and collect from the peasantry. The studies on the fiscal mechanism of the period are often passed off under the rubric of economic history, or more specifically as 'agrarian' history. Pioneering in the field was the British colonial official, W.H. Moreland, whose paradigm of a centralized fiscal despotism remains unchallenged.[6] Further, while Abu'l Fazl's statistical data in his *A'in-i-Akbari* are useful for projecting the power of the Great Mughals, other important sources and tools such as language, literature, paintings, and architecture which infused meaning and sustained the image of Mughal grandeur are generally ignored. In fact, while contemporary language and literature have hardly been utilized,[7] the scholars studying painting and architecture are considered marginal to the mainstream discourse on the history of the Mughals.[8]

So are those who choose to study the history of Sufism in the period. In this connection, the cases of two scholars, K.A. Nizami[9] and S.A.A. Rizvi,[10] who are otherwise known for their voluminous writings on religion and political culture in medieval India, may be cited here. While Rizvi is not counted at all amongst the scholars of the history of the Mughals, Nizami is often condemned as a reactionary Islamic scholar.

---

ed., *The Eighteenth Century in Indian History, Evolution or Revolution?* (Delhi, 2003). Also see, Richard B. Barnett, ed., *Rethinking Early Modern India* (Delhi, 2002).

[6] W.H. Moreland, *Agrarian System of Moslem India* (London, 1929). Also see, Irfan Habib, *The Agrarian System of Mughal India, 1556–1707* (Delhi, 1999).

[7] For a study of the Mughal attempt to promote Persian as the language of the empire, see Muzaffar Alam, 'The Pursuit of Persian: Language in Mughal Politics', *Modern Asian Studies* (hereafter *MAS*), Vol. 32, No. 2, 1998, pp. 317–49. Also see, Alam's recent work, *The Languages of Political Islam in India* (Delhi, 2004).

[8] Monica Juneja, 'Introduction', in her edited volume, *Architecture in Medieval India: Forms, Contexts, Histories* (Delhi, 2001).

[9] K.A. Nizami's major work pertains to the Sufis of the Delhi Sultanate, but see his *Akbar and Religion* (Delhi, 1989).

[10] S.A.A. Rizvi has also contributed immensely to the study of Sufism in medieval India, but see his *Muslim Revivalist Movements in Northern India in the Sixteenth and Seventeenth Centuries*, reprint (Delhi, 1993); idem, *Religious and Intellectual History of the Muslims in Akbar's Reign with Special Reference to Abul Fazl* (Delhi, 1975).

Indeed, any study of the Mughal ruling ideology would do well to explore the dichotomy of *shari'at* (Islamic law) and *zawabit* or *jahandari* (secular state laws), as also the relationship between the kings and the powerful Sufi orders (*silsilas*) such as the Chishtis and Naqshbandis. Apart from providing legitimacy, Sufis also sought to influence state policy in their bid to ensure that it was at least not in total contravention of the shari'at.[11] Ideally though they felt the need to implement the shari'at as the state law, but understood its limitations as well. These issues are of crucial import for any study of the state under the Muslim rulers of medieval India. Further, a comparative study of the history of contemporary Muslim polities in Central Asia and Iran will be invaluable for exploring new motifs and vistas of inquiry. More importantly, it can lead to a better understanding of the historical processes in the medieval Muslim world. Some reflections on the West Asian history of the earlier period will further enhance our knowledge of evolution of Muslim political institutions over time and space.

More fruitful will be a fresh look at the growth and development of political institutions of the Delhi Sultanate. Because of the importance given to the Mughals, the period of the Sultanate is marginal to the concern of historians. The general explanation for this neglect is said to be the lack of sufficient source material.[12] However, this relative lack

[11] For relevant discussions, see Muzaffar Alam, '*Shari'a* and Governance in the Indo-Muslim Context', in David Gilmartin and Bruce B. Lawrence, eds, *Beyond Turk and Hindu: Rethinking Religious Identities in Islamicate South Asia* (Delhi, 2002), pp. 216–45. Also see Muzaffar Alam, '*Akhlaqi* Norms and Mughal Governance', in Muzaffar Alam, Francois 'Nalini' Delvoye and Marc Gaborieau, eds, *The Making of the Indo-Persian Culture: Indian and French Studies* (Delhi, 2000).

[12] B.P. Saksena, 'General Presidential Address', *Proceedings of the Indian History Congress* (hereafter *PIHC*), 28th Session, Mysore, 1966, pp. I–XXXIV, especially p. XXIII. Not many people are however satisfied with this observation. For a cogent dissatisfaction with Mughal centrism in North Indian historiography, see Frank Perlin, 'State Formation Reconsidered', *MAS*, Vol. 19, No. 3, 1985, pp. 415–80, especially p. 423; C. Srinivasa Reddy, 'Approaches to the Mughal State', *Social Scientist*, Vol. 19, Nos 10–11, October–November 1991, pp. 90–6; Sanjay Subrahmanyam, 'The Mughal State: Structure or Process? Reflections on Recent Western Historiography', *Indian Economic and Social History Review* (hereafter *IESHR*), Vol. 24, No. 3, July–September 1992, pp. 291–321, especially pp. 293–5 for a criticism of the 'received wisdom' of the scholars of the 'Aligarh school'. The Aligarh historians' response is generally disseminated through verbal discourse.

of interest seems to stem from certain basic assumptions of historians, which are shaped by contemporary ideological issues leading to a projection of many ideas and categories onto the utterly different socio-political context of medieval India. Again, the celebration of Akbar's achievements in the age of 'intolerance' and 'fragmented' polities meant that the history of the earlier period was de-emphasized. The meagre material available on the Delhi Sultanate is largely based on the court-chronicles. These accounts are resolutely centred on the activities of the sultans, presenting a 'top down' view of history.[13]

The Sufi literature, mainly the *malfuzat* (compilations of conversations of a Sufi shaykh) and *tazkiras* (biographies), which offers a rich collection of historical data for an analysis of societal and mental structure, and power and process, besides presenting a 'bottom up' radiation of the perceptions of the disgruntled elites and the depressed commoners, have not been utilized. A valuable portion of this literature, which was in circulation in the middle of the fourteenth century and used by authorities such as Shaykh Jamali[14] and Abdul Haqq Muhaddis Dehlawi,[15] is now dubbed as 'forged' and hence considered to be devoid of any historical value. This demarcation of Sufi literature as 'authentic' and 'spurious' was done by M. Habib in an article published in 1950.[16] Subsequent scholars like M. Mujeeb, K.A. Nizami, and S.A.A. Rizvi, among others, have merely reiterated Habib's position. The abundance of anecdotes of miracles attributed to the Sufis is an important reason for the neglect of one set of sources. But then such

---

For a scholarly response however, see M. Athar Ali, 'Recent Theories of Eighteenth Century India', *Indian Historical Review* (hereafter *IHR*), Vol. 13, Nos 1–2, 1986–7, pp. 102–10; idem, 'The Mughal Polity: A Critique of Revisionist Approaches', *MAS*, Vol. 27, No. 4, 1993, pp. 699–710.

[13] For the evaluation of the narratives in the chronicles, see Mohibbul Hasan, ed., *Historians of Medieval India* (Meerut, 1968); Harbans Mukhia, *Historians and Historiography During the Reign of Akbar* (Delhi, 1976).

[14] Shaykh Jamali, *Siyar-ul-Arifin*, British Museum Ms. Or. 5853, OIOC, British Library, London.

[15] Abdul Haqq Muhaddis Dehlawi, *Akhbar-ul-Akhyar*, Ms. I.O. Islamic 1450, British Library, London.

[16] Muhammad Habib, 'Chishti Mystic Records of the Sultanate Period', *Medieval India Quarterly*, Vol. I, No. 2, (October 1950), pp. 1–42; reprinted in K.A. Nizami, ed., *Politics and Society During the Early Medieval Period: Collected Works of Muhammad Habib*, Vol. I (Delhi, 1974), pp. 385–433.

stories are to be found in the so-called genuine texts also. They are there for everybody to see, but for some reasons historians deny it.

In the considered opinion of the authorities, the accuracy and genuineness of the authentic sources are given. There is no need to critically evaluate and prove it. The other set of sources are treated as fabricated because (a) they contain principles and practices which are at variance with what is expounded in the authentic texts; (b) the narrators and compilers commit blunders about well-known facts and dates of Indian history; and c) they contain horrendous tales of miracles. Thus, the forged malfuzat was basically a 'light literature'—a mixture of mysticism, theology, and fiction, the last component comprising the bulk of the material—of little value commissioned by booksellers for 'honest trade'. Such remarks do not stand a critical scrutiny of the sources.

The value of malfuz literature and their dating do not create any problem for a researcher approaching them afresh. Let us have a quick look at some of them:

(1) *Dalil-ul-Arifin*—Conversations of Muʻin-ud-Din Chishti (d. 1236),[17] compilation attributed to Qutb-ud-Din Bakhtiyar Kaki (d. 1235);[18]

(2) *Fawaʼid-us-Salikin*—Conversations of Qutb-ud-Din Bakhtiyar Kaki, compilation attributed to Shaykh Farid-ud-Din Ganj-i-Shakar (d. 1265);[19]

---

[17] Born c. 1141 in Sijistan, Muʻin-ud-Din established the Chishti order of Sufism in the subcontinent. After travelling to the major centres of Islamic learning and culture in Central Asia, Iran, and the Middle East, Muʻin-ud-Din settled down in India in the advanced stage of his life. His tomb at Ajmer is a major centre of pilgrimage for Muslims and non-Muslims alike. For biographical material, see, Amir Khwurd, *Siyar-ul-Auliya* (Lahore, 1978), pp. 55–8. Also see, P.M. Currie, *The Shrine and Cult of Muin al-Din Chishti of Ajmer* (Delhi, 1989).

[18] Spiritual successor of Muʻin-ud-Din Chishti, Qutb-ud-Din was born at Ush in Transoxania. After long journeys undertaken with his preceptor, Qutb-ud-Din finally established himself in Delhi, despite the volatile political culture of the city in the early decades of the thirteenth century. For biographical material, see *Siyar-ul-Auliya*, pp. 58–67; *Siyar-ul-Arifin*, fols. 31b–43a. Also see S.A.A. Rizvi, *A History of Sufism in India, Vol. I, Early Sufism and its History in India to AD 1600* (New Delhi, 1978), pp. 133–8.

[19] Born in a respectable family some time in 1175 at Kahtawal, near Multan, Farid-ud-Din, then known as Masʻud, was mystically inclined even as a student,

(3) *Asrar-ul-Auliya*—Conversations of Farid-ud-Din Ganj-i-Shakar, compilation attributed to Shaykh Badr-ud-Din Ishaq (a successor and son-in-law of the shaykh);

(4) *Rahat-ul-Qulub*—Conversations of Farid-ud-Din Ganj-i-Shakar, compilation attributed to Nizam-ud-Din Auliya (d. 1325);[20]

(5) *Afzal-ul-Fawa'id*—Conversations of Nizam-ud-Din Auliya, compilation attributed to Amir Khusrau;[21]

(6) *Fawa'id-ul-Fu'ad*—Conversations of Nizam-ud-Din Auliya, Compilation attributed to Amir Hasan Sijzi;[22]

(7) *Khayr-ul-Majalis*—Conversations of Nasir-ud-Din Chiragh-i-Dehli (d. 1356),[23] compilation attributed to Hamid Qalandar.

---

which had earned him the sobriquet, *diwana bachcha*. He went on to be a leading saint of the Chishti order. His tomb is at Ajodhan, now called Pak Pattan, in Pakistani Punjab. For biographical material on the shaykh's life, see, *Siyar-ul-Auliya*, pp. 67–101; *Siyar-ul-Arifin*, fols. 43a–65b; Ali Asghar, *Jawahir-i-Faridi* (Lahore, 1884). Also see Khaliq Ahmad Nizami, *The Life and Times of Shaikh Farid-u'd-din Ganj-i-Shakar* (Aligarh, 1955); G.S. Talib, ed., *Baba Shaikh Farid—Life and Teaching* (Patiala, 1973); Richard M. Eaton, 'The Political and Religious Authority of the Shrine of Baba Farid', in *Moral Conduct and Authority—The Place of Adab in South Asian Islam*, ed., Barbara D. Metcalf (Berkley, 1984), pp. 333–56; Raziuddin Aquil, 'Episodes from the Life of Shaikh Farid-ud-Din Ganj-i-Shakar', *International Journal of Punjab Studies*, Vol. 10, Nos 1–2, January–December 2003, pp. 25–46.

[20] Successor of the Chishti saint Farid-ud-Din, Nizam-ud-Din was born c. 1243–4 at Badaun in a family that had migrated to northern India from Bukhara. After completing his education, with specialization in *hadis* (Tradition of the Prophet) and *fiqh* (jurisprudence), Nizam-ud-Din was looking for a job of *qazi* (judge) in Delhi before being introduced to Islamic mysticism by Farid-ud-Din's brother Najib-ud-Din Mutawakkil. For biographical material, see, Muhammad Jamal Qiwam, *Qiwam-ul-Aqa'id*, Urdu trans. Nisar Ahmad Faruqi (Rampur, 1994); *Siyar-ul-Auliya*, pp. 101–65; *Siyar-ul-Arifin*, fols. 75b–100b. Also see K.A. Nizami, *The Life and Times of Shaikh Nizam-u'd-din Auliya* (Delhi, 1991).

[21] For voluminous writings on Amir Khusrau in Urdu, see S.S. Abdur Rahman, *Hindustan Amir Khusau ki Nazr Mein* (Azamgarh, 1966); idem, *Amir Khusrau Dehlawi* (Azamgarh, 1979); idem, *Sufi Amir Khusrau* (Azamgarh, 1980); M. Wahid Mirza, *Amir Khusrau* (Delhi, 1986); Zoe Ansari and Abul Faiz Sahar, eds, *Khusro Shanasi* (Delhi, 1989).

[22] For Amir Hasan Sijzi, see his biography in Urdu, M. Shakil Ahmad Siddiqi, *Amir Hasan Sijzi Dehlawi: Hayat aur Adabi Khidmat* (Lucknow, 1979).

[23] Last of the five 'great' saints of the Chishti order, Chiragh-i-Dehli was born at Awadh (Ayodhya). His father, a textile merchant, died when the shaykh was still a young boy. He received his education in the traditional Muslim disciplines from

Now, since these malfuzat are supposed to be collections of conversations taking place between the shaykh and his disciples in the hospice (and in some cases corrected and edited by the saint himself), the cut-off date for the composition of a particular collection should be the date of the death of the Sufi in question. Thus even if we are not sure of the exact date of most of the compilation, we can infer that we are dealing with the material pertaining to the period c. 1235 (or slightly earlier) to 1356. I tentatively use the higher limit of 'mid-fourteenth century' because a) there is evidence from this period of the existence of these malfuzat and b) much of the material in these texts was incorporated by Amir Khwurd (d. 1368) in his *Siyar-ul-Auliya* (completed c. 1356).

Besides the explanations given above with regard to the alleged forgery and false-attributions of popular writings to the noted saints, historians also prefer to keep this literature aside in view of the popular assumption that the Sufis, in general, and those of the Chishti brotherhood, in particular, kept themselves aloof from politics and government of their times. Finally, for nearly four decades, the history of religions or ideas was a neglected stream, because of the dominance of 'Marxist' historians in the field of medieval Indian history. The historians of this 'school' did not see any role of the 'parasitic' Sufis in the political economy and hence their literature was considered to be of no value.[24]

We may briefly refer to the existing knowledge on the Sufi traditions of the Delhi Sultanate, which generally revolves around the questions concerning the Sufis' relationship with the rulers, their role in conversion or Islamicization, and their contribution to syncretism and synthesis in the field of religion and culture. As mentioned above, it is

---

the leading scholars of the place. He gave up his family business at the age of twenty-five so as to devote his time to prayers and meditation. Moving to Delhi at the age of forty-three, he became a disciple of Nizam-ud-Din Auliya. His tomb is in Delhi. For biographical material, see, *Siyar-ul-Auliya*, pp. 246–57; *Siyar-ul-Arifin*, fols. 126a–130b. Also see K.A. Nizami, *The Life and Times of Shaikh Nasir-u'd-din Chiragh* (Delhi, 1991).

[24] Irfan Habib's article, 'Slavery in the Delhi Sultanate, Thirteenth and Fourteenth Centuries: Evidence from Sufic Literature', *IHR*, Vol. 15, Nos 1–2, 1988–9, pp. 248–56, is disappointing in the sense that its concern is more to show the prevalence of slavery as a recognized institution than to understand how the Sufis themselves viewed it and worked for its abolition at least in a limited measure.

suggested that the Sufis kept themselves away from politics and government of their times for they believed that involvement in politics led to materialism and worldliness, which they wished to avoid. This distancing was also due to the consideration that the Sultanate was an illegal state with its resources being *haram* (prohibited) from the point of view of the shari'at. Thus, Sufi saints of the orders like the Chishtis not only refused to accept money or land grants from the rulers, but also declined to make a person their disciple till he had left government service, and sold all his possessions and distributed the amount amongst the poor. It is asserted that in no form was contact with the state tolerated. Further, the abhorrence to politics compelled the Sufis to stay away from the centres of political influence and establish their hospice (*jama'atkhana* or *khanqah*) in the localities inhabited by low caste Hindus. The spiritually hungry and depressed classes were amazed by the shining example of Islamic brotherhood and egalitarianism as reflected in the activities of the hospice such as the *langar* (free kitchen). This fascinating image of the true Islam represented by the Sufis paved the way for a revolution marked by large-scale conversion of the teeming lower classes. However, the Sufis, in general, and the Chishtis, in particular, were tolerant towards non-Muslim religious traditions. They were, therefore, indifferent towards conversion. In fact, it is noted that there was no evidence of even a single case of conversion in the mystic records of the Delhi Sultanate.[25]

Sufi sources of the period however reveal that the views summarized above need a drastic revision.[26] Also, the non-Persian sources

---

[25] Literature on Sufi cults produced on this line is numerous, but see, *Collected Works of Muhammad Habib*; Yusuf Husain, *Glimpses of Medieval Indian Culture* (Bombay, 1957); K.A. Nizami, *Some Aspects of Religion and Politics in India During the 13th Centuries* (Aligarh, 1961); Talib, ed., *Baba Shaikh Farid*; Rizvi, *A History of Sufism in India*, Vol. I; I.H. Siddiqui, 'The Early Chishti Dargahs', in C.W. Troll, ed., *Muslim Shrines in India—Their Character, History and Significance* (New Delhi, 1989); Carl W. Ernst and Bruce B. Lawrence, *Sufi Martyrs of Love: The Chishti Order in South Asia and Beyond* (New York, 2002). For a review of this literature, see Raziuddin Aquil, 'Sufi Cults, Politics and Conversion: The Chishtis of the Sultanate Period', *IHR*, Vol. 22, Nos 1–2, 1995–6, pp. 190–7; idem, 'Chishti Sufi Order in the Indian Subcontinent and Beyond', *Studies in History*, Vol. 21, No. 1, 2005, pp. 99–111.

[26] We shall return below with references to some recent writings which move away from the above formulations.

particularly the literature related to the 'monotheistic' or 'Bhakti' saints could well have been utilized for a more informed and accurate understanding of the history of the Sultanate period. There are some isolated studies on the saints and their works, mainly poetical compositions, but the material is not collated with Persian sources to attempt writing a social history of the period.[27]

Thus, the existing knowledge on the Sultanate period not only suffers from a faulty and scant source base, but also is both dated (major propositions were formulated in the late 1950s and early 1960s) and based on contradictory assumptions.[28] For instance, the defeat of the Hindus in the second battle of Tarain in 1192, leading to the establishment of the Sultanate, is attributed to the rigid caste system which allowed only an exclusive Rajput army to face the onslaught of an 'egalitarian' Islam, which comprised diverse Muslim groups such as the Turks, Afghans, and the Khaljis.[29] The premise that medieval Islam was egalitarian is questionable. The normative Islam might have certain ideals emphasizing equality in society, but as Islam spread in various regions, it got embedded in local social structures, and hierarchies based on birth, wealth, and power, became an integral part of the Muslim communities,[30] as is the case with caste amongst Muslims in India; Sufi ideals proved to be inadequate to fight inequalities in society.

[27] For the value of non-Persian sources, see recent studies by B.D. Chattopadhyaya, *Representing the Other? Sanskrit Sources and the Muslims, Eighth to Fourteenth Century* (Delhi, 1998); and Cynthia Talbot, 'Inscribing the Other, Inscribing the Self: Hindu-Muslim Identities in Pre-Colonial India', in *Comparative Studies in Society and History*, Vol. 37, No. 4, 1995, pp. 692–722. Also see, Pushpa Prasad, *Sanskrit Inscriptions of the Delhi Sultanate, 1191–1526* (Delhi, 1990).

[28] M. Habib and K.A. Nizami, eds, *A Comprehensive History of India, Vol. V, Part One, The Delhi Sultanate*, first published 1970, reprint (Delhi, 1992). For the history of the Sultanate period, see also A.B.M. Habibullah, *The Foundation of the Muslim Rule in India* (Lahore, 1945); K.A. Nizami, *Religion and Politics in India During the 13th Century; Collected Works of Muhammad Habib*; K.S. Lal, *History of the Khaljis* (Delhi, 1967); Agha Mahdi Husain, *Tughluq Dynasty* (Calcutta, 1963); Abdul Halim, *History of the Lodi Sultans of Delhi and Agra*, reprint (Delhi, 1974); I.H. Siddiqui, *Some Aspects of Afghan Despotism in India* (Aligarh, 1969).

[29] For the 'invidious caste distinctions' which affected, among other things, the military organization of the Indians, see Nizami, 'Foundation of the Delhi Sultanate', in Habib and Nizami, eds, *Comprehensive History*, pp. 132–6, 185–6.

[30] Louise Marlow, *Hierarchy and Egalitarianism in Islamic Thought* (Cambridge, 1997).

The Turkish reaction to what may be called the 'Hindustani outbreak' in the thirteenth and fourteenth centuries is too well known. The chronicler Ziya-ud-Din Barani, a disciple of the Chishti Shaykh Nizam-ud-Din Auliya, perceived this emergence of the converted Hindustani Muslims in the Delhi Sultanate as a perverse burlesque of society.[31]

Secondly, the Sultanate which was imposed after the victory of Muslim army (referred to in the sources as the *lashkar-i-islam*) is described as the 'Turkish Sultanate' and not as a Muslim Sultanate.[32] Certainly, we are not arguing for an Islamic state in medieval India, as two of the paths through which it could have been possible were not officially resorted to by the rulers, viz., imposition of the shariʻat in the strictly orthodox Sunni Hanafite sense of the term, and conversion of the entire population to Islam. Further, the point that a Muslim government need not necessarily be orthodox Islamic in character should not be ignored. Also, the general perception among Muslims in the Delhi Sultanate that it was 'their' government may be taken into account. The *ulama* (Muslim religious scholars) and *mashai'kh* (Muslim mystics) were consulted by the sultans in various policy matters. The ulama's understanding of the Sultanate as a Muslim polity often forced them to demand action against the Hindus.

Finally, the statement that the Turks established a centralized all-India government with Persian as the language of administration is partly contradicted by the suggestion that it was impossible to govern the country in an alien language without co-opting the existing political elite such as the *rana*s and *rawat*s.[33] Moreover, to view the Sultanate as a centralized all-India government is a tall claim, for it is found that

[31] For Barani's ideas, see his *Fatawa-i-Jahandari*, ed. Afsar Salim Khan, Lahore, 1972; Muzaffar Alam, '*Shariʻa* and Governance in the Indo-Muslim Context'; Raziuddin Aquil, 'On Islam and *Kufr* in the Delhi Sultanate: Towards a Re-interpretation of Ziya-ud-Din Barani's *Fatawa-i-Jahandari*', presented in 'Rethinking a Millennium: International Seminar in Honour of Prof. Harbans Mukhia', Delhi, 2004. See also Nizami, 'Foundation of the Delhi Sultanate', p. 189, for the contempt with which the Turkish slave-officers regarded persons from the 'tribes of Hindustan'.

[32] See for example, K.A. Nizami, 'The Early Turkish Sultans of Delhi', in Habib and Nizami, eds, *Comprehensive History*, p. 191.

[33] See for example, Nizami, 'Foundation of the Delhi Sultanate', pp. 180–1 (for language problem and difficulty in establishing a direct administration), and p. 187 (for centralized all-India administration).

it was only the region of Hindustan, comprising Punjab, the valleys of the Indus, the Yamuna and the Ganges, including the Doab, and parts of various Rajput strongholds such as Ajmer, Ranthambhor, Gwalior, and Kalinjar, that was subject to more or less uniform political influences during the period between the thirteenth and early sixteenth centuries.[34] The fortunes and political boundaries of various Muslim Sultanates and Hindu dynasties kept fluctuating during the period. Evidently, issues such as the nature and nomenclature of the Sultanate polity, and also the extent of their political influence, both in terms of actual boundary and indirect control, need to be reconsidered.[35]

In view of this backdrop, the publication of two recent works on the history of the Sultanate by André Wink[36] and Peter Jackson[37] is indeed most welcome. However, Wink's *Al-Hind*, Vol. II, focuses on the early phase of the Sultanate period. The volume recounts the tale of Muslim conquest of Hindustan, emergence of the Delhi Sultanate, and expansion of Islam in the subcontinent in a refreshing eco-friendly package of 'frontier history' imported only recently to India but with an already established 'market' in the US and China. There is a latent danger, however, that in the enthusiasm to capture the essence of medieval Indian history with this in-vogue model, the sources of the period as well as the secondary literature might get overlooked. Further, Wink cannot deny, though he seems reluctant to acknowledge, his debt to the contributions of historians such as A.B.M. Habibullah, M. Habib, and K.A. Nizami in the formulation of his own central argument, which means basically reinforcing older propositions.

---

[34] K.M. Ashraf, *Life and Conditions of the People of Hindustan* (Delhi, 1959), pp. III–IV. To follow Ashraf on this point does not necessarily mean that we buy any of his dated assumptions. Particularly unacceptable is his suggestion that the Sufis showed 'a more or less complete detachment from the life of the common people and their spiritual wants. They fight shy of recognizing the social changes which a closer association and mutual interaction of Hindus and Muslims were bringing about in Muslim society', p. XXI.

[35] For some discussion on relevant issues, see Raziuddin Aquil, 'Scholars, Saints and Sultans: Some Aspects of Religion and Politics in the Delhi Sultanate', *IHR*, Vol. 31, Nos 1–2, 2004, pp. 210–20.

[36] André Wink, *Al-Hind, The Making of the Indo-Islamic World, Vol. II, The Slave Kings and the Islamic Conquest, 11th–13th Centuries* (Leiden, 1997).

[37] Peter Jackson, *The Delhi Sultanate: A Political and Military History* (Cambridge, 1999).

Jackson's *Delhi Sultanate* is also disappointing as it covers only the first two centuries of the Sultanate, the thirteenth and fourteenth century, under the Turks. The author refers to the Afghan rule in passing in the brief Epilogue (c. 1400–1526).[38] This is typical of existing literature—to ignore or slight the subsequent period, the fifteenth and early sixteenth centuries, under the Saiyid, Lodi, and Sur rulers.

The present study seeks to draw attention to some of the important themes in religion and politics in the crucial, but neglected period of over a century, sandwiched between the Great Mughals and the 'greater' Delhi Sultanate of the Turks. The period of Afghan rule in the late fifteenth and early sixteenth centuries is generally portrayed as one of 'chaos' and 'anarchy'. It is assumed that the kings merely headed a decentralized-tribal confederacy of the Afghans. The Afghan rulers, it is said, set aside the usual medieval royal insignia such as the umbrella and the throne. Instead, they sat on a big platform, which they shared with their nobles who were generally members of their clans. The sovereign was content to be virtually one among the many clan chiefs. Thus the monarch, it is suggested, lacked both the ritual status and the requisite power to assert his authority and control over his ambitious nobles, ever in search of an opportunity to raise the banner of rebellion. The conflict between the sons of the outgoing sultans and the frequent revolts of powerful nobles eroded the king's power and position, generating, as it has been put, a crisis in society with immorality and perversion becoming rampant throughout the dominion. In such a situation even the Sufis, otherwise devoted to spiritual and otherworldly pursuits, began to aspire for political power. Indeed, it is reported, many of them behaved like kings.[39]

[38] Ibid., pp. 323–5.

[39] There exists a large body of literature on these lines, see, for instance, R.P. Tripathi, *Some Aspects of Muslim Administration*, reprint (Allahabad, 1972); S.M. Imamuddin, 'The Nature of Afghan Monarchy in India', *Islamic Culture*, Vol. 32, No. 4 (October, 1958), pp. 268–75; Halim, *History of the Lodi Sultans*; M.M. Haqq, 'The Shattari Order of Sufism in India and its Exponents in Bengal and Bihar', *Journal of the Asiatic Society of Pakistan*, Vol. XVI, No. 2 (1971), pp. 167–75. K.A. Nizami, 'The Lodis (1451–1526)', in Habib and Nizami, eds, *A Comprehensive History of India*, Vol. V, pp. 664–709. Iqtidar Alam Khan, 'The Turko-Mongol Theory of Kingship', *Medieval India: A Miscellany* (hereafter *MIAM*), Vol. II (1972), pp. 8–18; Dirk H.A. Kolff, *Naukar, Rajput and Sepoy: The Ethno-history of the Military Labour Market in Hindustan, 1450–1850* (Cambridge, 1990); Muhammad Zaki,

In the following pages, we shall examine existing propositions on the problem of politics and governance during the Afghan period. The nature of Afghan polity will be assessed with reference to the various symbols and rituals of sovereignty. The significance of religion in the articulation and projection of Afghan power will also be explored. For all this, we aim to return to the sources. Much of the primary material for the Afghan period was compiled under the Mughals. We shall see as to how this had a bearing on the history of the Lodi and Sur Afghans. Such an exercise will be worthwhile as the conclusions in secondary works, summarized above, seem to be based on premises which in our view do not get full support from the existing source material. On occasion, the use of evidence appears to be out of context. It will be appropriate to illustrate in detail the established proposition on the nature of Afghan polity with reference to R.P. Tripathi's authoritative work, *Aspects of Muslim Administration*. Tripathi suggests that the 'sturdy' Afghans with their love of 'tribal' independence did not recognize the idea of absolute sovereignty.[40] The author seems to agree with the fiction that the father of Sultan Bahlul Lodi (ruled 1451–89), Malik Kala had actually assumed 'sovereign power' and shared his throne with his leading nobles. Tripathi writes that in keeping with the sentiments of the Afghans and the tradition of his father, Bahlul Lodi claimed to be nothing more than one among the peers. He did not sit on the throne, nor issued any royal orders. Under him, the Afghan empire was a sort of confederation of tribes.[41]

Tripathi further states that Bahlul's son and successor, Sikandar Lodi (ruled 1489–1517) respected the susceptibilities of the Afghans and refrained from any radical change in the polity. Although the sultan sat on the throne and issued royal orders, the liberty-loving Afghans could not easily adapt themselves to this innovation.[42] Sikandar's successor, Ibrahim (ruled 1517–26) sought to curb the freedom and power of the nobles. The disaffected nobles not only rebelled but also invited the Mughals to attack Hindustan.[43] In Tripathi's opinion, unlike

---

Muslim Society in Northern India During the 15th and first half of the 16th Century (Calcutta, 1996).

[40] Tripathi, *Muslim Administration*, p. 80.

[41] Ibid., pp. 81, 83.

[42] Ibid., pp. 86–7.

[43] Ibid., pp. 89, 91.

Ibrahim Lodi, Sher Shah (ruled 1540–5), emerging as the 'leader of the Afghan national movement against the Mughals', resorted to a 'compromise between the early Turkish principle of absolute monarchy and tribal leadership of Bahlul'.[44]

Later authorities on the period have largely followed the same line.[45] However, S.M. Imamuddin has noted a difference between the Lodi and Sur polities. According to him, while the polity under the Lodi Afghans remained tribal, Sher Shah Sur succeeded in establishing a truly autocratic form of government which continued even under his son, Islam Shah Sur.[46] Reacting to the characterization of Afghan polity as 'tribal', I.H. Siddiqui takes another extreme position by calling it 'despotic'.[47] Making a more critical use of largely the same set of sources, Siddiqui highlights elements of absolutism in Afghan kingship. In doing so, however, the author tends to neglect the crucial linkages between religion and politics of the period, which to an extent restricted the power of the sovereign. The sources of the period refer to several anecdotes of bestowal of kingship on the rulers by the Sufi shaykhs, who enjoyed considerable political clout in the dominion. The evidence of the Sufis' involvement in the succession crisis, and in the conflict between the rival Muslim polities, is also available. The rulers' frantic attempts at placating the Sufis, through public protestation of respect and devotion, and offer of cash and land grants, betray their search for legitimacy.[48] These are some important issues, which should not be ignored while making an assessment of the nature of polity during the period.

The major propositions of the political history of the period seem to be primarily based on a reading of two late-sixteenth century Afghan chronicles, Abbas Khan Sarwani's *Tarikh-i-Sher Shahi*[49] and Muhammad Kabir's *Afsana-i-Shahan*,[50] without locating them in their

[44] Ibid., pp. 94–7.

[45] Halim, *History of the Lodi Sultans*, pp. 212–14; Nizami, 'The Lodis', pp. 664–6; Zaki, *Muslim Society in Northern India*.

[46] Imamuddin, 'Nature of Afghan Monarchy', pp. 268–75.

[47] Siddiqui, *Afghan Despotism*.

[48] See chapter five.

[49] Abbas Khan Sarwani, *Tarikh-i-Sher Shahi*, ed., S.M. Imamuddin, Vol. I (text), Dacca, 1964.

[50] Muhammad Kabir, *Afsana-i-Shahan*, British Museum, Ms. Add. 24,409, OIOC, British Library, London.

context. Writing after the collapse of Afghan power, Sarwani and Kabir were ruminating on the loss of a 'golden' past. Kabir's work has been found to be a dubious source suffering from 'glaring defects', and extremely anecdotal, though otherwise valuable for a study of Indo-Afghan cosmology during the period. Most of our historians have used Kabir in a very selective manner. For instance, while the anecdote about the Lodi sultans sitting on a large throne resembling a dais has been utilized as the basis for the central argument in several of these works, Kabir's suggestion that Bahlul Lodi's father Malik Kala was also a sultan of Delhi is generally glossed over. Kabir writes that Sultan Kala ruled the country for thirteen years, nine months, one day and five *gharis* (hours).[51] With such anecdotes in the *Afsana*, Kabir has to be read with caution.

Curiously, Kabir's accounts have often been preferred to those of Abbas Sarwani's. This is, however, not to suggest that Abbas is a safe guide either. On the contrary, any reliance on Abbas alone can be fraught with serious problems. The example of the alleged letter of Sultan Bahlul to the Afghan chiefs of Roh, mentioned by Abbas, may be noted here. Abbas has recorded that Bahlul Lodi, faced with a serious threat from the Sharqi sultan of Jaunpur, had sent a letter to the Afghan chiefs requesting them to come to the rescue of their fellow Afghans in Hindustan, adding that the captured booty and newly acquired territories would be shared with them as brothers. In response to this letter, Abbas adds, the Afghans came from all quarters like 'ants and locusts'.[52] Modern historians have used this account rather uncritically. According to them, the allusion to the 'share' of territories 'as brothers' is incompatible with sovereignty. In suggesting this, however, they ignore a crucial sentence in the so-called letter, which makes it clear to the Afghans that sovereignty shall no doubt be in Sultan Bahlul's name.[53] Further, the suggestion that in response to Bahlul's appeal the Afghans came from Roh like ants and locusts is also to be accepted with a pinch of salt. A comparison of the strength of the Lodi and Sharqi armies at this stage confirms the numerical superiority of the latter.[54] It may, however, be added here that there was nothing new

---

[51] Ibid., ff. 13b–14a.
[52] *Tarikh-i-Sher Shahi*, pp. 5–6.
[53] Ibid., p. 5.
[54] Siddiqui, *Afghan Despotism*, pp. 10–11.

or unusual in the 'invitation' to the Afghans to come to Hindustan. Even the Turkish rulers earlier had invited and settled the Afghans at strategic places. In fact, such push and pull dynamics had long been operative behind the immigration and settlement of the Afghans,[55] even as we need to remember that we are talking about a context when the boundaries of the modern nation states restricting the movements of people were nowhere in sight. The Afghan rulers of Hindustan generally invoked tribal lineages and customs for the purpose of mobilization and conquest. Once the purpose was served, the rulers were quick to set aside the tribal customary practices and instead asserted their sovereign power. Similarly, they used the bogey of Islam in the wake of the conflict with non-Muslim chieftains, but had little hesitation in ignoring the injunctions of the shari'at in matters of actual governance.

Instead, the Afghan kings like their predecessors drew upon the universal tropes of kingship. Muslim rulers before them, in India and elsewhere, had already appropriated from diverse traditions, a wide range of symbols of sovereignty for the enunciation of their power.[56] Though the sources do not provide much information on the elaborate court rituals representing the power of the Afghan kings, the right to place the crown upon the head, sit on the throne, include the name in the *khutba* (Friday sermons), mint coins (*sikka*) and collect revenue, vested with the kings and not with the 'tribal' chieftains. Similarly, *chatr* (royal umbrella), *aftabgir* (sun-umbrella), *naubat* (large kettle drum), and *naqqara* (kettle drum) were the paraphernalia of royalty, which were the special prerogatives of the sovereigns.

The titles, adopted by the kings after their enthronement, are also useful indicators of how they perceived their sovereignty and projected their power. Prince Nizam took up the title of Alexander or Sikandar and thus located himself in Islam's grand tradition, which had appropriated the symbols of sovereignty from divergent sources,

[55] For a relevant discussion see, Stewart Gordon, 'Legitimacy and Loyalty in Some Successor States of the Eighteenth Century', in his *Marathas, Marauders, and State Formation in Eighteenth-Century* (Delhi, 1994), pp. 64–81. Also see, Jos Gommans, *The Rise of the Indo-Afghan Empire, c. 1710–1780* (Leiden, 1995).

[56] For a refreshing study of Muslim kingship in general, see, Aziz Al-Azmeh, *Muslim Kingship: Power and the Sacred in Muslim, Christian and Pagan Polities* (London/New York, 1997).

including ancient Greece and Iran, as also from India. Earlier, the title was used by Sultan Ala-ud-Din Khalji (ruled 1296–1316). Farid Khan combined his two titles of Sher Khan and Shah Alam to be known as Sher Shah—asserting thereby that the lion was the king of the world. However, use of the lion or tiger-motif for the projection of the kingly power was not entirely an innovation of Sher Shah. The Saljuqids earlier had effectively utilized the title: lion-hearted.[57] Later Tipu Sultan of Mysore adopted the tiger-motif to project his power.[58] Further, the legends inscribed on the coins of the Afghan kings are also significant for the understanding of their power projection.[59] Whereas Bahlul Lodi claimed to be the *naib amir-ul-muminin* (deputy of the caliph),[60] Sher Shah counted himself amongst the rightly guided caliphs—Abu Bakr, Umar, Usman, and Ali—and referred to himself as the 'Just Sultan'.[61] Subsequently, the names of the first four caliphs were discarded by Sher Shah who claimed to be the caliph of the time (*khalifa az-zaman*).[62] Also significant was the *kalima* (the profession of faith in Islam) inscribed in a square on the obverse of Sher Shah's coins. On the other hand, he made his claims to power intelligible to his largely non-Muslim subjects by inscribing the legend, *Sri Ser Sah* or *Sri Ser Sahi* in Devanagari script on the reverse of the coin.[63]

It may be noted here that the paucity of coins of the Lodi period is attributed to the shortage of precious metals in the empire, to the extent that they were not available for minting coins.[64] This hypothesis ignores the reports of the huge treasures, which the Lodis had

---

[57] Ibid., p. 152.

[58] For Tipu Sultan, see Kate Brittlebank, *Tipu Sultan's Search for Legitimacy: Islam and Kingship in a Hindu Domain* (Delhi, 1997). Also see Janaki Nair's bold new forays in the field, 'Tipu Sultan, History Painting and the Battle for "Perspective"', *Studies in History*, Vol. 22, No. 1, 2006, pp. 97–143.

[59] For the value of coins for writing political history of the period, see Syed Ejaz Hussain's impressive data in his *The Bengal Sultanate: Politics, Economy and Coins, AD 1205–1576* (Delhi, 2003).

[60] H. Nelson Wright, *The Coinage and Metrology of the Sultans of Delhi*, reprint (Delhi, 1974), p. 246.

[61] Ibid., p. 264.

[62] Ibid., pp. 323–5.

[63] Ibid., pp. 263–89.

[64] Najaf Haider, 'The Lodi Coinage—Some Questions', *PIHC*, Golden Jubilee Session, Gorakhpur, 1989–90, pp. 229–35.

accumulated in the course of their conquests. It also neglects the impressive numbers of gold and silver coins issued by the contemporary rulers of the various regional kingdoms such as Kashmir, Malwa, Jaunpur, Bengal, and Gujarat. Even the rulers of the short-lived Sayyid dynasty had struck gold and silver coins.[65] Further, Babur (ruled 1526–30) was able to mint gold and silver coins after his conquest of Hindustan, and altogether eighty silver coins of the emperor survive from the period of his brief rule. Certainly the conqueror did not bring precious metals from outside for minting coins in India! In fact he refers to the vast Lodi treasury that had fallen into his hands in the aftermath of his victory at Panipat, a large portion of which was distributed amongst the nobles and well-wishers.

We understand that the Mughals had captured only a portion of the Lodi treasury, as the vast chunk of it was kept at forts like Chunar, which fell into the hands of Sher Khan not long after the sack of the Lodi Sultanate. The Afghan empire-builder himself issued gold and silver coins; and a large number of them, mainly silver, have survived.[66] This evidence clearly modifies the suggestion that there was a shortage of precious metals in the late-fifteenth and early-sixteenth centuries in North India that prevented the Lodis from striking gold and silver coins. The Lodi rulers' silver-mixed copper coins, known as billon, have survived. Though J.F. Richards agrees that there was no shortage of precious metals in the period, he attributes the debasement of coins under the Lodis to the decentralized, tribal nature of the administrative and political system, which curtailed the economic power of the sultans.[67] Simon Digby also notes that the 'Lodi Sultans of Delhi, less concerned with traditional Muslim concepts of sovereignty than their contemporary rivals, appear not to have issued gold or silver coins'.[68]

[65] John F. Richards, 'The Economic History of the Lodi Period: 1451–1526', in Sanjay Subrahmanyam, ed., *Money and the Market in India 1100–1700* (Delhi, 1994), pp. 137–55.

[66] Wright, *The Coinage and Metrology of the Sultans of Delhi*, pp. 263–90.

[67] Richards, 'Economic History of the Lodi Period', pp. 140, 153. Also see, John S. Deyell, 'The Development of Akbar's Currency System and Monetary Integration of the Conquered Kingdoms', in John F. Richards, ed., *The Imperial Monetary System of Mughal India* (Delhi, 1987), pp. 13–67.

[68] Simon Digby, 'The Currency System', in Tapan Raychaudhuri and Irfan Habib, eds, *The Cambridge Economic History of India, Vol. I: c. 1200–c. 1750* (Hyderabad, 1982), p. 99.

Such suggestions are not very convincing in the light of the fact that the Lodis were continuously asserting their power, using whatever tools of dominance they found effective. It appears that the silver and gold coins of the Lodis were taken out of circulation by the invading Mughals even as Babur issued coins in his own name.[69] After his death, coins were struck in the name of Humayun, and subsequently, as noted above, by Sher Shah. Whereas the Afghans of the previous generation did not care to preserve the Lodi coins partly because of their disenchantment with Ibrahim Lodi, they kept those issued by Sher Shah even as they cherished the memory of his 'just' rule.[70]

Together with coinage, the Afghan rulers also used architecture as a visual enunciation of their royal authority. Hectic building activities took place during the period. Sikandar Lodi laid the foundation of the city of Agra and made it the seat of his power so that he might exercise more effective control over the chiefs of the 'unruly' neighbourhood.[71] The historians of architecture, however, do not seem to be impressed with the building activities of the Afghan period in general. This again is influenced by the notion that Afghan polity was tribal in nature and, therefore, lacking in grandeur and magnificence. Percy Brown, for instance, wrote that the imperial power at Delhi had been of an unsubstantial nature under the Lodis. This is shown in the type of building erected during their period. Under their diminishing influence, 'all forms of constructive enterprise languished, and what

---

[69] The surviving coins may perhaps have been demonitized in the 1590s in accordance with a Mughal imperial order. For the Mughal attempt to expand its monetary regime, see Najaf Haider, 'Mughal and Mahmudis: The Incorporation of Gujarat into the Imperial Monetary System', *PIHC*, Diamond Jubilee (60th) Session, Calicut, 1999, pp. 270–86.

[70] For a different view, see, Deyell, 'Development of Akbar's Currency System', pp. 16–22. Also see, Marie H. Martin, 'The Reforms of the Sixteenth Century and Akbar's Administration: Metrological and Monetary Considerations', in Richards, ed., *Imperial Monetary System*, pp. 68–99.

[71] Suggesting that Sikandar Lodi shifted his capital to Agra in 1506, I.H. Siddiqui notes that formerly Agra was a *pargana* included in the *sarkar* of Biyana, but the sultan separated it with other nine parganas to constitute the sarkar of Agra. As the new city was to develop into the metropolitan city, it was reserved for *khalisa* and Mian Zaitun, the *shiqqdar* was assigned the duty of looking after its administration as well as development, 'Position of *Shiqqdar* under the Sultans of Delhi', *PIHC*, 28th Session, Mysore, 1966, pp. 202–8, especially pp. 204–5.

architecture was produced reflects the weakening spirit of the time'.
Brown further remarks that 'no great structural undertakings are
recorded, no capital cities were founded, no imperial palaces, no
fortresses, no mosques of importance, no colleges, and no public
buildings were erected'.[72] The author not only ignores the foundation
of the capital city of Agra by Sikandar Lodi but also contradicts his
own position by noting the construction of a number of mosques and
tombs under the Lodis that served as precedents first for Sher Shah,
and then for the Mughals. Yet, for Brown, the proliferation of tombs
under the Lodis is a sign of decline.[73] Another historian of architecture,
Catherine Asher, also attributes the proliferation of tombs under the
Lodis to the tribal polity of the Afghans, but does not ascribe the same
meaning to the continued construction of tombs under the Mughals.[74]
Tomb architecture has historically emphasized Mughal splendour.
Major landmarks in Mughal architectural tradition such as Humayun's
tomb in Delhi and Taj Mahal in Agra fall within this category.[75]

Fortunately for Sher Shah, historians of architecture have appreciated the construction of tombs and mosques under him. Sher Shah
had made it a custom to demolish existing royal structures in the
cities he conquered and build new mammoth forts and well planned
cities in their place. Indeed, there is a significant linkage between Sher
Shah's architecture and his desire for an exalted genealogy, and the
continuation of the Sur style and symbolism in Mughal architecture.[76]
Brown has noted that the octagonal plan of Lodi tombs, some of which
were of 'style and distinction', was developed further by Sher Shah
at Sahsaram[77] in a very splendid manner.[78] The tombs at Sahsaram

[72] Percy Brown, 'The Influence of Sher Shah Sur on the Islamic Architecture of
India', *PIHC*, 3rd Session, Calcutta, 1939, pp. 636–46, especially p. 638.

[73] Ibid., p. 638.

[74] Catherine Asher, *Architecture of Mughal India* (Cambridge, 1992), pp. 13–14.

[75] For useful references, see, ibid., pp. 335–56.

[76] Ibid., pp. 13–14.

[77] For Sahsaram, see B.P. Ambashthya, ed., *Beames' Contributions to the Political
Geography of the Suba of Awadh, Bihar, Bengal and Orissa in the Age of Akbar* (Patna,
1976), pp. 37–9; Irfan Habib, *An Atlas of the Mughal Empire, Political and Economic
Maps with Detailed Notes, Bibliography and Index* (Delhi, 1982), 10A, Notes.

[78] Brown, 'Influence of Sher Shah on Islamic Architecture', p. 639. For a study
of Sher Shah's tomb, see also, Catherine B. Asher, 'The Mausoleum of Sher Shah
Suri', *Artibus Asiae*, XXXIX, ¾ (1977), pp. 273–98.

represent 'the final flowering of that style and it is a florescence of notable size and splendour; so much so, that the principal example, that containing the remains of Sher Shah Sur himself, is an architectural production of which any country might be proud'.[79] What distinguishes the mausoleum of Sher Shah from the other buildings of this series at Sahsaram, built c. 1540, is that it has the almost unique location in the centre of a large artificial expanse of water. Such an unusual scheme adds very considerably to its romantic and monumental effect. Another tomb of the Sultanate period set in a lake is that of Ghiyas-ud-Din Tughluq (ruled 1320–5). However, the spirit of this tomb differed from that of Sher Shah. According to Asher, the Tughluq tomb utilized water like a moat around the fortress-like tomb with its high sloping pentagonal walls. By contrast, water at Sher Shah's wall-less tomb does not appear as a barrier but rather serves as a transition between the outside world and the tomb itself.[80]

The link between the architecture of the Sultanate and the Mughal periods is provided by the *Masjid-i-Qila-i-Kuhna*, another masterpiece of Sher Shah, built c. 1540 at Delhi. The structure of the mosque is enceinte with ideas, some of the past, others original and still more of an experimental order, so that few other buildings contain so many elements of tradition and promises of development.[81] Located inside the city founded by Sher Shah at Delhi, of which only the fort known as the Purana Qila and some of the gates have survived, the mosque also represented a crystallization of the forms and experiences seen in a series of small mosques built under the Lodis. Within the walled enclosure of the Purana Qila, in addition to the mosque, there was a concentration of secular buildings, palaces, courts, halls, and pavilions, most of which were 'swept away' by the Mughals. That these were

[79] Brown, 'Influence of Sher Shah on Islamic Architecture', p. 641.

[80] Asher, 'Mausoleum of Sher Shah', p. 278.

[81] Brown writes: 'above all it is supreme in the quality of its artistic treatment and intensely living in its architectonics, a composition well worthy of close and scientific study', in 'Influence of Sher Shah on Islamic Architecture', p. 645. R. Nath de-emphasizes the Sur influence on Mughal architecture. He doubts that such a fine architectural enterprise as the *Masjid-i-Qila-i-Kuhna* could have been undertaken by the Afghans and attributes it to Humayun, *History of Mughal Architecture*, Vol. I (Delhi, 1985), pp. 131–41. An earlier and more respectable authority, Sir Syed Ahmad Khan suggests that Sher Shah built the mosque in 1541, *Asar-us-Sanadid*, ed., Khaleeq Anjum, Vol. I (Delhi, 1990), pp. 335–6.

buildings of notable architectural merit is proved not only by the design of the mosque, but also by the exceptionally fine treatment of the gateways to the citadel. There can be little doubt that the palaces within were of the same high standard.[82] According to Brown, it was from this group of buildings that the Mughals obtained the spirit and incentive as well as many of the distinctive qualities of their own productions.[83]

Whereas the architecture served to enhance the grandeur of the Afghan kings, and also was a symbol of their might, the particular way in which royal orders (*farmans*) were to be received by the nobles also indicated the nature of Afghan monarchy. Referring to the imperial order issued to the nobles posted in the regions, Shaykh Rizqullah Mushtaqi records in his *Waqi'at-i-Mushtaqi* that they would go out on foot for two to six miles to receive the farmans. A platform was erected on which the bearer of the farman stood, and the noble standing below received it in the most respectful manner, placing it upon his head. If he was instructed to read it on the spot publicly, he did so; otherwise he took it with himself.[84] Nizam-ud-Din Ahmad adds in his *Tabaqat-i-Akbari* that if the order was that the farman should be read out in a mosque from near the pulpit, it had to be complied with.[85] The practice of paying respect to the royal orders continued under the Mughals. The elaborate reception of a farman demanded that the recipient act as if the king himself were arriving in person.[86] Further, the instruction that the order should be read out from the pulpit of a mosque was presumably intended also to lend to it a measure of sanctity and special authority. The insistence on the inclusion of the name of the ruler in the khutba was another significant step in this direction. It brought the sovereign in an enviable company of God, the Prophet, and the caliphs. The nobles, on the other hand, were relegated to the position of obedient servants of the monarch.

[82] Brown, 'Influence of Sher Shah on Islamic Architecture', p. 645.

[83] Ibid., p. 646.

[84] Shaykh Rizqullah Mushtaqi, *Waqi'at-i-Mushtaqi*, Ms. Or. 1929, OIOC, British Library, London, fol. 9a.

[85] Nizam-ud-Din Ahmad, *Tabaqat-i-Akbari*, Ms. I.O. Islamic 3320, OIOC, British Library, London, fol. 150a.

[86] J.F. Richards, 'The Formulation of Imperial Authority under Akbar and Jahangir', in his edited volume *Kingship and Authority in South Asia* (University of Wisconsin–Madison, 1978), pp. 252–85, especially, p. 274.

As mentioned above, it is often suggested that the Afghan kings had to share power with their nobles. P. Saran, a leading specialist of Mughal administration, recognizes that provincial boundaries which had hitherto been 'shifting and vague' were systematized by Sher Shah, and that the limits of the *subas* (provinces) defined by him remained practically unchanged after him. Akbar seemed to have maintained the *status quo* until he undertook a systematic reorganization of the empire into the provinces. Regarding the overall Afghan polity, however, Saran also follows the view that it was tribal and suggests that even under Sher Shah it continued to be so. He adds that the Afghan 'system' of division of the kingdom among nobles 'was not in the least altered or modified' by Sher Shah.[87] The sources, however, show that the nobility under Bahlul and his successors was quite broad-based, the non-Afghan Muslims and Rajputs each forming a fairly large group.[88] Also, the Afghan kings often asserted their supreme position by making such statements as: Just as two swords cannot be kept in one scabbard, two rulers cannot rule at one place simultaneously (*do shamshir dar yak niyam wa do hakim dar yak shahar aram nagirand*).[89] They also reminded their nobles that they should not expect a share in the government, as this was the kingdom of Hindustan where the law of the king and not the 'tribal' customs of Afghanistan constituted the law of the land.[90] The undisguised exercise of force in punishing the ambitious nobles who tried to defy royal power, and arbitrariness and innovations in carrying out the executions highlighted, in a measure, the unaccountability of the Afghan rulers.

Furthermore, the suggestion that the rulers before Akbar were inward-looking, or that they did not consider themselves as rulers of the same status as the Safavids or the Ottomans, is not entirely true in the case of at least Sher Shah, who died in an accident before his ambitious plans could reach their culmination. One of his major projects

---

[87] P. Saran, *Provincial Government of the Mughals, 1526–1658*, reprint (Bombay, 1973), pp. 55–6, 63 and 144–50. See also chapter three.

[88] I.H. Siddiqui, 'The Composition of the Nobility under the Lodi Sultans', *MIAM*, (1977), Vol. IV, pp. 10–66.

[89] *Tabaqat-i-Akbari*, fol. 197b; *Tarikh-i-Sher Shahi*, p. 46.

[90] *Tabaqat-i-Akbari*, fol. 198a; *Tarikh-i-Sher Shahi*, p. 50. M. Qasim Hindu Shah Astrabadi known as Farishta, *Gulshan-i-Ibrahimi* usually known as *Tarikh-i-Farishta*, Ms. I.O. Islamic 1251, OIOC, British Library, London, fol. 237b.

which remained unaccomplished was the colonization of the route to Afghanistan. The idea of having Afghan settlements along the route was significant not only for obstructing any invasion from the North-west, which often destroyed the political ecology of North India, but also for expansion in future. Sher Shah had even planned to send an emissary to the Ottoman sultan for a pact to undertake a joint campaign against the growing menace of the Qizilbash under the early Safavids. The idea was to engage the Qizilbash on two fronts simultaneously—on land and at sea, by the Ottomans and the Afghans. In fact, an order for the building of ships, though ostensibly for the *Hajj* pilgrims, had already been issued. Mir Rafi-ud-Din, a leading saint of that time, was to leave for Rum as an envoy. Evidence for the two projects are found in Ni'matullah Harawi's *Tarikh-i-Khan-i-Jahani wa Makhzan-i-Afghani*[91] and Mulla Abdul Qadir Badauni's *Muntakhab-ut-Tawarikh*,[92] which merit respect from the scholars, and cannot be rejected as a mere fanciful imagination of Abbas Khan Sarwani, the bete noire of scholars of Mughal history.

The author of the *Tawarikh-i-Daulat-i-Sher Shahi* gives a plausible reason for Sher Shah's animosity against the Safavids. According to him, Sher Shah had sent an ambassador to the court of Shah Tahmasp, requesting him to capture Hamayun and hand him over to his men. Instead of obliging the Afghan king, Shah Tahmasp cut off the ears and nose of the Indian envoy. Sher Shah, as a reprisal, ordered the mutilation and expulsion of all the Qizilbash nobles who had links with the Mughals, and were still living in any part of his dominion. Further, he ordered all the Persian inhabitants of his kingdom to be expelled and their properties to be attached to the state; anyone offering them help or protection was to be treated as an outlaw.[93]

In the light of the evidence of a relentless imperialistic project under the Afghans, it is difficult for us to agree with the 'tribal-anarchy' hypothesis. Furthermore, to evaluate the Afghan polity in a more nuanced perspective we may refer to a few models of state in medieval

[91] Khwaja Ni'matullah Harawi, *Tarikh-i-Khan-i-Jahani wa Makhzan-i-Afghani*, 2 Vols, ed., S.M. Imamuddin (Decca, 1960–2): Vol. I, p. 335.

[92] Mulla Abdul Qadir Badauni, *Muntakhab-ut-Tawarikh*, 3 Vols, eds, Ahmad Ali, Kabir al-Din Ahmad and W. Nassau Lees (Calcutta, 1864–9): Vol. I, pp. 369–70.

[93] Riazul Islam, *Indo-Persian Relations: A Study of the Political and Diplomatic Relations Between the Mughal Empire and Iran* (Tehran, 1970), p. 202.

India.[94] These include: (a) Marx's notion of oriental despotism and the Asiatic mode of production, which concedes to the 'unchanging' state a strong centralized coercion for external warfare and internal exploitation of the village communities. (b) The Indian historiographical model of a rather unitary centrally organized and territorially defined kingdom with a strong bureaucracy. (c) The Marxist-inspired model of Indian feudalism of a decentralized and fragmented feudal state. (d) The model of the segmentary state, which locates the early medieval state between the tribal 'stateless' form of government and a patrimonial state. (e) The patrimonial state, which depicts the Mughal empire as household-dominated, rather than a highly structured bureaucratically-administered state.[95] Some scholars have stressed the presence of a powerful centralized bureaucracy as the vital characteristic of historical empires. While accepting the idea of a bureaucratic dominance, some other scholars have asserted that the diffusion of firearms, especially siege artillery, explains the aggregation of central power, which brought the Mughal empire into being.[96] This view, termed as the 'gunpowder empire hypothesis', is not applicable to the empire-building activities of the Afghans as they almost entirely depended upon the cavalry for their conquests. Indeed, as we shall see below, the use of gunpowder could at times have disastrous consequences.

Besides these major concepts of the state in medieval India, there exist a considerable number of what is characterized as the 'non-aligned' contributions, which emphasize processes of state formation rather than the state as a given entity. These are attempts at an analysis of political processes and the changes in the structure of polity in medieval India, and perceive political changes through centralization and integration. Even though these changes tended to be restricted to certain periods and regions, they regularly relapsed, usually during dynastic crisis, but normally did not fall back into status quo ante. Thus a certain degree of structural alterations survived these dynastic changes.[97] They also underscore the series of processes, for example,

[94] Herman Kulke, ed., *The State in India, 1000–1700* (Delhi, 1995).

[95] Kulke, 'Introduction: The Study of the State in Pre-modern India', in his edited volume, *The State in India*, pp. 1–47, especially pp. 1–2.

[96] Douglas E. Streusand, *The Formation of the Mughal Empire* (Delhi, 1989), pp. 9–10.

[97] Kulke, 'Introduction', p. 40.

extension of agrarian society through peasantization of tribal groups; improvement of trading networks; emergence and spatial extending of ruling lineages by so called 'Kshatriyaization' or 'Rajputization'; 'greater penetration of the royal will into local arenas of power'; and never-ending though rarely successful attempts to centralize administrative functions, particularly revenue collection, etc.[98] Another major topic of various recent studies is the role played by religious institutions in the process of state formation. They take into account various aspects of medieval socio-religious developments, for example, religious and socio-political integration through religious networks, royal legitimization and expansion of royal influence through patronage and management of temples and shrines.[99]

Among these, the contributions which highlight the processes of state formation with the significant role played by religious institutions are valuable for an appreciation of the Afghan polity. Indeed, the sources suggest that religion was an important factor in the articulation and projection of Afghan power. It ensured that the Afghan king was both absolute and limited. Being a representative of God on earth, he enjoyed certain discretionary powers and was accountable to 'Him' only. But if he failed to ensure peace and order in the realm, and oppressed the subject, he could lose his 'job' on account of the prayer of a saintly person, for example, a Sufi shaykh. The sources mention several anecdotes in which a reigning king was removed from the throne by the Sufi saint, and kingship was bestowed upon some one who was portrayed as a more deserving person. It is no wonder then that the rulers tried to keep the saints in good humour, and in return, sought legitimacy from them. Significantly, in this connection, Sher Shah is said to have insisted upon his nobles to maintain dignity in public and to fear God.[100] Thus, any study of Afghan polity must necessarily take into account the role of religion in it. The Sufis' involvement in politics with all their visions and miracles was of particular significance.

The intermingling of religion and politics does not imply that Afghan polity was theocratic in nature. The rulers' dependence on the ulama and the Sufis for support and legitimacy was crucial in a political tradition without a strong rule of primogeniture. Moreover,

[98] Ibid., p. 41.
[99] Ibid., pp. 42–3.
[100] For details see chapter two.

the support of the minority Muslim population, whose political understanding was informed by the religious institutions like the mosques and the hospices of the Sufis (khanqahs), was also necessary for the king who projected himself as the protector of the faith. The Muslims did feel secure and comfortable in such a dispensation even as they were aware of the fact that the rulers did not make any serious attempt to implement the shari'at as the law of the land. On the other hand, the Afghan rulers understood that a strict adherence to the shari'at was impracticable for ruling the vast majority of non-Muslim population.

The sources need therefore to be read afresh for an apposite appreciation of the period. Of the so-called Afghan chroniclers, only Abbas and Kabir belonged to that *qaum* or *biradari*. Employed in the service of the Mughals, they did not stand to gain by extolling the achievements of the enemies of their masters. Abbas Sarwani himself, in his composition presented as a gift to Akbar, emerges as an apologist for Sher Shah seeking favours from the Mughal emperor. The memory of the reverses the Mughals encountered at the hands of the Afghans under Sher Shah continued to haunt them for long. In his *Ma'asir-ul-Umara*, Shah Nawaz Khan has recorded that Akbar was always apprehensive of Daulat Khan Lodi, known as one of the bravest men of his age. When the news of his death was conveyed to Akbar he heaved a sigh of relief, and said, 'This day Sher Khan Sur has departed from the world (*im-roz sher khan sur az alam raft)*.[101] Indeed, the Mughals spared no efforts to marginalize the Afghans after the restoration of their rule.[102]

The Mughal chroniclers have invariably voiced their masters' hostility in their panegyric accounts of the reign of Humayun. Prominent amongst them is Abu'l Fazl who presents the Afghans in his *Akbarnama* as the dangerous 'other', totally unreliable since 'treachery' of their leader Sher Shah had cost the Mughals their dominion. Incidentally, Abu'l Fazl did not recognize Sher Shah as the *badshah* of Hindustan, as he has used the Afghan king's earlier title of Sher Khan throughout.

[101] Nawab Samsam-ud-Daula Shah Nawaz Khan, *Ma'asir-ul-Umara*, Ms. I.O. Islamic 2443, OIOC, British Library, London, fol. 202b.
[102] For the representation of the Afghans in Mughal imperial service, see Afzal Husain, *The Nobility under Akbar and Jahangir: A Study of Family Group* (Delhi, 1999); Firdos Anwar, *Nobility under the Mughals, 1628–1658* (Delhi, 2001); M. Athar Ali, *The Nobility under Aurangzeb* (Delhi, 1997).

Moreover, he has used his stock of abusive epithets for the Afghans generally, and for Sher Shah in particular.

The Mughal or Akbari hegemony continued to shape the texture of subsequent historiography. The history of the Afghan period became a victim of this hegemony. Mostly produced under the Mughals, the texts dealing with the Afghans have generally been utilized in ways that do not conform to the standards of source criticism and the methodological demands of dispassionate appreciation of the material. When the choice is, for instance, between the conflicting accounts of Abbas and Kabir, the latter is generally preferred. When both these Afghan authorities concur on a point, the divergent opinion of either Abu'l Fazl or Jauhar Aftabchi (another 'His Majesty's voice') is considered to be 'authentic'.[103] The Mughal chroniclers enjoy such a pervasive influence on modern scholarship that while Aftabchi is said to have recorded everything 'faithfully',[104] Abbas Sarwani's intentions are often doubted.[105] We may submit that the account of Abbas Sarwani needs to be treated more carefully. Short of hyperboles, an earlier authority, Rizqullah Mushtaqi, corroborates his account. Another writer, Nizam-ud-Din Ahmad, who is generally respected for his balanced narrative, further confirms the account of Abbas Sarwani to a great extent. Abdul Qadir Badauni not only supports Abbas Sarwani but also actually glorifies the history of the earlier period. He takes pride in the fact of his birth in the 'blessed' reign of Sher Shah.[106] Other scholars such as Ni'matullah Harawi and Ahmad Yadgar[107] have produced a more balanced narrative even as they have drawn on Abbas Sarwani's work and have reflected the perception that perhaps the Afghan rulers had greater regard for justice, which is generally defined in terms of the concern for the welfare of the people and the respect for the norms of the grand traditions of Islam, as we shall see in chapter three.

[103] Jauhar Aftabchi, *Tazkirat-ul-Waqi'at*, or *Tarikh-i-Humayun Shahi*, British Museum Ms. Add. 16711, OIOC, British Library, London.

[104] I.H. Siddiqui, *History of Sher Shah Sur* (Aligarh, 1971), p. 54.

[105] Cf. Alam and Subrahmanyam, 'Introduction', in their edited, *The Mughal State*, p. 19.

[106] *Muntakhab-ut-Tawarikh*, Vol. I, p. 363.

[107] Ahmad Yadgar, *Tarikh-i-Salatin-i-Afaghina*, ed., M. Hidayat Hosain (Calcutta, 1939).

Glorification of Akbar's achievements sometimes leads to the vulgarization and belittling of Afghan exploits. Mention may be made here of the circulation of the scandalous report that Sher Shah had occupied the strong Ruhtas fort by sending armed soldiers inside the citadel disguised as women in palanquins. Unable to digest Sher Shah's capture of one of the most impregnable forts, Abu'l Fazl writes that by a hundred flatteries and deceptions the simple-minded Hindu chief of the place was conned by that trickster, Sher Shah.[108] Later writers have also followed Abu'l Fazl's account.[109] The circulation of this story must have considerably affronted the Afghans as it clearly amounted to an insult and expressed contempt for their capabilities as honourable warriors. Abbas, for one, rejects it as 'simply false and slanderous'.[110] In this connection, the example of Abu'l Fazl's propagation of an alleged statement of Babur that Sher Shah's eyes betrayed 'turbulence' and 'strife-mongering' may also be mentioned.[111] It is evidently the *Akbarnama* from which Ni'matullah borrows Babur's alleged remark that the eyes of that Afghan named Sher Khan betrayed turbulence and strife mongering (*chashman in afghan sher khan nam dalalat bar fitna wa shor-angezi mi-kunand*).[112]

The Mughal court painters were not behind in getting the message through such treatment; some of them were, indeed, quick to grasp this image of Sher Shah. A portrait of the Afghan ruler existing from, at least, as early as the reign of Jahangir, clearly depicts his eyes itching for '*fitna*' (turbulence) and '*shor-angezi*' (strife mongering).[113] Conversely, as J.F. Richards points out, in more than fifty paintings directly portraying emperor Akbar, 'the artists contrast the divine order, self-control, and harmony of the emperor as the illumined person, with

[108] Abu'l Fazl, *Akbarnama*, Ms. I.O. Islamic 4, OIOC, British Library, London, fol. 84b.

[109] *Tarikh-i-Khan-i-Jahani wa Makhzan-i-Afghani*, Vol. I, pp. 293–5; *Tarikh-i-Salatin-i-Afaghina*, pp. 187–9. Firishta adds that the merit of the invention of this strategy of sending soldiers in the guise of women is not due to Sher Shah; the fort of Asir in the Deccan having been long before acquired in the same manner by Nasir Khan Faruqi, ruler of Khandesh, *Tarkh-i-Farishta*, fol. 239b.

[110] *Tarikh-i-Sher Shahi*, p. 110.

[111] *Akbarnama*, fol. 82a.

[112] *Tarikh-i-Khan-i-Jahani wa Makhzan-i-Afghani*, Vol. I, p. 275.

[113] Portrait published in Gulbadan Begam, *Humayun-Nama*, ed. and trans. A.S. Beveridge, reprint (Delhi, 1983), facing p. 133.

the turgid, struggling disorder of those unwieldy masses of men and mankind seen in the remainder of the painting'.[114]

A logical follow up of all this is also the general representation of the Afghans as rustic people always engaged in pillage and undue aggrandizement. Though the Afghans themselves provided some of the material for the dissemination of their image as 'foolish rustics',[115] much of it was invented by the Mughals in the wake of their all out effort to discredit the Afghan rulers. To illustrate this point further, let us take the case of the reconstruction of Sher Shah's early life by K.R. Qanungo. The author suggests that during his student days at Jaunpur, Sher Shah (then Farid), a 'robust and daring youth', operated as 'part time thief', graduating in course of time as a 'bandit chief'.[116] This is in flagrant disregard of the evidence in the Persian sources which state that Sher Shah had utilized his period of stay at Jaunpur in not only studying the standard texts on statecraft and history, but also in cultivating himself in the company of the noted ulama and the mashai'kh of the area (*dar suhbat ulama wa mashai'kh an diyar ba tahzib-i akhlaq mashghul bud*).[117]

Qanungo, however, cites Rizqullah Mushtaqi and Abu'l Fazl as his authorities in this connection. The latter has recorded that after the death of his father, all his property fell into Farid's hands, and he began to create trouble in the territory of Sahsaram and in the jungles of Chaund by indulging in such crime as theft, robbery and murder.[118] Qanungo corrects Abu'l Fazl and suggests that Farid practised theft and robbery (omits murder) *not after* (emphasis original) the death of Hasan but during his lifetime probably in places other than 'Sahsaram and the jungles of Chaund'.[119] I.H. Siddiqui differs from Qanungo to

---

[114] Richards, 'Formulation of Imperial Authority', p. 262.

[115] See, for instance, the deliberately enacted idiotic behaviour of the followers of Bahlul in the latter's quest to capture power at Delhi, *Waqi'at-i-Mushtaqi*, ff. 4a-b; *Tabaqat-i-Akbari*, fols. 133b–134a; Abdullah, *Tarikh-i-Dau'di*, ed., Sk. Abdur Rashid (Aligarh, 1954), pp. 8–9.

[116] K.R. Qanungo, *Sher Shah and his Times* (Bombay, 1965), pp. 32–3.

[117] *Muntakhab-ut-Tawarikh*, Vol. I, p. 357. See also *Tarikh-i-Sher Shahi*, p. 14; *Tabaqat-i-Akbari*, fol. 196a; *Tarikh-i-Khan-i-Jahani wa Makhzan-i-Afghani*, Vol. I, pp. 263–4; *Tarikh-i-Salatin-i-Afaghina*, p. 173; *Tarikh-i-Dau'di*, p. 108.

[118] *Akbarnama*, fol. 82a.

[119] Qanungo, *Sher Shah Sur and his Times*, p. 43.

suggest that Farid 'had taken to robbery' after having been removed
from the position of shiqqdar of the parganas, and not as a student in
Jaunpur.[120] We have already drawn attention to the dubious nature of
Abu'l Fazl's account of this period. Any reliance on him alone can be
disastrous. Let us turn to Mushtaqi's narrative. He reports that while
campaigning in the region of Malwa, Sher Shah told Mallu Khan that
in his early life he had associated himself with the dacoits and high-
waymen and plundered the country all around.[121] On the basis of this
evidence, Qanungo suggests that as 'even the most taciturn of men,
prone to excessive reserve, are known to indulge in their lighter moods
in old age when in the company of kindred spirits, when they can
well afford to laugh at their own juvenile follies, we have no reason to
distrust Sher Shah's alleged confession' to Mallu Khan.[122] The use of
such phrases as the 'lighter mood' and 'the company of kindred spirits'
by the author clearly shows that Qanungo first accepts Abu'l Fazl's version and then reads Mushtaqi to locate a corroborative evidence, di-
vesting the reference to brigandage here of its context.

Mallu Khan, it must be noted, was one of the few warlords who
had refused to accept Sher Shah as the king of Hindustan even after
the latter's victory over the Mughal emperor, Humayun. The former
had even pretended to be a sovereign in his own right, styling himself
as Qadir Shah.[123] It is to chastise him, and also the 'Purabia'[124] upstart
Puranmal that Sher Shah had to undertake his Malwa campaign (to
be discussed in chapter four below). Mallu Khan, however, surrendered
before Sher Shah soon after the arrival of the latter at Sarangpur.
The subsequent account of the treatment meted out to Mallu Khan, a
captive in Sher Shah's camp, shows a deliberate attempt on the part of
the king to terrorize him with the purpose of driving home the point
that kingship was not his glass of wine. The army's march to Ujjain,
fully equipped with arms and weapons, with the soldiers putting on

[120] Siddiqui, *History of Sher Shah Sur*, p. 20.

[121] For references to Mallu Khan in the *Waqi'at-i-Mushtaqi*, see ff. 52a–53b.

[122] Qanungo, *Sher Shah and his Times*, p. 33.

[123] *Waqi'at-i-Mushtaqi*, ff. 52a–b. Upendra Nath Day, *Medieval Malwa—
A Political and Cultural History 1401–1562* (Delhi, 1965), pp. 330–4.

[124] Iqtidar Alam Khan, 'Re-examining the Origin and Group Identity of the
so-called Purabias, 1500–1800', PIHC, Diamond Jubilee (60th) Session, Calicut,
1999, pp. 363–71.

iron armour in the 'hot sun', the leading nobles faking an attack on Sher Shah during the march and their ensuing submission and saluta-tion, and the narration of the hardships faced in early life including the reference to dacoity and plunder were designed to instil terror in the Khan's mind. The strategy actually worked on the desired line. A completely astounded Mallu Khan fled away in the direction of Gujarat. Having done away with the pretender, at least for the time being, Sher Shah turned his attention to the slightly more powerful Puranmal. Sher Shah's action against Puranmal and his Rajput followers, who were reportedly massacred at his command, has been condemned as 'treacherous' by modern scholars. The evidence is generalized to prove his 'failure' to break the shackles of Islamic orthodoxy, as also his inability to incorporate the Rajputs in the Indo-Muslim political network.

It may however be mentioned here that the criticism of the Afghan rulers' alleged intolerance in existing historiography seems influenced by an enthusiasm to establish that Akbar commenced the policy of tolerance towards non-Muslims. Our own reading of the sources suggests that hardly any ruler of the Delhi Sultanate attempted to annihilate the non-Muslim population, or used force to convert them to Islam and impose the shari'at as the basis of governance. On the contrary, the emphasis was on integrating the regional warlords in an imperialistic project.[125] The sources throw invaluable light on much more than the military campaigns of the Muslim rulers. Much of the material available therein actually elucidates the early Muslim endeavour to come to terms with the local reality through rapproche-ments and appropriations. Awfi's *Jawami-ul-Hikayat*, completed sometime after 1230, comprises a whole section on counsels for 'good government, stable administration and welfare of the subjects'. Further, a farman of Ala-ud-Din Khalji stresses the minimum use of violence

---

[125] J.F. Richards suggests that the increasing employment of unconverted free Indian nobles by the Muslim rulers was not 'solely a matter of increased "toler-ance" on the part of the Muslims, but the end result of forced Hindu acceptance of a harsh reality', in 'Introduction', in his edited *Kingship and Authority*, p. X. For the problems faced by the early Delhi sultans in establishing their authority, see also, Peter Hardy, 'The Growth of Authority over a Conquered Political Elite: The Early Delhi Sultanate as a Possible Case Study', in Richards, ed., *Kingship and Authority*, pp. 192–214.

and bloodshed both for conquest and enforcement of 'law'. Dictionaries compiled by the middle of the fourteenth century incorporate non-Persian words and terms indicating a quest for an acceptable politico-cultural idiom. The translation of the Arabic classics in the thirteenth century and the Persian adaptation of the ancient Indian tales such as the *Basatin-ul-Uns* of Malik Ikhtisan, completed in 1325–6, may also be viewed in terms of the willingness to adapt to, or incorporate from, diverse sources of tradition. [126]

The Afghan kings encouraged Rajputs and other non-Muslims to join imperial service, thereby broadening the base of the government apparatus. If the rulers aimed to establish direct rule throughout Hindustan, this would have called for the extirpation of the indigenous chieftains, which in turn implied large-scale loss of soldiers. The more viable option was to make the chieftains accept their suzerainty and allow them to run the local administration on the condition that it was to be closely supervised by the imperial governors. This arrangement was useful on several counts. Acceptance of Afghan paramountcy meant expansion of Afghan power in Rajput strongholds without much resistance. It also ensured undisturbed flow of revenues from the countryside. Further, the military support of the Rajput allies could enhance the prospects of conquest and control of new/hostile regions. The Afghan rulers found this more suitable. Their policy towards the Rajputs was thus aimed primarily at incorporating them in their imperial projects. Thus the local institutions and ideals were assimilated in the process. Some of the liberal trends, which are generally attributed to Akbar, actually owe their origin to the policies pursued by the Afghans.[127]

As we shall see in chapter six, the role played by the Sufis in this process of assimilation was particularly significant. Existing historiography does highlight their role in the building of a syncretic medieval culture. The doctrine of *wahdat-ul-wujud* (monism as a reality) had brought the Sufis close to certain streams of non-Muslim thought. Amongst the supporters of the doctrine was the leading Chishti shaykh,

---

[126] For relevant sources, see I.H. Siddiqui, *Perso-Arabic Sources of Information on the Life and Conditions in the Sultanate of Delhi* (Delhi, 1992). Also see, Muhammad Nizamu'd-Din, *Introduction to the Jawama'ul-Hikayat wa Lawami'ur-Riwayat of Sadidu'd-Din Muhammad Al-'Awfi* (London, 1929).

[127] For a detailed treatment of this problem, see chapter four.

Abdul Quddus Gangohi. Another mystic, Saiyid Muhammad Ghaus Gwaliori, popularized yogic practices in Sufi circles and drew attention to the similarities in the spiritual terminologies of various mystical traditions. Further, the contribution of the Sufis to the growth and development of vernacular literature and devotional music is equally noteworthy. At times, however, the Sufis could take as fanatical a position as that of any 'orthodox' *alim* (religious scholar) from medieval India. Elsewhere, we have analysed some stories of miraculous encounters between the Sufis and the non-Muslim spiritual power-holders such as the brahmanas and the yogis. These anecdotes are a valuable source material for a better understanding of the complexities of religious tensions in medieval India.[128] The Sufis' pursuit of an authoritative position in society brought them in contact with the rulers, as we shall see in chapter five. We have noted above how some modern scholars suggest that the period witnessed 'spiritual anarchy' because the Sufis of various orders (silsilas) hankered after power and wealth. This formulation is based on a premise that the Sufis, in particular the Chishtis of the earlier period, that is, the thirteenth and fourteenth centuries, maintained distance from the politics of their time. This assumption has already been questioned in some recent researches. The role of the Sufis in politics, including those of the Chishti order, is no longer viewed as something profane and soul-pollutant.[129]

To sum up the main points of the foregoing, we examined the existing propositions in secondary works, which delineate that the period of the Afghan rule witnessed the disintegration of the 'central-ized' political structure of the Delhi Sultanate resulting in a general

---

[128] Raziuddin Aquil, 'Conversion in Chishti Sufi Literature'.

[129] For the Sufis' role in politics, see, Richard M. Eaton, *Sufis of Bijapur, 1300–1700, Social Roles of Sufis in Medieval India* (Princeton, 1978); Simon Digby, 'The Sufi Shaykh as a Source of Authority in Medieval India', *Purushartha*, 9 (1986), 55–77; idem, 'The Sufi Shaikh and the Sultan: A Conflict of Claims to Authority in Medieval India.' *Iran*, 28 (1990), 71–81; Carl W. Ernst, *Eternal Garden: Mysticism, History and Politics at a South Asian Sufi Centre* (Albany, 1992); I.A. Zilli, 'Early Chishtis and the State', in Anup Taneja, ed., *Sufi Cults and the Evolution of Medieval Indian Culture* (Delhi, 2003), pp. 54–108; Raziuddin Aquil, 'Sufi Cults, Politics and Conversion'; idem, 'Miracles, Authority and Benevolence: Stories of *Karamat* in Sufi Literature of the Delhi Sultanate', in Taneja, ed., *Sufi Cults and the Evolution of Medieval Indian Culture*, pp. 109–38.

crisis. The suggestion in these works that this disintegration was caused by the 'tribal' character of Afghan polity has also been reconsidered. Contrary to the notion that the Afghan polity was tribal in nature, and that a decentralized-tribal polity is incompatible with peace and stability, the primary material indicates that rather than depending upon tribal lineages and customs only, the Afghan rulers drew on the universal tropes of kingship for the articulation of their power. This is clearly reflected, among other things, in the relentless campaigns for the expansion of their dominion, issuing of coins, insistence on the inclusion of their names in the khutba, grand architectural plans and their projection as the shadow of God on earth. Further, the details about governance recorded by the medieval authorities point to a kind of 'welfare monarchy' in the period. As we shall see in chapter three, sixteenth century narratives have portrayed the Afghan kings as ideal rulers, whose welfare mechanism, personal piety and revenue-free grants to holy-men were much celebrated. These accounts cannot be dismissed as mere imaginations of Afghan historians, for non-Afghan writers have also presented largely similar pictures of the period. There are thus some serious lacunae in the historiography of the Afghan period. Studies on the nature of polity and the role of religion in it seem to be heavily influenced by the 'hegemonistic' and imperialist Mughal discourse. We may submit that the issues relevant to religion and politics need to be reconsidered not only for a balanced and empirically sustainable picture of the period, but also for a more accurate understanding of the growth and development of political ideals and institutions under the Mughals in the second half of the sixteenth century. For this purpose, a study of the Afghan imperialistic project under Sher Shah will be a worthwhile exercise. It may be noted that the Afghan empire-builder is often dismissed by the historians as a 'warlord'-turned-'sultan', equal in rank perhaps to such 'Purabia' upstart as Puranmal. As a matter of fact, the status and prestige of the 'sultan' had considerably declined by the early sixteenth century. Muslim rulers were increasingly styling themselves as badshahs in their own right.

PART I

STRUGGLE FOR POWER AND DOMINANCE

1

The Making of a Badshah
Emergence of Sher Shah Sur

Do not raise anyone of the Surs to the rank of *amir* because they have got ambition for sovereignty.

Sultan Bahlul to his son, Nizam, later Sultan Sikandar[1]

AMBITION WAS INDEED THE HALLMARK of many an Afghan adventurer who travelled to far-off places in search of *naukari* or *chakari* (service), and if possible a *wilayat* where the dignity or honour of the clan and the tribe could be safeguarded. While some remained petty horse dealers, or ordinary soldiers, others rose dramatically to carve out vast kingdoms of their own.[2] In this chapter we shall attempt to describe the circumstances leading to the emergence of Sher Shah as the badshah of Hindustan. Though we shall primarily depend on Abbas Sarwani's *Tarikh-i-Sher Shahi*, other works which deal with the period will also be taken into account. Further, the works of the Mughal chroniclers like Jauhar Aftabchi and Abu'l Fazl will be consulted with the qualification that, from the Afghan point of view, theirs is basically a text of 'othering'. The Mughals sought to vulgarize and marginalize

---

[1] According to Rizqullah Mushtaqi, Sultan Bahlul advised his son: *hich sur ra amir na-kuni ke dimagh badshahi darand*, *Waqi'at-i-Mushtaqi*, fol. 47b.

[2] See for instance Stewart Gordon, 'Legitimacy and Loyalty in Some Successor States', for Dost Muhammad Khan who migrated from Afghanistan in 1703, and enlisted in the Mughal army as an ordinary soldier and went on to establish his own kingdom of Bhopal. Other Afghan kingdoms which emerged in the eighteenth century, including Rohilkhand, evidently benifitted from the availability of the Afghan soldiers in the North Indian labour market. For the rise of Rohilkhand, see Gommans, *The Rise of the Indo-Afghan Empire*.

the Afghans after returning to power in the second half of the sixteenth century.

The existing literature on the rise of Sher Shah Sur is undoubtedly of considerable value, but it also needs reconsideration. We have indicated in the Introduction as to how the sources of Afghan history have been utilized arbitrarily. This is true for the story of the emergence of Sher Shah as well. As we shall point out at relevant places during the course of this chapter, whereas the modern authorities are very critical of the Afghan historians, there is not much appreciation of the problems which one confronts in the accounts of the late sixteenth century 'faithful' Mughal chroniclers. The formulations in the second- ary literature appear to have been influenced by the dominant Mughal ideology. Further, the chronology of events of the early phase of Sher Shah's career is yet to be ascertained satisfactorily. Modern scholars have tried to establish the dates of important events, leading at times to bizarre results. This again is due to the defects and inconsistencies in the extant sources. Another important problem in modern writings is the virtual neglect of the involvement of religion in politics. The sources cannot be blamed for this, as they record anecdotes which provide significant insights into the Afghan attempts at empire- building. Several stories of bestowal of kingship to Sher Shah by the Sufi shaykhs are narrated in the chronicles and Sufi literature. Reports of supernatural beings fighting on behalf of Sher Shah in the battles against Humayun and during the campaigns against Rajput chieftains are not uncommon. Modern scholars have ignored these reports. Ishwari Prasad refers in a footnote to Humayun's suggestion that he had seen supernatural beings fighting at Qannauj, but rejects it as useless: 'These statements are not to be taken literally. They are only medieval modes of describing victories and defeats'.[3] In view of all this, it seems that the story of the career of Sher Shah remains to be told afresh.

Iqtidar Husain Siddiqui's researches have provided considerable sophistication to our understanding of Afghan history. Siddiqui has exposed the received wisdom in the existing historiography by a more careful reading of the sources. We have referred above to his *Afghan Despotism* in which he has cogently argued against the characterization

---

[3] Ishwari Prasad, *The Life and Times of Humayun* (Allahabad, n.d.), p. 150.

of Afghan polity as 'tribal'. However, as we have noticed, the author ignores the crucial linkages between religion and politics in the period of our study. Also, Siddiqui's recently published *Sher Shah Sur and his Dynasty* does not show much improvement over its earlier version entitled *Sher Shah Sur*.[4] Amongst other things, discrepancy in the chronology remains unresolved; this we will notice in the course of our narrative. At times, it also seems that the methodology pursued with reference to the utilization of the sources is inconsistent. Referring to Muhammad Kabir's *Afsana-i-Shahan*, Siddiqui himself notes that the author 'seems to have been ignorant even of the elementary facts of history. He was not at all a historian by inclination. There are neither dates of important events nor the sequence of events is well-arranged'.[5] Yet Siddiqui not only follows Kabir for the chronology of events in the early phase of Sher Shah's career, but often assigns specific dates to certain events. In doing so, he rejects the more important Afghan source, *Tarikh-i-Sher Shahi* of Abbas Sarwani, as unreliable. Also, in a few cases, when both these Afghan historians corroborate each other, the contrary opinion of Mughal chroniclers such as Jauhar Aftabchi or Abu'l Fazl is preferred. At times, as we shall illustrate below, Siddiqui ignores a whole corpus of sources in favour of a solitary evidence which provides a different picture.

Further, Siddiqui's political narrative on Sher Shah's career abruptly ends on the eve of the battle of Chausa. The two battles at Chausa and Qannauj have not been examined. Thus, such an important theme as the causes of Humayun's defeat remain unaddressed. Siddiqui is apparently satisfied with the existing formulations on Humayun's encounter with Sher Shah, as he notes that the battles have been 'discussed by the modern scholars at length'. This is surprising because the earlier studies by Ishwari Prasad and K.R. Qanungo need to be thoroughly revised. We shall identify the problems in the writings of the two authorities at relevant places during the course of our own analysis of the battles. Modern writings on Sher Shah's subsequent campaigns in various regions such as Malwa and Rajasthan should also be reconsidered. Such an exercise will be of great value, as the Afghan empire-builder's later image is largely shaped by an uncritical

[4] I.H. Siddiqui, *Sher Shah Sur and his Dynasty* (Jaipur, n.d.).
[5] Ibid., pp. 3–4.

reading of the medieval accounts of his action against certain Rajput chieftains. Our own reading of the sources reveal that a reappraisal of these issues will be a legitimate exercise. A fresh study of Sher Shah's conflict with Humayun and later with a section of the Rajputs will be more meaningful if we also take into account the galloping early career of the empire-builder. Even though we will be using much of the known material, a careful perusal of the chapter will show our differences with the earlier authorities.

We may however submit that our attempt to trace the career graph of Sher Shah is very tentative. Given the nature of extant sources, we have refrained from assigning fixed dates to important events. We are also reluctant to draw conclusions on points on which different sources provide divergent and conflicting accounts. Thus the attempt is to highlight the complexities of the political arena of early sixteenth century Hindustan, and point to the various factors which facilitated the rise of Sher Shah. Though ambition and adverse circumstances induced extraordinary courage, the Afghan empire-builder exploited the conditions through sheer hard work and craftiness to emerge as the sole leader who could mobilize the Afghans to drive out the Mughals from Hindustan. His first task was to unite the Afghans who were riven with clan rivalries and conflicts. Bahlul's suggestion quoted in the prescript shows how Sher Shah's own Sur clan was sidelined in the Lodi Sultanate. Within the clan, Muhammad Khan was trying to reduce others to subjection. There were bigger players in the field too. The Afghan pretender Sultan Mahmud, the Nuhanis of Bihar, the Rajput chieftains, and the ruler of Bengal were closely watching the political developments and trying to fish in troubled waters. They were eliminated from the scene one by one, and Sher Shah with his large Afghan force was in a position to give Humayun a run for his money. In recounting these events we have avoided passing value-judgements on Sher Shah's actions—to which modern historians often resort to.

The refrain that the Afghans came from all quarters like 'ants and locusts' may be an exaggeration. But the fact that the push and pull dynamics behind Afghan immigration into India continued to be active under the Lodis cannot be denied.[6] Attracted by the material wealth of Hindustan as so extravagantly displayed and splurged by

---

[6] For details, see chapter two.

Sultan Bahlul Lodi, Sher Shah's grandfather, Ibrahim, joined a group of Afghans at Roh[7] who were packing their bags for the 'broad and rich' country of Hind. Soon after his arrival, Ibrahim Khan entered the service of a Lodi noble, and took up his residence at Bajwara.[8] Later, Ibrahim came into the service of Jamal Khan Sarangkhani at Hisar Firuza[9] and got several villages in pargana Narnaul[10] as *iqta* (assignment of land) for maintenance of forty horsemen.[11] Nizam-ud-Din Ahmad and Abdullah write that Hasan's father Ibrahim came to Hindustan in the wake of Sultan Bahlul's call, and joined the service of one of his nobles. He was based at Hisar Firuza for some time, and later at Narnaul.[12] Ni'matullah does not mention Narnaul.[13] The official Mughal chronicler Abu'l Fazl suggests that Ibrahim was an ordinary horse dealer, who resided in a village called Shamla in the territory of Narnaul.[14]

Meanwhile, Sher Shah's father, Mian Hasan, joined the service of Umar Khan Sarwani,[15] a close confidant of Sultan Bahlul. However,

[7] For Roh, see Hussain Khan, 'The Genesis of Roh (The Medieval Homeland of the Afghans)', *JASP*, Vol. XV, No. 3, 1970, pp. 191–7; idem, 'The Political and Economic Conditions of Roh', *JASP*, Vol. XVI, No. 2, 1971, pp. 177–82.

[8] Located in the Harhana, or Hariana, tract Bajwara was particularly known for the cavalry horses which were reckoned equal to the Iraqi breed, Habib, *Atlas*, 4 A & B, Notes.

[9] Under Akbar, Hisar Firuza was a sarkar of suba Delhi. Area: 12,445 square miles, Jama: 52,554,905 *dams*, Habib, *Atlas*, Table I and 4 A, Notes. The name Hisar Firuza is derived from Sultan Firuz Shah Tughluq who is said to have founded the place, see M.M. Juneja, *History of Hisar from Inception to Independence, 1345–1947* (Hisar, 1989).

[10] Headquarters of the sarkar of the same name, suba Agra under Akbar. Area: 4125 square miles, Jama: 51,046,711 dams, Habib, *Atlas*, Table I and 4 A & B, Notes.

[11] *Tarikh-i-Sher Shahi*, pp. 8–9.

[12] *Tabaqat-i-Akbari*, fols. 195b–196a; *Tarikh-i-Dau'di*, p. 107.

[13] *Tarikh-i-Khan-i-Jahani wa Makhzan-i-Afghani*, Vol. I, pp. 261–2.

[14] *Akbarnama*, Eng. trans. Vol. I, pp. 326–7. For other views see also Badauni, *Muntakhab-ut-Tawarikh*, Vol. I, p. 357. Farishta writes that Ibrahim came to Delhi in quest of military service and was employed by one of the nobles of the court of Sultan Bahlul, *Farishta*, fol. 236b. Siddiqui has suggested that Ibrahim Sur came along with his son, Hasan, to India in 1452, but has not cited any specific evidence from the sources to this effect, in his *History of Sher Shah Sur*, p. 4; idem, *Sher Shah Sur and his Dynasty*, pp. 5–6; cf. Qanungo, *Sher Shah and his Times*, p. 6.

[15] Abbas refers to him as Khan-i-Azam Umar Khan Sarwani Kakbur, *Tarikh-i-Sher Shahi*, p. 9.

when Ibrahim passed away at Narnaul, Mian Hasan was granted his father's iqta with the fresh addition of several villages. Jamal Khan was impressed by Hasan's loyalty and devotion towards him. When he got charge of Jaunpur[16] in the reign of Sikandar Lodi with orders to maintain two thousand horsemen and grant territorial assignments, he gave the parganas of Sahsaram and Khwaspur Tanda[17] to Mian Hasan for maintaining five hundred horsemen.[18] A divergent picture is painted by Abu'l Fazl. According to him, Ibrahim's son Hasan acquired the qualities of a nobleman and switched over from trading to soldiering. He was in the service of Raimal (the grandfather of Raisal, a noble in Akbar's court) before he went to Chaund[19] in the territory of Sahsaram where he became a servant of Nasir Khan Luhani, an officer of Sikandar Lodi. By his loyal service and ability Hasan surpassed his colleagues, and when Nasir Khan died, he entered the service of his brother Daulat Khan. He subsequently joined Biban, who was one of the grandees of Sikandar Lodi, and achieved distinction as an accomplished administrator.[20] Siddiqui has pointed out that Hasan was in Jamal

[16] According to local traditions, the name Jaunpur is derived from Jamadagni, a famous *rishi*, and the place was earlier called Jamadagnipura. The supposed dwelling place of the rishi at Jamaitha, on the right bank of the Gomati about half way between Jaunpur and Zafarabad, is referred to in support of this claim. Others suggest that the present name is of Muslim origin, and it is derived from Juna, later known as Muhammad bin Tughluq, in whose honour the place was founded by Firuz Shah Tughluq. It is said that when the latter was building the new city, his dead cousin (Juna) appeared to him in a dream and begged the sultan to commemorate his memory by naming the city after him, *Uttar Pradesh District Gazetteers, Jaunpur* (Lucknow, 1986), p. 1. For the history of Jaunpur in the period of our study, see ibid., pp. 26–35. Also see chapter three of this book.

[17] Now a large village, known as Tanda Kalan, stands on the right bank of the Ganges, seventeen miles north-east of the district headquarters of Varanasi and eighteen miles north of Chandauli, the *tahsil* headquarters, *Uttar Pradesh District Gazetteers, Varanasi* (Lucknow, 1965), p. 427; cf. Habib, *Atlas*, 8 A.

[18] *Tarikh-i-Sher Shahi*, pp. 10–12; *Tabaqat-i-Akbari*, fol. 196a; *Muntakhab-ut-Tawarikh*, Vol. I, p. 357; *Farishta*, fol. 236b; *Tarikh-i-Khan-i-Jahani wa Makhzan-i-Afghani*, Vol. I, pp. 262–3; *Tarikh-i-Salatin-i-Afaghina*, p. 173.

[19] One of the eighteen *mahals* of sarkar Ruhtas, suba Bihar under Akbar, the pargana headquarters is now known as Chainpur. Other important parganas of Ruhtas for the history of our period included Bhojpur, Sahsaranw or Sahsaram and Fathpur Bihiya, *Beames' Contributions to Political Geography*, pp. 37–9; Habib, *Atlas*, 10 A, Notes.

[20] *Akbarnama*, Eng. trans. Vol. I, p. 327; *Ma'asir-ul-Umara*, Vol. II, p. 564.

Khan's service between 1498–9. He had received the iqta of Sahsaram and Khwaspur Tanda, which were full of 'turbulent' Rajput and Chero zamindars, after 1510 from Khan Azam Ahmad Khan Lodi Sarangkhani, and not from his father, Jamal Khan.[21]

The Afghan tradition claims that Sher Shah was born to an Afghan wife of Mian Hasan in the reign of Sultan Bahlul, and was named as Farid.[22] There is a great deal of confusion among historians regarding the date of birth of Farid. For instance, Siddiqui notes that 'Farid was born sometime after 1486 and 1490 may be suggested as the approximate date of his birth'.[23] Qanungo gives a precise 1486 as the date of his birth.[24] These dates are however hypothetical as the authors have not cited any specific evidence from the sources. Also, there is some controversy concerning the place of birth of Farid. Modern scholars are increasingly inclined in favour of Narnaul.[25] The local tradition at Sahsaram claims that Farid was born there. In the early nineteenth century, Francis Buchanan visited the ruins of the house where the Afghan empire-builder was said to have been born. He found that a small *math* had been built at the place, and the *mahant* lived chiefly by an image of Hanuman.[26] We shall refer below to a parallel Rajput tradition which claimed that Farid was born to a Rajput wife of Mian Hasan.[27] Abbas claims that Farid was very ambitious from childhood itself and wanted to join military service even as a young boy.[28]

Mian Hasan had seven other sons, six of whom were born of concubines. Hasan neglected Farid's mother on account of his weakness

---

[21] *History of Sher Shah Sur* , pp. 10–11. However, Siddiqui has not cited any evidence in support of the claim that by 1485 Hasan Sur had been more than 20 years of age, *Sher Shah Sur and his Dynasty*, pp. 9–10.

[22] *Tarikh-i-Sher Shahi*, pp. 9, 13. Nizam-ud-Din Ahmad refers to Farid's Afghan mother, but does not mention as to when and where he was born, *Tabaqat-i-Akbari*, fol. 196a. Nimatullah says that Farid was born at Hisar Firuza, but does not mention the date/year of birth, *Tarikh-i-Khan-i-Jahani wa Makhzan-i-Afghani*, Vol. I, p. 262. Ahmad Yadgar also writes that Farid was born at Hisar, *Tarikh-i-Salatin-i-Afaghina*, p. 73.

[23] Siddiqui, *Sher Shah Sur and his Dynasty*, p. 11.

[24] Qanungo, *Sher Shah and his Times*, p. 9.

[25] Ibid., pp. 9–10; Siddiqui, *History of Sher Shah Sur*, p. 8.

[26] Francis Buchanan, *An Account of the District of Shahabad in 1812–13* (Delhi, 1986), p. 87.

[27] See chapter four.

[28] *Tarikh-i-Sher-Shahi*, p. 10.

for the slave-girls, and according to reports, at least one of whom exercised tremendous influence on him. Also, at the time of assigning the responsibilities for administering the parganas he showed less favour to Farid. Annoyed with his father's behaviour, Farid left home to chart out an independent career for himself. Mian Hasan, learning that Farid had gone to Jaunpur, wrote to Jamal Khan that Farid had become angry without reason, and should be sent back so that he could arrange for his education at Sahsaram. When Jamal Khan suggested that Farid should return to Sahsaram and pursue his education, he retorted that Jaunpur was a better place for the purpose and he would therefore receive his education there. Jamal Khan agreed with the proposal and Farid concentrated on his studies.[29] His training at Jaunpur went a long way in providing him a theoretical framework for tackling the complex problems of warfare and statecraft. As noted above, K.R. Qanungo ignores the authorities cited above and follows Abu'l Fazl in suggesting that Farid indulged in theft and robbery at this stage.

It may be mentioned here that Sikandar Lodi's reign is significant in the history of medieval Indian education, mainly because of three steps taken by him. One was an insistence on a certain educational level for all his civil and military officers. Secondly, he substituted Persian for Hindi as the language of the lower administration, forcing non-Muslim administrative officials belonging to such communities as the Kayasthas to learn Persian. For that purpose schools, were set up which were not attached to the mosques, leading to the secularization of education. Thirdly, in the educational policy of Sikandar Lodi, there was a growing emphasis on rational sciences (*maqulat*), although the chief preoccupations of a Muslim scholar were still largely the traditional subjects (*manqulat*). The sultan himself occasionally attended the courses of a scholar, Abdullah Tulanbi. He established new schools in several places and invited scholars from other parts of the Muslim world.[30]

[29] Ibid., pp. 13–14; *Tabaqat-i-Akbari,* fol. 196a; *Tarikh-i-Khan-i-Jahani wa Makhzan-i-Afghani,* Vol. I, pp. 263–4; *Tarikh-i-Dau'di,* p. 108; *Muntakhab-ut-Tawarikh,* Vol. I, p. 357; *Tarikh-i-Salatin-i-Afaghina,* p. 173; *Farishta,* fol. 236b. For a list of books taught in the *madrasas* of the fifteenth century and other relevant information, see M. Zaki, 'Organization of Islamic Learning under the Saiyids and Lodis', *MIAM,* Vol. IV, pp. 1–9.

[30] For a brief but useful survey of Muslim education in medieval India, see Aziz Ahmad, *An Intellectual History of Islam in India* (Edinburgh, 1969), pp. 52–7,

Mian Hasan while on a visit to Jaunpur where Farid was receiving his education was reproached by his friends and relatives for having sidelined his son out of consideration for a slave-girl. He was persuaded to appoint Farid as the shiqqdar of the two parganas held by him. A reluctant Farid agreed to meet his father and accept the assignment.[31] Nizam-ud-Din Ahmad mentions Hasan's arrival at Jaunpur after two or three years, and the patch-up between the father and the son led to the latter getting the charge of the parganas (*daroghgi jagir*).[32] Ahmad Yadgar refers to the bestowal of kingship to Farid by a ragged darwesh at Jaunpur. The darwesh is said to have asked Hasan as to why he was terrorising (*dilgir*, lit. seizing the heart, terrifying) the king (badshah) of Delhi. The Afghans present there were astonished and Hasan handed over the administration of the parganas to Farid.[33] It may be noted that the anecdotes of dreams, miracles, and prophecies were an integral part of the Afghan political discourse. Dreams and prophecies had their own significance in the story of the Afghan resurgence under Sher Shah Sur. Modern historians have generally neglected such anecdotes in both the chronicles and the Sufi sources. It is claimed that these anecdotes were 'mostly fictional without any grain of truth'.[34] It may be that Hasan had appointed Farid not because of any 'persuasion' or the competence of the latter, but because the political condition required his absence from the parganas for a long time.[35]

especially pp. 53–4. Also see Yusuf Husain, *Glimpses of Medieval Indian Culture* (Bombay, 1957), pp. 69–96.

[31] *Tarikh-i-Sher-Shahi*, pp. 14–16. Also see, *Tarikh-i-Khan-i-Jahani wa Makhzan-i- Afghani*, Vol. I, pp. 263–4; *Tarikh-i-Dau'di*, p. 108; *Muntakhab-ut-Tawarikh*, Vol. I, p. 357; *Farishta*, fol. 236b. For the office of the shiqqdar, see Siddiqui, 'Position of the *Shiqqdar* under the Sultans of Delhi'.

[32] *Tabaqat-i-Akbari*, fol. 196a.

[33] *Tarikh-i-Salatin-i-Afaghina*, p. 174.

[34] Siddiqui, *Sher Shah Sur and his Dynasty*, pp. 4, 88. For an appreciation of such anecdotes, see Simon Digby, 'Dreams and Reminiscences of Dattu Sarwani', *IESHR*, Vol. II, No. 1 (January, 1965), pp. 52–80 & Vol. II, No. 2 (April, 1965), pp. 178–94.

[35] Qanungo, *Sher Shah and his Times*, pp. 39–41. Siddiqui has suggested that Farid was appointed as the shiqqdar in 1512 or 1513, already twenty-two or twenty-three years old by then, in his *A History of Sher Shah Sur*, p. 3. Qanungo suggests that Farid started for Sahsaram in January 1518, *Sher Shah and his Times*, p. 41.

Before leaving for Sahsaram, the fresh Jaunpur graduate brimming with self confidence reportedly lectured his father on the responsibilities of a ruler whose dispensation of justice and punishment prevented the country from plunging into chaos. Mian Hasan, glad to hear his views on the ideal society and government where the soldiers and the *raiyat* were not oppressed, leading to prosperity and expansion of the kingdom, gave him leave to proceed towards the two parganas.[36] Soon after assuming charge, Farid held a series of meetings with the *muqaddams*, the *patwaris*, the cultivators, and the soldiers in the different parts of the parganas. Abbas suggests that Farid had held a joint meeting of the cultivators, chiefs, and the village officials, which may not have been possible. Pointing this out, Siddiqui infers that the term raiyat should be read as muqaddams, not common peasantry, and *muzari* as petty *zamindars*.[37] Nurul Hasan suggests that thousands of peasants could not have gathered together along with the village dignitaries, and thus Farid did not make any direct contact with the cultivators.[38] If it is assumed that Farid made a tour of the parganas and held meetings with the cultivators, officials, and chiefs, separately or village-wise, the confusion will be over.[39] In these meetings, he announced that he would take measures for augmenting the agrarian economy, in which the profit would be theirs, while the good name would be his. He fixed the revenue to be paid by the raiyat, to the tune of 1/3 of the produce.[40] The soldiers and tax-gatherers were warned that if they forced the raiyat to pay more than the agreed share, he would punish them severely. He also directed his father's officers to

[36] *Tarikh-i-Sher Shahi*, pp. 16–21; *Tabaqat-i-Akbari*, fols. 196a–b, *Tarikh-i-Khan-i-Jahani wa Makhzan-i-Afghani*, Vol. I, p. 264; *Tarikh-i-Dau'di*, p. 108; *Farishta*, fol. 236b.

[37] *A History of Sher Shah Sur*, pp. 14–15.

[38] Nurul Hasan, 'Revenue Administration of the Jagir of Sahsaram by Farid (Sher Shah)', *PIHC*, Ranchi, 1964, pp. 102–7.

[39] Qanungo, *Sher Shah and his Times*, p. 48.

[40] In fact it has also been suggested by P. Saran that the land was divided into several classes and the rate was fixed accordingly, 'Revenue System of Sher Shah', in his, *Studies in Medieval Indian History* (Delhi, 1952), pp. 67–89, especially pp. 85–7. For a discussion of how 1/3rd of the produce and not 1/4th was levied by Sher Shah, except in the case of Multan, see also, Satish Chandra Misra, 'Revenue System of Sher Shah', *PIHC*, 15th Session, Gwalior, 1952, pp. 232–8, especially, pp. 234–8.

ensure that the raiyat was protected from the excessive exactions by the zamindars, otherwise collecting taxes from them would be an act of injustice.[41]

Further, as P. Saran points out, in telling his father about the oppression of the muqaddams, Farid had displayed his acquaintance with the working of the existing systems of assessment and had decided to reform them. Being thus resolved to introduce the system of measurement he had no need to discuss it with the peasants. He proceeded straight to the question of the mode of payment, in which, by giving them an option, he could facilitate their work. Thus, Saran concludes that Farid, in his administration of the parganas of his father, adopted the system of measurement in assessment of land revenue, and secondly, that he offered to the peasants an option in the mode of payment and not in the method of assessment.[42] S.C. Misra, however, suggests that though Sher Shah might have preferred the system of measurement he did not press his choice except in areas where the system could work without much trouble to the cultivator.[43]

Farid then decided to take action against the refractory zamindars and muqaddams of the two parganas who had not shown their faith in him. The nobles wanted to wait for Mian Hasan to return from Jaunpur with his army, but Farid quickly assembled a party of young Afghans and horsemen and launched a lightning attack on the rebels, slaughtered them, captured and sold their women and children, and brought cultivators from outside to settle there. Such a drastic step against one set of rebels served as deterrence to others. Farid's action paved the way for a regular flow of revenue, and populousness and cultivation in the parganas. His achievement was appreciated by Mian Hasan and

---

[41] *Tarikh-i-Sher Shahi*, pp. 21–3.

[42] Saran, 'Revenue System of Sher Shah', p. 79.

[43] Misra adds that the king was no doubt trying to extend the sphere of his authority and therefore desired a wider application of measurement. Islam Shah continued the work of his father and under him the administration became more centralized than ever. So it seems to have been Islam Shah who was responsible for what Abu'l Fazl calls, freeing Hindustan from the systems of *ghalla-bakhshi* and *muqtai*. He had more time than his father, he was more disregardful of the established usages, the nobles as a land-owning power collapsed under his rule and their place was taken by the king's bureaucracy, 'Revenue System of Sher Shah', p. 234.

other notables of the region.[44] This delicate balance between the 'regular flow of revenue' and 'prosperity' of the raiyat was ensured by establishing a more aggressive and sophisticated administrative machinery based on the principles of Islamic political theory and experiences of early Islam in India. Qanungo hails Farid's administration as 'the rule of a strong-willed and well-meaning autocrat sincerely working for the betterment' of the peasantry. He adds that Farid 'built up a well-knit revenue administration at this time, which was to become the archetype of the revenue system of his empire, and which again was to be passed on to the Mughal and the British Empires, to come down to Free India almost intact'.[45]

Mian Hasan, however, was compelled to remove Farid from his position, as it is alleged that his success was disliked by Mian Hasan's Indian slave-girl (*kanizak hindi*), whose name has not been mentioned in the sources, and her two sons from him. The slave-girl persuaded Hasan to remove Farid from his position, and give the responsibility to her son, Sulaiman. When Farid heard that Hasan was finding faults with him in order to dismiss him, he himself sent his resignation letter asking for an enquiry into the mismanagement or corruption, if any, during his tenure as the shiqqdar. The embarrassed father explained to Farid that it was not because of any fraud that he was being removed, adding that it was, actually, to avoid the nuisance created by Sulaiman and his mother that he was forced to take this step.[46] Ni'matullah notes that Hasan had reportedly promised her that he would give the charge

---

[44] *Tarikh-i-Sher Shahi*, pp. 24–30; *Tabaqat-i-Akbari*, fol. 196b; *Tarikh-i-Khan-i-Jahani wa Makhzan-i-Afghani*, Vol. I, pp. 265–6; *Tarikh-i-Dau'di*, pp. 108–9; *Tarikh-i-Salatin-i-Afaghina*, p. 174; *Farishta*, fol. 236b. Badauni also appreciates Farid's achievements as the administrator of his father's *jagir*, *Muntakhab-ut-Tawarikh*, Vol. I, p. 357.

[45] *Sher Shah and his Times*, pp. 52, 63.

[46] *Tarikh-i-Sher Shahi*, pp. 30–9; Ni'matullah mentions that it was under the influence of the slave-girl, mother of Sulaiman and two others, that Hasan had to remove Farid from his position, *Tarikh-i-Khan-i-Jahani wa Makhzan-i-Afghani*, Vol. I, p. 266. In his *Sher Shah Sur and his Dynasty*, Siddiqui incorrectly notes on p. 26 that Sulaiman was the son of Hasan Sur's 'favourite wife', but on p. 35 he corrects himself by suggesting that Sulaiman was 'born of a slave girl'. Ishwari Prasad also makes the mistake of referring to Sulaiman's mother as Hasan's favourite wife, *Life and Times of Humayun*, pp. 101–2. R.P. Tripathi refers to Sulaiman's mother as Hasan's 'youngest wife', *Rise and Fall of the Mughal Empire* (Allahabad, n.d.), p. 115.

of the parganas to her sons after they had grown up. Thus he was being pressurised to fulfil his promise.[47] In an extremely prejudiced account of the period, Abu'l Fazl suggests that Farid pained his father by his arrogance and evil disposition.[48]

Farid left home a second time. As noted above, Siddiqui suggests that Farid had taken to robbery after being removed from the position of shiqqdar. According to the sources, however, Farid proceeded towards Agra where he sought the patronage of Daulat Khan and complained against his father. Referring particularly to the latter's weakness for a slave-girl and the consequent mismanagement in the parganas, Farid requested that the assignment be given to him.[49] Daulat Khan apprised Sultan Ibrahim of the activities of Mian Hasan, and suggested that the parganas be allotted to Farid. The sultan found Farid's complaint against his father to be in bad taste and rejected his request (*badshah farmud ke bad mardist ke shikayat wa gila pidar-i-khwud mikunad*).[50] Daulat Khan, however, assured Farid not to lose heart, increased his daily allowances (*wazifa-i-yaumiya*) and tried to keep him in good humour.[51]

Meanwhile Mian Hasan passed away.[52] On the third day, Sulaiman, Hasan's son from his favourite slave-girl, put on his father's turban

[47] *Tarikh-i-Khan-i-Jahani wa Makhzan-i-Afghani*, Vol. I, p. 266. Also see *Tabaqat-i-Akbari*, fols. 196b–197a; *Farishta*, fols. 236b–237a; *Tarikh-i-Dau'di*, p. 9. Badauni writes that the circumstances led to an estrangement between Farid and his father, *Muntakhab-ut-Tawarikh*, Vol. I, p. 357.

[48] *Akbarnama*, fol. 82a.

[49] *Tarikh-i-Sher Shahi*, pp. 40–1; *Tarikh-i-Khan-i-Jahani wa Makhzan-i-Afghani*, Vol. I, pp. 267–8; *Tarikh-i-Dau'di*, pp. 109–10; *Tarikh-i-Salatin-i-Afaghina*, p. 175. Badauni notes that Farid complained against his father and brothers without referring to Hasan's weakness for the slave-girl, *Muntakhab-ut-Tawarikh*, Vol. I, p. 357. Nizam-ud-Din writes that Farid asked Daulat Khan that the assignment of the parganas be given to him and his brother (Nizam, though his name is not mentioned), *Tabaqat-i-Akbari*, fol. 197a. Also see *Farishta*, fol. 237a.

[50] *Tarikh-i-Sher Shahi*, p. 42. *Tabaqat-i-Akbari*, fol. 197a. See also, *Tarikh-i-Khan-i-Jahani wa Makhzan-i-Afghani*, Vol. I, p. 268; *Tarikh-i-Dau'di*, p. 109; *Tarikh-i-Salatin-i-Afaghina*, p. 175; *Muntakhab-ut-Tawarikh*, Vol. I, pp. 357–8; *Farishta*, fol. 237a. cf. Sayid Muhammad Nurul Hasan, *Asar-i-Sharf* (Patna, A.H. 1282), p. 23.

[51] *Tarikh-i-Sher Shahi*, p. 42; *Tabaqat-i-Akbari*, fol. 197a; *Farishta*, fol. 237a.

[52] Siddiqui has suggested that Mian Hasan died c.1524, *A History of Sher Shah Sur*, p. 7.

(*dastar*) symbolizing his succession as the incharge of the parganas. Mian Nizam, Farid's younger brother, not only challenged Sulaiman's decision to take his father's place but also informed Farid of the turn of events. Farid briefed Daulat Khan about his father's death and matters relating to Sulaiman. Daulat Khan brought the news of Mian Hasan's death to the knowledge of Sultan Ibrahim, and procured the farman conferring the government of the two parganas on Farid.[53] Reflecting the Mughal imperial attempts at slandering a powerful Afghan challenge to their authority, Abu'l Fazl writes that after Hasan's death his property fell into Farid's hands, and, as noted above, he began to create trouble in the territory of Sahsaram and in the jungles of Chaund by resorting to theft, robbery and murder. In a short time, the Mughal chronicler alleged, by craft and unrighteousness Farid surpassed the 'rebel of the age', gathering many 'rascals' and 'vagabonds' around him.[54]

The Afghan narrative has it that when Farid arrived in the parganas all his kinsmen (*azizan*: literally, near and dear ones) obeyed the farman. As Sulaiman could not face Farid, he went to Muhammad Khan Sur who held the pargana of Chaund and commanded fifteen hundred horses. As Muhammad Khan bore some grudges against Mian Hasan, he desired that the two brothers should fight and become dependent upon him. He asked Sulaiman to wait for the outcome of the battle at Panipat (April 1526), adding that if the Mughals emerged victorious he would snatch the parganas from Farid by force and give them to him; in case Ibrahim Lodi turned out triumphant he (Sulaiman) would have to go to the sultan and lodge a complaint against Farid.[55]

---

[53] *Tarikh-i-Sher Shahi*, pp. 42–3; *Muntakhab-ut-Tawarikh*, Vol. I, p. 358; *Tarikh-i-Khan-i-Jahani wa Makhzan-i-Afghani*, Vol. I, p. 268; *Tarikh-i-Dau'di*, p. 110; *Tarikh-i-Salatin-i-Afaghina*, p. 176. Nizam-ud-Din Ahmad writes that the charge of the government of Sahsaram and Khawaspur Tanda was given to Farid and his brother, *Tabaqat-i-Akbari*, fol. 197a; *Farishta*, fol. 237a. Mushtaqi's account differs with those of the later authorities. According to him, Farid left his father during the reign of Ibrahim Lodi and came to the sultan in Agra, where Daulat Khan, the *naib-i-arz*, suggested him to go to Darya Khan who was building up an army in Bihar. Farid thus returned to Bihar, *Waqi'at-i-Mushtaqi*, fol. 48a.

[54] *Akbarnama*, fol. 82a.

[55] *Tarikh-i-Sher Shahi*, p. 44. Also see *Tabaqat-i-Akbari*, fol. 197a; *Farishta*, fol. 237a; *Tarikh-i-Dau'di*, p. 110; *Tarikh-i-Khan-i-Jahani wa Makhzan-i-Afghani*, Vol. I, pp. 268–70; *Tarikh-i-Salatin-i-Afaghina*, pp. 175–6.

The Afghans were defeated at Panipat.[56] According to the late sixteenth century Afghan narrative, their major weakness lay in the fact that they lacked an able leader who could unite the Afghans for a common cause. Their disunity led to the occupation of most of the eastern territories by the Mughals who plundered and massacred even the general population in the cities and towns they captured. This generated widespread hostility and hatred against the 'foreign' invaders.[57] The Afghan leaders, however, failed to capitalize on it. The show of resistance clearly betrayed the Afghan belief, at this stage, in fishes' justice: that big fish sought to destroy the smaller ones. We shall return to this problem in the next chapter and see how Sher Khan emerged as the sole leader of the Afghans who effectively mobilized them for a fightback against the Mughals.

Ibrahim Lodi's defeat at Panipat and Muhammad Khan's threatening posture compelled Farid to enter into the service of Bahar (or Pahar) Khan, son of Darya Khan Nuhani (or Luhani).[58] Soon Farid endeared himself to Bahar Khan, and was rewarded for his capabilities (*nawazish yaft*).[59] It is said that one day he had gone for a hunting excursion (*shikar*) with Bahar Khan when a lion (*sher*) appeared there. Farid killed

---

[56] For a detailed discussion of the first battle of Panipat, see A. Halim, *History of Lodi Sultans*.

[57] *Babur-Nama*, Memoirs of Babur, translated from the original Turki text of Zahir ud-Din Muhammad Babur Padshah Ghazi by Annette Susannah Beveridge, Vol. I & II, first published in 1922, reprint (Delhi, 1997); Shaikh Rukn-ud-Din, *Lataif-i-Quddusi* (Delhi, nd), p. 63 as cited in Siddiqui, *A History of Sher Shah Sur*, p. 22.

[58] *Tarikh-i-Sher Shahi*, pp. 46–7; *Tabaqat-i-Akbari*, fol. 197b; *Muntakhab-ut-Tawarikh*, Vol. I, p. 358; *Tarikh-i-Khan-i-Jahani wa Makhzan-i-Afghani*, Vol. I, p. 270; *Tarikh-i-Salatin-i-Afaghina*, p. 176; *Farishta*, fol. 237a. *Tarikh-i-Dau'di*, p. 111, Abdullah has also copied Mushtaqi's suggestion that Sultan Muhammad had asked Farid to conquer the fort of Chaund. According to Mushtaqi, Farid and Nizam went to Darya Khan who showed them much consideration and favour. He told Farid that he would assign him the fort of Chaund if he could seize it from Muhammad Khan Sur. Sher Khan accepted the assignment and marched towards the fort of Chaund, and defeated Muhammad Khan. Farid joined Darya Khan after this victory, *Waqi'at-i-Mushtaqi*, fols. 48a–b. Ishwari Prasad identifies Darya Khan's son as Bihar Khan, named after 'the country he ruled', *Life and Times of Humayun*, p. 104. R.P. Tripathi calls him 'Bahadur Khan Nuhani', *Rise and Fall of the Mughal Empire*, p. 117.

[59] *Muntakhab-ut-Tawarikh*, Vol. I, p. 358.

the lion. Bahar Khan, who had by then assumed the title of Sultan Muhammad and had struck coins and caused the khutba to be read in his name, conferred upon Farid the title of Sher Khan and appointed him as the deputy to his son Jalal Khan.[60] Ahmad Yadgar adds that the lion had gone on a rampage, killing or injuring most of the men in the hunting-party (aksar mardum ra kusht-o-zakhami gardanid).[61] Local lore in modern day Narnaul claims that it was while hunting in the neighbourhood of this southern district of Haryana that Farid had killed a lion (sher) and was thus called Sher Khan.[62]

Mushtaqi differs with other authorities cited above. According to him, one day Darya Khan ordered Daulat Khan Nuhani, his uncle's son, to lead a military expedition. He expressed his unwillingness to do the job. Upon this, Darya Khan called Farid and told him about Daulat Khan's refusal to undertake the expedition, adding that he was now being deputed to do so. If carried out successfully, the title of Daulat Khan's father, Sher Khan, who was killed by the Rajput zamindars of Kara[63] in 1495, would be granted to him. Farid gained victory in the campaign, and in return got the title of Sher Khan.[64] Also, S.H. Askari draws attention to an inscription which suggests that Darya Khan Nuhani was amongst the earliest patrons of Farid.[65]

---

[60] Tarikh-i-Sher Shahi, p. 47; Tabaqat-i-Akbari, fol. 197b; Muntakhab-ut-Tawarikh, Vol. I, p. 358; Tarikh-i-Khan-i-Jahani wa Makhzan-i-Afghani, Vol. I, p. 270; Farishta, fol. 237a. Modern authorities deny that Farid had got the title Sher Khan because of actually killing any lion, Siddiqui, Sher Shah Sur and his Dynasty, pp. 35–6. Qanungo, Sher Shah and his Times, pp. 71–2.

[61] Tarikh-i-Salatin-i-Afaghina, p. 177.

[62] Gyan Swarup Bhardwaj, 'Maharishi Chyawan ki Tapobhumi Raha hai Shahar Narnaul', Dainik Tribune (Hindi), Chandigarh, Thursday, 9 June 1997, p. II.

[63] With the foundation of Allahabad under Akbar, Kara, more frequently referred to Kara-Manikpur, ceased to possess any political significance. It is now a small village, about eight km. north of the Grand Trunk Road, sixty-six km. north-west of Allahabad and ten km. north-east of Sirathu, the tahsil headquarters. The village contains archaeological remains of considerable importance; the oldest Muslim building being the tomb of Qurbullah Shah, known as Khwaja Karak, who died in 1309, Uttar Pradesh District Gazetteers, Allahabad (Lucknow, 1968), pp. 34–42, 381–3. For Khwaja Karak (or Gurg), see Simon Digby, 'Anecdotes of a Provincial Sufi of the Dehli Sultanate, Khwaja Gurg of Kara', Iran, Vol. XXXII, 1994.

[64] Waqi'at-i-Mushtaqi, fol. 48b; Tarikh-i-Dau'di, pp. 111–12.

[65] S.H. Askari, 'Bihar in the Time of the Last Two Lodi Sultans of Delhi', PIHC, 18th Session, Calcutta, 1955, pp. 148–57, especially p. 155.

The rule of the Nuhanis in Bihar under Darya Khan and his son Bahar Khan styled as Sultan Muhammad may briefly be outlined here. Appointed as the *muqta* of Bihar in 1495–6 by Sikandar Lodi, Darya Khan, son of Mubarak Khan Nuhani who held high position in the Lodi nobility and was governor of Kara-Manikpur, is hailed in Afghan memory for his glorious role in uprooting the base of the Sharqis in Bihar and compelling the zamindars to submit to his power. Darya Khan either reconciled the powerful zamindars to the Afghan rule or destroyed them. He also won over the local Sufis and the ulama to his side by making large landgrants as well as establishing matrimonial relations with them. Pleased by his efforts to integrate Bihar within the Lodi dominion, Sikandar Lodi seems to have rewarded him with the honorary title of *wazir-i-mamalik*. Darya Khan got the credit not only for offsetting Sultan Husain Sharqi's influence in Bihar, but also reportedly endeared himself to the people by his just rule. He enjoyed so much authority that no zamindar of Bihar helped Husain Sharqi when he rose for the last time soon after the death of Sikandar Lodi. Though Husain Sharqi had got military support from the rulers of Bengal and Orissa, his campaign could not succeed because the zamindars, aware of Darya Khan's strength, decided to remain aloof.[66]

Darya Khan could not maintain good relations with Sikandar's son and successor, Ibrahim Lodi. Though he had participated in a campaign in 1519 against Islam Khan Sarwani, his son-in-law, who had rebelled against the sultan and was killed by Darya Khan's men at Kara, the rebellion of Nasir Khan, his elder brother and administrator of Ghazipur,[67] in 1524 destroyed his relation with the sultan. He had thirty thousand *sawars* under him at this time as the nobles posted by the king in different parts of Bihar were subordinate to him. Ibrahim Lodi had won over a few nobles of the region including Kamal Khan Kamba and Husain Khan who held the rank of six thousand sawars, and asked them to kill Darya Khan. But as the latter got an inkling of the matter the pro-sultan nobles had to flee to Agra to save their own lives. Soon afterwards, however, Darya Khan passed away leaving his son, Bahar Khan as his successor. All the rebellious Afghan nobles who escaped

[66] Iqtidar Husain Siddiqui, 'Nuhani Rule in Bihar', *PIHC*, 32nd Session, Jabalpur, 1970, pp. 282–7, especially, pp. 282–3.

[67] Sarkar Ghazipur, suba Allahabad, under Akbar occupied 1,475 square miles with the jama being 13,431,325 dams, Habib, *Atlas*, Table I and 8 A, Notes.

from Ibrahim Lodi got refuge in Bihar at this time. Assured of their help, Bahar Khan assumed the title of Sultan Muhammad Nuhani and began to have the khutba read in his own name.[68]

Ibrahim Lodi sent a large force under the command of Mustafa Farmuli, the muqta of Awadh,[69] to crush the Afghan rebels. Mustafa Farmuli cleaned all the territories from Qannauj[70] to Ghazipur, but fell ill and died soon after entering Bihar. Bayazid Farmuli, Mustafa's younger brother and Firuz Khan Sarangkhani who continued the imperial campaign against the rebels, could not make any headway, even as Ibrahim Lodi died fighting against the Mughals at Panipat in 1526. The fall of the Lodi Sultanate provided Sultan Muhammad Nuhani with an opportunity to build up his power in the eastern region of the Lodi empire. He succeeded in creating from the wreckage of the Lodi army, a large but disorderly formation. Thus, it is reported that he could detach forty to fifty thousand men to occupy the eastern region upto Qannauj; himself remaining in Bihar. However his occupation of the eastern territories remained partial as the forts like those of Chunar,[71] Jaunpur, and Awadh were still held by nobles who did not recognize his authority. Without getting their possession, the supporters of Muhammad Nuhani were not in a position to check the Mughal expansion in the east. With the Mughal prince Humayun occupying the eastern territory rapidly, despite localized resistance, the Nuhani rule was limited to Bihar and a few parganas of Jaunpur.[72]

[68] Siddiqui, 'Nuhani Rule in Bihar', pp. 283–4. Also see, S.H. Askari, 'Bihar in the Time of the Last Two Lodi Sultans of Delhi', pp. 154–7; idem, 'Establishment of the Nuhani Kingdom in Bihar', in *Medieval Bihar: Sultanate and Mughal Period*, fourth volume of Prof. S.H. Askari's Collected Works (Patna, 1990), pp. 42–63.

[69] Suba Awadh under Akbar comprised five sarkars, including Awadh, Gorakhpur, Bahraich, Khairabad and Lucknow, covering 26,463 square miles with an estimated jama of 201,364,203 dams, Habib, *Atlas*, Table I and 8 A, Notes; *Beames' Contribution to Political Geography*.

[70] Qannauj or Kanauj was a sarkar (Area: 5215 square miles; jama: 52,584,620.5 dams) of suba Agra under Akbar, Habib, *Atlas*, Table I and 8 A, Notes.

[71] The fort and the town of Chunar are located on the southern bank of the Ganges, at a distance of twenty one miles from Mirzapur and nineteen miles from Banaras, *Uttar Pradesh District Gazetteer, Mirzapur*. Mirzapur has not been located by Habib, though Chunar (Area: 1561 square miles; jama: 5,810,604 dams) is mentioned as a sarkar of suba Allahabad under Akbar, *Atlas*, Table I and 8 A, Notes.

[72] Siddiqui, 'Nuhani Rule in Bihar', p. 284.

As noted above, Sher Khan enjoyed a good reputation under Sultan Muhammad, but once having taken leave from him, he went to his parganas and overstayed there, which Sultan Muhammad resented. Sher Khan's rival for the leadership of the Surs, Muhammad Khan, took this opportunity to uphold the cause of Sulaiman, and requested the sultan that the charge of the two parganas be taken away from Sher Khan, and allotted to Sulaiman. The sultan, however, rejected the proposal in view of Sher Khan's service to him, and suggested that as a responsible member of the clan, the Khan should ensure that peace and equity were established in the family.[73] Another report has it that Sultan Muhammad had ordered Muhammad Khan Sur to see to it that Sher Khan's brothers got their share in the management of the parganas.[74] Coming back to Chaund, Muhammad Khan sent a representative to Sher Khan directing him to do justice with his younger brothers and reminding him that Afghan laws and customs were not hidden from him (*qa'ida rasume afghani az shuma makhfi nist*). Sher Khan retorted that this land was not the country of Roh that he should divide and distribute it amongst his brothers. He added that the country of Hind was completely under the laws of its king who, after the death of a noble, confers the charge of his iqta upon one of his sons who would be considered to be the ablest of all and the remaining brothers would have no share in it. He reminded that the two parganas were conferred upon him by Sultan Ibrahim, and it was not proper for the Khan to expect the handing over of Tanda and Balhu,[75] which were situated near Banaras, to Sulaiman.[76]

---

[73] *Tarikh-i-Dau'di*, p. 112.

[74] *Muntakhab-ut-Tawarikh*, Vol. I, p. 358; *Tabaqat-i-Akbari*, fols. 197b–198a; *Tarikh-i-Khan-i-Jahani wa Makhzan-i-Afghani*, Vol. I, p. 271; *Farishta*, fols. 237a–b.

[75] *Uttar Pradesh District Gazetteer, Varanasi*, p. 387, refers to village Balua (Pargana Mahuari, Tahsil Chandauli), located on the right bank of the Ganges about fourteen miles away from Varanasi and about thirteen miles from Chandauli. An unmetalled road about six miles in length linked Tanda Kalan with Balua, ibid., p. 427. Ishwari Prasad has Tanda and Malhar and identifies the former as a 'city', *Life and Times of Humayun*, pp. 105–6.

[76] *Tarikh-i-Sher Shahi*, pp. 49–50; *Tabaqat-i-Akbari*, fol. 198a; *Tarikh-i-Dau'di*, p. 113; *Tarikh-i-Khan-i-Jahani wa Makhzan-i-Afghani*, Vol. I, pp. 271–2. Also see *Farishta*, fol. 237b.

Enraged by Sher Khan's response, Muhammad Khan sent a big army to capture Tanda and Balhu. Sukka, Khawas Khan's father who was the shiqqdar of the place and who had under him a considerably large part of Sher Khan's forces, was killed while defending the territory. His defeated army came to Sher Khan at Sahsaram.[77] Sher Khan, however, was not in a position to stay there any longer. Although some persons advised him to go to Sultan Muhammad, Sher Khan chose to join Sultan Junaid Barlas, the Mughal governor of Kara-Manikpur, and brought along large presents. The Mughal official, in turn, sent his force to accompany Sher Khan. Muhammad Khan and Sulaiman, having failed to withstand the onslaught, fled to the hills of Ruhtas.[78]

Sher Khan recovered not only his own territories but also captured Chaund and several other parganas previously belonging to the crown (*khalisa*). Subsequently, he wrote to the Afghans who had fled away to the hills to come back, assuring that their iqtas would not only be restored, but also doubled. The Afghans came flocking to him. When he found that many of the Afghans had collected around him, he offered handsome presents to the Mughals and sent them back to Sultan Junaid. Sher Khan then wrote an emotionally charged letter to Muhammad Khan addressing him as an uncle (*am*), clarifying that his purpose was to avenge his brother. He also suggested to him that unification of the 'kinsmen' was the need of the hour. He should forget the past differences, come out of the hills and return to Chaund. Muhammad Khan did so and gratefully took possession of his pargana.[79]

---

[77] *Tarikh-i-Sher Shahi*, p. 51; see also, *Tabaqat-i-Akbari*, fol. 198a; *Muntakhab-ut-Tawarikh*, Vol. I, p. 358; *Tarikh-i-Dau'di*, p. 113; *Tarikh-i-Khan-i-Jahani wa Makhzan-i-Afghani*, Vol. I, pp. 272–3; *Tarikh-i-Salatin-i-Afaghina*, p. 178; *Farishta*, fol. 237b.

[78] *Tabaqat-i-Akbari*, fols. 198a–b; *Farishta*, fol. 237b; *Muntakhab-ut-Tawarikh*, Vol. I, pp. 358–9; *Tarikh-i-Dau'di*, pp. 113–14; *Tarikh-i-Khan-i-Jahani wa Makhzan-i-Afghani*, Vol. I, p. 273. Ahmad Yadgar mentions that Sher Khan went to the Mughal governor of Jaunpur, *Tarikh-i-Salatin-i-Afaghana*, p. 178.

[79] *Tarikh-i-Sher Shahi*, pp. 52–4. See also, *Tabaqat-i-Akbari*, fol. 198b; *Muntakhab-ut-Tawarikh*, Vol. I, p. 359; *Tarikh-i-Dau'di*, p. 114; *Tarikh-i-Khan-i-Jahani wa Makhzan-i-Afghani*, Vol. I, pp. 273–4; *Tarikh-i-Salatin-i-Afaghina*, p. 178; *Farishta*, fol. 237b.

Relieved of the apprehension from Muhammad Khan, Sher Khan went to Sultan Junaid,[80] who took him to Babur's court at Agra. Later, he accompanied the emperor in his Chanderi expedition.[81] During his stay with the Mughals, Sher Khan came to know of their methods of warfare, their style of governance, and the ways of their nobles. Often in the gatherings of the Afghans, he would talk about his capabilities and intention to expel the Mughals from Hindustan. Even as the senior Afghans would dismiss him as an ambitious and loud-mouthed 'bachcha' (child), Sher Khan would explain that the Mughals had no firmness and stability in warfare. Their king did not pay attention to the administration of the dominion, which was in the hands of his nobles who could be purchased by gold. Therefore, it was easy to drive the Mughals out of Hindustan (*mughalan ra az hindustan badar kardan asan ast*).[82] As we shall further see below Sher Khan exploited these weaknesses of the Mughals during the period of his conflict with Humayun. Curiously, Siddiqui denies that the details about Sher Khan's observations on the Mughals and his subsequent flight from Agra contain any 'factual basis'.[83]

[80] Nizam-ud-Din Ahmad says Sher Khan gave the charge of the jagir to his brother Nizam, and went to Sultan Junaid Barlas at Kara, from where he was taken to Babur's court, *Tabaqat-i-Akbari*, fol. 198b. According to Siddiqui, Sher Khan went to Junaid Barlas, the Mughal governor of Jaunpur who happened to be in Bhatta (Modern Rewa) after the battle of Khanwa was over (1527). He joined Babur in January 1528 when the latter was preparing to march on Chanderi for its conquest, *A History of Sher Shah Sur*, p. 27.

[81] *Tarikh-i-Sher Shahi*, p. 54; *Tabaqat-i-Akbari*, fol. 198b; *Muntakhab-ut-Tawarikh*, Vol. I, p. 359; *Tarikh-i-Dau'di*, p. 114; *Tarikh-i-Khan-i-Jahani wa Makhzan-i-Afghani*, Vol. I, p. 274; *Tarikh-i-Salatin-i-Afaghina*, p. 179; *Farishta*, fol. 237b. Babur has noted that Chanderi was in the possession of Rana Sanga who had captured it from the Mandu sultans. He stormed Chanderi in 934/1527–8 and by 'God's pleasure; took it in a few hours; in it was Rana Sanga's great and trusted man Medni Rao; there was a general massacre of the Pagans in it, and converted what for many years had been a mansion of hostility, into a mansion of Islam', *Babur-Nama*, pp. 483–4. See also pp. 589–98 for the details of the 'holy-war' against Chanderi and its capture. For a history of the region in this period, see U.N. Day, *Medieval Malwa*.

[82] *Tabaqat-i-Akbari*, fols. 198b–199a. See also, *Tarikh-i-Sher Shahi*, pp. 55–6; *Tarikh-i-Dau'di*, p. 114; *Muntakhab-ut-Tawarikh*, Vol. I, p. 359; *Tarikh-i-Khan-i-Jahani wa Makhzan-i-Afghani*, Vol. I, p. 275; *Tarikh-i-Salatin-i-Afaghina*, p. 179; *Farishta*, fols. 237b–238a.

[83] *A History of Sher Shah Sur*, pp. 27–8; idem, *Sher Shah Sur and his Dynasty*, p. 38.

Amongst the highlights of Sher Khan's exploits in the Mughal camp is included the story of Babur taking his meal in the company of his nobles. Sher Khan was also there. A kind of fish-curry (*ash-mahicha*) was placed before him. Not knowing the proper way of taking it, Sher Khan cut the fish into pieces with his knife and ate it easily. Babur saw this and was surprised at his ingenuity. He ordered the *wazir* to immediately arrest Sher Khan as he was a man of expedients and in whose forehead the marks of royalty were clearly visible. The wazir, however, suggested that Sher Khan's arrest might lead to the alienation of the Afghans and disorder in the kingdom. The emperor was silenced. Sher Khan, however, realized that Babur wanted to harm him. Shortly after the meal was over, Sher Khan fled on his horse in the direction of Bihar. When Babur learned that Sher Khan had left the army, he scolded the wazir for not arresting him at that very moment, adding that something terrible was going to happen.[84] According to Badauni, Babur observed Sher Khan behaving in a way which deserved royal censure and wanted to punish him. Those present on the occasion related the particulars of his independence and arrogance.[85] In Abu'l Fazl's considered opinion, Sher Khan was too inferior a creature to be invited for a meal with Babur, hence the meal-episode has not been mentioned by him. He writes that one day Sultan Junaid introduced Sher Khan, with two other Afghans who were in his service, to the emperor. As soon as the 'farseeing glance of his majesty' fell upon Sher Khan, he remarked, as quoted above, that the eyes of this Afghan indicated 'turbulence' and 'strife-mongering'. He should be arrested immediately. The emperor received the other two favourably. Sher Khan got apprehensive on seeing the emperor's look and fled before he was arrested.[86]

[84] *Tarikh-i-Sher Shahi*, pp. 56–7; See also *Tabaqat-i-Akbari*, fol. 199a; *Tarikh-i-Salatin-i-Afaghina*, pp. 179–80; *Farishta*, fol. 238a.

[85] *Muntakhab-ut-Tawarikh*, Vol. I, p. 359.

[86] We have also mentioned above that Ni'matullah borrows from Abu'l Fazl, Babur's alleged remarks on Sher Khan's eyes betraying 'turbulence' and 'strife-mongering'. Siddiqui notes that Sher Khan deserted Babur in 1529 and joined Sultan Mahmud Lodi, *A History of Sher Shah Sur*, p. 28. R.P. Tripathi omits the details of the meal-episode and Babur's reported remarks. He writes that Sher Khan was in Babur's army for fifteen months, and adds, perhaps inaccurately, that the emperor 'was also pleased to restore to Sher Khan his lost *jagir* (1528–9)', *Rise and Fall of the Mughal Empire*, p. 118.

After reaching Sahsaram, Sher Khan promptly sent huge presents to Sultan Junaid with a letter couched in apologetic terms (*khat ma'zirat amiz*). He explained that he was informed that Muhammad Khan Sur and his step-brother Sulaiman had persuaded Sultan Muhammad to forcibly seize the parganas as he (Sher Khan) had joined the Mughals. Sher Khan added that when the news reached him he could no longer stay in Babur's camp and left without permission. He also informed that on earlier occasions when he had sought leave from the emperor, it was not granted to him. Finally he assured the Mughal noble that he was always available at his service.[87] On the other hand, he told his men that he had lost faith in the Mughals and the latter likewise had lost confidence in him, and was therefore going over to Sultan Muhammad. Aware of his competence, the sultan was pleased to have Sher Khan in his service and again appointed him as the deputy of his son, Jalal Khan.[88] Another report says that Sultan Junaid, realising that Sher Khan had offered a lame excuse (*bahana*) for leaving the emperor's court, did not respond to his letter. Disappointed and suspecting a disciplinary action (*mayus wa mutawahhim*), Sher Khan was compelled to join Sultan Muhammad. The Nuhani ruler not only welcomed him but also restored him as the *ataliq* (guardian) of his son.[89]

It will be interesting to turn to an anecdote concerning Sher Khan's ambitious plan at this stage. One day Sultan Muhammad asked the servants inside the palace to see whether there was anybody present in the audience hall. The servants found that Sher Khan was offering *namaz-i-chasht* (forenoon prayer) at that time. They informed him of the presence of Sher Khan. The sultan called him inside and said: 'You have seized Sahsaram and Chaund. Now you offer namaz-i-chasht. Do you want to seize my Bihar also?' Sher Khan tied a knot in his belt

---

[87] *Tarikh-i-Sher Shahi*, pp. 57–8. Also see *Tabaqat-i-Akbari*, fol. 199a; *Muntakhab-ut-Tawarikh*, Vol. I, pp. 359–60; *Tarikh-i-Dau'di*, p. 115; *Tarikh-i-Khan-i-Jahani wa Makhzan-i-Afghani*, Vol. I, p. 276; *Tarikh-i-Salatin-i-Afaghina*, p. 180; *Farishta*, fol. 238a.

[88] *Tarikh-i-Sher Shahi*, p. 58; *Muntakhab-ut-Tawarikh*, Vol. I, p. 360.

[89] *Tarikh-i-Khan-i-Jahani wa Makhzan-i-Afghani*, Vol. I, p. 276; *Tabaqat-i-Akbari*, fol. 199a; *Tarikh-i-Dau'di*, p. 115. Siddiqui has suggested that Sher Khan was appointed deputy of Jalal Khan by Dudu in 1529 and not by Sultan Muhammad who had died in 1527, *A History of Sher Shah Sur*, p. 32, f.n.3.

and said: 'The day you become the king of Delhi, I shall be given Bihar'.[90] Sultan Muhammad, however, was not destined to become the king of Hindustan. In his natural death,[91] Sher Khan found a powerful contender for the leadership of the Afghans removed from the scene. However, a more formidable and legitimate aspirant for the leadership of the Afghans, Sultan Mahmud Lodi, son of Sultan Sikandar Lodi, was still lurking around. Also, the ruler of Bengal, in the wake of the rebellion of the Afghan nobles against Ibrahim Lodi and the latter's defeat at the hands of Babur, was contemplating to expand westward, as we shall see below. After Sultan Muhammad's death, his son Jalal Khan was placed on the throne of Bihar. Jalal's mother Dudu ruled the kingdom on his behalf and allowed Sher Khan to act as her son's deputy. When Dudu also passed away, Sher Khan continued to be the guardian of Jalal Khan. The kingdom of Bihar virtually fell into his lap.[92] Abu'l Fazl does not mention that Sher Khan was in the service of the Nuhanis. He suggests that after the death of the governor of Bihar who was one of the Nuhani nobles, there was no one to discharge his duties. Taking advantage of the situation, Sher Khan raided the area and grabbed much property.[93] Mushtaqi writes that after Sultan Muhammad's death Sher Khan began to plan the annexation of Bihar, and soon brought the region under his control.[94]

During this period, Sher Khan also allied with a rebellious Makhdum Alam, administrator of Hajipur[95] and a brother-in-law of the sultan of Bengal, Ghiyas-ud-Din Abu'l Muzaffar Mahmud Shah,

[90] *Waqi'at-i- Mushtaqi*, fol. 48b; *Tarikh-i-Salatin-i-Afaghina*, p. 177.

[91] According to Siddiqui, the Nuhani power was curtailed with the death of Sultan Muhammad in 1527. His widow and son, Jalal Khan, were deserted by most of his allies who joined Mahmud Lodi, son of Sikandar Lodi, who visited Bihar after the battle of Khanwa, 'Nuhani Rule in Bihar', p. 285.

[92] *Tarikh-i-Sher Shahi*, p. 59; *Tabaqat-i-Akbari*, fol. 199a; *Muntakhab-ut-Tawarikh*, Vol. I, p. 360; *Tarikh-i-Dau'di*, p. 115; *Tarikh-i-Khan-i-Jahani wa Makhzan-i-Afghani*, Vol. I, p. 276; *Tarikh-i-Salatin-i-Afaghina*, p. 180; *Farishta*, fol. 238a. Some of the authorities have confused Dudu with Lad-o-Malika, calling the latter as Jalal Khan's mother, see for instance, *Asar Sharf*, p. 22.

[93] *Akbarnama*, fol. 82a.

[94] *Waqi'at-i-Mushtaqi*, fol. 48b.

[95] Hajipur (Area: 2479 square miles; Jama: 27,331,030 dams) was a sarkar of suba Bihar under Akbar, *Beames' Contribution to the Political Geography*; Habib, *Atlas*, Table I and 10 A, Notes.

son of the more illustrious Sultan Ala-ud-Din Husain Shah. The displeased sultan not only wanted to remove Makhdum Alam, but also to seize Bihar from the Afghans. A large force was dispatched under Qutb Khan, the Bengali administrator of Mungir,[96] for the purpose. Sher Khan wrote to the sultan to behave properly and avoid a fight (*sher khan basyar tariq iltamas sulah kard*) without success. In the fierce battle (*jang-i-azim*) that followed, Sher Khan routed the Bengal army and seized a large booty of treasures, horses and elephants, etc.[97] Mushtaqi however provides a different reason for the Bengali attack. According to him, after consolidating his hold over Bihar, Sher Khan decided to conquer Bengal. He kept four hundred sawars ready for march, while another four hundred were sent to raid the territories of Bengal. To counter these raids, the king of Bengal deputed Qutb Khan against the wilayat of Bihar.[98] Sher Khan's material power was further enhanced by Makhdum Alam's property which the latter had given him shortly before being attacked by the Bengal army for not fighting against Sher Khan in the previous encounter.[99] Ghulam Husain Salim suggests that after Qutb Khan was killed in the battle, Makhdum Alam rebelled again with a view to capture the throne of Bengal, and was killed fighting with Sultan Mahmud Shah.[100]

Sher Khan's refusal to share the newly acquired treasure and territories with the Nuhanis induced serious differences between them

[96] One of the sarkars of suba Bihar, Mungir (or Monghyr) had 31 mahals under Akbar (Area: 7745 square miles; Jama: 29,625,981.5 dams), Habib, *Atlas*, Table I and 10 A, Notes. C.f. *Beames' Contribution to the Political Geography*, pp. 27–30.

[97] *Tarikh-i-Sher Shahi*, pp. 60–1; *Tabaqat-i-Akbari*, fols. 199a–b. Badauni suggests that the Bengali attack was to overthrow Makhdum Alam and Sher Khan had marched to his aid, *Muntakhab-ut-Tawarikh*, Vol. I, p. 360; *Tarikh-i-Khan-i-Jahani wa Makhzan-i-Afghani*, Vol. I, pp. 276–8; *Farishta*, fol. 238a; Ghulam Husain Salim, *Riyaz-us-Salatin*, Eng. trans. Abdus Salam, first published 1903, reprint (Delhi, 1975), p. 138. Siddiqui has pointed out that the time of Qutb Khan's invasion of Bihar implicit in Abbas Khan's work was not correct. Abbas suggests that this event took place before Sher Khan's occupation of Chunar fort and the battle of Do-rah, but the invasion took place, according to Siddiqui's calculation, in 1532–3, *A History of Sher Shah Sur*, pp. 38–40.

[98] *Waqi'at-i-Mushtaqi*, fols. 48b–49a. Abdullah borrows Mushtaqi's account, *Tarikh-i-Dau'di*, p. 116.

[99] *Tarikh-i-Sher Shahi*, pp. 61–2.

[100] *Riyaz-us-Salatin*, p. 138.

because of which the latter began plotting to kill him. The Nuhanis however were not totally united. Some of them came to Sher Khan and told him about the plot. In order to curb Sher Khan's power, Jalal Khan and his supporters decided to approach the sultan of Bengal for help. As part of this plan, Jalal Khan sent Sher Khan towards his pargana of Sahsaram, while he himself went over to the sultan. When Sher Khan heard about it, he was pleased and remarked that the kingdom of Bihar had now come into his hands (*chun sher khan shunid ke jalal khan pesh badshah bangala raft khush-hal shud wa guft ke mulk bihar ba-dast man amad*).[101]

The king of Bengal asked Ibrahim Khan, son of Qutb Khan who was killed in the previous campaign against Sher Khan, to accompany Jalal Khan with a huge army. Meanwhile, Sher Khan recruited a large number of Afghan soldiers and marched towards Bengal. The two armies met at a place identified as Surajgarh,[102] where Sher Khan had built a fortress of unburnt bricks. Sher Khan was very particular about fortification from the very early phase of his career. His action against the zamindars was marked by mud fortification at every stage of the march. This practice of fortification during a campaign had become

[101] *Tarikh-i-Sher Shahi*, pp. 62–72. See also, *Tabaqat-i-Akbari*, fol. 199b; *Muntakhab-ut-Tawarikh*, Vol. I, p. 360; *Tarikh-i-Dau'di*, pp. 116–17; *Tarikh-i-Khan-i-Jahani wa Makhzan-i-Afghani*, Vol. I, pp. 278–79; *Tarikh-i-Salatin-i-Afaghina*, pp. 180–1. Also see *Farishta*, fol. 238a. According to Siddiqui, Sher Khan had suppressed the Nuhanis and became the undisputed master of Bihar after the death of Dudu in 1529–30. Failing in their design to kill Sher Khan in retaliation to his high-handedness, the Nuhanis took Jalal Khan with them to Bengal, sometime in 1530, *A History of Sher Shah Sur*, pp. 32–3.

[102] *Tarikh-i-Sher Shahi*, p. 72. 'Surajgarh' has been mentioned by Abu'l Fazl, which according to him is the boundary of the territory of the ruler of Bengal and where Sher Shah won a victory against the Bengalis, *Akbarnama*, fol. 82a. Siddiqui suggests that Ibrahim Khan was defeated near Ghayaspur along the river Punpun in 1534. Surajgarh, according to him, was captured some time in the middle of 1535, *A History of Sher Shah Sur*, pp. 42, 46. B.P. Ambashthya puts the place (and date of the battle) to Surajgarh (October 1530), *The Decisive Battles of Ser Sah* (Patna, 1977), pp. 9–30 Cf. Qanungo, *Sher Shah and his Times*, pp. 137–8. Though other medieval authorities have referred to the Bengali campaign led by Ibrahim Khan, they do not mention the site of the battle, *Tarikh-i-Khan-i-Jahani wa Makhzan-i-Afghani*, Vol. I, p. 279; *Muntakhab-ut-Tawarikh*, Vol. I, p. 360; *Farishta*, fol. 238a. Abdullah suggests that the Bengal army was led by Jalal Khan. Ibrahim is not mentioned, *Tarikh-i-Dau'di*, pp. 117–18.

'customary' for him as we shall see subsequently. Ibrahim, having a large number of elephants and artillery, under-estimated Sher Khan's strength, and could not harm him on account of the mud fortress. The Afghans fought back Ibrahim's forces who came close to the fortress. None of the two contending forces could gain an upper hand. The vastness of their army, elephants and artillery enabled the Bengalis to hold the field till then.[103]

Ibrahim Khan was forced to raise the siege and ask the king of Bengal for reinforcements as his present force was not sufficient to dislodge Sher Khan from his earthen fortress. Sher Khan, on the other hand, realising that any delay in an open fight might enable reinforcements to arrive for the Bengalis, decided for a pitched battle.[104] Also, the awe about the strength of the Bengalis had disappeared from the heart of the Afghans. According to Abbas, Sher Khan not only invoked the martial ethos of his Afghan forces but also told them to have faith in the Quranic verse which says that a handful of chosen persons vanquished large numbers by divine command. While the term *jihad* was avoided, the 'handful of chosen persons' must be righteous enough to get this 'favour' from God. Further, as we shall see below, in the battles against Humayun also, the bogey of jihad was avoided but those killed, either Afghans or Mughals, were said to have attained martyrdom. The term jihad was used only for campaigns against the Rajputs.

Sher Khan found that the Afghans were sufficiently motivated for the fight. Also, the young and proud Ibrahim Khan was anxious for an open engagement without raising a fortress for his own safety. Sher Khan therefore announced his decision to fight an open battle. Ibrahim Khan formally accepted the challenge.[105] The number of elephants,

---

[103] For the position taken by the Afghans in the earthen fortress constructed by Sher Shah and the skirmishes which followed, see also *Tabaqat-i-Akbari*, fol. 199b; *Tarikh-i-Khan-i-Jahani wa Makhzan-i-Afghani*, Vol. I, p. 279; *Tarikh-i-Dau'di*, p. 117; *Tarikh-i-Salatin-i-Afaghina*, p. 181; *Farishta*, fol. 238a. In a superficial and misleading account of the encounter of Sher Khan with the Bengalis, Badauni writes that Sher Khan fought from within the fort everyday, *Muntakhab-ut-Tawarikh*, Vol. I, p. 360.

[104] *Tabaqat-i-Akbari*, fols. 199b–200a.

[105] Badauni writes that Sher Khan was compelled to fight as the Bengalis had already received large reinforcements (*madad-i-azim*), *Muntakhab-ut-Tawarikh*, Vol. I, p. 360.

artillery and the infantry in Ibrahim Khan's army was very large. Sher Khan planned to first destroy the order in which Ibrahim had arranged his forces, so that the Bengal cavalry was drawn away from their artillery and infantry, and the elephants mixed up with the horsemen to create confusion. Accordingly, he brought his selected horsemen in the open, while the rest of the forces were stationed behind the hill. When the forces of Ibrahim Khan appeared, a division of the Afghan horsemen marched against the enemy and, after having discharged one volley of arrows, turned back. The Bengal horsemen thought that the Afghans had fled, and ran in pursuit leaving their ranks behind, as calculated by Sher Khan. When the Afghans who were in hiding saw this, they came out and charged upon the Bengal cavalry from behind. The fleeing Afghans also turned around and then they all fell upon the Bengali horsemen. Ibrahim Khan saw many of his nobles fleeing but decided to fight on and was slain. Jalal Khan who was seriously injured in the fight fled back to Bengal. Sher Khan who emerged victorious seized huge amounts of treasures, elephants, equipages and artillery. The Afghan leader now became the uncrowned king of Bihar.[106]

A seventeenth century Ujjainiya narrative claims that Gajpati, the Maharaja of Bhojpur, fought for Sher Khan in this battle and his two thousand followers joined the vanguard of the Afghan forces in front of the Bengal army. It is also suggested that Ibrahim Khan was slain by Gajpati himself and was amply rewarded by Sher Khan for his bravery.[107] The Ujjainiya report that Sher Khan's army had three divisions is supported by Ahmad Yadgar.[108]

Meanwhile Sher Khan was also able to capture the fort of Chunar where Sultan Ibrahim Lodi had kept the royal treasury on the eve of Babur's invasion, having entrusted it to the custody of Taj Khan Sarangkhani. Taj Khan had handed over the management of the fort and the forces to his favourite wife Lad Malika. His sons from his other wives resented this. One of them attempted to murder Malika, and when Taj Khan protested over it, he was attacked fatally. Subsequently,

---

[106] *Tarikh-i-Sher Shahi*, pp. 72–9; Ni'matullah adds that thus with one stroke of the pen the whole of Bihar came into the possession of Sher Khan, *Tarikh-i-Khan-i-Jahani wa Makhzan-i-Afghani*, Vol. I, p. 280; *Tabaqat-i-Akbari*, fol. 200a; *Farishta*, fols. 238a–b. Cf. *Tarikh-i-Dau'di*, pp. 117–18.

[107] Ambashthya, *Decisive Battles*, pp. 20–2.

[108] *Tarikh-i-Salatin-i-Afaghina*, pp. 181–2.

as Taj Khan's sons were troubling her, the three Turkoman brothers loyal to Malika persuaded her to marry Sher Khan and hand over the fort to him. She agreed to the proposal and invited Sher Khan to Chunar. When Sher Khan reached there, Lad Malika married him and presented a huge amount of gifts, apart from the Lodi treasury. Sher Khan also annexed the territories around the fort.[109] Badauni says that Sher Khan grabbed the fortress of Chunar together with its vast treasures from Taj Khan's sons, and took in marriage his wealthy and beautiful wife, fuelling his ambitions further.[110] Another tradition has it that Sher Khan, aware of the affairs at Chunar, proposed a treaty of marriage with Lad Malika, which was soon concluded.[111] Sher Khan's marriage with Lad Malika was followed by another marriage with Hargusain, a young and wealthy Brahmin widow of Nasir Khan Nuhani, 'one of the great nobles' of Sikandar Lodi. The three hundred *mans* of gold which she gave to Sher Khan,[112] together with the treasure received from Lad Malika, enabled him to quickly build up a huge army. The military labour market of Hindustan was available for employers who were willing to recruit and pay honestly and generously. We shall return in the next chapter to Sher Khan's purchasing power at this stage.

The feeble Afghan-Rajput resistance to the invading Mughals has been mentioned above. The Afghans, supported by Hasan Khan Mewati and Rana Sanga, had proclaimed Sultan Mahmud Lodi, son of Sultan Sikandar Lodi, as the king, fought a battle with Babur at Khanwa near Fatehpur-Sikri, and were defeated.[113] Sher Khan was compelled to join Sultan Mahmud, only to desert him soon. Babur wrote on 28 February

---

[109] *Tarikh-i-Sher Shahi*, p. 84. Also see *Tabaqat-i-Akbari*, fols. 200a–b.

[110] *Muntakhab-ut-Tawarikh*, Vol. I, pp. 360–1.

[111] *Tarikh-i-Khan-i-Jahani wa Makhzan-i-Afghani*, Vol. I, pp. 281–3; *Tarikh-i-Dau'di*, p. 118; *Tarikh-i-Salatin-i-Afaghina*, pp. 182–3; *Farishta*, fol. 238b. Abu'l Fazl writes that Sher Khan took Jamal Khan's widow as his wife and thus occupied the fortress, *Akbarnama*, fol. 70a. R.P. Tripathi suggests that Taj Khan was killed, or died, in 1530, and through 'intrigue, bribery, and even treachery, Sher Khan got possession of the fort, as well as the wife of Taj Khan', *Rise and Fall of the Mughal Empire*, p. 69.

[112] *Tarikh-i-Khan-i-Jahani wa Makhzan-i-Afghani*, Vol. I, p. 283; *Tarikh-i-Sher Shahi*, pp. 84–5.

[113] *Tarikh-i-Sher Shahi*, p. 85; *Muntakhab-ut-Tawarikh*, Vol. I, p. 361. *Tabaqat-i-Akbari*, fol. 200b; *Farishta*, fol. 238b.

1529 that Sher Khan whom he had favoured the previous year with the gift of several parganas had joined the Afghans led by Sultan Mahmud. Later Babur mentioned on 3 March 1529 having received 'dutiful letters' from him.[114] After the defeat, Sultan Mahmud left with Rana Sanga for Chittor,[115] from where he moved to Bhata or Bihta. Shortly after Babur's death (1530), the Afghan chiefs led by Mian Biban and Mian Bayazid Farmuli again put Sultan Mahmud to the throne at Bihta, and marched to Bihar. Sher Khan could not oppose them as they had a much larger force and following, while he himself did not command sufficient respectability among the Afghans till then. He was, therefore, compelled to enter into Sultan Mahmud's service. The Afghans divided the territory of Bihar amongst themselves. Sultan Mahmud assured Sher Khan that he would grant him the kingdom of Bihar after capturing Jaunpur from the Mughals. A farman or *qaulnama*[116] was also issued to this effect, after receiving which Sher Khan took permission to leave for Sahsaram.[117] Ni'matullah says that Sultan Mahmud was enthroned for the second time during Babur's reign. Babur, however, died before the sultan's march towards Jaunpur.[118]

Sultan Mahmud, marching towards Jaunpur, issued a farman to Sher Khan asking him to turn up immediately. Sher Khan wrote back that he would do so after arranging his forces. The nobles, aware of his 'false pretences', 'fox-like strategem' and his alliance with the Mughals, suspected his intention (*sher khan mard mukhil wa makkar ast*). They suggested to the sultan not to believe in his statement, and rather to march to Sahsaram and compel him to accompany the army. The advice was approved. Thus, Sher Khan's ploy failed. He now readied his men for the march and himself went to receive the sultan and his entourage,

---

[114] *Baburnama*, pp. 652, 659.

[115] Sarkar Chittor (Area: 15,953 square miles; Jama: 34,637,649 dams) of suba Ajmer was under the direct control of the Mughals in 1595. Subsequently in 1615, Chittor with all its 26 or 28 parganas was assigned to Kunwar Karan, the son of Rana Amar Singh, ruler of Mewar, Habib, *Atlas*, Table I and 6 A, Notes. For Sher Shah's Chittor campaign, see chapter four.

[116] *Tabaqat-i-Akbari*, fol. 200b; *Farishta*, fol. 238b.

[117] *Tarikh-i-Sher Shahi*, pp. 86–7; *Tabaqat-i-Akbari*, fol. 200b; *Farishta*, fol. 238b. See also, *Muntakhab-ut-Tawarikh*, Vol. I, p. 361.

[118] *Tarikh-i-Khan-i-Jahani wa Makhzan-i-Afghani*, Vol. I, pp. 284–5; *Tarikh-i-Dau'di*, p. 119.

offering them a warm welcome and a good deal of hospitality. Sultan Mahmud soon marched towards Jaunpur with Sher Khan in his company. When they arrived near Jaunpur, the Mughals fled away without a fight. Large swathes of eastern territories up to Lucknow[119] came under the control of the Afghans.[120]

When Sultan Mahmud learned that Humayun was advancing towards him, he too marched from Jaunpur and the two armies clashed near Lucknow. Sher Khan realized that the defeat of the Afghans was imminent as there was no order in the army. He also disliked the leadership of Biban and Bayazid. Therefore, he wrote to the Mughal general Hindu Beg that he was brought up by the Mughals (*man az khaq bar-awardah-i-mughalanam*) and he had been forced to accompany the sultan (*mara bazor hamrah khwud awardah and*), but on the day of battle he would retreat without fighting. He also requested Hindu Beg to apprise Humayun of the service (*khidmat*) he would thus render resulting in the Afghans' defeat. When informed, Humayun responded that Sher Khan should not fear for having accompanied Sultan Mahmud and if the plans outlined in his letter took shape, he would be rewarded. Accordingly, Sher Khan withdrew his soldiers without a contest leading to the defeat of the Afghans. Most of Mahmud's nobles were either killed or separated from him. The sultan fled, giving up the desire for kingship.[121] Badauni says that Sultan Mahmud fled away to Orissa, identified by him as the frontier of the desert of non-existence (*sarhad-i-sahra-i-adam*).[122] It augered well for Sher Khan as another

[119] Headquarters of the sarkar of Lucknow (Area: 5883 square miles; Jama: 80,716,160 dams) in the suba of Awadh under Akbar, Habib, *Atlas*, Table I. One of the stories on the origin of Lucknow relates that the place is named after an *ahir* or milk-seller named Lakhna, who as a result of the spiritual blessings of a Sufi saint had become rich and founded the city, *Uttar Pradesh District Gazetteer, Lucknow* (Lucknow, 1959), p. 1. For a history of Lucknow in our period, see ibid., pp. 32–4.

[120] *Tarikh-i-Sher Shahi*, pp. 88–90; *Tabaqat-i-Akbari*, fols. 200b–201a; *Muntakhab-ut-Tawarikh*, Vol. I, p. 361; *Tarikh-i-Dau'di*, p. 119; *Tarikh-i-Khan-i-Jahani wa Makhzan-i-Afghani*, Vol. I, pp. 285–6; *Farishta*, fols. 238b–239a.

[121] *Tarikh-i-Sher Shahi*, pp. 90–2; *Tabaqat-i-Akbari*, fol. 201a; *Tarikh-i-Dau'di*, p. 120; *Tarikh-i-Khan-i-Jahani wa Makhzan-i-Afghani*, Vol. I, pp. 286–8; *Tarikh-i-Salatin-i-Afaghina*, pp. 184–5. *Farishta*, fol. 239a.

[122] *Muntakhab-ut-Tawarikh*, Vol. I, pp. 361–2. Ishwari Prasad incorrectly notes that abdicating his claims to the throne, Sultan Mahmud settled down as a '*Jagirdar*' at Patna, *Life and Times of Humayun*, p. 113.

powerful and legitimate rival for the leadership of the Afghans was removed from the scene. Abu'l Fazl places this victory of Humayun over the Afghans in 939/1532–3, after the siege of Chunar, which in fact was conducted later. Also he does not mention the role played by Sher Khan in Humayun's victory.[123] Siddiqui rejects the suggestion that Sher Khan's withdrawal had led to Sultan Mahmud's defeat as baseless and a later concoction.[124] Ishwari Prasad passes the judgement: 'It was an act of sheer treachery on the part of Sher Khan'.[125] Prasad in fact condemns Sher Khan for his 'treachery' on several occasions, as we shall note at appropriate places.

Humayun, instead of rewarding Sher Khan for his role in the battle, assigned Hindu Beg to take over Chunar from him.[126] When Sher Khan refused to hand over Chunar, Humayun himself marched to seize the fort. Sher Khan meanwhile left the fort in the hands of his son Jalal Khan, later known as Islam Shah Sur, and went away with his family and followers towards Bharkunda in the hills. The Mughals laid siege of the fort, which was bravely defended by Jalal Khan and his soldiers.[127] Sher Khan knew that Humayun would have to go back soon as he had received information from his spies that Sultan Bahadur of Gujarat had seized Mandu and had resolved to capture Delhi, for which he would set out shortly. Suggesting that the awareness of worldly affairs or knowledge, brings power, Abbas Khan writes that Sher Khan had sent spies all over for obtaining information.[128]

[123] *Akbarnama*, fol. 70a. Jauhar Aftabchi is also silent about the role played by Sher Khan in the defeat of the Afghans, who were led by, according to him, Biban, Bayazid and Ibrahim Khan Lodi. All of them were killed, *Tazkirat-ul-Waqi'at*, fols. 3b–4a.

[124] Siddiqui, *A History of Sher Shah Sur*, pp. 35–7; idem, *Sher Shah Sur and his Dynasty*, p. 48.

[125] Prasad, *Life and Times of Humayun*, p. 113. Also see, Tripathi, *Rise and Fall of the Mughal Empire*, p. 70.

[126] *Tabaqat-i-Akbari*, fol. 201a; *Farishta*, fol. 239a.

[127] *Tarikh-i-Sher Shahi*, pp. 92–3. See also, *Tarikh-i-Khan-i-Jahani wa Makhzan-i-Afghani*, Vol. I, pp. 288–9; *Muntakhab-ut-Tawarikh*, Vol. I, p. 362; Abdullah borrows details from *Waqi'at-i-Mushtaqi* pertaining to the second siege of Chunar, *Tarikh-i-Dau'di*, pp. 121–2; *Tarikh-i-Salatin-i-Afaghina*, pp. 185–6. Cf. *Akbarnama*, fol. 70a; *Tazkirat-ul-Waqi'at*, fol. 4a.

[128] *Tarikh-i-Sher Shahi*, p. 94. C.A. Bayly has recently suggested that there existed a flexible and at times penetrating, but labile and thinly spread network of surveillance in medieval India; the British colonial government on the other hand

Humayun had also become aware of Sultan Bahadur's plans. Seeking to exploit Humayun's predicament, Sher Khan sent a *wakil* or agent with a letter reminding him of his past services, including the more recent 'service' in the battle at Lucknow, and requested that the fort of Chunar be given to him. Addressing himself as an old slave (*ghulam-i-pir*), Sher Khan added that the emperor may keep his son Qutb Khan as a hostage. Sultan Bahadur's intention of marching to Delhi, coupled with the news that Mirza Muhammad Zaman had managed to escape from the Bayana fort[129] and was causing trouble in the region, compelled Humayun to accept Sher Khan's proposal, and leave for Agra.[130] Ishwari Prasad criticizes Humayun for lifting the siege. He writes that by capturing Chunar he would have destroyed the very foundation of Sher Khan's rising power. Thus, he adds, the Mughals would never have been expelled from India. In condemning Humayun for the 'cardinal error', Prasad contradicts himself by suggesting that Bahadur Shah 'was too wealthy, too ambitious, and too clever not to be dangerous in the highest degree'. He also admits that 'the news from the south was sufficiently serious to have given anyone pause'.[131]

Sher Khan took the opportunity of Humayun's absence to recruit a large number of Afghan soldiers, in some cases even forcibly as we shall see in the next chapter, trained them and paid monthly salary in cash. With their support, he wiped off all opposition in Bihar (*wilayat bihar ra saaf sakhta*).[132] Impressed by his triumph, a large number of Afghan chiefs, who had earlier scorned him, came to join him. Emboldened by

---

created a sophisticated 'information order' in modern times, *Empire and Information: Intelligence Gathering and Social Communication in India, 1780–1870* (Cambridge, 1996). Cf. Muhammad Zamiruddin Siddiqui, 'The Intelligence Services under the Mughals', *MIAM*, Vol. II, 1972, pp. 53–60.

[129] The *dastur*-circle of Bayana, sarkar Agra, is much noted in the economic history of Mughal India for high quality indigo production, Habib, *Atlas*, 8 A & B, Notes.

[130] *Tarikh-i-Sher Shahi*, pp. 94–5. See also *Tabaqat-i-Akbari*, fol. 201b; *Muntakhab-ut-Tawarikh*, Vol. I, p. 362; *Tarikh-i-Khan-i-Jahani wa Makhzan-i-Afghani*, Vol. I, p. 289; *Tarikh-i-Dau'di*, p. 122; *Tarikh-i-Salatin-i-Afaghina*, p. 186; *Farishta*, fol. 239a. Also see, *Tazkirat-ul-Waqi'at*, fols. 4a–b. According to I.H. Siddiqui the Mughals besieged Chunar in November 1531. The siege lasted for one month, *A History of Sher Shah Sur*, pp. 37–8.

[131] Prasad, *Life and Times of Humayun*, pp. 61, 69.

[132] *Tabaqat-i-Akbari*, fol. 201b. Also see *Farishta*, fol. 239a.

his success and the recognition of his capabilities by the senior Afghans, Sher Khan assumed the title of *Hazrat-i-Ala*.[133] Ni'matullah refers to the bestowal of kingship to Sher Khan by a *majzub* at a market place in Patna during this period.[134] It is reported that when Sher Khan heard this prophecy his desire for sovereignty increased further.

Based on a coin preserved in the AMU library and the indications in Kabir's *Afsana-i-Shahan*, Iqtidar Husain Siddiqui has suggested that Sher Khan had assumed the titles of Sultan and Shah, and had begun to strike coins in that capacity in 1535. In arriving at this conclusion, Siddiqui ignores a whole range of sources which provide a different picture. Referring to the silence of the chroniclers on the issue of Sher Khan assuming kingship at this stage, Siddiqui explains that 'Jauhar and Mushtaqi who are the earliest writers, were not in a position to hear of the assumption of sovereignty by Sher Shah as his activities were confined to Bihar and Bengal, far away from their home towns'. The author adds that Sher Shah himself might have tried to keep the people of North India in the dark by not giving publicity to this fact as he could not afford to fight against both Humayun and Sultan Mahmud of Bengal at the same time.[135] Siddiqui's explanation of the silence of the chroniclers is not very convincing. As noted above, rapid information flow was possible in medieval India, and it is unlikely that the news of such a serious matter as Sher Khan's claiming sovereignty could not have travelled from Bihar to Agra. Catherine Asher, on the other hand, has made it clear that she would agree with Siddiqui only after the publication of the legends inscribed on the coin.[136]

S.C. Misra gives the details of a silver coin of Sher Shah dated 942/ 1535–6, preserved in the AMU. On the obverse, within a square, Sher Shah's name, his regnal titles and the year are given: *sultan sher shah khallad-allah mulkuhu 942*. Outside the square, the full sequence of the same is mentioned: *as-sultan-al-adil abul muzaffar farid-ud-duniya*

---

[133] *Tarikh-i-Sher Shahi*, pp. 95–6. For the title *Hazrat-i-Ala* used for Sher Khan, also see *Waqi'at-i-Mushtaqi*, fol. 49a.

[134] He writes: *guyand dar in hin shabe dar bazar qasba-i-patna sair kunan ba do-sah kas as yaran wa makhsusan mi guzasht, majzube nashista bud. Chun nazr bar sher khan uftad, haq ta'ala bar zuban-i-u jari sakht, wa guft binid ke badshah-i-dehli piyada mi ayad, Tarikh-i-Khan-i-Jahani wa Makhzan-i-Afghani*, Vol. I, p. 290.

[135] *A History of Sher Shah Sur*, pp. 44–5; *Sher Shah Sur and his Dynasty*, p. 62.

[136] Asher, 'Mausoleum of Sher Shah'.

wad-din. In the fourth segment, there appear some Devanagari characters which are not very clearly read, but is apparently the ruler's name in that script. On the reverse, within a square appears the kalima. In the four segments, the names of the four pious *khalifas* are placed.[137] The presence of the 942/1535–6 silver piece and other pre-946/1539–40 coins, mainly copper, is not a sufficient evidence for suggesting that Sher Shah's accession had taken place before the battle of Chausa. As Misra rightly points out, Sher Khan issued his first coins without waiting for a formal coronation ceremony, without assuming the royal titles and royal status except insofar as his coins were concerned and without having the khutba read in his name. Hence, despite the presence of the coins, there is no mention of 'coronation' by the chroniclers.[138] The title Hazrat-i-Ala which he assumed publicly was not high enough to be an affront either to the Afghan sentiments or to Mughal pretensions—but adequate enough to allow its holder to exercise undisputed authority.[139]

Though by issuing the coins, Sher Shah claimed sovereign status, he refrained from legitimising it with an 'accession' ceremony. His leadership had yet to acquire the charisma which could enable the steps to be easy and generally acknowledged, his acceptance as the leader by the older Afghan nobility being too recent. Sher Shah could hardly afford to jeopardise his status as the undisputed Afghan leader for a step which would have the stigma of ill-judged ambition and unscrupulousness. Only when he had restored the Afghan power, could he hope to have his elevation to the supreme position accepted by the Afghans. Thus, as Misra suggests, this splitting of the royal prerogatives and the exercise of one without proper credentials was an innovation of Sher Shah, 'a supreme example of his pragmatic genius'. For him it was a solution of an impasse in which he found himself. He could not yet ascend the throne or have the khutba read in his name, nor could he keep the issue of coinage in abeyance for long.[140]

---

[137] S.C. Misra, 'The *Sikka* and the *Khutba*: A Sher Shahi Experiment', *MIAM*, Vol. I, 1969, p. 39.

[138] Ibid., p. 45.

[139] Ibid.

[140] Ibid., pp. 46–7. For Sher Shah's 'accession' and 'coronation', see Rama Sankar Avasthy, 'Sher Shah—His Accession and Coronation', *PIHC*, Second Session, Allahabad, 1938, pp. 368–75.

At this stage, Sher Khan's coffers were further enriched when he succeeded in winning over Bibi Fath Malika, who was the daughter of Mian Muhammad Kalapahar Farmuli, Sultan Bahlul's sister's son, with all her wealth and retainers. The lady had earlier considered going over to the *raja* of Bihta for protection after the death of her illustrious brother-in-law, Mian Bayazid, in the last encounter between Humayun and Sultan Mahmud at Lucknow. When she learned that the raja had become hostile towards the Afghans and was robbing them, she decided not to go to him. Sher Khan, knowing this, conceived the design of bringing her under his control. The Bibi, after getting a promise on solemn oath of her safety under Sher Khan, came over to him.[141] Her arrival in Sher Khan's protection was particularly fortuitous for the latter, as he took three hundred *maunds* of gold from her. Incidentally, this reminds us once again of some numismatists' claim that there was a physical shortage of precious metals in the period. Also, it may be that the precise amount of three hundred maunds which he was said to have received from the various ladies was metaphorical, though we are not in a position to explain it at present. In any case he used the amount for recruiting and equipping his army before embarking on the conquest of Bengal.

In Abbas Sarwani's account, when Nasib Shah, the ruler of Bengal died, the nobles enthroned Sultan Mahmud.[142] He could not control the affairs of the kingdom leading to the outbreak of trouble there. Sher Khan now felt tempted to seize the kingdom. He busied himself in conquering Bengal and brought the entire region west of Garhi under his control.[143] On the other hand, leaving the Gujarat campaign incomplete, Humayun had to rush to Agra as Mirza Askari and Yadgar

[141] *Tarikh-i-Sher Shahi*, pp. 96–100; see also *Tarikh-i-Khan-i-Jahani wa Makhzan-i-Afghani*, Vol. I, p. 283, for Sher Khan receiving 300 *maunds* of gold from the Bibi. According to Siddiqui, she came to Sher Khan towards the close of 1533 after Makhdum Alam's death under whose protection Bayazid Farmuli had kept her at Hajipur, *A History of Sher Shah Sur*, pp. 41–2.

[142] Ghulam Husain Salim identifies Nasib Shah of the chronicles as Nasir-ud-Din Abu'l Muzaffar Nasrat Shah (son of Ala-ud-Din Husain Shah) of the coins and inscriptions. He also notes that after his death the nobles had helped his son Firuz Shah to ascend the throne. The latter ruled for three years before being killed by one of his eighteen uncles who captured the throne and styled himself as Sultan Mahmud, *Riyaz-us-Salatin*, pp. 134, 137.

[143] *Tarikh-i-Sher Shahi*, pp. 100–1. See also, *Tarikh-i-Dau'di*, p. 122; *Tarikh-i-Salatin-i-Afaghina*, p. 186; *Muntakhab-ut-Tawarikh*, Vol. I, p. 348. For a slightly different account of Sher Khan's Bengal campaign at this time, see *Farishta*, fol. 239a.

Nasir Mirza had rebelled.[144] At Agra, he was informed of the mobilization of the Afghans under Sher Khan who had by then captured the whole of Bihar and large parts of Bengal. The emperor did not march against Sher Khan immediately. Instead, he sent Hindu Beg towards Jaunpur instructing him to send a report on the activities of Sher Khan. Gulbadan Begam refers to Humayun staying in Agra for one year before turning to the affairs of Sher Khan.[145] Farishta records that after his return from Gujarat, Humayun indulged in excessive use of opium and neglected public business. Taking advantage of the death of Sultan Junaid Barlas, the Afghans of the eastern territories, whom he had kept in subjection, revolted and joined Sher Khan.[146] In sharp contrast to this, the Mughal chronicler Jauhar Aftabchi suggests that some time after his arrival from Gujarat, Humayun was informed that Sher Khan had taken possession of the strong fortress of Ruhtas. He was also told that Sher Khan was besieging Gaur,[147] the capital of Bengal, and it was expected he would capture the city shortly. Humayun therefore decided to march to Chunar.[148]

Sher Khan, on knowing Humayun's moves against him, sent huge offerings to Hindu Beg and submitted that he had adhered to the promise made to the emperor. He also requested him to send a favourable report regarding his loyalty, so that Humayun would not march against him. The Afghan narrative suggests that Hindu Beg, lured by the presents sent by Sher Khan, wrote to Humayun that the Afghan leader was a loyal servant who strikes coins and reads khutba in the name of the exalted emperor. Mushtaqi however differs on this point, saying that Sher Khan could not influence Hindu Beg through his *peshkash* of

---

[144] Gulbadan Begam, *Humayun-Nama*, p. 39. Also see, *Tazkirat-ul-Waqi'at*, fols. 7b–11b. Mirza Haidar Dughlat, *Tarikh-i-Rashidi*, Eng. Trans. N. Elias, revised and edited by Denison Ross, reprint (Patna, 1973), p. 470.

[145] *Humayun-Nama*, p. 39. Nizam-ud-Din Ahmad also wrote: *chun jannat ashiyani ba agra rasidand yaksal qarar girafta ba aish wa nishat guzranidand*, *Tabaqat-i-Akbari*, fol. 175b.

[146] *Farishta*, fols. 234b–235a.

[147] Also known as Lakhnauti and Jannatabad, Gaur was a mass of ruins already in the seventeenth century, though its 66 mahals under Akbar gave the Jama figure, 18,846,967 dams, Habib, *Atlas* Table I and 11 A, Notes; *Beames' Contribution to the Political Geography*, pp. 67–72.

[148] *Tazkirat-ul-Waqi'at*, fols. 12a–b. See also, *Tarikh-i-Rashidi*, p. 470; *Tarikh-i-Khan-i-Jahani wa Makhzan-i-Afghani*, Vol. I, p. 290; *Tarikh-i-Dau'di*, p. 122; *Tarikh-i-Salatin-i-Afaghina*, p. 187.

a few maunds of gold. Sher Khan had written to the Mughal noble pledging his loyalty and denying claims to any part of the king's wilayat. He had requested to be allowed to retain Bengal and also to hold the fort of Chunar on lease, in lieu of which he would continue to pay revenue, and sincerely perform royal service. Moreover, one of his sons would be in Humayun's service with four hundred sawars, but he himself would not attend the court.[149]

Mushtaqi further records that Hindu Beg was not moved by Sher Khan's claims and suggestions, responding that if he wanted to serve Humayun, he should proceed in person and obtain a *khil'at* and horse.[150] It was wrong on his part to demand the assignment of the wilayat to be conveyed to him from the court in writing. Dismissing Sher Khan's claim for the wilayat of Bengal, Hindu Beg explained that since the badshah honoured the country of Hindustan with his residence, he considered every part as belonging to him, whether it was Delhi, Bengal, Gujarat, or the Deccan. It was the privilege of the emperor to grant territory to any of his servants.[151] In response to this reply of Hindu Beg, Sher Khan wrote that having tasted his salt he would not be disloyal to him, but if Humayun marched against him he would leave Chunar and Bihar and proceed to Bengal. If followed there also, he would leave for some other place. Sher Khan also added that the badshah was very careless and given to pleasure-seeking, and on reaching Gaur, would indulge in pleasure, not caring for anything. During this period, he would wreak havoc in the wilayat.[152]

Humayun was alarmed by the increasingly threatening posture of Sher Khan. He was informed that the number of Sher Khan's sawars was increasing rapidly as he was continuously recruiting them. When Humayun had started for Gujarat, Sher Khan had only six thousand horsemen in his service, now he had as many as seventy thousand paying them twelve crore *tankas* as monthly salary. These figures may be inflated, but they certainly point to the rise of Sher Khan as a major power to be reckoned with. He was no longer a 'bachcha' in the early sixteenth century struggle for political power and dominance in North

---

[149] *Waqi'at-i-Mushtaqi*, fol. 46a.

[150] For the significance of khil'at in medieval Muslim politics and society, see Stewart Gordon, ed. *Robes and Honor: The Medieval World of Investiture.* 2000. New York. Palgrave.

[151] *Waqi'at-i-Mushtaqi*, fols. 46a–b.

[152] Ibid., fol. 46b.

India. Humayun was warned that if he would not march against Sher Khan that year, the latter might himself start against him.[153] Humayun however delayed in starting the campaign. Sher Khan, on the other hand, deployed his son Jalal Khan and Khawas Khan Senior along-with other *umara* to seize Bengal. When they entered Bengal, Sultan Mahmud found himself powerless against them and shut himself up inside the fort of Gaur. The Afghans surrounded and attacked the fort.[154] Humayun started his march the following year and decided to occupy the fort of Chunar first, giving ample time to Sher Khan to complete the conquest of Gaur.[155] Siddiqui suggests that Humayun left towards Chunar in the autumn of 1537, adding that the emperor was wise in occupying Chunar on his way to Gaur.[156]

Sher Khan left Ghazi Khan Sur and Sultan Barawaqi inside the fort of Chunar and carried away his family and retainers to the fortress of Bharkunda, but could not accommodate all of them there. He there-fore occupied the bigger and safer fort of Ruhtas by, according to later traditions, sending armed Afghans soldiers inside the fort in the guise of women in *dolis* and thus capturing it.[157] Leaving his family in the fort, Sher Khan himself moved in the hills of Bharkunda, never linger-ing at any place. Even as Sher Khan was persuading the raja of Ruhtas for his access to the summit of the fort, much water had flowed down the delta of Bengal. Khawas Khan Senior was drowned in a ditch at Gaur. His brother Shihab Khan was conferred the title of his elder brother, that is, Khawas Khan, and sent by Sher Khan to capture the fort of Gaur at the earliest. He seized the fort in a lightening attack. Sher Khan's son Jalal Khan, who had wanted to delay the final attack, wrote to his father an account of the conquest of Gaur, praising Khawas Khan's valour and determination.[158]

---

[153] Ibid.

[154] Farishta notes that Sher Khan had to return to Bihar, leaving his soldiers to press the siege, as one of the zamindars was creating trouble (*chun dar bihar yake az zanindaran fitna angekhta bud*), *Farishta*, fol. 239a.

[155] Qanungo notes that 'Humayun's grand army was probably set in motion by the first week of November 1537', and that the regular siege of the fort of Chunar began on 10th January 1538, *Sher Shah and his Times*, pp. 175–6.

[156] *A History of Sher Shah Sur*, pp. 51–2.

[157] See Introduction, p. 30.

[158] For Abbas Sarwani's detailed account of Sher Khan's capture of the forts at Gaur and Ruhtas, see *Tarikh-i-Sher Shahi*, pp. 101–11.

Meanwhile, Humayun came to Banaras[159] after the capture of the fort of Chunar which was surrendered by the Afghans in March 1538.[160] Significantly, even after the besieged had surrendered on the condition of their lives being spared, the hands of about two thousand persons, according to Abu'l Fazl, or three hundred selected artillerymen, according to Jauhar, were cut off by the Mughals. Abu'l Fazl, however, denies that it was done on Humayun's order. The chronicler gives a clean chit to the emperor even as the treatment meted out to the besieged went against the 'noble qualities and weighty ethics' of the Mughals. Jauhar's suggestion that Humayun was angry with Rumi Khan over this incident is contradicted when he said that the Khan 'received royal favours' for his achievement.[161]

Meanwhile, Sher Khan was summoned before Humayun at Banaras. The Afghan leader, although unwilling to obey, wrote back that he wanted to serve him, and that he had amassed the Afghans around him and was successful in conquering the fort of Gaur. He offered Humayun the territory of Bihar if he agreed to grant him Bengal with its limits as it existed in the time of Sikandar Lodi. Further, he assured the dispatch of ten lakh rupees annually from Bengal provided Humayun returned to Agra. The emperor accepted the overture and sent a horse and special robes of honour to Sher Khan with the direction to carry out the proposal immediately.[162] Gulbadan Begam writes that the peace-talks were disrupted as the wounded king of Bengal

---

[159] For its location and history in the period of our study, see *Uttar Pradesh District Gazetteer, Varanasi*, pp. 1, 46–50.

[160] For the details of the siege of Chunar and its capture, see *Tazkirat-ul- Waqi'at*, fols. 12b–14a. *Humayun-Nama*, p. 39; *Akbarnama*, fols. 82b–83b; *Tabaqat-i-Akbari*, fols. 176a, 201b; *Muntakhab-ut-Tawarikh*, Vol. I, p. 348; *Tarikh-i-Khan-i-Jahani wa Makhzan-i-Afghani*, Vol. I, pp. 290–2; *Tarikh-i-Dau'di*, p. 122; *Farishta*, fol. 235a; Siddiqui, *A History of Sher Shah Sur*, p. 52.

[161] *Tazkirat-ul Waqi'at*, fols. 14a–b. For Humayun's appreciation of Rumi Khan's achievement, also see *Tabaqat-i-Akbari*, fol. 176a.

[162] *Tarikh-i-Sher Shahi*, pp. 113–14. Jauhar suggests that Sher Khan was asked to send the umbrella, the throne and the treasure of Bengal, evacuate the fort of Ruhtas, and give up possession of the territory he had taken; in exchange for which he might have the fort of Chunar, the city of Jaunpur, and any other place he chose. Sher Khan, however, declined to give up Bengal, which had cost him years of struggle and loss of a large number of soldiers in its conquest, *Tazkirat-ul-Waqi'at*, fols. 15a–b.

came to Humayun's court.[163] Abu'l Fazl does not refer to the attempts at peace but mentions that the injured ruler of Bengal, identified as Nasib Shah, came to the world-protecting court, and sought assistance against Sher Khan.[164]

On the other hand, Jauhar suggests that Humayun marched towards Bengal after hearing that Sher Khan who was already at Gaur had not only rejected the peace proposal, but also was proceeding by the hill road with all the treasures towards Ruhtas.[165] Indeed, learning that Humayun was marching towards Bengal, Sher Khan took an untraversed route and having rushed through the jungle, appeared before Gaur all of a sudden (*az rahi ke kasi gahi narafta ast az rah jangal yakayak bamuqam gaur rasid*).[166] By the time Humayun could reach Bengal, Sher Khan had evacuated it, carrying away to Ruhtas all the treasures through the forest.[167] Mughal writers claimed that Humayun had 'conquered' Bengal, and Sher Khan had 'fled' from there fearing the imperial army.[168]

According to reports, Sher Khan had not only left the inner wings of the palace undisturbed, but had deliberately left some beautiful

---

[163] *Humayun-Nama*, p. 39.

[164] *Akbarnama*, fol. 83b; *Tabaqat-i-Akbari*, fol. 176a. Farishta identified the injured ruler of Bengal as Sultan Mahmud, *Farishta*, fol. 235a. According to Abbas, shortly after the dispatch of the wakil of Humayun to Sher Khan the envoy of Sultan Mahmud, the ruler of Bengal, came to the emperor and informed him that the Afghans had captured the fort, but most part of the country was still under the control of the sultan. He requested the emperor not to trust Sher Khan's words and march towards Bengal to expel the Afghans. Having heard these submissions, Humayun ordered the army to move towards Bengal, *Tarikh-i-Sher Shahi*, pp. 114–15.

[165] *Tazkirat-ul-Waqi'at*, fol. 15b.

[166] *Waqi'at-i-Mushtaqi*, fol. 49a.

[167] *Tarikh-i-Sher Shahi*, pp. 122–4. Ghulam Husain Salim notes that on hearing about the approach of the Mughal forces, an anxious Sher Khan removed the treasures of the rulers of Gaur and Bengal and fled towards Radha (western region of Bengal) and Jharkhand, *Riyaz-us-Salatin*, p. 142.

[168] *Tazkirat-ul-Waqi'at*, fols. 16a–17a; *Humayun-Nama*, p. 40, *Tarikh-i-Rashidi*, p. 470; *Akbarnama*, fols. 84a–b. Also see *Tabaqat-i-Akbari*, fol. 176b. Though Ghulam Husain Salim has referred to Sher Khan's anxiety over Humayun's march to Bengal, he notes as a matter of fact that the Mughal emperor captured the city of Gaur, the capital of Bengal, without any opposition. The ports of Sonargaon and Chatgaon, too, were part of the territories which came to be occupied by the Mughals, *Riyaz-us-Salatin*, p. 142.

young women for Humayun's entertainment. The Mughal ruler shut himself up in the palace for several months and did not grant audience to anybody.[169] Abu'l Fazl explains that actually Humayun stayed back enjoying Bengal's pleasant climate (*hazrat jahanbani hawai bangala ra khwush kardah ba aish wa shadmani nashistand*).[170] He also renamed Gaur (grave) as Jannatabad (paradise).[171] Sher Khan, on the other hand, gained time not only to consolidate his position, but also captured Mughal territories.[172] When circumstances necessitated Humayun's return,[173] it was too late for him to check the Afghan onslaught. Sher Khan gave a rude shock to the Mughals, who received two successive drubbings at Chausa[174] and Qannauj to be discussed in the next chapter. The ambitious Afghan's dream of driving the Mughals out of the country came true. From Bengal to Punjab and Agra to Mandu, several small time chieftains were subjugated. Sher Khan from a petty chieftain had become the badshah of Hindustan. The Mughals attributed their shocking defeats to the hand of God or the treachery of the Afghans. They ignored Sher Khan's cool, calculated use of opportunities and resources which came in his way. He not only recruited and mobilized the Afghans, but also led them to victory employing strategies and tactics which were truly ingenious.

[169] *Waqi'at-i-Mushtaqi*, fols. 46b–47a; *Tarikh-i-Dau'di*, pp. 123–4. Nizam-ud-Din notes that Humayun stayed in Bengal for three months, *Tabaqat-i-Akbari*, fols. 176b, 202a. Also see *Tazkirat-ul-Waqi'at*, fol. 17a.

[170] *Akbarnama*, fol. 84b; *Muntakhab-ut-Tawarikh*, Vol. I, p. 349; *Ma'asir-ul-Umara*, Vol. II, p. 728.

[171] *Humayun-Nama*, p. 40; *Tabaqat-i-Akbari*, fol. 176b; *Tarikh-i-Rashidi*, p. 470; *Tarikh-i-Khan-i-Jahani wa Makhzan-i-Afghani*, Vol. I, p. 296; *Farishta*, fol. 235a; *Riyaz-us-Salatin*, p. 142. R.P. Tripathi writes that after reaching Gaur in September 1538 the Mughal emperor utilized his three or four months of stay in establishing law and order. The fall of the Husaini dynasty must have brought chaos and confusion in Bengal, *Rise and Fall of the Mughal Empire*, p. 93. For this statement Tripathi does not indicate any particular evidence he has used and there is no support for this in the sources which we have consulted.

[172] *Tazkirat-ul-Waqi'at*, fol. 17a; *Akbarnama*, fols. 84b–85a; *Tarikh-i-Sher Shahi*, pp. 125–6; *Tarikh-i-Dau'di*, p. 125.

[173] *Humayun-Nama*, pp. 40–4; *Waqi'at-i-Mushtaqi*, fols. 47a, 49b; *Akbarnama*, fols. 85a–86b; *Muntakhab-ut-Tawarikh*, Vol. I, pp. 349–50; *Tarikh-i-Rashidi*, p. 470; *Riyaz-us-Salatin*, pp. 142–3; *Tarikh-i-Sher Shahi*, p. 126; *Tarikh-i-Khan-i-Jahani wa Makhzan-i-Afghani*, Vol. I, pp. 297–8; *Tarikh-i-Dau'di*, p. 125.

[174] For its location, see chapter two.

2

Mughal-Afghan Interface
Battles and Mobilization

THE BATTLES

Sher Khan knew all kinds of machinations, deception, duplicity and strata-
gem which are never treated as forbidden in war and that he knew how to
begin the fight and how to conclude it.

Abbas Khan in *Tarikh-i-Sher Shahi*[1]

SHER KHAN'S COMPETENCE AS A military commander is praised by both
contemporary and later authorities in superlative terms. His credentials as a capable leader came to the fore in his battles against the
Bengalis and the Mughals whose armies were both numerically and
technologically superior to his. The victories in these battles through
his mind-boggling strategies and enervating tactics catapulted him to
the *badshahat* of Hindustan. The battle against the Bengal army not
only made him the sole leader of the region of Bihar but also a powerful force along with Sultan Bahadur of Gujarat who could offer an
'indigenous' resistance to the 'foreign' rule of the Mughals.

Though the exact strength of the two armies in the battle of Surajgarh
cannot be determined, the military differentials were clearly loaded in
favour of the Bengalis. Particularly advantageous was their use of artillery which had elevated them in the estimation of both the Afghans
and the Mughals. Besides, the elephants could well have been used to

---

[1] Abbas wrote: *sher khan anwa haila wa makr wa fareb wa khada ke dar harb
makruh nist mi-danist wa madakhil wa makharij jang didah bud, Tarikh-i-Sher
Shahi*, p. 137.

trample the Afghan troopers in the eventuality of the latter deciding to fight to the finish and barge into the Bengali ranks. Sher Khan could hope of a victory against the Bengalis only in the case of an encounter involving the mounted-archers and sword-weilding sawars. His tactics ensured that this was the case in this battle, with the shocked Bengal troopers, elephants, and artillery rendered useless.[2] The outcome of the battle speaks volumes of Sher Khan's abilities as a military commander who could turn the tables on the enemies even in extremely adverse conditions. Conversely, he was shrewd enough to exploit the enemy's weakness to the hilt as in the battle against Humayun at Chausa. The two battles which he fought against Humayun sealed the fate of the first Mughal kingdom of Hindustan. Though the idiosyncracies of their 'young' ruler contributed in part to the failure of the Mughals, Sher Khan's brilliant qualities as a military commander with his thoroughly pragmatic approach to warfare too gave him a definite edge.

The Battle of Chausa

During the period when Humayun was preoccupied with the pleasures of the flesh in the pleasant atmosphere of the palace at Gaur, renamed Jannatabad, Sher Khan not only blocked the route to Bengal, but also was busy capturing Mughal territories. Banaras was conquered and most of the Mughals were slain. Khawas Khan was sent to Mungir where Khan-i-Khanan Lodi had been holding charge on behalf of Humayun. He captured the town in a sudden attack, and, after putting Khan-i-Khanan in chains, brought him to Banaras. Haibat Khan Niyazi, Jalal Khan Jalu, Sarmast Khan Sarnabi, and other chiefs captured Bahraich[3] and Sambhal.[4] Another force was sent to Jaunpur where the Mughal officer-in-charge was slain in action. The Mughals who were in the town of Kara fought, but were defeated. Thus all the areas as far as Qannauj and Sambhal were occupied by Sher Khan.[5] Our earliest

[2] For the battle of Surajgarh, see previous chapter.

[3] Bahraich (Area: 4,137 square miles; Jama: 2,41,20,525 dams) formed one of the five sarkars of suba Awadh under Akbar, Habib, *Atlas*, Table I and 8A&B, Notes.

[4] Sambhal (Area: 5,585 square miles; Jama: 6,69,41,431 dams) constituted one of the six sarkars of suba Delhi under Akbar, had a mint issuing copper money and was noted for tobacco and mango, Habib, *Atlas*, Table I and 8A & B, Notes.

[5] *Tarikh-i-Sher Shahi*, p. 126. For the capture of Jaunpur, also see *Akbarnama*, fol. 85a.

Persian authority, Rizqullah Mushtaqi writes that during the period of Humayun's indulgence at Gaur, Sher Khan carried on raids and humiliated the Mughals, moving as far as Awadh. According to Jauhar, while the king had given himself up to pleasure and indolence, Sher Khan had killed seven hundred Mughals, had laid siege to the fortress of Chunar, and taken the city of Banaras. Also, he had sent an army along the bank of the Ganges to take Qannauj, seized the families of several of the officers, and sent them as prisoners to Ruhtas.[6] Further, Khan-i-Khanan Lodi who was sent by Humayun to Mungir at the time of the emperor's return march from Bengal was imprisoned by an Afghan detachment, and was sent to Sher Khan.[7] Later Askari, who was sent to obtain information on Sher Khan's activities, informed from Kahalgaon[8] that the Afghans were besieging Chunar and Jaunpur, and had actually occupied the country up to Qannauj. Askari also informed that Sher Khan had collected a large army in the vicinity of Ruhtas, and had completely blocked the road to the western provinces.[9] Siddiqui ignores the above evidence in suggesting that Jaunpur was not occupied by the Afghans before the battle of Chausa, and Sambhal remained under the Mughals till the battle of Qannauj in 1540.[10]

On the other hand, Mirza Hindal had killed a leading Sufi of the time, Shaykh Bahlul, and proclaimed himself as the king at Agra. According to Abu'l Fazl, Humayun had sent Shaykh Bahlul from Bengal with the message for Hindal that he should refrain from rebellious activities.[11] Nizam-ud-Din Ahmad writes that Hindal commenced hostilities in Agra and executed Shaykh Bahlul for allegedly conspiring with the Afghans. He then had the khutba read in his name.[12] Humayun

---

[6] *Tazkirat-ul-Waqi'at*, fol. 17a.

[7] Ibid., fols. 18b–19a. As noted above, this evidence is corroborated by Abbas Sarwani, but Qanungo does not take it into account to suggest that when Humayun crossed the Ganges at Mungir the Khan-i-Khanan was waiting there for him, *Sher Shah and his Times*, p. 195.

[8] One of the 31 mahals of sarkar Mungir, suba Bihar under Akbar, *Beames' Contribution to the Political Geography*, p. 28.

[9] *Tazkirat-ul-Waqi'at*, fol. 20a; *Tarikh-i-Khan-i-Jahani wa Makhzan-i-Afghani*, Vol. I, pp. 295–6; *Tarikh-i-Dau'di*, p. 125; *Riyaz-us-Salatin*, p. 142.

[10] *A History of Sher Shah Sur*, p. 58, fn. 1.

[11] *Akbarnama*, fol. 85a.

[12] *Tabaqat-i-Akbari*, fols. 176a, 202a. Farishta follows Nizam-ud-Din's account, but refers to Shaykh Bahlul as the preceptor of Humayun, *Farishta*, fol. 235a.

on receiving this news proceeded from Bengal. His army being in great disorder, and in view of the urgency to reach Agra, the emperor had to leave Sher Khan behind.[13] Jauhar Aftabchi complains that instead of marching straight through the northern bank of the Ganges, Humayun followed Muwaiyad Beg's advice to cross the river near Mungir. According to him, the Chausa disaster could have been averted if the emperor had marched through the northern bank.[14]

Sher Khan was aware of the fact that utter confusion and distress prevailed in the Mughal army, while his own soldiers were well equipped. Also, the morale of the Afghan nobles and soldiers was very high. He therefore decided to pursue the Mughals. Accordingly, he came out of the hills of Ruhtas and proceeded towards the Mughals, raising earthen forts and marching leisurely. When Humayun learnt that Sher Khan was coming, he turned and marched in his direction.[15] The nobles suggested to Humayun not to march against the foe since the army was not equipped. They added that the emperor should halt somewhere and recruit soldiers and then crush the enemy. However, Humayun rejected their advice.[16] Sher Khan, learning that Humayun

---

[13] For the rebellion in Agra and Humayun's decision to march straight to the capital along with his small and disorganized army, *Tarikh-i-Sher Shahi*, p. 127; *Tarikh-i-Rashidi*, pp. 470–1; *Akbarnama*, fols. 85a–86b. Also see, *Muntakhab-ut-Tawarikh*, Vol. I, p. 350; *Tarikh-i-Khan-i-Jahani wa Makhzan-i-Afghani*, Vol. I, pp. 297–8; *Riyaz-us-Salatin*, pp. 142–3; *Tazkirat-ul-Waqi'at*, fols. 18a–b.

[14] *Tazkirat-ul-Waqi'at*, fols. 20b–21a. Following Jauhar, Qanungo writes that 'Providence, as it were, now delivered the unfortunate Emperor into the hands of Sher, who till then had no intention of fighting the Emperor, or of retarding his march to Agra along the northern route', *Sher Shah and his Times*, p. 195. Siddiqui differs to suggest that Sher Khan was aware of the plight of the Mughal army and was therefore 'determined to measure strength with the Mughals at this time; the change of route by his rival could not deter him. As the son of the soil, he could choose any place to halt the Mughals for the battle', which 'was certain to take place', *Sher Shah Sur and his Dynasty*, pp. 81–2.

[15] *Tarikh-i-Sher Shahi*, pp. 127–9; *Akbarnama*, fols. 86b–87a; *Tabaqat-i-Akbari*, fol. 177a.

[16] Abu'l Fazl blames destiny for Humayun's rejection of the advice and the subsequent failure of the Mughals, *Akbarnama*, fol. 87a. According to Jauhar Aftabchi, when the Mughal army had reached Maner, a crier was sent around the camp to proclaim that the soldiers should be on their guard, as the enemy was expected. In fact, some of them appeared the next day, and a skirmish took place between the advance parties. The following day, during the march, it was reported

was marching towards him, sent a messenger suggesting that he would strike coins and read the khutba in the emperor's name if Bengal was granted to him. At the same time, he came to Chausa and encamped in a large village called Sahya with a stream of twenty-five yards separating the two forces.[17] Jauhar Aftabchi records that on the fourth day after the Mughals had encamped near Chausa, Sher Khan's advancing army came in sight. Humayun consulted the nobles to chalk out an appropriate course of action. Qasim Husain suggested that as the Afghans had marched for thirty-six miles that day, and their horses must also be tired, it was advisable to attack them immediately. However, Muwaiyad Beg again differed, suggesting that there was no need to hurry. Humayun agreed with him, and consequently the army encamped. Sher Khan also settled down but threw up an entrenchment around his camp.[18]

Sher Khan summoned Khawas Khan who had been deputed against Maharath Chero. On the other hand, having received the representation (*ariza*) of Sher Khan who had transgressed his limits (*az had khwud tajawuz kardah*) as he had been camping in the face of the emperor, with only a river intervening between them, Humayun warned him to march back as an act of showing respect to him (*adab badshahi nigah darad*), so that the formalities for the grant of Bengal to him could be completed. He was also asked to vacate the passage of the river so that

that the enemy had seized the boats laden with the guns that had been used at the siege of Chunar, *Tazkirat-ul-Waqi'at*, fol. 21a.

[17] *Tarikh-i-Sher Shahi*, p. 129; According to Abu'l Fazl, the Mughal army came face to face with Sher Khan at the village of Bihiya in Bhojpur, with the 'black' river Karamnasa flowing between them. *Akbarnama*, fols. 87a–b. Ni'matullah has mentioned that Sher Khan arrived at Chausa with a large army and constructed an entrenchment around his camp, *Tarikh-i-Khan-i-Jahani wa Makhzan-i-Afghani*, Vol. I, p. 298.

[18] *Tazkirat-ul-Waqi'at*, fols. 21a–b. For a change, Qanungo does not agree with Jauhar. He writes that 'throughout his whole career Mu'yyid Beg unwittingly gave sound advice only on this occasion, and that if Humayun ever showed any wisdom, it was on this occasion, when he acted upon the advice of Mu'yyid Beg. An attack on him across this muddy stream is what Sher himself wanted the Mughals to attempt, thus placing Humayun in the predicament of "the elephant in the mire". There is therefore no point in lamenting over the fact that Humayun failed to grasp the opportunity for a decisive victory over Sher', *Sher Shah and his Times*, p. 200. Siddiqui agrees with Qanungo in his *Sher Shah Sur and his Dynasty*, pp. 83–4.

Humayun might cross it and be able to make a show of pursuing him by two or three stages and then retrace his steps. The Afghan leader accepted the terms and, after vacating the passage of the river, marched back. Humayun then threw a bridge on the river and crossed it with his harem, and ordered the pitching of the imperial tents (saraparda-i-badshahi).[19] Jauhar adds that the armies faced each other for nearly two months, but skirmishes took place everyday with soldiers being killed on both sides. At this juncture, heavy rains set in, submerging Sher Khan's camp and forcing him to shift to a foothill five or six miles westward, but the encounters continued.[20] Badauni suggests that the two armies confronted each other for three months.[21]

Humayun then sent Shaykh Khalil, a descendant of the thirteenth-century Chishti Sufi, Shaykh Farid-ud-Din Ganj-i-Shakar, to Sher Khan with the order to proceed immediately to Ruhtas. The emperor would move in pursuit of Sher Khan, and then turn back. After this a farman would be issued granting the kingdom of Bengal to the Afghan leader. According to Abbas, Shaykh Khalil came to Sher Khan, conveyed the order, and exhorted him to conclude peace. During the consultation, however, the shaykh appealed to the Afghans to fight and defeat the Mughals.[22] Later the shaykh privately told Sher Khan that great disorder prevailed in the Mughal army, that Humayun's brothers had rebelled, and the emperor had proposed peace out of necessity. Sher Khan should take this precious opportunity to confront the enemy.[23]

---

[19] *Tarikh-i-Sher Shahi*, p. 130.

[20] *Tazkirat-ul-Waqi'at*, fols. 21b–22a. Abu'l Fazl asserts that though the royal army was small and ill-equipped, it won in every skirmish, and slaughtered the Afghans on every side, *Akbarnama*, fol. 87b.

[21] *Muntakhab-ut-Tawarikh*, Vol. I, p. 350. Also see *Tabaqat-i-Akbari*, fol. 177a.

[22] According to Abbas, Sher Khan considered this advice of the shaykh as a good omen and decided to fight. He then gave to the shaykh a huge amount of money and the merchandize from Bengal and captivated his heart by these presents. Thereafter, he summoned Shaykh Khalil in private and talked of the close relationship which existed between the Afghans and the family of Shaykh Farid-ud-Din Ganj-i-Shakar. Pointing to a common nativity and making promises, Sher Khan asked the shaykh to counsel him in the matter of combat or peace with Humayun. The shaykh then suggested that Sher Khan should fight against the Mughals, *Tarikh-i-Sher Shahi*, pp. 130–1.

[23] *Tarikh-i-Sher Shahi*, pp. 131–2. According to Jauhar, when Shaykh Khalil was sent to Sher Khan for settling the treaty, the latter agreed for peace on condition of

From the Mughal point of view, the shaykh's advice to Sher Khan amounted to treachery. The shaykh however absolved himself of blame by informing Humayun that though the Afghan leader had agreed for peace, he might suddenly attack the Mughal camp. The Mughals clearly did not pay any heed to the shaykh's report, as evinced from the 'faithful' Mughal servant Jauhar Aftabchi's account.[24] We shall return to the implications of the Sufis' involvements in politics in chapter five below.

Suggesting that the agreement between Humayun and Sher Khan over Bengal with the latter including the emperor's name in the khutba and the sikka was ratified by an oath on the Quran, Badauni writes that Shaykh Khalil was actually sent by Sher Khan. Prior to this, Humayun had sent Mulla Muhammad Aziz, an old friend of Sher Khan, as an ambassador. At the time of the arrival of the Mulla, Sher Khan was busy preparing the fort and entrenchment. When the Mulla came near, he ordered a tent to be pitched and sat on the ground unceremoniously. After hearing the message from Humayun, Sher Khan asked the messenger to remind the emperor that he was itching for a battle, whereas his army was reluctant. On the other hand, Sher Khan further said, he was trying to restrain his own army which was ready to kill.[25] Ni'matullah also absolves Shaykh Khalil of the charge of treachery by suggesting that he was the preceptor of Sher Khan and was sent by the latter to Humayun with the peace proposal.[26] Nizam-ud-Din Ahmad also notes that Sher Khan had sent his spiritual guide Shaykh Khalil to attend on the emperor. It was determined that he should relinquish all his territories except Bengal, and he confirmed the terms by an oath on the Quran. Sher Khan had also agreed to include Humayun's name

---

Chunar with its adjoining areas being given to him. Humayun was finally obliged to accept his demands and peace was concluded, *Tazkirat-ul-Waqi'at*, fol. 22a.

[24] *Tazkirat-ul-Waqi'at*, fol. 22b.

[25] *Muntakhab-ut-Tawarikh*, Vol. I, pp. 350–1. Earlier, according to the same authority, Sher Khan wrote a letter to Humayun saying that his Afghan followers are basically servants and retainers of his Majesty. It will be good if he favours them with the grant of jagirs, otherwise hunger will drive them to open revolt. He added that he had kept them in check for long, but now they no longer obey him, and the proverb is well known: The hungry man will throw himself upon the sword. For the rest whatever the king says is law, ibid., Vol. I, p. 349.

[26] *Tarikh-i-Khan-i-Jahani wa Makhzan-i-Afghani*, Vol. I, pp. 298–9.

in the public prayer and the coin.[27] Curiously, in suggesting that any peace treaty between Sher Khan and Humayun was impossible at this stage, Siddiqui ignores altogether the above evidence in the sources.[28]

Though Sher Khan had marched from Ruhtas with the intention to fight against Humayun, making most of his predicament, he lacked the courage to go for a direct set-piece battle against the legitimate ruler of Hindustan. The venerated shaykh's advice gave him the much needed legitimacy for this momentous step. He thus began preparations for the battle. Yet the Sufi's suggestion, and the bestowal of kingship to him by the Prophet as seen by him in a dream on the night before the battle, were not sufficient to motivate him for a pitched battle in broad day-light. He decided to sweep the Mughal camp at a time when the soldiers and the guards were to be lost in the sweet summer morning slumbers in the cold breeze on the bank of a junction of the two rivers—Ganges in the north and Karamnasa in the west—with the southern hill overlooking the camp. Meanwhile, Sher Khan spread the rumour that the local chief Maharath Chero was marching against him. Therefore, he marched with his forces in that direction. When he had gone three or four *karoh*s from his encampment, he ordered his soldiers to turn back saying the spies had brought the news that Maharath was still at a distance. This mock campaign was organized the next day also. At about midnight he summoned his nobles and addressed them. The contents of his address, recorded by Abbas Khan, provide the late sixteenth century Afghan justification of the scandalous attack on Humayun's camp.

Sher Khan's speech traces the story of his loyalty and service to the Mughals, and the humiliation and torture that he received from them in return. A brief summary of Sher Khan's statement will help us understand his subsequent actions, as also of his Afghan followers, in a better perspective. Sher Khan informed his men that he had promised to conclude peace with the emperor, but as an afterthought he felt that all his services rendered to him had been in vain. He complained that despite his loyalty to him which led to the defeat of Sultan Mahmud Lodi in the battle at Lucknow, Humayun subsequently demanded the fort of Chunar, and on his refusal, marched to take it by force. He,

---

[27] *Tabaqat-i-Akbari*, fols. 177a, 202b. Also see *Farishta*, fols. 240a, 235b.
[28] *A History of Sher Shah Sur*, p. 62.

however, had to turn back following the news of the revolt in Agra, and of Sultan Bahadur's march to Delhi. He (Sher Khan) had then the opportunity and ability to capture the Mughal territories up to Jaunpur, but did not do so out of loyalty to the emperor. He also pointed out that after returning from Gujarat, Humayun arranged his forces and marched against him. All his sincere expression of loyalty and services proved futile. He lost all hope and became apprehensive of his evil designs when Humayun marched to Bengal. Now he was negotiating for peace out of necessity as his army was in shambles and his brothers had become hostile. After dealing with his brothers, he would come with a larger force. Quoting the Prophetic tradition that a faithful does not allow the scorpion to sting more than once, Sher Khan concluded that he would fight the emperor reposing faith in the greatness of God.[29]

It may be mentioned here that the use of the term jihad was avoided by Sher Khan, in the case of the battle against the Bengalis. Yet the victory was attributed to the will of God. The Mughals also attributed their failure to destiny or the will of God, but continued to harp on Sher Khan's treachery and his violation of oath on the Quran. At the time of dismissing them, Sher Khan asked the nobles to get ready after making full preparations, as if he was still anxious on account of Maharath. Early in the morning he marched in the direction of Maharath, and after advancing two and half karohs halted and announced that he had been riding out for two days and then returning with the sole objective that this would make the emperor off the guard. Motivating the soldiers by appealing to their martial ethos, and reputation, he asked them to turn and march in all haste towards the forces of Humayun.[30]

The Mughal narrative has it that soon after the peace-treaty was concluded, the 'treacherous' Sher Khan summoned his principal officers and challenged them to storm the Mughal camp if they were brave enough. One of them, Khawas Khan offered to undertake the task with a detachment of good soldiers and a number of war elephants. Pleased as he was, Sher Khan gave him a select band of troops and elephants. Although the detachment left the camp in the forenoon, the cunning warlord, Khawas Khan, loitered about till night before

[29] *Tarikh-i-Sher Shahi*, pp. 133–5.
[30] Ibid., pp. 135–6.

sweeping the Mughal camp early next morning.[31] Abu'l Fazl writes that Sher Khan sometimes sent influential persons for peace, and sometimes cherished wicked thoughts of war. Finally, leaving a body of infantry and inefficient men, together with his artillery in front, he himself marched two stages to the rear and then encamped. The royal army did not understand the game. Abu'l Fazl laments that when an event is destined to happen, carelessness does occur. Thus, great lapses ensued in keeping watch, as Muhammad Zaman Mirza showed utter negligence on a night when he was posted to keep vigil. That fox (Sher Khan) who was waiting for an opportunity, marched through the night and landed at the rear of the Mughal camp early in the morning.[32] The Afghan army was arranged in proper order.[33] It was divided into three units (tob), one led by Sher Khan himself, one by his son Jalal Khan, and another by Khawas Khan.[34]

On hearing that the Afghans had attacked the Mughal camp, Humayun ordered his forces to fight back, saying that he would join them after his ablutions.[35] Ni'matullah says that Humayun was reciting Quran at the time of the Afghan attack.[36] The Mughals had not emerged from their tents when the Afghan forces swiftly made their way to the stable and broke their ranks. Realising that it was too late to fight, Humayun immediately fled from the camp.[37] Jauhar suggests that when the Afghans entered the rear of the Mughal camp, Humayun ordered the kettle-drums to be beaten, and soon about three hundred cavalry assembled around him. However, finding that the Afghans had thrown everything in confusion, his soldiers refused to obey the order to advance. Humayun personally attacked an Afghan elephant marching against him, but an archer seated on the elephant struck an arrow on his arm. When the enemy began to surround him, one of his followers came and led him away to the bank of the river.[38] By then, the

---

[31] *Tazkirat-ul-Waqi'at*, fols. 22a–b, 23b.

[32] *Akbarnama*, fol. 87b.

[33] *Tarikh-i-Sher Shahi*, p. 136.

[34] *Akbarnama*, fol. 87b.

[35] *Tarikh-i-Sher Shahi*, p. 136.

[36] *Tarikh-i-Khan-i-Jahani wa Makhzan-i-Afghani*, Vol. I, p. 302.

[37] *Tarikh-i-Sher Shahi*, pp. 137–38; *Akbarnama*, fol. 87b.

[38] *Tazkirat-ul-Waqi'at*, fols. 23b–24a. Gulbadan Begam also refers to Humayun's arm getting wounded, *Humayun-Nama*, p. 41.

bridge had been destroyed, either by the Afghans,[39] or by the sudden pressure on it of the desperate Mughals running for their lives.[40]

A large number of Mughals were drowned in the river while trying to escape. This was not enough. Nizam-ud-Din Ahmad writes that the Afghans from their boats speared the Mughal soldiers whom they found in water.[41] Humayun plunged his horse into the river, but it soon drowned. Just when he was drowning, Nizam, a water-carrier, rescued him with a distended leather bag. Accompanied by a few others, including Mirza Askari, he rapidly proceeded to Agra.[42] Sher Khan thanked God for his victory,[43] and wrote a verse on the occasion which summed up the situation:[44]

Farid hasan ra tu shahi dehi
Sipahe humayun ba-mahi dehi

(You give sovereignty to Farid the son of Hasan
You give the army of Humayun to the fish)

Abbas Khan avoids the embarrassing details of the flight of the Mughals and in a face-saving description, suggests that the Afghans had plunged the Mughal camp into such a confusion that Humayun had to flee towards Agra leaving his family behind, intending to return with a stronger army.[45] Further, the Afghan narrative says that after Sher Khan's victory in the battle, the Mughal queen along with the entire harem of the emperor followed by a crowd of women turned up before him. Sher Khan showed due respect to them. Soldiers were ordered not to imprison the women and children, and bring them to the Mughal queen's camp. It is also highlighted that Sher Khan's order was strictly followed. Later these women, including the queen, were

---

[39] *Tabaqat-i-Akbari*, fol. 177a; *Muntakhab-ut-Tawarikh*, Vol. I, p. 351; *Tarikh-i-Khan-i-Jahani wa Makhzan-i-Afghani*, Vol. I, p. 302.

[40] Abu'l Fazl writes that when Humayun came to the bridge, he found it broken, *Akbarnama*, fol. 88a.

[41] *Tabaqat-i-Akbari*, fol. 177a.

[42] *Tazkirat-ul-Waqi'at*, fols. 24a-b; *Tabaqat-i-Akbari*, fol. 177a; *Akbarnama*, fol. 88a; *Muntakhab-ut-Tawarikh*, Vol. I, pp. 351–2; *Tarikh-i-Khan-i-Jahani wa Makhzan-i-Afghani*, Vol. I, pp. 302–3; cf. *Tarikh-i-Dau'di*, p. 125; *Farishta*, fol. 235b.

[43] *Tarikh i-Sher Shahi*, p. 139.

[44] *Muntakhab-ut-Tawarikh*, Vol. I, p. 352. Curiously, Siddiqui gives two dates for this event: 26 June 1539 and 7 June 1539, *A History of Sher Shah Sur*, pp. 57 and 62.

[45] *Tarikh-i-Sher Shahi*, p. 138.

sent under protection to Agra with money for their expenses during the journey.[46] Unable to digest the humane treatment meted out to the ladies of the Mughal harem, Abu'l Fazl is at pains to explain that divine protection and defence was their surety and safeguard.[47] Gulbadan Begam, however, laments that several noble ladies were consumed in that disaster. Their fate could not be ascertained.[48]

Though the Mughal defeat had far-reaching consequences, with Humayun running for his life and Sher Shah enthroned as the new king of Hindustan,[49] the events on that fateful summer morning at Chausa can hardly be described as a battle in the sense of two armies facing each other in an open ground in broad daylight. It was more of a guerrilla attack on an army camp exposed to danger from all sides. Abu'l Fazl reflected the sentiments of the Mughals by characterizing it as a *qissa-i-purghussa*.[50] To begin with, there was no fortification around the camp, so that the army was vulnerable from three directions, the south, east and, the north. The over-flooded river in the west blocked the possibility of an escape route for the Mughals. The solitary bridge thrown in haste could be useless if large numbers of people suddenly rushed on to it. It would have collapsed, even if the Afghans were unable to destroy it. This brings to notice the burden of keeping the followers and harems by the emperor and his nobles during a campaign. Being useless in battle, they considerably curtailed the army's efficiency and mobility. Sher Shah's shrewd attack on the most vulnerable part of the camp in the rear created a commotion all around. This happened at Qannauj as well as we shall see below. Yet it is clear that the Mughals were not attacked only in the rear,[51] as two of the three Afghan divisions simultaneously ran into the Mughal stable and the

---

[46] Ibid., p. 139; *Tarikh-i-Khan-i-Jahani wa Makhzan-i-Afghani*, Vol. I, pp. 304–5. Abdullah inaccurately says that they were sent to Kabul, *Tarikh-i-Dau'di*, p. 126.

[47] *Akbarnama*, fols. 87b–88a.

[48] *Humayun-Nama*, pp. 41–2.

[49] *Tarikh-i-Sher Shahi*, pp. 140–3. A. Karim suggests that Sher Shah's accession had already taken place in Shergarh, a fort built by him near Sahsaram during the period between his occupation of the country upto Qannauj and Humayun's march from Gaur, that is, from February to March 1539 (Ramazan to Shawwal 945), 'Date and Place of Sher Shah's Accession', *Journal of the Asiatic Society of Pakistan*, Vol. V, 1960, pp. 63–71.

[50] *Akbarnama*, fol. 88a.

[51] Cf. *Tazkirat-ul-waqi'at*, fol. 23b.

imperial enclosure reaching very close to Humayun. Also the loyalty of Muhammad Zaman Mirza, the official responsible for keeping watch that night,[52] was doubtful. His death was no compensation for the disaster.

To sum up, the leadership qualities of Humayun and Sher Shah contributed a great deal to the outcome of the event. It will be interesting to turn to the assessment made by an Afghan author, presented for the appreciation of Humayun's more respected son Akbar. Abbas Khan writes that emperor Humayun was brave and gallant as a lion. Having subjugated many notable warriors he brought the entire Hind in his possession. However, being proud of his young age, lineage, and abundance of followers and retinues, Humayun despised the number and strength of Sher Khan's forces. He ignored the essential requisites for the battle and neglected the disorganized condition of his army.[53] On the other hand, adds Abbas, Sher Khan employed all kinds of unscrupulous means in war knowing how to begin the fight and how to conclude it to his advantage.[54] Following the Mughal authorities, Ishwari Prasad condemns Sher Shah for his 'treachery', which according to him, 'played a great part in deciding the issue of the battle'. Prasad adds that Sher Shah 'felt no qualms of conscience at breaking his word and sanctioning arrangements which were contrary to his declared intentions'.[55] This reads literally like the charges levelled by the Mughal chroniclers.

The Battle of Qannauj

Though the victory at Chausa was followed by Sher Shah's enthronement, the thought that Humayun had escaped alive, and a large part of the country was still under him kept disturbing this new king of Hindustan. Thus, while the Afghans all over were celebrating the 'revival' of their rule,[56] Sher Shah busied himself with conquering new

[52] For Abu'l Fazl's criticism of the complete negligence (*ghaflat-i-tamam*) shown by Muhammad Zaman Mirza, see *Akbarnama*, fol. 87b.

[53] *Tarikh-i-Sher Shahi*, pp. 136–7.

[54] See f.n. 1 above.

[55] Prasad, *Life and Times of Humayun*, p. 133. It may also be noted here that Prasad's details on the location of the camps of Mughal and Afghan armies do not support the two charts provided by him, ibid., pp. 125–32.

[56] For the week-long celebration, see, *Tarikh-i-Sher Shahi*, pp. 143–4.

territories and consolidating his hold on the existing ones. Bengal was captured by the Afghans with its Mughal governor Jahangir Quli Beg lured into a 'false treaty' and killed.[57] According to another report, after defeating Humayun at Chausa, Sher Khan did not immediately push forward to the capital, but resolving to leave no enemy behind, returned to Bengal. Jahangir Quli Beg was defeated and killed. After reoccupying Bengal, Sher Khan assumed the title of Sher Shah and ordering coins to be struck and khutba to be read in his name, marched with his army towards Agra the next year.[58] Farmans were sent to the rulers of Malwa and Gujarat to march against the Mughals. Their refusal to cooperate with the Afghans led to the death of Sher Shah's son Qutb Khan in an encounter with a Mughal detachment. According to reports, Qasim Husain Sultan Uzbek, together with Yadgar Nasir Mirza and Iskandar Mirza, fought with the Afghans near Kalpi, and slew a son of Sher Shah who was commanding the army. His head was sent to the 'service' of the emperor.[59]

Though Qutb Khan's death was a big blow for Sher Shah, Humayun's condition was all the more precarious. After his ignominious flight from Chausa and arrival at Agra, it appeared for a time that the brothers would be able to thrash out their differences.[60] But this was not to be, as Mirza Kamran grew suspicious of Humayun's attitude towards him and left for Lahore with his soldiers. Much of the problem was Humayun's own creation. For instance Kamran took strong exception to Humayun's hilarious decision to enthrone the water carrier Nizam with strict orders to the nobles and Mirzas to attend the court and make obeisance to him at a time when the fate of the kingdom was hanging in balance. Kamran's cryptic response to the enthronement of Nizam was timely. Gulbadan Begam quotes him questioning the emperor's bizarre indulgence at the time when Sher Khan was fast approaching the Mughal camp (*dar in waqt ke sher khan nazdik rasida*

---

[57] *Akbarnama*, fol. 88b; *Tarikh-i-Khan-i-Jahani wa Makhzan-i-Afghani*, Vol. I, pp. 305–6; *Riyaz-us-Salatin*, p. 144.

[58] *Tabaqat-i-Akbari*, fol. 202b; *Muntakhab-ut-Tawarikh*, Vol. I, p. 352; *Farishta*, fol. 240a.

[59] *Tarikh-i–Sher Shahi*, pp. 146–7; *Tabaqat-i-Akbari*, fol. 178a; See also *Akbarnama*, fol. 88b; *Muntakhab-ut-Tawarikh*, Vol. I, p. 354; *Tarikh-i-Rashidi*, p. 472.

[60] *Tazkirat-ul-Waqi'at*, fols. 25a–26a.

in che kar ast ke hazrat mikunand).[61] Sher Shah had already marched up to Lucknow by this time. Moreover the rejection of the proposal that Humayun should stay in Agra and Kamran would undertake the expedition against the advancing Sher Shah further alienated the prince.[62] To top it all, Kamran accused Humayun of trying to eliminate him by poisoning.[63]

Thus, with a hurriedly arranged army at Agra, Humayun marched against Sher Shah. According to reports, Humayun had one hundred thousand cavalry at this time,[64] whereas the Afghan army did not exceed fifty thousand.[65] When he reached Qannauj, Sher Shah, who had already taken up position on the other side of the Ganges, sent his envoy to Humayun asking him as to which side of the river the battle should take place. Humayun, who, according to Abbas, never took any serious notice of Sher Shah in his view, considered it below his dignity to 'withdraw' before the enemy and decided to cross the river.[66] Thus he again made the tactical error of choosing to fight with the river on his back, with serious consequences, though the decision to cross the river may also have been aimed at checking the desertion in his army. It is reported that Muhammad Sultan Mirza and his sons acted 'treacherously' at this time and fled from the army without any cause. The force which Kamran had left behind to reinforce Humayun's troops also fled, and this became a fashion, a large number of the soldiers became dispersed, and fled to different parts of Hindustan.[67]

---

[61] *Humayun-Nama*, p. 45. See also *Tazkirat-ul-Waqi'at*, fol. 25b. According to Abu'l Fazl, Humayun had promised to Nizam, after he was rescued, that he would enthrone him for half-a-day, *Akbarnama*, fol. 88a.

[62] *Tazkirat-ul-Waqi'at*, fol. 26b; *Muntakhab-ut-Tawarikh*, Vol. I, p. 353.

[63] *Muntakhab-ut-Tawarikh*, Vol. I, pp. 353–4; *Tabaqat-i-Akbari*, fol. 177b; *Farishta*, fol. 236a.

[64] *Muntakhab-ut-Tawarikh*, Vol. I, pp. 353–4; *Farishta*, fol. 236a.

[65] *Tabaqat-i-Akbari*, fol. 178a; *Farishta*, fol. 236a.

[66] *Tarikh-i-Sher Shahi*, p. 148. Qanungo argues that though 'the battle of Kanauj might pass muster in medieval times, it is positively misleading to the present generation with a better sense of geography. So it is to be corrected as the Battle of Bilgram, because Bilgram existed in the time of Sher and Akbar, and it exists even now, and because the battle was fought somewhere nearer to Bilgram than to Kanauj', *Sher Shah and his Times*, p. 242.

[67] *Tabaqat-i-Akbari*, fol. 178a; *Farishta*, fol. 236a; *Muntakhab-ut-Tawarikh*, Vol. I, p. 354; *Tarikh-i-Rashidi*, p. 474; *Akbarnama*, fol. 90b.

When Sher Shah receded away from the Ganges, Humayun threw a bridge on the river, and crossed it. When only half of the army of Humayun had crossed the river, Sher Shah was advised by his nobles to attack them. He, however, rejected the suggestion, as he felt that at this stage he possessed a very large army, there was unity amongst the Afghans, and they had emerged victorious against the Mughals in recent encounters; therefore, there was no need to resort to such a step. Sher Shah's decision not to attack the Mughals while crossing the Ganges must have been influenced by the realization that his victory over Humayun would have any meaning only if he were able to fight a decisive set-piece battle, both from the point of view of legitimacy and as a strong warning to other warlords watching the situation. It may be noted here that the chiefs of Malwa such as Mallu Khan and Puranmal had not acknowledged his status as the new sovereign of Hindustan till then. Sher Shah declared that in spite of his advantages, he would keep his word and would fight a just war, leaving the outcome to God.[68] Later, on the day of the battle, having put his forces in order, Sher Shah exhorted the Afghans to fight bravely, declaring that he himself would come out alive from the battlefield only when he was triumphant.[69] Incidentally, the battle took place on the 10th of Muharram (947/1540).[70] The significance of this date in Islamic history is well known. The battle of Karbala was fought on this date between two Muslim armies, leaders of both claiming that they were 'just' in the eyes of Allah. In tune with the Shi'ite lamentation, the Mughals coined the following chronogram after their defeat at Qannauj: *kharabi-i-mulk-i-dilli* (desolation of the kingdom of Delhi).[71] Earlier one of the chronograms invented to record the date of accession of Humayun was *khayr-ul-muluk*, i.e. best of kings (937/1530).[72]

When Sher Shah knew that the entire force of Humayun had crossed the river, he encamped close by and constructed earthen embankments as was his custom. After some days, Khawas Khan also turned up. On the very day of his arrival, he intercepted the supply line of the Mughals,

---

[68] *Tarikh-i-Sher Shahi*, pp. 148–9.

[69] Ibid., pp. 150–3.

[70] *Akbarnama*, fol. 90b; *Tabaqat-i-Akbari*, fol. 178a; *Tazkirat-ul-waqi'at*, fol. 27a.

[71] *Muntakhab-ut-Tawarikh*, Vol. I, p. 354.

[72] Ibid., Vol. I, p. 344.

capturing three hundred mules and camels and a large convoy of bullocks.[73] Humayun's problems were aggravating with every passing day. To add to the desertion in his army, and cutting off of supplies to the remainder in the camp, a heavy pre-monsoon downpour submerged the Mughal camp located in the catchment area of the Ganges and forced him to shift to a higher location.[74]

Sher Shah had arranged his forces in five divisions with himself occupying the centre along with Azam Humayun Sarwani, Isa Khan Sarwani, Qutb Khan Lodi, Haji Khan, Buland Khan, Saif Khan Sarwani, Bijli Khan Sarwani, and others. The fore-centre led by Sher Shah's son, Jalal Khan, was occupied by Sarmast Khan, and the Niyazis, including Haibat Khan who later received the title of Azam Humayun. The right wing comprised Mubariz Khan, Bahadur Khan, Rai Husain Jalwani and the Kararanis. The left wing had two subdivisions: while the immediate left was led by Khawas Khan, Barmazid Kaur, and others; the extreme left was led by Sher Shah's son, Adil Khan, Qutb Khan Naib, and others. Facing them were the Mughals led by Humayun in the centre. In close proximity to him on his left hand side was stationed the experienced general and friend Mirza Haidar Dughlat followed by twenty-seven *tugh*-bearing amirs. In front of the centre were placed over seven hundred carriages and mortars, and small guns. The command of the artillery was given to Muhammad Khan Rumi and other sons of Ustad Ali Quli, Ustad Ahmad Rumi and Husain Khalifa. They placed the carriages and mortars in their proper position and stretched chains between them. Hindal led the fore-centre, Askari the right wing, and Yadgar Nasir Mirza the left flank.[75]

---

[73] *Tarikh-i-Sher Shahi*, p. 149.

[74] Mirza Haider Dughlat writes that the Afghans had attacked the Mughal army while it was marching in battle array to occupy a more elevated and suitable place for a regular pitched battle, *Tarikh-i-Rashidi*, p. 475. Badauni suggests that the Mughals were attacked before they had shifted to the high ground, *Muntakhab-ut-Tawarikh*, Vol. I, p. 354; *Tarikh-i-Khan-i-Jahani wa Makhzan-i-Afghani*, Vol. I, pp. 308–9: *Farishta*, fol. 236a.

[75] For the arrangement of the various divisions of the two armies and the battle which ensued, *Tarikh-i-Rashidi*, pp. 474–7; *Tazkirat-ul-waqi'at*, fols. 27a–b; *Tarikh-i-Sher Shahi*, pp. 149–50, 153–4; *Akbarnama*, fols. 90b–1a. *Tarikh-i-Khan-i-Jahani wa Makhzan-i-Afghani*, Vol. I, pp. 309–11. Cf. Prasad, *Life and Times of Humayun*, pp. 140–6; Qanungo, *Sher Shah Sur and his Times*, pp. 227–37; Ambashthya, *Decisive Battles*, pp. 138–54.

The first encounter took place between the fore-centres of the two armies. The Afghans were defeated with their commander Jalal Khan falling from the horse while engaged in a hand to hand combat. Yet Jalal Khan aided by Mian Ayub Kakbur Sarwani and Ghazi Mahali continued to hold their ground. Meanwhile, the Mughal left wing ran into the right division of the Afghans, driving them to join their centre which was under the command of Sher Shah himself. On the other hand, the two subdivisions of the Afghan left wing jointly fell upon the Mughal right wing and compelled them to retreat. Sher Shah was observing from the centre the success of his left wing and the failure of the right. He wanted to go to the aid of the latter in person. He was however, advised against leaving his position as the soldiers might think that their centre had suffered defeat.

Thus, when Sher Shah was advancing straight, the Mughal forces which had defeated the Afghan right wing attacked the centre of Sher Shah's forces. But they suffered defeat and moved backward to join their own centre. Sher Shah, then personally engaged in the fight, drove away the Mughal fore-centre which earlier had an upper hand against the Afghan fore-centre. The success of the Afghan left wing has also been noted above. The right wing which was compelled to retreat and was pushed to the centre rallied again. The Mughals were thus surrounded from all the three sides. In their rear was the crowd of the camp followers, and behind them was the swollen river. With many Mughal officers losing their ground and camp followers pressed by the Afghans, pushing from the rear, the centre of the army had broken. The whole Mughal army, including a considerable number of followers who were useless, in fact a liability during battle as in the case of Chausa, plunged into chaos. All the exits for them were closed by the Afghans who were constantly pressing from all sides. They ran blindly for safety and a large number of them were killed in the stampede. An equally large number jumped into the Ganges and were drowned. Seeing the disaster, Humayun had also fled to the bank of the river, crossed it on the back of an elephant, rushed towards Agra, and was joined by the Mirzas during the flight. Evidently, no lessons were learned from the defeat at Chausa!

Abbas tried to please the Mughals by suggesting that Humayun showed such feats of bravery and heroism as were beyond description. He also added that God had decreed that His creation would ultimately flourish under that auspicious king (Humayun) and his progeny, who would prove to be the ideal rulers. Abbas attributed Humayun's defeat to 'the men of invisible world' (*mardan-i-ghayb*), who were fighting his horses. He concludes that this tragedy occurred because of the hostility among Humayun's brothers, otherwise it was beyond Sher Khan's power to become a match for that valiant Mughal emperor.[76] Abu'l Fazl adds that though it was not reckoned that the king himself should fight, such rules could not be adhered to at that time of testing manhood. Hence Humayun twice attacked the enemy and threw it into confusion. Two lances were broken in his hands testifying to his endeavour and courage.[77] The above assessments ignore the massive mobilization of anti-Mughal forces by Sher Khan who successfully led them to victory in the battles.

MOBILIZATION AND RECRUITMENT

The Afghans will be able to turn away the Mughals on the very day that they got a leader of their own and the entire Afghan race could be one with him. You are that fortunate leader.

Azam Humayun Sarwani to Sher Khan
on the eve of the battle of Chausa[78]

From dismissal as an ambitious Sur bachcha in Babur's camp barely a decade ago to the rise of Sher Shah as the badshah of Hindustan was a long journey. Nobody had really thought then that the Mughals with all their military might would ever be defeated and driven away by the Afghans led by, of all the people, Sher Khan, a person of no consequence. And all these happened so quickly that Sher Khan's success was considered to be a miracle. A thoroughly shocked fugitive Humayun, who continued to undermine Sher Khan's capabilities and resources, kept repeating that the Afghans had not defeated his forces, as he had seen some supernatural beings fighting at Qannauj and turning away the heads of the imperial horses indicating that they must

---

[76] *Tarikh-i-Sher Shahi*, pp. 154–5.

[77] *Akbarnama*, fol. 91a.

[78] According to Abbas, Azam Humayun observed: '*afghanan waqte mughalan ra az hind khwahad baraward ke sardar afghanan yak bashad wa qaum afghanan ba-u muttafiq bashad wa an sahib-i-daulat tui*', *Tarikh-i-Sher Shahi*, p. 128.

make good their escape. Abbas Khan records that Humayun told this to Amir Sayyid Rafi-ud-Din in Agra and Majd-ud-Din Sarhindi in Sarhind.[79] Abu'l Fazl explains that god 'withdrew' Humayun from the battlefield and the defeat actually laid 'the foundation of the righting of the worlds', as he was sending Akbar to do the job.[80]

Not only the Mughals but the Afghans as well attributed Sher Khan's success to the will of God. A report was circulated to the effect that in the night before the decisive battle, Sher Khan had seen a dream. He saw that in a wrestling bout between him and Humayun the latter had brought him down and was trying to turn him over but could not do so because Sher Shah clutched the ground with his fingers and held on. Sher Khan's narration of this dream had caused a considerable panic amongst his nobles. And not without reason, as any run of the mill interpreter of dreams would have prophesied Humayun's victory in the ensuing battle. Assuming the role of the interpreter himself, Sher Khan asked his men not to worry as the dream actually symbolized his success inasmuch as the battle would enable him to grab the land,[81] that is, Hindustan. Popular Muslim cosmology treats kingship as a gift from God. It is believed that Sher Khan received it on account of his piety. Humayun lost because he had devoted himself to wine, women, and opium. Ni'matullah refers to yet another dream of Sher Khan on the eve of Chausa in which both he and Humayun were brought to the presence of the Prophet who informed Humayun of the bestowal of kingship to Sher Khan. The royal crown was thus taken away from Humayun and handed over to the Afghan leader with the instruction to do justice (adl-wa-insaf) with the people.[82] Significantly, the leading ulama and the Sufis had begun to desert the Mughals.

Another favourite Mughal explanation of their defeat was the 'treachery' of the wretched Afghans and their leader Sher Khan who kept reassuring Humayun till as late as the time when the emperor was half way through the march to Bengal that he was an old servant (ghulam-i-pir) of the Mughals and thus could not betray his salt

---

[79] Tarikh-i-Sher Shahi, pp. 156–7; Tarikh-i-Khan-i-Jahani wa Makhzan-i-Afghani, Vol. I, pp. 311–12. Also see Tazkirat-ul-Waqi'at, fol. 27b.

[80] Akbarnama, fols. 91a–b.

[81] Tarikh-i-Khan-i-Jahani wa Makhzan-i-Afghani, Vol. I, pp. 309–10. Abdullah says that Sher Khan saw this dream on the eve of Chausa, Tarikh-i-Dau'di, p. 125.

[82] Tarikh-i-Khan-i-Jahani wa Makhzan-i-Afghani, Vol. I, p. 303.

(*namak*). This frequent referring to namak and ghulami testified to his loyalty and submissiveness which convinced Humayun that Sher Khan would not 'dare' to cross the limit. The references to the 'treachery' of the 'evil-minded', 'black-hearted' and 'wretched' Afghans led by that 'fox' Sher Khan are too numerous in Abu'l Fazl's account to be cited here. According to Jauhar Aftabchi, Humayun could not imagine that Sher Khan would attack imperial territories and kill several hundred Mughals while he was for several months immersed in pleasure and indolence.[83] Thus, when report of Sher Khan's attack on Mughal territories and large scale massacre of imperial soldiers was brought to him in the 'pleasant' milieu of Bengal, he did not take them seriously. As we saw above, his return march was hastened by the rebellions of his brothers, the latest being Hindal Mirza reading khutba in his own name at Agra. According to Mushtaqi, Humayun came out of the palace after hearing the news that his preceptor Shaykh Bahlul was killed by Mirza Hindal at Agra on the charge that he was in league with Sher Khan.[84]

This brings us to the third explanation for the Mughal failures. It is suggested that the problems of Humayun were compounded by the Mongol theory of kingship which envisaged the division of the kingdom amongst the sons of the deceased king, leading to 'decentralization' and fratricidal warfare.[85] Thus, Humayun's position was considerably weakened by the rebellions of Kamran and Hindal. Askari also seized the opportunity to bargain for himself as much as he could.[86] Mirza Haider writes that Kamran's refusal to join Humayun in his march against Sher Khan before the battle of Qannauj and his departure to Lahore on the pretext of illness 'was the turning point in the

---

[83] *Tazkirat-ul-Waqi'at*, fols. 17a–b.

[84] *Waqi'at-i-Mushtaqi*, fols. 46b–47a, 49b; for the accusation that the shaykh was supplying arms to Sher Khan, see *Humayun-Nama*, pp. 40, 44.

[85] Iqtidar Alam Khan in his, 'Turko-Mongol Theory of Kingship' suggests that Humayun was defeated by Sher Khan due to the inherent weakness in the Mongol theory of kingship.

[86] For the continued bickerings among Humayun's brothers before and after the battle of Qannauj, see, *Humayun-Nama*, pp. 45–9. For Askari bargaining for a huge sum of money from Humayun before complying with the emperor's order to march from Bengal and report on the activities of Sher Khan, see *Tazkirat-ul-Waqi'at*, fols. 19b–20a.

rise of Sher Khan, and in the downfall of Chaghtai power'.[87] Describing the failure of the attempts to unite the Mirzas, Abu'l Fazl records that the rebellious Kamran privately sent Qazi Abdullah, his *sadr*, to Sher Khan to establish friendly relations. He sought the fulfillment of his desires with help from enemies, and wrote a letter to the effect that if Punjab were secured to him he would facilitate Sher Khan's success.[88]

Following the Mughal narrative, Ishwari Prasad attributes Humayun's failure to Sher Khan's treachery and discontentment of the Chaghtai *amirs*.[89] Further, Qanungo does not blame Humayun's incapacity as a military commander for his defeat. He writes that it was the '*ill-luck* (emphasis original) of the Emperor in the shape of an untimely shower that flooded his camp in mid-summer. But for this accident, Humayun would not have chosen to shift from his invulnerable entrenched camp'.[90] Noting that Humayun was 'an able military commander' and 'quite capable of extraordinary exertion', R.P. Tripathi also suggests that the Mughal emperor was 'the victim of an inexorable fate'. Tripathi cites, among other incidents, the 'unanticipated and usually heavy downpour of rain in the middle of May' which flooded his camp at Qannauj, placing him at a 'great disadvantage and contributed largely to his defeat'.[91]

By attributing Humayun's failure to 'fate' we will be neglecting several tactical errors committed by him. We have already indicated the danger of fighting the battle with the river on the back. Also, though it may be difficult to show the consistency of the pre-monsoon rains in the early sixteenth century, Humayun did not consider this possibility in choosing a place for encampment. Further, he was not able to keep his soldiers in control as the authorities report of widespread desertion from the camp. He could not take even his brothers in confidence, though Tripathi suggests that none of 'his brothers, not even Kamran, can be held responsible for the collapse of the Mughal power'.[92] In Tripathi's opinion, one major weakness of Humayun was his 'unsuspecting nature'. According to him, the 'tragedy of Chausa might

---

[87] *Tarikh-i-Rashidi*, pp. 471–85, especially p. 472.
[88] *Akbarnama*, fols. 93a–b.
[89] Prasad, *Life and Times of Humayun*, p. 149.
[90] Qanungo, *Sher Shah Sur and his Times*, p. 237.
[91] Tripathi, *Rise and Fall of the Mughal Empire*, pp. 110–11.
[92] Ibid., pp. 109–10.

have been averted had he refused to place trust in Sher Shah, and acted with caution'.[93] All these explanations put a question mark on his capabilities as a military commander at that stage of his career.

On the other hand, Sher Shah emerges as a shrewd campaigner, who mobilized vast resources, both men and material, within a span of a decade and emerged victorious. He recruited professional Afghan soldiers, organized the entire qaum settled throughout Hindustan, and exploited their 'hatred' against the Mughals. Many of these Afghans had arrived in the reign of Bahlul, who is said to have sent letters to the tribal chiefs of Roh inviting them to the rescue of the nascent Afghan kingdom of Delhi against Sultan Mahmud Sharqi's siege of the capital.[94] As noted above, Abbas informs that on receipt of the letters a huge number of the Afghans started from Roh. When they arrived near Delhi, the forces of Sultan Mahmud Sharqi gave a fight to them. Fateh Khan Harawi who was leading the Sharqi army, had a massive force with huge elephants, but they were soon routed. As we shall see below, Sultan Mahmud who was engaged in the siege of Delhi fled without having a contest. Also, Bahlul had issued orders to his nobles that any Afghan who came from Roh in search of employment should be presented before him so that he may grant him jagir to his satisfaction. He had warned the nobles to ensure that no Afghan immigrant should return to his homeland for want of livelihood and employment. Abbas adds that when the Afghans heard this news and saw the grant of favours made by the sultan, they began to stream into the country in large numbers, were employed as soldiers or nobles and received maintenance grants.[95]

The establishment of Mughal rule had meant joblessness and migration, though some Afghan and non-Afghan nobles were slowly joining the service of the new rulers.[96] Yet, there was a widespread

[93] Ibid., p. 111.

[94] *Tarikh-i-Sher Shahi*, pp. 5–7.

[95] Ibid., pp. 7–8. For the immigration of the Afghans, see also *Tarikh-i-Dau'di*, p. 107. Also see, Iqbal Husain, 'Afghan Immigration into India—A Case Study of Some Afghan Families, 16th–19th Centuries', *PIHC*, 55th Session, 1994, pp. 237–48.

[96] Mention may also be made here of Humayun's reported conversation with Shah Tahmasp in which he referred to the presence of a massive and hostile Afghan population everywhere, *Zakhirat-ul-Khawanin*. For Humayun's relation with Shah Tahmasp, also see, Riyazul Islam, *Indo-Persian Relations*, pp. 22–47.

hostility amongst the Indian Muslims and non-Muslim groups such as the Rajputs against the newly established rule of the Mughals. It must be remembered that the invading Mughals had not only defeated the Afghan and Rajput armies, but had also sacked the cities and villages killing and looting the general population. The Mughals were aware of this hostility as Humayun in his return march from Bengal refused to recruit soldiers in the wake of an impending fight against Sher Khan at Chausa.[97] The fugitive imperial party was attacked by the non-Muslim villagers (*gawaran*) after the defeat at Qannauj at a place not far from Agra.[98] In a tantalizing example of a communal reading of this incident by a modern Hindu nationalist historian, Ishwari Prasad notes that though 'thirty thousand men of the contiguous country districts rose up in arms to oppose' the Mughals who were continued to be treated as 'foreigners', this was not sufficient to throw them out. In fact, the author writes that the Rajputs should have set aside their differences in 'national interests' to form a coalition and exploit the opportunity to 'drive both the Afghan and the Mughal out of the country'. Prasad however concludes that the Rajputs 'had failed in similar crisis before; it was futile to expect anything better of them in 1540'.[99] However, the evidence of attack on the retreating Mughal army indicates that the non-Muslim chieftains were not entirely indifferent.

Sher Khan exploited the hatred against the Mughals to make a case for the dislocation of the political ecology of early sixteenth century Hindustan. We have seen in the previous chapter how Sher Khan's rivals for the leadership of the Afghans were gradually eliminated from the scene. During the period when Humayun was engaged in tackling Sultan Bahadur, Sher Khan got respite to wipe off whatever opposition was left in Bihar, and started mobilising the Afghans against the Mughals. According to Abbas Khan, those Afghans who had taken to mendicancy and indolence on account of their misfortune, were forced to enlist again as soldiers, on pain of death. When the Afghans heard

[97] Abu'l Fazl blames destiny for Humayun's turning down of the advice to stop somewhere to recruit soldiers and then turn to crush the enemy, *Akbarnama*, fols. 87a–b.
[98] *Humayun-Nama*, p. 47; *Akbarnama*, fol. 92a.
[99] Prasad, *Life and Times of Humayun*, pp. 151–2.

that Sher Khan was trying to organize them, they flocked to him from all quarters.[100]

When Sultan Bahadur, after meeting with reverses, proceeded towards Surat, the Afghan chiefs and soldiers who were in his service switched over to Sher Khan. Even those Afghan nobles who out of pride had earlier scorned to come into the service of Sher Khan, changed their position on seeing his growing prosperity, and entered his service. Thus, Isa Khan, the son of Azam Humayun Sarwani, Mian Biban Shahu-Khail, Qutb Khan Mauj-i-Khail, Mian Maruf Farmuli, Azam Humayun the son of Sultan Alam Shahu-Khail, in short all the prominent Afghans came over to him.[101] It is worth mentioning here that his leading nobles belonged to obscure families whose members had not occupied any important position in the Lodi Sultanate. Their contingents comprised fierce soldiers, also belonging to ordinary families. As they owed their dignified position to Sher Khan, they had a sense of gratitude, to serving him with unwavering loyalty. Their support was crucial for Sher Khan's rise to sovereignty.[102] Also important is the degree of discipline Sher Khan was able to maintain in his army through the payment of a fixed monthly salary to the soldiers kept in different forts all over Hindustan. In the case of troops maintained by the nobles, he was very strict about their branding (*dagh*) and ensured that fraud, so rampant in the previous regimes, was checked. We shall return to these issues later in this section.

It will be pertinent to recapitulate here the gradual increase in the material strength of Sher Khan taking into account, amongst other things, treasures and forts captured by him, and how he used them to mobilize and recruit large numbers of Afghan soldiers. Reference has already been made to the regular flow of revenue ensured by Sher Khan's measures in the parganas. This regular source of income increased with the expansion of his territorial control. His strict order

---

[100] *Tarikh-i-Sher Shahi*, pp. 95–6. Cf. Iranian emperor's suggestion to fugitive Humayun that after his return to Hindustan he should try to divert the Afghans towards trade and industry, *Zakhirat-ul-Khawanin*. The cases of soldiers turning to asceticism are often found in the tazkiras. For instance, Badauni refers to Shaykh Muhammad Qalandar who served in the army of Ibrahim Lodi, but later became an ascetic, *Muntakhab-ut-Tawarikh*, Vol. III, p. 25.

[101] *Tarikh-i-Sher Shahi*, p. 96.

[102] Siddiqui, *A History of Sher Shah Sur*, pp. 43–4.

to the soldiers not to destroy cultivation during the march of the army was significant not only from the point of view of logistics, as the cultivators could have been approached for the supply of grains in the eventuality of crisis, but also for the projection of the image of Sher Khan as the protector of all.[103] Further, this came in handy for the collection of revenue soon after the area had come under his control. The demand of land-tax in Mughal territories shortly after their annexation at the time when Humayun was stuck in Bengal is a case in point.

Apart from this regular source of income, always increasing with territorial expansion, Sher Khan enhanced his wealth and following in various other ways as well. The invocation to the Afghan tribal lineages was one. Addressing the Afghan chiefs belonging to various clans he would raise the question of their plight in the wake of the Mughal invasion, which was the result of their own bickerings. At a narrower level he would coax the chiefs of his own Sur clan to unite under his leadership. During his first journey to Agra, Sher Khan, then Farid, had halted at Kanpur where according to Abbas Khan, the rank-holding Sarwani Afghans, including Azam Humayun, were staying. Those Sarwanis who were related to Farid's father Mian Hasan, offered their hospitality. One of the chiefs, Shaykh Ismail was also present there. Introducing him to Farid, the Sarwanis suggested that he was a Sarwani, and then added that he was a Sur like him (Farid) and was Sarwani from his mother's side. Farid asked Ismail as to why he did not say that he was a Sur. Ismail replied that he had never said that he was a Sarwani, and was not responsible for their claiming him as one. Farid suggested to Ismail and Ibrahim (later known as Shuja'at Khan and Sarmast Khan respectively) to accompany him with their followers to Agra.[104] Later, as we have seen above, he also won over the powerful Muhammad Khan Sur of Chaund to his side by first displacing him with the help of the Mughals and subsequently addressing him as uncle.

His friendship with Makhdum Alam has already been noted above. When the sultan of Bengal sent a force against him, reportedly for not coming to the aid of Qutb Khan, Makhdum Alam sent all his

---

[103] *Waqi'at-i-Mushtaqi*, fol. 52a.
[104] *Tarikh-i-Sher Shahi*, p. 40.

belongings to Sher Khan, saying that he would take them back if he won, and if not they should better remain with him instead of going to others. Sher Khan, in return, was expected to come to his assistance; he did not, however, find it worth going personally. Makhdum Alam was killed in the battle, and his wealth remained in the hands of Sher Khan. He also received in quick succession, as we saw above, at least three fairly rich, young, and beautiful widows of powerful nobles of the Lodi Sultanate, by either marrying them quietly or exploiting their condition to lure them into his 'protection'. These trophy women brought immense wealth including the imperial Lodi treasury, prestige amongst the Afghans, and in one case provided incentive to non-Muslim groups to join his bandwagon. Contrarily, the Ruhtas fort was captured by force from the Hindu raja, though the Mughal chroniclers highlighted deception as the means to capture it.

Thus Sher Khan had become rich enough to emerge as the second biggest employer of soldiers from the military labour pool of Hindustan. As noted above, according to an estimate, Sher Khan had 'seventy thousand sawars paying them twelve crore tankas', before Humayun decided to march against him. Nizam-ud-Din Ahmad records that Sher Khan had acquired great power and strength by this time as he had taken possession of the provinces of Bihar and Jaunpur, and the fortress of Chunar. Humayun, realising that it was extremely necessary to destroy Sher Khan at once, marched from Agra with a well equipped army on 14 Safar 942/14 August 1535.[105] Sher Khan, on the other hand, considered himself powerful enough to warn Humayun of dire consequences in the eventuality of his decision to march towards Bengal. According to Abbas, Sher Khan threatened that Humayun's march would bring him only remorse and repentance, as the Afghans were united again and all the discord and disunion that previously existed among them had disappeared (*dar in ayyam afghanan muttafiq and wa khilaf wa naza ke ba yak digar dashtand kulli rafa shuda ast*). The Mughals could capture the country from the Afghans because of the latter's internal feud and differences.[106] Comparing the resources of Firuz Shah Tughluq and of the Mughal emperor Akbar, P. Saran has estimated Sher Shah's annual income to

---

[105] *Tabaqat-i-Akbari*, fols. 175b–176a.
[106] *Tarikh-i-Sher Shahi*, pp. 115–16.

be little over sixteen crores tankas.[107] Saran has also given a rough idea of how vast and varied the total annual expenditure of Sher Shah's government must have been.[108]

Sher Shah kept a huge amount of wealth and stationed armies in the major forts in various parts of his empire. According to the earliest available account, he had twenty five thousand footmen and matchlock-men (tufangdars) under his personal command; seven thousand tufangdars were stationed in the fort of Mandu, three thousand at Chittor, one thousand and six hundred at Ranthambore, five hundred at Bayana and one thousand at Gwalior; and two thousand footmen, adept in archery, in the fort of old Ruhtas. Similarly a garrison, consisting of sawars and footmen, was stationed in every fort. Besides, he always had one lakh and fifty thousand sawars under his personal command. He had at least three thousand elephants in his pilkhana (stable for elephants). The main treasure was kept in Ruhtas under the charge of Ikhtiyar Khan Batini. In the country of Gakkhars he built an extensive and impregnable fort on a hill and gave it also the name of Ruhtas. He kept sufficient treasure and a large force there under the joint command of three leading nobles.[109]

Following the dictum that a hungry soldier would not lay down his life on the day of battle, Sher Khan fixed a monthly salary for his soldiers and paid them in cash. Several references to his giving training to the soldiers are also to be found in the sources. Discipline in the army was maintained through the rule that the families of the soldiers would either stay in their own houses or in the forts held by Sher Khan. Thus the exceptionally mobile, disciplined and trained professional soldiers mounted on horses presented a sharp contrast to the Mughal army in which soldiers were outnumbered by the servants and slave-girls of the emperor and his generals, presenting the spectacle of a slow moving bazaar.[110]

---

[107] P. Saran, 'Annual Income and Expenditure of Sher Shah', in *Studies in Medieval Indian History* (Delhi, 1952), pp. 90–5.

[108] Ibid., pp. 95–103.

[109] *Waqi'at-i-Mushtaqi*, fols. 50b–51a. See also, *Tarikh-i-Sher Shahi*, pp. 212–16, 218; *Tarikh-i-Dau'di*, p. 130.

[110] Mirza Haider complains against the presence of a large number of servants and slaves (ghulam) of the emperor and those of his amirs who 'render no assistance to their master and have no control over themselves' on the day of battle,

Thus Sher Shah maintained a highly efficient army directly controlled by him. Yet a caveat here is in order as the nobles also maintained their own soldiers whose loyalty may have been primarily to the nobles, and not to the king. However, it was possible for the soldiers to approach the king directly and complain against the high-handedness of the noble such as the non-payment of their salaries. The case of the disenchantment of some two thousand horsemen posted by Sher Shah under Shuja'at Khan on the Deccan frontier may be cited here. The noble had tried to usurp parts of the maintenance grants of the soldiers. When their request for justice was turned down, they sent a wakil to Sher Shah. The latter reproached the noble for acting against his laws, advising him to maintain dignity in public and fear God. The noble, being humbled, apologized to the horsemen for his misconduct.[111] Denying that the military organization under the Lodi and Sur kings was 'tribal' in character, Siddiqui suggests that this was true for the period prior to the advent of Bahlul Lodi as the sultan of Delhi when 'the military generals and their dependent *sawars* were behaving like a disorderly rabble in the military campaigns for more than a hundred years'.[112]

The above-mentioned 'law' pertains to the system of branding which was aimed at checking the corruption of the nobles, and to ensure that they maintained the stipulated number of soldiers and paid them their dues. The system of branding was revived by Sher Shah to ensure that the nobles maintained the requisite number of soldiers in accordance with their ranks, and did not bring other men and horses at the time of fixing their monthly emoluments. The descriptive rolls of the soldiers and horses were to be recorded before they were brought to him, and he personally checked their weapons. For branding of horses in

---

adding that 'in whatever place there was conflict the *ghulam*s were entirely ungovernable. When they lost their masters, they were seized with panic and blindly rushed about in terror'. This, he said, happened at Qannauj as well. However, his statement that though the Mughals were defeated 'not a man, either friend or foe, was wounded. Not a gun was fired and the chariots were useless' is incorrect, *Tarikh-i-Rashidi*, pp. 470–7.

[111] *Tarikh-i-Sher Shahi*, pp. 228–31.

[112] I.H. Siddiqui, 'The Army of the Afghans Kings in North India (AD 1451 to AD 1555)', *Islamic Culture*, Vol. 39, July 1965, pp. 223–43. Military historians, however, tend to treat all medieval armies as 'tribal' or 'disorderly rabbles', see, Stephen Peter Rosen, *Societies and Military Power: India and its Armies* (Delhi, 1996).

the armies posted on the frontiers of his dominion, he appointed *munsifs* and did the inspection personally when he happened to be in the vicinity.[113] The authorities suggest that the system of dagh was 'introduced' by Sher Shah. As Ni'matullah points out, 'revived' would have been a better word as Sultan Ala-ud-Din Khalji is known to have taken steps in this direction.[114]

Rizqullah Mushtaqi relates some interesting anecdotes concerning the branding of soldiers and marking their horses possibly using hot iron-stamps, under the supervision of Sher Shah. The episodes throw significant light on the belief in the paranormal abilities of the king and the style of his governance. One day when he was overseeing the branding of horses, a man turned up, riding a Tazi horse. Sher Shah fixed four *badrah*s as his monthly salary. The saint Shaykh Khalil who was present there, asked the king as to why such a young and skilful rider with a good horse should receive only four badrahs. Sher Shah replied that he did not deserve more than that. To convince the shaykh, he ordered the young man to draw the bow, but he repeatedly failed to do so. On Sher Shah's proving that the young man did not have the basic skills of a soldier, the shaykh remarked that the king possessed miraculous ability to 'see the interior of men'.[115]

Another account illustrates that the method of branding could be very arbitrary. It was the turn of the dagh of Ahmad Khan Sur. A bearded Sarbini Afghan in his contingent who received four badrahs as his monthly allowance demanded that he should be paid higher as his uniform (*yakta-i-daraz*) was twice as costly as the coarse one (*tigochia*) worn by others who were better paid than him. The ruler however said that his yakta was cheap, but he would get additional four badrahs for his beard. The amount fixed was eight badrahs; four in his name and the remaining four for his beard, and it was accordingly entered in the register.[116]

Such occasional gestures, deep interest in the affairs of the soldiers, constant interaction with them, invocation of their martial ethos, and payment of fixed monthly salary to them were important factors for

[113] *Waqi'at-i-Mushtaqi*, fol. 51a; *Tarikh-i-Sher Shahi*, p. 208; *Tarikh-i-Dau'di*, pp. 212–13.

[114] *Tarikh-i-Khan-i-Jahani wa Makhzan-i-Afghani*, Vol. I, p. 338.

[115] *Waqi'at-i-Mushtaqi*, fol. 51a.

[116] Ibid., fol. 51b.

their loyalty towards the ruler. The expression of loyalty and the spirit of sacrifice in his amirs such as Qutb Khan, Haibat Khan Niyazi, Jalal Khan Jalu, Shuja'at Khan and Sarmast Khan at the time when Sher Khan was contemplating a direct armed conflict against Humayun at Chausa may be seen in a statement attributed to Azam Humayun Sarwani. He said that the Mughals could earlier defeat the Afghans due to their disunity. Now that they were united, they had lost all fear of the Mughals. He reiterated the saying of his elders that Afghans were never inferior to the Mughals in combat. He addressed Sher Shah as that fortunate leader who would lead the Afghans to victory.[117]

The loyalty of the Afghans towards Sher Khan and their spirit of sacrifice was reflected further in the statement attributed to Saif Khan Sarwani who met Sher Khan during his march towards Bengal, while being hotly pursued by Humayun. This is also evident from his decision to fight the advancing Mughals so that the distance between them and Sher Khan increased further, thus providing the latter more time.[118] Though Siddiqui notes that Kabir has also described with added details Saif Khan's encounter with the Mughals in his *Afsana-i-Shahan*, he rejects it as unauthentic because the Mughal chronicler Jauhar Aftabachi 'who mentions everything faithfully' has not recorded this.[119] Siddiqui's formulation has two problems. Firstly, he assumes that as a faithful Mughal servant Aftabchi has recorded everything related to Humayun's activities. Secondly, whatever the writer recorded was authentic. Clearly, these assumptions raise serious questions on how the sources have been utilized by the established authorities. This case sufficiently illustrates the fact that even if the two Afghan chroniclers, Abbas and Kabir, corroborate each other, the contrary opinion of Mughal chroniclers such as Jauhar or Abu'l Fazl is preferred. This is an example of reading the story of the Mughal-Afghan conflict from the point of view of the Mughals. Also neglected in this connection is the fact that Abu'l Fazl drew on Jauhar's account, and the latter recounted the events much later than they had actually occurred. Even if it is assumed for a while that the old servant was very 'objective', the possibility of his forgetting or ignoring some of the events cannot be

---

[117] *Tarikh-i-Sher Shahi*, pp. 128–9.
[118] Ibid., pp. 119–22.
[119] *A History of Sher Shah Sur*, p. 54; idem, *Sher Shah Sur and his Dynasty*, p. 74.

denied. Moreover, Saif Khan's sacrifice for an Afghan cause was not as significant for the loyal Mughal servants Jauhar and Abu'l Fazl as it was for the late sixteenth century Afghan writers Kabir and Abbas, and indeed for the Afghan memory, in general.

Returning to the question of mobilization, Sher Shah was not only generous in his patronage towards the members of his Sur clan who lived in Hindustan or came from Roh either for service or in expectation of some favour, but also showered gold on every Afghan visitor. Allowances or stipends to be paid anually were fixed by him.[120] His public position to do away with clan loyalties and mobilize the entire Afghan qaum under his leadership is aptly portrayed in an anecdote in which he is shown to be extremely disturbed and anguished (*bisyar ranjida wa dilgir mi shud*) when he heard anybody asking an Afghan visitor to which clan he belonged. According to him, the visitor's identity as an Afghan (or Pathan) was sufficient. He asserted that all Afghans were equal in the eyes of God. Any attempt to divide them was not only a sin, but also smacked of impertinence (*fazul*) and stupidity (*himaqat*).[121] Thus, the entire Afghan population whether Batini, Sarbini, or Gharghashti were united as brothers and motivated to drive away the Mughals and capture the kingdom of Hindustan. Sher Shah used their support to emerge victorious against the Mughals in two successive encounters within the span of a year. The late sixteenth century Mughal imperial discourse attributed Humayun's failure to the divine intervention, negligence of his officers, ambitions of his brothers and nobles and above all to the treachery of the Afghans and their leader Sher Shah Sur. Even though the Mughals had returned to establish their dominion on a firm footing, the presence of a courageous Afghan soldier was a constant threat to them. Indeed, Mughal history is haunted by a fear psychosis of an Afghan resurgence under 'Sher Khan'. No wonder then that they had marginalized and vulgarized the Afghans. Overawed by their grandeur and magnificence, most historians have hitherto followed the Mughal narrative in portraying the Afghans as uncultured and wicked people.

Contrary to this representation of the Afghans as the dangerous 'other', a large corpus of writings in the Persian language—some of

---

[120] *Tarikh-i-Sher Shahi*, p. 227. See also *Tarikh-i-Dau'di*, p. 223; *Tarikh-i-Khan-i-Jahani wa Makhzan-i-Afghani*, Vol. I, p. 337.

[121] *Tarikh-i-Khan-i-Jahani wa Makhzan-i-Afghani*, Vol. I, pp. 337–8.

them composed by the beleaguered Afghans themselves—celebrated the good old days under the Afghan rulers. The period of the Lodi and Sur sovereigns was clubbed together and perceived as one long tradition, fractured by the advent of the Mughals. It is this attempt to salvage a 'golden' past to which we shall refer to in the next section. Having shown above that the story of the Mughal-Afghan interface in particular and Afghan history in general need to be reconsidered, we shall now focus on the material concerning the problem of governance and Afghan-Rajput relations.

PART II

POLITICAL IDEALS
AND INSTITUTIONS

3

Norms of Governance and Aspects of Administration

As regard his justice on this earth, I say that none gives pain even to a creeping ant. Even Nausherwan who has been described as a great judge could not equal Sher Shah in giving right decisions. When he dispenses justice like Umar, the entire world looks up with admiration and praises him. None has the courage to touch even a nose-ring lying (without its mistress); people scatter gold along the road, the cow and the lion move by one path, and the two drink water at one place.

Malik Muhammad Jai'si in *Padmavat*[1]

MALIK MUHAMMAD JAI'SI'S REMARKS ARE significant not only for the evaluation of the norms of governance under the Afghans, but also because it highlights an important feature of the history of Muslim polity, namely the integration of diverse non-Islamic political ideals in classical Islam. The Afghan rulers drew on the ideals and institutions of medieval Indo-Persian tradition of governance, which were evolved over centuries of interaction between the classical Islamic norms on the one hand, and those of the Persians on the other. This process of appropriation had begun within the first century of Islam. The limitation of the shari'at for ruling the fast expanding Muslim frontier was already realized by the early caliphs. Also, the slow but gradual incorporation of the *Ajami*s or non-Arabs paved the way for the replacement of the tribal-Arab forms of government with a more sophisticated method drawn from the Byzantine and Sasanid political systems.

[1] Malik Muhammad Jai'si, *Padmavat*, in Ramachandra Shukla, ed., *Jaisi Granthawali* (Varanasi, 1935), p. 5 (*stutikhand*). English translation of the passage in Dasharatha Sharma, 'The Earliest Extant Account of Sher Shah', *The Indian Historical Quarterly* (henceforth *IHQ*), Vol. 8: 2, June 1932, pp. 302–4.

It may be worthwhile to note here the significance of the celebration of pre-Islamic Iranian legends in the late-tenth- and the eleventh-century Persianate world attempting to do away with the hegemony of Arabic Islam. It may also be important to keep in mind the political context of the period in which Iran formed a part of the empire established by the Turks of the Central Asian steppes with their base in Ghazna, now in Afghanistan. In this connection, the need to take into account the periodic upsurge of the Afghans in Eastern Islam may also be mentioned. Confronted by the dominance of the chauvinistic Arabs (who in a typical example of 'Othering' had disdainfully dubbed the Persians as a dumb people), adventurous Turks, and the resurgent Afghans, the Iranian self-perception hinged on the glorification of the militaristic and political achievements of the ancient kings. The Turkish Sultan Mahmud (ruled 998–1030) to whom Abu'l Qasim Firdausi presented his celebrated *Shahnama* was not particularly amused by the accounts of the military exploits of pre-Islamic Persian warlords. No wonder, the sultan was not so parsimonious with other poets recording the exaggerated narratives of his own achievements, particularly his much-celebrated 'holy wars' in India.[2]

It must also be said to the credit of Sunni Islamic orthodoxy that it strove hard for ensuring what it viewed as the pristine purity of Islam, condemning 'innovations' and deviance from the true path. Ironically, however, the orthodoxy succumbed to the forces of history to adopt elements from non-Islamic traditions, and even to bear with the emergence of *saltanat* and badshahat. Yet the shari'at was not entirely replaced by secular, or customary laws. The Muslim rulers were expected to maintain a delicate balance between the two. At least, a public declaration of respect and adherence for the shari'at was expected from the rulers.[3]

---

[2] For some such discussions, see the voluminous writings of Allama Shibli Numani, C.E. Bosworth, A.K.S. Lambton and M. Nazim. For a recent study of Abu'l Qasim Firdausi's *Shahnama* (AD c. 1000), see Kumiko Yamamoto, *The Oral Background of Persian Epics: Storytelling and Poetry* (Leiden and Boston, 2003). For a sanitized version of Sultan Mahmud's Indian expeditions, see M. Habib's classic little monograph. Also see, Romila Thapar, *Somanath: The Many Voices of a History* (Delhi, 2004).

[3] For recent treatments of the theme, see Muzaffar Alam, '*Akhalaqi* Norms and Mughal Governance'; idem; '*Shari'a* and Governance in the Indo-Islamic

The balance between the sacred and the secular is very well reflected in the 'mirror for princes' literature and the *akhalaq* digests. The authors of these works, though Muslims, borrowed from the views and sayings of ancient Greek masters, and supplemented them with stories and anecdotes from Persia. Conversely, they invoked the shari'at and illustrated their discourses with anecdotes from classical Islam in cases where they found support in them for their ideals, thereby enhancing the acceptability of their views in Muslim orthodox circle. The prime duty of the ideal ruler, in their opinion, was to ensure the well being of the people of diverse groups, and not of Muslims alone.[4]

The views of the early Muslim political theorists, like Imam Ghazali and Nizam-ul-Mulk Tusi, who defended the transformation of the caliphate into kingship, may be mentioned here. Defending the rule of the sultan, Imam Ghazali wrote that the decline of the caliphate does not mean that the people should stop obeying the law, dismiss the qazis (jurists), declare all authority to be valueless, and pronounce the acts of those in high places to be invalid. The office of government in different regions was legally executed by the sultans, who professed allegiance to the caliph, by mentioning the latter's name in the sermons, khutba, and the coins, sikka, and maintained stability and order. Ghazali also recommended support for and submission to even an unjust and ignorant ruler, as the attempt to depose him might prove counter-productive. Further, Ghazali also effected a fusion of the Islamic ethic and the Sasanian norms of governance.[5]

Context'; idem, *Languages of Political Islam*; Aziz Al-Azmeh, *Muslim Kingship*; Ira M. Lapidus, 'State and Religion in Islamic Societies', *Past and Present*, May 1996, pp. 3–27. Also see the classic study by A.K.S. Lambton, *State and Government in Medieval Islam* (Oxford, 1981).

[4] Alam, 'Akhalaqi Norms and Mughal Governance'.

[5] For a detailed exposition of Ghazali's views on good governance, see F.R.C. Bagley, *Ghazali's Book of Counsel for Kings* (Oxford, 1964). The noted historian Ibn Khaldun has also defended the transformation of the caliphate into kingship, as the qualities of the caliphate survived in the preference for Islam and its ways, and adherence to the path of truth. The only change which became apparent was in the restraining force which had been in religion and was now changed into asbiyat (lit: party-spirit; love of kindred or country) and the sword, Lambton, *State and Government in Medieval Islam*, p.173. For Ibn Khaldun's life and works, see also M. Talbi, 'Ibn Khaldun', *Encyclopaedia of Islam* (New Edition), Vol. 3, Leiden, 1971, pp. 825–31.

Like Ghazali, Nizam-ul-Mulk Tusi also attempted to combine some-thing of the Islamic ideal with the Persian notion of the ideal ruler.[6] Curiously, Lambton suggests that in spite of their attempt to create an amalgam of Islamic and pre-Islamic ideals, Imam Ghazali and Nizam-ul-Mulk Tusi, by their emphasis on the absolute power of the ruler and his unaccountability except to God, helped to perpetuate the fundamental disharmony between the ideal of Islam and the ideal of pre-Islamic Persia.[7] In doing so, the author ignores the continuation of a shared cultural heritage, particularly in religion and politics of the medieval Middle East. Islam also appropriated from the existing forms of Christianity and Judaism, which the polemics of the later times tended to ignore. Jesus, the most towering personality in Christianity, remains perhaps the second most respected figure in Islam.[8]

To return to the political ideas, the king, having projected himself as a vice-regent, or shadow of God on earth, was not expected to dis-criminate between Muslims and non-Muslims in providing protec-tion and justice to his subjects. A section of the ulama, however, continued to emphasize the necessity of complying with the letter of the law. The opinion of the mid-fourteenth century chronicler and political theorist of the Delhi Sultanate, Ziya-ud-Din Barani, on this matter is not without value. In a passage that shows his remarkable understanding of the context of time and space, Barani has suggested that the total annihilation of the innovators and opponents of the shari'at, was not possible, either through the teachings of the Quran or through the swords of the sultans. According to him, they can at most be kept suppressed and disgraced, and debarred from high offices, as they pose a grave threat to the honour of Islam. Patronage to these would be tantamount to discrediting the pious Muslims, the high-born and the God-fearing. Thus, while Barani's ideal polity demanded marginalization of the infidels and deviant Muslims, the ruler being a

---

[6] Nizam-ul-Mulk Tusi, *The Book of Government or Rules for Kings, The Siyasat-nama or Siyar al-Muluk of Nizam-ul-Mulk*, translated from the Persian by Hubert Darke (London, 1960).

[7] Lambton, *State and Government in Medieval Islam*, p. 26.

[8] For an interesting recent study on the depictions of Jesus as a Prophet in classical Arabic literature and his veneration in devotional Islamic traditions, like Sufism, see Tarif Khalidi, *The Muslim Jesus: Sayings and Stories in Islamic Literature* (Cambridge Mass. and London, 2001).

representative of God was expected to personify his basic attributes like mercy, forgiveness, justice and equity. There was no question of discrimination on the basis of religion in such matters as protection and justice (adl-wa-insaf) to the people. More significantly, the limitation of the parameters of the shari'at in tackling the complexities of the contemporary problems has been noted, and the need to follow more effective secular state laws (*zawabit-i-mulki*) emphasized.[9] Indeed, the Delhi sultans were hardly to be found as shari'at-bound. They adopted Persian theory of kingship and flouted the statutes of the shar'iat in matters of government, but paid lip service to Islam.[10]

Mention may be made here, for instance, of Ghiyas-ud-Din Balban, who ruled from Delhi for over forty years from about the middle of the thirteenth century—acting first as *naib* (deputy) of the puppet Sultan Nasir-ud-Din Mahmud (1246–66)[11] and subsequently ascending the throne of Delhi as sultan (1266–87) in his own right. Balban came to power at a time when the Mongols had ravaged the major part of the Muslim world. Having sacked Punjab, they were threatening to take Delhi by storm. Balban's aggressive Mongol policy protected the Sultanate from the depredation of the Mongol hordes.[12] The suppression of the 'rebellious' elements in the regions and the protection of trade routes were other achievements of Balban, which brought great prestige to the throne.[13] If Ziya-ud-Din Barani is to be believed, the king also thwarted political upheavals in the capital by providing a veneer of divinity to his rule. He called himself the shadow of God on earth (*zillullah*), and proclaimed that kingship was the vice-regency of God (*niyabat-i-khudai*). Tracing his genealogy to the mythical Afrasiyab, the sultan emulated the customs and ways of life of the pre-Islamic

---

[9] For Ziya-ud-Din Barani's provocative ideas, see his *Fatawa-i-Jahandari*. Also see, Aquil, 'On Islam and *Kufr* in the Delhi Sultanate'.

[10] For a general political history, see Habib and Nizami, eds, *The Delhi Sultanate (AD 1206–1526)* Delhi, 1970. For a review of the literature on the Sultanate period, see Raziuddin Aquil, 'Scholars, Saints and Sultans'. The expression 'shari'at-bound' is derived from Annemarie Schimmel, *Islam in the Indian Subcontinent* (Leiden-Koln, 1980).

[11] Ziya-ud-Din Barani notes that Sultan Nasir-ud-Din was a mere *namuna*, as the reins of power were in the hands of Balban then known as Ulugh Khan, *Tarikh-i-Firuz-Shahi*, fols. 12b–13a.

[12] Ibid., fols. 23b–24a.

[13] Ibid., fols. 26a–28a, 38a–45a.

Sasanid rulers of Persia. Elaborate court rituals, including *sijda* (pros-
tration) and *paibos* (kissing of feet) were introduced and forcibly implemented. Seen in the backdrop of anarchy in the aftermath of the death
of Iltutmish, Balban's measures restored the authority of the crown.[14]
Significantly, as an all-powerful noble under Nasir-ud-Din Mahmud,
Balban was a devotee of Farid-ud-Din Ganj-i-Shakar, khalifa of Qutb-
ud-Din Bakhtiyar Kaki.[15] Ali Asghar, himself a descendant of the shaykh,
recorded in the early seventeenth century that the saint had married
Balban's daughter Bibi Huzaira and had six sons and three daughters
from her.[16] Earlier, Amir Khwurd had noted that the shaykh had several
wives and had five sons and three daughters.[17] The saint's favourite son,
Nizam-ud-Din (not to be confused with his khalifa, Nizam-ud-Din
Auliya) had joined Balban's army and died fighting the Mongol invaders in Punjab.[18]

The above example suggests that politics and governance under
the sultans were not completely secular in orientation.[19] Indeed, there
appears to be a critical interdependence between the ulama and the rulers.
This was because most of the institutions engaged in training and
employment of religious scholars were established by the political elites
and funded through charities and grants. By and large, the ulama acted
as paid servants of the state. They generally interpreted the shari'at to
suit the policies of the sultans, and were employed in administration to
act as judges and religious advisors to make the Muslim subjects believe
that the Sultanate was an Islamic state. They also legitimized the rulers'
campaigns against non-Muslim chieftains by characterizing them as
jihad.[20] The khutba read in mosques presented the rulers as protectors

[14] Ibid., fols. 13b–17b.

[15] *Siyar-ul-Auliya*, pp. 89–90; *Siyar-ul-Arifin*, 56b-57a; *Jawahir-i-Faridi*, pp. 204,
214–15. For Balban's religiosity and his veneration of the Sufi saints generally, see
Tarikh-i-Firuz-Shahi, fols. 21b–22a.

[16] *Jawahir-i-Faridi*, pp. 215–18. Also see *Khazinat-ul-Asfiya*, Vol. I, p. 301.

[17] *Siyar-ul-Auliya*, pp. 76, 195.

[18] Ibid., pp. 100, 200.

[19] For more examples and a fuller discussion, see Raziuddin Aquil, 'From *Dar-
ul-Harb* to *Dar-ul-Islam*?: Chishti Sufi Accounts and the Emergence of Islam in
the Delhi Sultanate', in Satish Saberwal and Mushirul Hasan, eds, *Assertive Religious Identities: India and Europe*, Delhi, 2006.

[20] For a militaristic interpretation of the concept of jihad, see. E. Tyan, 'Djihad',
Encyclopaedia of Islam (New Edition), Vol. 2, Leiden, 1991, pp. 538–40.

and promoters of Islam and Muslims. The same need for legitimacy led early sultans to seek investiture (*manshur*) from the caliphs.[21] At the practical level, the ruler was expected to provide relief to his subjects from tyranny, irrespective of their religion, suppress crime, and ensure prosperity of the realm, safety on highways, comfort to traders, soldiers and travellers. Thus, the ideal include both a non-sectarian concern for the general welfare of the subjects across their religious affiliation and also for the statutes of the shari'at, which served as a major source of legitimacy. There was a constant vigil to maintain a balance between the two, but it would often be dislocated as well. We shall look at these problems in some details with reference to the Afghan period.

The sixteenth century writers have not only appreciated the 'good' deeds of the Afghan kings, but also highlighted their image as pious Muslim rulers. Shaykh Jamali and Shaykh Rizqullah Mushtaqi, for instance, almost exaggerate the rulers' veneration of the Sufi shaykhs. Jamali wrote in his *Siyar-ul-Arifin* that after the death of Bahlul Lodi his preceptor (*pir*), Shaykh Sama-ud-Din Kamboh Suhrawardi visited the sultan's grave. After reciting the *fatiha* (prayers for the dead), he meditated for a while. Shortly afterwards the shaykh raised his head and remarked that on account of his devotion to the friends of God the sultan was successful both in this world and the hereafter.[22] Later, Mushtaqi noted in his *Waqi'at-i-Mushtaqi* that Sultan Bahlul held the learned and pious men in respect. He personally heard the complaints of the people and passed suitable orders. From the very beginning of his reign, he attended religious sermons, and used to go to mosque on Friday for congregational prayers. Mushtaqi went on to narrate some anecdotes, which highlight the sultan's attitude towards the holy men of the realm.[23] He traced the sultan's devotion towards religion since

---

[21] For ulama's relationship with the rulers, see Nizami, *Religion and Politics in India*; Mujeeb, *Indian Muslims*; Ahmad, *An Intellectual History of Islam in India*; I.H. Qureshi, *The Muslim Community of the Indo-Pak Subcontinent, 610–1947* (Delhi, 1985); idem, *The Ulema in Politics* (Delhi, 1985). In consulting these modern authorities, their affiliations to 'liberal' and 'separatist' traditions of Indo-Islamic scholarship may be kept in mind. For a useful discussion on the concerns of the Indo-Muslim monarchy, see also, J.F. Richards, 'Introduction', in his edited volume, *Kingship and Authority in South Asia*, pp. 1–12.

[22] *Siyar-ul-Arifin*, fols. 144b–145a.

[23] *Waqi'at-i-Mushtaqi*, fols. 6a–b.

his childhood, and narrated an incident in which the sultan's uncle, Islam Khan, had prophesied that the child would bring power and glory to his family.[24] The author also refers to the bestowal of kingship to Bahlul by a majzub (a saintly person who is supposed to have renounced the world) when he was a young man.[25]

Writing in the reign of Akbar, Nizam-ud-Din Ahmad recorded in his *Tabaqat-i-Akbari* that Bahlul Lodi was adorned not only with personal piety, but was also completely bound in obedience to the laws of the Prophet. In all matters, he followed the path of the law and was very enthusiastic in attending to justice and equality. He passed a great part of his time in the society of the learned and in the company of the *faqir*s or holy men; and considered it right to show kindness to the poor and the needy.[26] In his *Khulasat-ut-Tawarikh* (composed in the late seventeenth century), Sujan Rai copied from Nizam-ud-Din Ahmad's account, highlighting Sultan Bahlul's religiosity and concern for the welfare of his subjects.[27]

The sixteenth-seventeenth century Persian sources lavish equal praise on Sikandar Lodi. The sultan's friend and philosopher Shaykh Jamali hailed his noble qualities including his interest in poetry and devotion towards men of religion.[28] Later, Rizqullah Mushtaqi's estimate of the reign of Sikandar Lodi is both detailed and full of praise. He has noted that he wrote the *Waqi'at-i-Mushtaqi* to describe the events of the reign of Sikandar Lodi along with the attainments of some Sufis and nobles who were his contemporaries. According to him, Sikandar Lodi was a great king devoted to the shari'at. He loved justice and was unmatched in bravery and generosity. During his reign people were prosperous. Agriculture and construction activities increased considerably. Mushtaqi further added that the soldiers enjoyed immense prestige under Sikandar Lodi. The traders used to travel in the dominion with a sense of security. The artisans and the peasants had

---

[24] Ibid., fol. 3a.

[25] Ibid., fol. 3b; Muhammad Qasim Hindu Shah known as Farishta, *Tarikh-i-Farishta*, Royal Asiatic Society (RAS) Persian Mss. No. 61 (Microfilm), p. 292.

[26] *Tabaqat-i-Akbari*, fol. 133b. Also see, Shaykh Abdul Haqq Muhaddis Dehlawi, *Tarikh-i-Haqqi*, RAS Persian Mss. No. 47 (Microfilm), p. 106.

[27] Sujan Rai, *Khulasat-ut-Tawarikh*, RAS Persian Mss No. 53 (Microfilm), p. 337. Also see, *Tarikh-i-Farishta* (RAS Microfilm), p. 299.

[28] *Siyar-ul-Arifin*, fols. 73b–74a.

such peace and order in the wilayat that even robbers and highway-men submitted on their own, became law-abiding and settled down to live peacefully. If anyone turned from the path of obedience, the sultan either got him beheaded or banished from the empire.

Highlighting the sultan's religiosity, Mushtaqi further wrote that in every city and territory, Islam prospered considerably and its laws were enforced. The mosques and Sufi institutions, like jama'atkhanas and khanqahs were full. *Muhtasibs* (superintendents of police, who exam-ined weights, measures and provisions, and prevented gambling, drink-ing, etc.) were chosen from amongst the competent persons. Scholars and teachers were appointed in the madrasas (Islamic seminaries), and nobles, their sons and soldiers kept themselves busy with acquiring knowledge and learning, and in performing religious acts. Every man who was *ahl-i-nisab*, that is, under religious obligation to pay the tax *zakat*, paid it. Food grains, clothes, cattle and other essential items were cheap. In every city, huge amount of money was disbursed from royal treasury amongst the scholars, learned men, widows and the needy. The officers were ordered to prepare the list of deserving persons in the localities under their charge. They regularly sent to each whatever was fixed for him. In the farmans (royal orders) issued to the nobles regarding the assignment of the parganas and the territories, it was specifically mentioned that the *imlak* and *wazaif* (land grants to holy-men) were excluded.[29]

Mushtaqi virtually portrayed Sikandar Lodi as a religious bigot and claimed that no territory in his kingdom could be called a *dar-ul-harb*, or 'the land of war'.[30] He wrote that the sultan banned and abolished

---

[29] For Rizqullah Mushtaqi's appreciation of the reign of Sikandar Lodi, see *Waqi'at-i-Mushtaqi*, fols. 8b–9a. Later Ni'matullah also noted that during the time of Sikandar Lodi there was plenty of rain and there was no deficiency of food-grain throughout the dominion. The people lived in peace and tranquility, *Tarikh-i-Khan-i-Jahani wa Makhzan-i-Afghani*, Vol. I, p. 212. However, famine did occur in some parts of North India under Sikandar Lodi. Elsewhere, Ni'matullah suggests that the sultan in order to mitigate the hardships of the famine stricken people of his time remitted the payment of zakat (religious cess) in corn. Henceforth, the system of paying corn as zakat was abolished, ibid., Vol. I, pp. 186–7; A. Rashid, 'Famine in the Turco-Afghan Period', *PIHC*, Ranchi Session, 1964, pp. 84–9, especially p. 87.

[30] A. Abel, 'Dar al-harb', *Encyclopaedia of Islam* (New Edition), Vol. 2, Leiden, 1991, p. 126.

innovations in religion. Hindus were prevented from taking a ritual bath in public at Mathura. He also wanted to destroy the tank at Kurukshetra where Hindus gathered on religious occasions for bathing. The ulama, however, prevented him from doing this by denouncing it as an un-Islamic act. Further, people were stopped from worshipping goddess Shitla (the goddess of small-pox). The sultan's reformist zeal also saw the banning of the procession of the spear of Salar Mas'ud Ghazi and the demolition of 'fake' graves.[31]

Mushtaqi also records a story to substantiate his claim about the sultan's religiosity. He relates that when the ruler fell seriously ill before his death, he ordered his *imam* Shaykh Ladhan, son of Shaykh Sama-ud-Din Kamboh Suhrawardi, to prepare an estimate of the *kaffara* (compensation) for unlawful acts committed by him such as neglecting prayer (*namaz*) and not keeping fast during the month of Ramazan, shaving off his beard, taking wine and also inflicting unlawful punishments like severing the ears of the criminals. The shaykh did accordingly, noting down in detail the compensation for every sin, and submitted it to the king. The latter also prepared a list of the sins he had committed from the period of adolescence onwards, and handed it over to the shaykh asking him to calculate the amount due as compensation. When the shaykh finally submitted his report containing the sultan's sins and the equivalent amount, the sovereign ordered the *khazanadar* (treasurer) to take out the money from that section of the treasury that was considered lawfully earned and give it away to the ulama. The latter praised the ruler for his wisdom.[32] Mushtaqi's nephew

---

[31] *Waqi'at-i-Mushtaqi*, fols. 9a–b. It is also suggested that the sultan prevented the women from visiting the shrines and the graveyards, *Tarikh-i-Khan-i-Jahani wa Makhzan-i-Afghani*, Vol. I, pp. 216–17. The image of Sikandar Lodi as a bigot was further highlighted by Sujan Rai, *Khulasat-ut-Tawarikh* (RAS Microfilm), p. 339. For a recent study of the cult of Salar Mas'ud Ghazi, see Shahid Amin, 'On Retelling the Muslim Conquest of North India', in Partha Chatterjee and Anjan Ghosh, eds, *History and the Present* (Delhi, 2002), pp. 24–43. Also see, Tahir Mahmood, 'The Dargah of Sayyid Salar Mas'ud Ghazi in Bahraich: Legend, Tradition and Reality', in Christian W. Troll, ed., *Muslim Shrines in India: Their Character, History and Significance* (With an Introduction by Marc Gaborieau), first published 1989 (Delhi, 2003), pp. 24–43; Iqtidar Husain Siddiqui, 'A Note on the Dargah of Salar Mas'ud in Bahraich in the Light of Standard Historical Sources', in Troll, ed., *Muslim Shrines in India*, pp. 44–7.

[32] *Waqi'at-i-Mushtaqi*, fol. 27b.

Abdul Haqq Muhaddis Dehlawi, himself a leading scholar, also praised Sikandar Lodi in his *Tarikh-i-Haqqi* for his piety and to it he seems to attribute the prosperity of his reign. According to him, the king was particularly devoted towards the saints, scholars, and other noble men—a large number of whom had come from Arabia and other parts of the Islamic world during his reign.[33]

Reflecting the Mughal imperial attempt to discredit the earlier rule, Nizam-ud-Din Ahmad suspected much of the material on Sikandar Lodi to be a product of exaggeration and cited the merit of his own work being nearest to the reality.[34] He has, however, closely followed Mushtaqi's account of the assessment of the reign of the sultan.[35] It is also suggested by him that Sikandar Lodi possessed information about the condition of his subjects (raiyats) and soldiers to such a degree that even details of the domestic affairs of the people reached him, so that it was suspected that the ruler had a *jinn* (benevolent supernatural being) who was intimate with him, and gave him information of what was to occur in future.[36] In fact, the sources alluded to the sultan's ability to perform miracles.[37] Such claims concerning Sher Shah will be referred to below. The Sufis also wrote *qasida* (panegyrics) in praise of the rulers, and *marsiya* (elegy) on their death, and dedicated their works to them, as we shall see in chapter five.

The Sufis not only highlighted the virtuous deeds of the sovereigns, but also often praised them for being very handsome or good looking. Mushtaqi has noted that Prince Nizam, later Sultan Sikandar, was known for his excellent temperament and remarkable personality. Anyone who possessed a heart and looked upon him, had his heart

[33] *Tarikh-i-Haqqi* (RAS Microfilm), pp. 108–9. Also see, Shaykh Abdul Haqq Muhaddis Dehlawi, *Akhbar-ul-Akhyar*, Urdu trans. Subhan Mahmud and Muhammad Fazil (Delhi, 1990), pp 470–1.

[34] *Tabaqat-i-Akbari*, fol. 148b. Later, Farishta quoted Nizam-ud-Din Ahmad's statement concerning the exaggerated phraseology of previous authors, *Tarikh-i-Farishta* (RAS Microfilm), p. 309.

[35] *Tabaqat-i-Akbari*, fols. 148b–149b.

[36] Ibid., fols. 149b–150a; *Tarikh-i-Khan-i-Jahani wa Makhzan-i-Afghani*, Vol. I, p. 219; *Khulasat-ut-Tawarikh* (RAS Microfilm), p. 340.

[37] *Akhbar-ul-Akhyar* (Urdu trans.), pp. 470–1. A. Halim writes that innumerable and sometimes incredible stories are extant regarding Sikandar Lodi including the one in which he is credited with the resurrection of a dead body, *History of the Lodi Sultans*, p. 111.

captivated at the very sight.[38] Mushtaqi has illustrated his point with the story of Shaykh Hasan, the grandson of Shaykh Abu Lala, who had fallen in love with the prince.[39] Abdul Haqq also recorded an abridged version of this story in his *Akhbar-ul-Akhyar*.[40]

The above episodes recorded mainly by Jamali and Mushtaqi, and recounted and elaborated by subsequent authors, served to strengthen the image of the Lodi rulers as pious. They sought company of, and blessings from, the religious leaders, and were concerned also to establish the 'holy law' in their realms. It would appear that the Lodi kings also contributed to the projection of such an image in their quest to legitimize their ceaseless efforts to build an empire. This was particularly necessary in view of their long drawn struggle with the Sharqis of Jaunpur. A number of Sufis actually threw their lot in favour of the Lodis as they felt that the cause of Islam would be served better under them. However, according to a later report, Sikandar Lodi also planned to pull down the Jama Masjid of Jaunpur, identified with the glory and power of the Sharqis, after his conquest of the city. The ulama present there dissuaded the sultan from doing so, and thus the mosque was spared. Further, some of the details in the sources actually illustrate how at times Sikandar Lodi could be indifferent to the dictates of the shari'at and mock at the power and prestige enjoyed by the religious leaders.

Thus, the invocation of the 'holy law' was more or less a matter of convenience with the Lodis and so was the case with Sher Shah subsequently. The accounts in Afghan histories from the late-sixteenth century onwards justified Sher Shah's actions during his campaign in Malwa and Rajasthan. It may also be that the ruler himself provided religious colour to the cold-blooded massacres of the Rajputs by keeping the ulama and Sufis in good humour. The sources suggest that his welfare mechanism, personal piety and revenue-free land-grants (*madad-i-ma'ash*) to holy men also made him fit in the image of an ideal ruler. Long passages on statecraft attributed to Sher Shah from the very early days of his career, to be found in Abbas Khan Sarwani's *Tarikh-i-Sher Shahi* show that the ruler's vision of an ideal government was quite broad-based. It may be that he had imbibed these ideas,

[38] *Waqi'at-i-Mushtaqi*, fol. 13a.
[39] Ibid., fols 13a–b.
[40] *Akhbar-ul-Akhyar* (Urdu trans.), p. 575.

as a student at Jaunpur, where he was probably exposed to the early 'mirror for princes' literature. The passages recorded by Abbas Sarwani and their summarized versions in other texts clearly echo the views of such political theorists as Imam Ghazali and Nizam-ul-Mulk Tusi.

As noted in chapter one, before taking up the assignment of the shiqqdar of the two parganas, Sahsaram and Khwaspur Tanda, Sher Shah, then known as Farid Khan, had lectured his father on the need to maintain law and order in the realm, and the way to ensure it. According to Abbas Sarwani, Farid harped on the need to establish justice as it led to consolidation and expansion of the kingdom, growth of the exchequer, and populousness of villages and towns. Conversely, tyranny caused destruction of the empire and the ruin of the country, leading to damnation in this world and the next. Thus, prosperity and survival of the kingdom was based on the well being of the raiyat, and that was possible when the nobles stopped committing oppression. Further, the suggestion that the affluence of a country depended upon the dispensation of justice and punishment was illustrated through an interesting simile in which the state was referred to as a plant, and the administration as water. Hence it was obligatory to keep the roots of the tree of the kingdom alive with the water of justice and chastisement so that the people could enjoy the fruits of peace and order.[41]

Later, as a shiqqdar, Farid again stressed the need to augment cultivation and warned the corrupt revenue officials and zamindars to stop exploiting the peasantry, as cultivation was not possible if tyranny were not done away with.[42] Much of it appears to be literally quoted from the writings of Imam Ghazali and Nizam-ul-Mulk Tusi. Even if we assume that the above statements are not the original words of Farid, they are evidently drawn from the discussions on justice and prosperity in the works of medieval Muslim political theorists. Such adaptations may also be noticed in Abdullah's *Tarikh-i-Da'udi*[43] and Ni'matullah Harawi's *Tarikh-i-Khan-i-Jahani wa Makhzan-i-Afghani*.[44]

Further, sixteenth century writers extol Sher Shah's methods of administration and public works. In particular, the focus is on his

[41] *Tarikh-i-Sher Shahi*, pp. 16–21.
[42] Ibid., pp. 21–3.
[43] *Tarikh-i-Da'udi*, p. 108.
[44] *Tarikh-i-Khan-i-Jahani wa Makhzan-i-Afghani*, Vol. I, p. 264.

justice and charity. It is difficult to get direct evidence of the influence of the early Muslim political theorists on Sher Shah's ideals, even though we know that some of the classical texts were known in the period.[45] We also know about Sher Shah's training at Jaunpur in the company of the ulama and Sufis of the place.[46] It may be that the Afghan empire builder evolved his own style of governance on the basis of his long experience as an administrator at various levels. Impressed by his public works and charitable endeavours, and also by the late sixteenth century intellectual milieu, which provided the postulates for evaluating good governance, the chroniclers probably attributed to Sher Shah what they found in the works of the theorists.

A brief summary of the details given by the authorities can serve to illustrate how Sher Shah's rule was perceived by his contemporaries, and by the near-contemporaries even in the aftermath of the hostile Mughals returning to power with a vengeance. We shall also assess as to what extent the history of his style of governance is a construction of the late sixteenth century Afghan chroniclers. It is stated that his administrative measures wiped off poverty from the realm as he spent a lot in charity, and was always concerned about the well being of the people.[47] In order to check the occurrence of famine, Sher Shah had arranged for state-stores of grain from where it could be sent to famine-stricken areas.[48] He built rest-houses for the poor and public-kitchen (langar) was started where food was available for them all the time. The royal kitchen was also open to the public. Sher Shah himself took his food in the company of the ulama and the Sufis.[49]

The sources also note that peace and order reigned supreme in Sher Shah's reign. The muqaddam or the village chief was responsible for any crime in the area. If it occurred anywhere, the head of the village concerned was arrested. Consequently, the rural chieftains became cautious and ensured that no such cases occurred in their vicinity.[50]

[45] Alam, 'Akhalaqi Norms and Mughal Governance'.

[46] See Introduction, p. 31.

[47] Waqi'at-i-Mushtaqi, fol. 49b. Also see Tarikh-i-Da'udi, pp. 216–21; Tarikh-i-Sher Shahi, pp. 224–6; Tarikh-i-Khan-i-Jahani wa Makhzan-i-Afghani, Vol. I, pp. 333–7.

[48] Rashid, 'Famine in the Turco-Afghan Period', p. 87.

[49] Waqi'at-i-Mushtaqi, fol. 49b; Tarikh-i-Sher Shahi, p. 225.

[50] Waqi'at-i-Mushtaqi, fol. 49b; Tarikh-i-Da'udi, pp. 218–19.

According to Abbas Sarwani, Sher Shah was convinced that theft and highway robbery were committed either at the instance of the village chiefs or at least they had full information about them.[51] Sher Shah also issued orders to his *amils* or revenue and administrative officials to mete out good treatment to the travellers and merchants and ensure that they were protected from the ravages of the thieves and dacoits.[52]

The construction of roads with posts (*dakchaukis*) and inns (*sarais*), coupled with the rules concerning highway-robbery, should be viewed not merely as aspects of public welfare, but as measures clearly designed to ensure the state's control of the regions. The highways could facilitate rapid movement of the army for campaigns in the regions as part of the imperialistic project. Further, the attempt to maintain law and order on the roads ensured increased trade and commerce in the dominion, with the subdued petty chiefs refraining from harassing the merchants.[53] Abbas Sarwani concluded that Sher Shah was a unique personality of his age. In a very short period he brought the country under his control, restored peace and order on the road, provided an efficient government and gave to the peasantry and soldiers peace and tranquility.[54]

It would be incorrect to assume that such a portrayal of the Afghan regime, in general, and that of Sher Shah, in particular, is to be found only in the Afghan histories of the Mughal period. The non-Afghan Persian authorities of the period corroborate Abbas Sarwani's account of Sher Shah's achievement in the field of politics and administration. One of them, Mulla Abdul Qadir Badauni, goes on to celebrate his good fortune of having been born in the blessed reign of so just a sovereign as Sher Shah. Undoubtedly, this celebration was particularly heightened by Badauni's dissatisfaction with Akbar's unorthodox ways.[55] Moreover, the Afghan chronicler, Abbas Sarwani, was not the

---

[51] *Tarikh-i-Sher Shahi*, pp. 220–2.

[52] Ibid., p. 222.

[53] For more details on Sher Shah's administrative and welfare measures, and their appreciation by the medieval authorities, see *Waqi'at-i-Mushtaqi*, fols. 50a–51a. Also see, *Tarikh-i-Da'udi*, pp. 216–21; *Tarikh-i-Sher Shahi*, pp. 216–18; *Tabaqat-i-Akbari*, fol. 205a; *Tarikh-i-Haqqi* (RAS Microfilm), p. 120; *Tarikh-i-Farishta* (RAS Microfilm), p. 376.

[54] *Tarikh-i-Sher Shahi*, p. 239.

[55] *Muntakhab-ut-Tawarikh*, Vol. I, p. 363.

first to give all the details about Sher Shah's administrative measures and welfare mechanism. Rizqullah Mushtaqi, a non-Afghan, gives a similar report. Abbas Sarwani has evidently drawn on the account in the *Waqi'at-i-Mushtaqi*. It may be that these authorities, influenced by advances made under Akbar and yet in search of an ideal ruler, have projected backward in time some of the later developments. However, such a proposition is not entirely accurate in view of an almost verbatim account of Sher Shah's reign in a work produced in the reign of the ruler himself, *Padmavat* of Malik Muhammad Jai'si.

Some of the details given by Jai'si can probably help us understand the ruler's image in his own time. The author wrote that even Nausherwan who was described as a great judge could not equal Sher Shah in giving right decisions. The latter's attempt to dispense justice like the caliph Umar was admired by the whole world. Further, highlighting the king's charitable endeavours Jai'si claimed that God had made him extremely liberal. Bali and Vikrama were said to be very charitable, and Hatim and Karna very generous. But even these could not satisfy the people to the same extent as Sher Shah. Even a performer of ten *asvamedha* sacrifices did not equal him in merit and liberality.[56]

Jai'si's statement again reveals the integration of political ideals from diverse traditions, including Persian, Indic and classical Islam. Also, Jai'si's account of Sher Shah's justice and charity may be exaggerated, but what will be difficult to disprove is the fact that the image of Sher Shah as a benevolent ruler had already spread within the first couple of years of his short reign. More significantly, the process of his deification had also started within his lifetime. This may be found in the description of the beauty of his physical form and the paranormal power attributed to him.

---

[56] *Padmavat*, pp. 5–6. English translation of the passage in Dasharatha Sharma, 'Earliest Extant Account of Sher Shah', pp. 303–4. Once again, comparison with Hatim (the much celebrated Yemenite prince) for generosity and with Nausherwan (the Sasanid ruler of pre-Islamic Iran) for justice is a standard trope in Persian writings on good governance. As late as 1780s, Ghulam Husain Salim noted in the preface to his history of Bengal that he wrote the work at the behest of his British master, George Udny, who is referred to as the Hatim and Nausherwan of the age, *Riyaz-us-Salatin*, pp. 2–4. For a modern, separatist Muslim observation on Jai'si's appropriations of the Hindu ideals, see chapter six below.

Supernatural power is generally attributed to the Sufis. In a significant reversal, however, Rizqullah Mushtaqi makes the noted Sufi,
Shaykh Khalil, suggest that the kings possessed miraculous powers,
while others saw only the outward things. The shaykh was impressed
by the ruler's ability to catch the fraud in the course of branding (dagh),
as noted in the previous chapter. This anecdote of the ability of Sher
Shah of performing miracles is supplemented by the frequent suggestion that the monarch was a representative of God on earth. This is
further substantiated by the dreams in which the Prophet is said to
have bestowed kingship on Sher Shah following an order from God
with the direction to establish justice (adl-wa-insaf) in the realm.
Further, reports of bestowal of kingship to Sher Shah by wandering
dervishes are also to be found in Persian histories.[57] Whatever happened
in the subsequent period, despite serious attempts at vulgarization by
the Mughals, constitutes an interesting study in the growth of the legend
of Sher Shah. A recent visit to Sahsaram was an eye opener as it was
found that Sher Shah is venerated there as a local saint. His tomb is
taken as a shrine, called the 'roja' (rauza: mausoleum) in local parlance,
which people frequent to seek blessings and benedictions, and place
ritual Sufic chadar (decorated sheets of cloth and flowers) on the grave.
The image of the philanthropic monarch and a thaumaturgic Sufi is
subsumed in the personality of the king. Conversely, a large number
of Sufis are found to be deeply involved in the politics of the period.[58]
To return to the problem of governance, we shall briefly discuss some
of the views on the administrative structure under Sher Shah. This will
further help us understand political ideals and institutions of
governance under the Afghans, as also in a measure under the Mughals
in the second half of the sixteenth century.

ADMINISTRATIVE SET-UP

It was Sher Shah who for the first time essayed seriously and with success to define the territorial limits of the provinces and to establish a
uniform system of government.[59]

[57] For the account of bestowal of kingship to Sher Shah, see *Tarikh-i-Khan-i-
Jahani wa Makhzan-i-Afghani*, Vol. I, p. 290.

[58] See chapter five.

[59] Parmatma Saran, *The Provincial Government of the Mughals*, pp. 55–6.

Parmatma Saran writes that Sher Shah consolidated his government by making his provincial governors (called *iqtadars* or *muluk-i-tawaif*) realise that they were liable to punishment for the least violation of the statutes and that they had no claims to any particular iqta or jagir. Thus under Sher Shah the provinces attained, both territorially and administratively, a definite stage in their evolution which became the substructure of Akbar's administrative edifice.[60] Though Iqtidar Husain Siddiqui dismisses what he calls Saran's 'sweeping generalizations', he himself goes on to state that certain far-reaching changes were set in the administrative system of the wilayat of Sher Shah, and that they served as a model for Akbar when he organized his empire by grouping sarkars into subas.[61] Much earlier, William Erskine had suggested that many of Sher Shah's revenue regulations were retained or renewed by Akbar, and seemed to have been incorporated into Todarmal's improved system of finance.[62] Later, recognizing the 'exceptional' aspiration of Sher Shah for large-scale state-building, J.F. Richards notes that during 'that brief period his energetic administration forecast many of the centralizing measures in revenue assessment and military organization that would be carried to completion by the Mughals'.[63]

Any discussion on Sher Shah's administrative set-up must take into account the fact that he ruled the country merely for about five years and that the Surs were shortly afterwards succeeded by the Mughals who were not expected to acknowledge any of his achievements and were in fact ready to decimate anything which portrayed the Afghans in good light. Thus, though the issues concerning the territorial divisions of Sher Shah's empire and their administrative organizations have been debated by historians for a long time now, lack of sufficient material in the sources prevents us from believing that a very sophisticated 'system' or 'structure' of administration existed under him. Nor do we actually view the sixteenth century administrative history in terms of a rigid, unchanging structure, including that of the latter half

[60] Ibid.

[61] *A History of Sher Shah Sur*, pp. 104 and 122.

[62] William Erskine, *A History of India Under the Two First Sovereigns of the House of Taimur, Babur and Humayun*, Vol. II, London 1854, reprint (Delhi, 1973), p. 446; Qanungo, *Sher Shah and His Times*, p. 52.

[63] *The Mughal Empire*, pp. 11, 81.

under Akbar with which we are not immediately concerned.[64] The chronicles reveal that Sher Shah was constantly making experiments in different regions and at various levels of his dominion. Instead of rejecting his administrative innovations and reforms as ad-hoc arrangements, they need to be studied as part of the historical processes with all their tensions and turbulence. Our aim here is however limited. We shall give a general outline of the various territorial divisions of Sher Shah's empire and the duties of the officials appointed by him to run the administration.

Sher Shah's dominion extended from Sonargaon in the east to the Gakkar country in the north-west, the western boundary being formed by a line joining Balnath Jogi on the Jhelum in the north to Khushab nearly a hundred miles south-west, and hence running across the Jhelum along the bank of the Indus down to Bhakkar. In the south, his territories were bound by the Vindhya and Karakoram ranges, as he had brought within his sway practically the whole of western Rajputana, Malwa and Kalinjar.[65] The whole empire was divided into nine provinces called wilayat, more popularly known under the Mughals as subas, comprising the territory from Delhi to the western boundary of Rohilkhand, from Rohilkhand as far as Awadh and Jaunpur, Bihar, Bengal, Malwa, Ajmer including Jodhpur and Nagaur, Punjab, Multan including the Gakkar country, and Sindh. Though the traditionally defined boundaries of the provinces were more or less retained by Sher Shah, what is of particular interest is his efforts to establish a uniform administrative machinery in the kingdom. Thus the regions which were formerly outside the control of the Delhi sultans, particularly in the fifteenth and early decades of the sixteenth centuries, were integrated into a larger, increasingly centralized network of administration. The permanent and hereditary military fiefs, or iqtas, gave way to a more sophisticated territorial division of the empire into provinces. As mentioned above, while Saran recognizes that the provincial boundaries were systematized or defined by Sher Shah, he suggests that the polity under him continued to be 'tribal', and the 'system' of division of the kingdom among the leading nobles 'was not in the least altered or

---

[64] For a different view, see Ibn Hasan, *The Central Structure of the Mughal Empire and its Practical Working up to the Year* 1657, first published 1936, reprint (Delhi, 1970).

[65] Saran, *Provincial Government*, p. 44.

modified by Sher Shah'.[66] Ibn Hasan also notes that 'Sher Shah favoured the centralization of power' and his 'reforms suggested certain lines of action to his successors', but it was 'reserved for Akbar to take up the work of reconstruction in the light of the lessons and experiments recorded by three centuries of Muslim rule in Northern India'.[67]

The provincial governors appointed by Sher Shah were variously called *hakims*, muqtas, or *faujdars*. They enjoyed vast powers for collection of revenues, to deal with insurrections and maintain law and order in the province. Like in the imperial court, they held grand darbars in their provincial headquarters, and extended patronage to scholars and religious mendicants. But they were expected to remain within bounds and not act against the king's wishes, or else be prepared for punishment which included a transfer, demotion in rank and posting to a smaller inconsequential wilayat, imprisonment and death.[68] Most of the administrative arrangements were made by Sher Shah in the course of his conquests. In a measure which speaks of the exigencies of the time and was aimed at keeping the nobles in check, the governorship of certain provinces was given to more than one person. For instance, Punjab was entrusted to at least three nobles with 'same authority and powers to control the administration',[69] before Sher Shah had to cut short his campaign in the west and rush to check the rising tide of rebellion of Khizr Khan in Bengal. Saran mentions five nobles Haibat Khan Niyazi, Khawas Khan, Isa Khan Niyazi, Habib Khan and Rai Husain Jalwani, as being incharge of the whole country between Lahore and the frontier.[70] Similarly at the time of the initial conquest the territories of Rajasthan were given to the charge of Khawas Khan and Isa Khan who were assisted by some other nobles.[71]

Understandably, this arrangement was conditioned by the rebellious activities of Khizr Khan in Bengal as well. Khizr Khan was appointed as the supreme muqta of Bengal in 1539. Sher Shah however had to rush

[66] See Introduction, p. 24.

[67] *The Central Structure*, pp. 50–1.

[68] For more details on wilayats and their muqtas, Siddiqui, *A History of Sher Shah Sur*, pp. 122–5; Saran, *Provincial Government*, pp. 51–4.

[69] Siddiqui, *A History of Sher Shah Sur*, p. 123.

[70] *Provincial Government*, p. 52.

[71] Ibid., p. 54.

to Bengal within a couple of years and remove the governor, though the latter had pledged his loyalty. With a view to minimising the chances of rebellion, the province was split up into 'manageable sarkars', or sub-provinces.[72] The administrators of these smaller units were independent of one another, but responsible to the emperor through an *amin*, who was given the responsibility for supervising and controlling the general administration of the province. The post of amin was created with the object of keeping internal turbulence in check, and for protecting the province from ambitious neighbours. As a 'trustee' he was responsible to the emperor for the province as a whole. Saran suggests that the amin's office roughly resembled that of the later Mughal viceroys of the Deccan under whom several minor provinces were combined into a single viceroyalty with the same object in view, namely to facilitate the control of a distant province and keep in check the fissiparous tendencies of the local chiefs.[73] Perhaps the experiment did not work smoothly as the amin of Bengal, Qazi Fazilat, was lampooned by his detractors, in a pun of words, as Qazi Fazihat;[74] *fazihat* (disgrace, ignominy or stigma) being the opposite of *fazilat* (excellence, virtue or dignity). Returning to the issue of Sher Shah's keeping more than one governor in the same province, this arrangement did not last for long. Constantly engaged in administrative reshuffles, and realizing that the arrangement did not function successfully, Sher Shah gave the charge of the whole of Punjab including Multan to Haibat Khan. Other nobles were withdrawn. Haibat Khan was to be assisted by Fateh Jang, who in turn was given the charge of Multan. Other provinces such as Bihar and Malwa also came to have faujdars, answerable directly to the emperor.

As in the case of Bengal, the provinces were divided into sarkars. The executive head of the sarkar was called a faujdar, muqta, or *shiqqdar-i-shiqqdaran*. The faujdar was an important military officer who wielded authority over all the government servants in the *shiqqs* under the Delhi sultans. Sher Shah revived the institution of *faujdari* just after he had established his sway over the vast territories in North India. In all the sarkars reserved for the khalisa, faujdars were posted as the head of the government. The muqta, who also appears to have held the charge of

---

[72] Siddiqui, *A History of Sher Shah Sur*, p. 123. Saran, *Provincial Government*, p. 51.

[73] *Provincial Government*, pp. 49–50.

[74] *Tarikh-i-Sher Shahi*, p. 216.

certain sarkars, enjoyed a higher status in the nobility than the faujdar, and for this reason they were assigned almost the full or a major portion of the revenue, yielded in a sarkar.[75] The references to the designation shiqqdar-i-shiqqdaran for the head of the sarkar are also to be found in the sources.[76] Saran likens the sarkar to the present day Commissioner's division, serving as a medium of communication between the provincial government and the district (pargana) and as an agency of general supervision over the pargana administration. He notes that the executive head of the sarkar was the shiqqdar-i-shiqqdaran or chief shiqqdar, with whom the office of faujdar was also generally combined.[77] Siddiqui doubts whether Sher Shah created the office of the shiqqdar-i-shiqqdaran. He suggests that Rizqullah Mushtaqi referred to shiqqdar-i-shiqqdaran because the officer being the executive-cum-military head of the sarkar held authority over so many pargana shiqqdars in his sarkar and forgot to indicate his real designation of faujdar or muqta. Later authorities Abbas Khan and Abdullah have merely quoted from Mushtaqi. Thus, Siddiqui concludes, in the absence of any independent source other than Mushtaqi's it cannot be presumed that shiqqdar-i-shiqqdaran was ever adopted by Sher Shah as an official appellation to be used for the head of the sarkar government.[78]

The head of the sarkar who combined in himself the functions of the military and those of the executive officer was expected to provide military support required, if any, in the realization of revenue, and to maintain law and order. Together with *munsif-i-munsifan*, the supreme judicial officer in the sarkar who handled revenue matters as well, he kept himself posted with the affairs of the parganas. According to the Afghan chronicler, Abbas Sarwani, they ensured that no injustice was committed against the raiyat. Further, they were to settle boundary-disputes between the amils of the parganas. Finally, when the raiyat created trouble in the collection of revenue, they were to subdue them by exemplary punishment which would serve as a deterrent.[79] Under Akbar

---

[75] Siddiqui, *A History of Sher Shah Sur*, pp. 117–19.

[76] *Waqi'at-i-Mushtaqi*, fol. 50b; *Tarikh-i-Sher Shahi*, p. 211; *Tarikh-i-Da'udi*, p. 213.

[77] *Provincial Government*, pp. 69–70.

[78] *Sher Shah Sur*, pp. 121–2.

[79] *Tarikh-i-Sher Shahi*, p. 211. Abdullah also records that the shiqqdar-i-shiqqdaran and the munsif-i-munsifan were expected to ensure that the raiyat was not oppressed and the revenue was not embezzled, *Tarikh-i-Da'udi*, p. 213.

the head of the sarkar known as the faujdar was to assist the *amalguzar* (incharge of revenue) in the realization of revenue. His main function was to guard the rural areas of his sarkar. In the army he regularly inspected the local militia and kept it well-equipped and in good trim.[80]

The *daroghas* or *thanedars*, who could have the ranks even of one thousand sawars, were posted in the *thanas* established at strategic points for the protection of highways from the robbers. The thanas were also to be found in small towns. In the big cities such as Lahore, the officer in charge of the police administration was known as the *kotwal*. The post of the kotwal was civil in nature. He had quite a large staff at his disposal, and was responsible for the maintenance of law and order in the city. The kotwal's soldiers could be seen patrolling the city at night. Another official with varying responsibilities posted in the cities was the shiqqdar. While, he looked after the civil and police administration of the city of Delhi, he was responsible for the development of the new city at Qannauj and keeping the roads safe from the highway-robbers.[81] Besides, a network of courts was said to be functioning from the province downwards, in every sarkar and pargana headquarters.[82]

Finally, to turn to the lowest unit of Sher Shah's administration, the sarkars were further divided into parganas. Sher Shah's reforms, innovations, and efforts for the efficient functioning of the general administration of the pargana, including its revenue administration, has been appreciated by scholars.[83] However, R.P. Tripathi has a different opinion. Though he recognizes Sher Shah's 'aim to revitalize the government and introduce efficiency', Tripathi suggests that it was 'unhistorical to say that Sher Shah created any new pargana machinery of the government unknown to the early Sultans. What he is credited with having done he had already found in operation when he took the charge of his father's Jagir. Sher Shah was not an innovator'.[84] By contrast, our

[80] Saran, *Provincial Government*, p. 193.

[81] *Tarikh-i-Sher Shahi*, pp. 213–14; Siddiqui, *Sher Shah Sur*, pp. 118 and 122.

[82] Saran, *Provincial Government*, pp. 198 and 337.

[83] H.N. Sinha, 'Sher Shah's Parganas and their Administrative Officials', *IHQ*, Vol. XVI, No. 1, March 1940, pp. 166–9; Saran, *Provincial Government*; Qanungo, *Sher Shah and his Times*; Ishwari Prasad, *The Life and Times of Humayun*.

[84] Tripathi, *Muslim Administration*, p. 356. See also, Siddiqui, *Sher Shah Sur*, p. 104.

earliest Persian authority, Rizqullah Mushtaqi suggests that in every pargana Sher Shah appointed a shiqqdar, a munsif, a khazanadar, a *munsif-i-khazana*, a Persian writer (*parsi-nawis*) and a Hindvi writer (*hindi-nawis*).[85] Following him, Abdullah mentions shiqqdar, amin, *khotadar*, clerk (Hindvi), and clerk (Persian), but drops munsif-i-khazana from the list of officials at pargana level.[86] The Afghan historian, Abbas Sarwani also does not refer to munsif-i-khazana in his list of officials which included a shiqqdar, an amin (or an amil), a *fotahdar*, a *karkun* (clerk) to write in Hindi, a karkun to write in Persian, and a *qanungo*.[87]

The shiqqdar being the executive head of the pargana was incharge of the general administration, including law and order and criminal justice.[88] The terms amil, amin, and munsif, were synonymous in the administrative terminology of Sher Shah's time. The official was responsible for the mandatory annual assessment and realization of revenue from the pargana. Besides, he also assisted the shiqqdar together with the headmen of the villages in maintaining law and order and punishing the miscreants.[89] Being a lucrative post with a number of incentives, a revenue officer was posted in the pargana for a maximum period of two years.[90] The revenue collected from the pargana was to be kept in the treasury the incharge of which was called the khazanadar, khotadar or the fotahdar, as noted above.[91] The

[85] *Waqi'at-i-Mushtaqi*, fol. 50b.

[86] *Tarikh-i-Da'udi*, p. 213.

[87] *Tarikh-i-Sher Shahi*, pp. 210–11.

[88] According to Siddiqui, under Sher Shah, the shiqqdars governed the parganas and cities entrusted to their charge, and suppressed the rebels by cleaning the dense forests which they used as hideouts. They dispensed justice to all without discrimination. To make the shiqqdar more active in suppressing the criminals, Islam Shah held him responsible like the muqaddam for every crime committed within his jurisdiction, Siddiqui, 'Position of *Shiqqdar*', p. 206. However, Irfan Habib has suggested that the shiqqdar performed the role of the revenue collector only, 'Evidence for Sixteenth-Century Agrarian Conditions in the Guru Granth Sahib', *PIHC*, 25th Session, Poona, 1963, pp. 186–94, especially p. 191.

[89] Saran, *Provincial Government*, p.196. Irfan Habib suggests that the munsif seemed to be in control only over the assessment process, 'Evidence for Sixteenth-Century Agrarian Conditions', p. 191.

[90] *Tarikh-i-Sher Shahi*, p. 211.

[91] Under the Mughals the standard khazandar was retained, Saran, *Provincial Government*, p. 269.

reference to the munsif-i-khazana as a pargana official is to be found only in the *Waqi'at-i-Mushtaqi*. If such an officer existed he would be an inspector of treasuries and would belong to a bigger unit than a pargana.[92] The karkun was 'a sort of camp clerk and accountant in one', both to the chief amil and to the one in the pargana, who accompanied them on their tours of assessment. He maintained a record of the transaction which took place between the officials and the cultivators at the time of assessment, on behalf of the government so that the collector might compare his accounts with those of the headman and the patwari.[93] For a convenient functioning of the local administration, a duplicate set of clerks for the purpose of keeping records in Hindvi was appointed. The qanungo referred to by Abbas Khan was probably a semi-government official who kept a record of the past and present state of agriculture in the pargana and was expected to indicate the future prospects as well.[94] He was paid by means of a commission of one per cent of the assessed revenue.[95] In every village there was a muqaddam and a patwari. The former assisted the revenue officials in the collection and served as a link between them and the peasantry within his jurisdiction. For this service he was given a percentage of the revenue allowed to him by the government. The patwari kept all the agricultural records of the village. He also received one per cent commission for his service.[96]

Though it will be difficult to establish that the intermediary headmen were completely removed and direct links were forged with the cultivators at the pargana level throughout the empire, it is clear that the attempts made by Sher Shah witnessed a larger degree of diffusion of the state authority at the local level. J.F. Richards points out that Sher Shah's revenue measures were flawed by excessive uniformity.

[92] Ishtiaq Husain Qureshi, *The Administration of the Sultanate of Delhi*, fifth revised edition (Delhi, 1971), p. 260.

[93] Saran, *Provincial Government*, p. 270.

[94] *Tarikh-i-Sher Shahi*, p. 211. According to Saran, he was in a way the head of the patwaris of his pargana since he had to keep the same records for the pargana as the patwari had to keep for the village, *Provincial Government*, p. 274.

[95] According to Saran, under Akbar the qanungos were paid cash salaries from the public treasury, *Provincial Government*, p. 274.

[96] For muqaddam and patwari, see Tripathi, *Muslim Administration*, p. 354. For patwari, also see, Saran, *Provincial Government*, pp. 259 and 275.

When his officials tried to fix near-uniform rates of assessment on the harvest across the entire domain, they generated considerable resistance. Converting harvest into cash with a single schedule for a large portion of North India was impracticable and created enormous inequities, as it ignored the differences in fertility between localities. Later, Todarmal understood and addressed this problem with more complete area and production statistics collected from the qanungos.[97]

Commenting on Sher Shah's administrative set-up, Parmatma Saran observes: 'It was this administrative organization which Akbar found in existence when he ascended the throne, and we are not told that he made any noteworthy modification in it. Nor was it possible or necessary for him to do so as Sher Shah's machinery was a very elaborate and well-tried one.... There were over a hundred Sarkars and three thousand parganas or mahals in the empire (of Akbar) in the year 1596 (40 regnal year). Excepting the adoption of new names for certain old offices and the introduction of some new functionaries, Akbar does not seem to have thought it advisable to make any material alterations in the framework of the sarkar or pargana government'.[98] In the light of the foregoing, it may not be unfair to say that even if the idealized portrayal of the Afghan rule in our sources is to be taken with some reservations, it is clear from the evidence adduced that Sher Shah's age, as suggested recently, formed a significant stage in the evolution of what we often tend to attribute to Akbar.[99] And this was not simply in administrative institutions. In the genealogy of the Indo-Persian ideals of governance too, the Afghan regime represented a notable stage. What is more significant is the fact that despite the overwhelming presence of the dominant Mughals for centuries after, Sher Shah seems to be remembered as the just and ideal ruler.[100] Important in this connection was the incorporation of non-Muslims in the Afghan attempts at empire-building.

[97] *The Mughal Empire*, pp. 83–4.

[98] *Provincial Government*, p. 70.

[99] Muzaffar Alam and Sanjay Subrahmanyam, 'Introduction', in their edited volume, *The Mughal State*.

[100] See for instance, S.H.Askari, '*Mirat-ul-Muluk*: A Contemporary Work Containing Reflections on Later Mughal Administration', *Indica*, The Indian Historical Research Institute Silver Jubilee Commemoration Volume, Bombay, 1953, pp. 27–37.

4

The Afghans and the Rajputs
Conflict and Accommodation

Common misfortune had brought the young *yavan* horseman Farid Khan
and the Ujjainiya prince Badal close together. Both of them having swords
in their hands, took vows to remain friendly to each other all through their
lives and to help each other in times of misfortune.

Bodhraj in Ujjjainiya ki Varta[1]

MODERN STUDIES CONCERNING HINDU-MUSLIM interactions in medieval
India have largely been conducted on two lines. On the one hand are
those historians whose approach implies virtual denial of the existence of separate Hindu-Muslim identities prior to the British rule. They
hold that the incidents of temple destruction were limited to a very
brief and early phase of encounter, the motivation being economic
aggrandizement rather than religious zeal. In their views, all the ills in
this connection emanate from the British colonial construction.[2] On

---

[1] Bodhraj, *Ujjainiya ki Varta*, Eng. trans, B.P. Ambashthya, in *Non-Persian
Sources of Indian Medieval History* (Delhi, 1984), p. 22. Bodhraj belonged to Pugal
in Bikaner. He was a contemporary of Nain Singh, the author of the famous *Khyat*,
and the Prime Minister of Jodhpur in the second-half of the seventeenth century.
Bodhraj travelled a lot in search of the material for his history of the Pramaras,
and visited Jagdishpur in Shahabad district of Bihar in 1719 V.S/AD 1663, where
he stayed for six months, ibid., foreword, pp. I–IV. Also see Brahmadeva Prasad
Ambashthya, 'Tradition and Genealogy of the Ujjainiyas in Bihar', *PIHC*, 24th
Session, Delhi, 1961, pp. 122–7.

[2] This is clearly reflected in the numerous writings of, among others, M. Habib,
M. Mujeeb, K.A. Nizami and S.A.A. Rizvi. For example, Mujeeb refers to the in-
stallation of Sanskrit inscriptions in mosques and other buildings as evidence of
communal harmony in the Delhi Sultanate, *Islamic Influence on Indian Society*

the other hand, there has existed a group of 'separatist' and 'communal' scholars. The Muslims among them believe that Hindus and Muslims are two different 'nations'. For this view, they seek legitimacy in
the writings and activities of the Naqshbandi Sufi, Mujaddid Alf-i-Sani
Shaykh Ahmad Sirhindi in the early seventeenth century, if not in
Muhammad bin Qasim's conquest of Sindh in 711–12.[3] The Hindu
historians in this group assert that medieval India under Islamic rulers, with large-scale destruction of temples and constant humiliation
faced by the Hindus represented a dark phase of India's history. From
this perspective, most of the evils facing the Hindus today are a legacy
of Muslim rule in India.[4]

In recent years there have also been some attempts independent of
these two rigidly demarcated approaches, but they are limited to a few,
even though very important, aspects.[5] In the following pages we have
extended, in a measure, this approach in a more comprehensive manner. Such an exercise is necessary as the diverse views on the question
of Hindu-Muslim relations and forms of religious identities in medieval India need to be reconsidered and revised in a large measure. It
appears that religious identities, in their various forms, did exist in the
period. It is also clearly visible that in the conflict over political control
of a territory, mobilization on religious lines was not uncommon; also,
religious symbols were frequently used. Muslims seemed to be engaged

---

(Meerut, 1972), pp.114–27. For a more recent assertion of Hindu-Muslim harmony, see M. Ifzal-ur-Rahman Khan, 'The Attitude of the Delhi Sultans Towards
non-Muslims: Some Observations', *Islamic Culture*, Vol. 69: 2, April 1995, pp. 41–
56. Also see, Romila Thapar, *Somanatha*.

[3] A leading exponent of this separatist narrative is I.H. Qureshi, *The Muslim
Community of the Indo-Pakistan Subcontinent*. For a 'liberal' Muslim attack on
the 'reactionary' and 'Sunni fanatic' Shaykh Ahmad Sirhindi who 'sought to whip
up communal frenzy' in medieval India, see Rizvi, *Muslim Revivalist Movements
in Northern India*. For criticisms on similar lines and dismissal of the shaykh's
influence over the Mughal political elite as unimportant, see also, Mujeeb, *Indian
Muslims*.

[4] See, for example, K.S. Lal, *The Legacy of Muslim Rule in India* (Delhi, 1992).

[5] Muzaffar Alam, 'Competition and Coexistence'; idem, 'Assimilation from a
Distance'; Richard Eaton, 'Temple Desecration and Indo-Muslim States', in idem,
Essays on Islam and Indian History (Delhi, 2000), pp. 94–132; Carl W. Ernst, 'Ad-
miring the Works of the Ancients: The Ellora Temples as Viewed by Indo-Muslim
Authors', in Gilmartin and Lawrence, eds, *Beyond Turk and Hindu*, pp. 198–220.

in a recurrent jihad against the *kuffar*[6] (sing. *kafir*) or infidels/Hindus in India, with hordes of *ghazis* (victorious soldiers) and *shahids* (martyrs) indulging in large-scale loot and plunder, including razing of temples, gaining thereby rich rewards both 'here' (in this world) and 'hereafter' (in the next).

The experience of Indian Islam, however, was special in the sense that here the Muslims had come to live with the infidels albeit in the dominant position as rulers. The Muslim rulers with all their pretensions of following the shari'at had not converted the conquered territories into *dar-ul-Islam*[7] in the strictly orthodox sense of the term, nor did they convert the entire local population to Islam. In peaceful context, non-Muslims were given the status of the *zimmi*s or *ahl-i-kitab*.[8] The zimmi is defined as against the Muslim and the idolater (kafir). Originally only Jews and Christians were involved. Subsequently, it became necessary to consider Zoroastrians, a number of minor faiths in Central Asia and the Hindus in the subcontinent. The inhabitants of India were treated as zimmis, though classical Quranic exegesis did not regard them as Ahl-i-Kitab or the People of the Book. This expansion of the concept entailed a compromise with idolatry that was not acceptable to all the schools of jurisprudence (*mazahib*). The Shafi'i and Hanbali jurists (*fuqaha*) counted only Jews, Christians and Zoroastrians as zimmis. On the other hand, the Malikites and the Hanafites included among them all non-Muslims (even idolaters) who were not Arabs or apostates (*murtad*). The preponderant Hanafite position enabled medieval Indian rulers to legally justify a tolerant policy or attitude towards the Hindus. Significantly, the decision to

[6] The word *kafir* is used in the Quran with reference to the unbelieving Meccans who endeavoured to refute and revile the Prophet. Not only were the non-believers threatened with God's punishment and help for denying or 'concealing' his blessings, the Muslims were ordered to keep apart from them, and to defend themselves from their attacks and even to take the offensive against them. W. Bjorkman, 'Kafir', *Encyclopaedia of Islam* (New Edition), Vol. 4 (Leiden, 1978), pp. 407–9.

[7] Dar-ul-Islam, 'the land of Islam' is the whole territory in which the law of Islam prevails. In the classical doctrine, everything outside dar-ul-Islam is dar-ul-harb or 'the land of war', A. Abel, 'Dar al-Islam', *Encyclopaedia of Islam* (New Edition), Vol. 2 (Leiden, 1991), pp. 127–8.

[8] G. Vajda, 'Ahl al-Kitab', *Encyclopaedia of Islam* (New Edition), Vol. 1 (Leiden, 1986), pp. 264–6.

categorize Indian idolaters as zimmis is attributed to Muhammad bin Qasim, the early eighth century Arab conqueror of Sindh, who had reportedly stated that the idol-temples of the Hindus were similar to the churches of the Christians, synagogues of the Jews and fire-temples of the Zoroastrians. Despite occasional demands for strict regulations, the status of the Hindus as zimmis was not questioned in a serious way.[9] Yet, the 'virtual consensus' on the legal standing of the Hindus did not preclude the emergence of great variations in Muslim attitudes towards them in a more general sense. These attitudes range from 'utmost hostility to almost total acceptance of Hindu religious beliefs'.[10]

Further, it will be important to keep in mind the fact that the evolution of ideas in this regard in classical Islamic thought has shown two aspects at once different and interdependent. On the one hand are the doctrinaires, found mainly among the jurists and the judges, who have interpreted the regulations in a restrictive way seeking to develop a programme which, if not one of persecution, is at least vexatious and repressive. From time to time a sovereign, either through Islamic zeal or through the need for popularity amongst Muslims, ordained measures to the doctrinaires' satisfaction. Sometimes, also, there were outbursts of popular anger against the zimmis, which in some cases arose from the places occupied by them in the higher ranks of administration, especially that of finance. Several examples can be given in the medieval Indian context of the articulation of such protests, for instance, by Ziya-ud-Din Barani, Abdul Quddus Gangohi, Abdul Qadir Badauni and Shaykh Ahmad Sarhindi. But indeed, on the other hand, current practice fell very much short of the programme of the purists, which was hardly ever implemented. Moreover, the different schools of jurisprudence are not all in agreement and some of them reiterate rules without any practical effect.[11]

Islam tolerated the religion of the zimmis subject to the following restrictions: it was forbidden to insult Islam and to seek to convert a Muslim. Both the preacher and the apostate could receive death

---

[9] Yohanan Friedmann, 'Islamic Thought in Relation to the Indian Context', first published in 1986, reprinted in Richard M. Eaton, ed., *India's Islamic Traditions, 711–1750* (Delhi, 2003), pp. 52–3.

[10] Ibid., p. 53.

[11] Cl. Cahen, 'Dhimma', *Encyclopaedia of Islam*, New Edition, Vol. 2 (Leiden, 1991), pp. 227–31.

penalty. Existing places of worship were protected, construction of new buildings forbidden and reconstruction of old buildings fallen into decay opposed by the rigorists. There were also various limitations on the outward expression of worship, such as processions and the use of bells, though these were not strictly implemented in the early centuries of Islam. The same is true for the Delhi Sultanate. But in the contemporary Mamluk state, due to pressures from various factors including the Crusades, Mongol invasions and the campaigns by Muslim religious leader like Ibn Taimiyya, various regulations concerning the zimmis were implemented with varying degree of success. This included a distinguishing type of dress, mounts were to be reduced to nothing better than a donkey and a new restriction, with an Italian parallel, forbade them to possess houses higher than those occupied by Muslims.[12] This may perhaps explain generally the non-descript nature of Hindu places of worship in medieval India, compared to the grandeur of mosques, tombs and palaces of the Muslims. In Muslim context, the building of the mosque should be higher than those of the residential quarters of the neighbourhood.

The zimmis of a territory conquered by the Muslims had to pay a tax (*jizya*) which, from the point of view of the latter, was material proof of their subjection. It is also suggested that for the inhabitants it was merely a continuation of the taxes paid to earlier regimes. In classical Islam, jizya was to be levied only on those who were male, adult, free, capable and able bodied, so that children, old men, women, invalids, slaves, beggars, the sick and the mentally deranged were excluded.[13] Though at times a pietistic sovereign seemed to be concerned about the violations of the rules by the zimmis, the occasional intolerance was often due to political and economic factors, or for the need for legitimacy.

The nature of relationship between the Afghans and the Rajputs in our period of study is an important problem, which needs careful consideration. Generally, rulers like Sikandar Lodi and Sher Shah are condemned in the historiography as bigots. Undoubtedly, the Persian sources from the Mughal period have contributed to the making of such an image of the Afghan rulers. Sikandar Lodi is reported to have

---

[12] Ibid.

[13] See the entries on 'Djizya' by Cl. Cahen, Halil Inalcik and P. Hardy in *Encyclopaedia of Islam* (New Edition), Vol. 2 (Leiden, 1991), pp. 559–67.

levelled to the ground all the places of worship of the kafirs. Though they recognize the exaggerated phraseology of the chroniclers, most modern authorities pick up the examples of intolerance from the sources to illustrate the fanaticism of the rulers. In the case of Sikandar Lodi the examples which are cited include (a) his desire as a youth to put an end to the bathing festival at Kurukshetra; (b) the execution in his reign of a Brahman who had declared that 'Islam was true, but his own religion was also true', and had refused to convert to Islam; (c) at Mathura and other places, he wanted to convert some temples into mosques; (d) release of a Hindu prisoner from jail and giving an important assignment on the condition of his embracing Islam; (e) he banned the worship of goddess Shitla; (f) display of ta'ziyas (replicas of the shrines of Hasan and Husain, grandsons of Prophet Muhammad) during Muharram and the annual procession of the standard of Salar Mas'ud Ghazi were stopped; (g) women were forbidden to visit the tombs; and (h) barbers were prevented from shaving the Hindus at Mathura.[14] However, the incidents, which portray Sikandar Lodi's uncompromising attitude do not point to a definite and persistent policy of persecution of non-Muslims. The acts of violence recorded in early Persian sources were linked to rebellions in the regions, or were a part of political subjugation. Yet, modern historians ignore the context and condemn Sikandar Lodi as a bigot.[15]

The chieftains who accepted the suzerainty of the Afghan kings and paid tributes were allowed to administer the territories under their control. Several examples can be given from the reign of Bahlul Lodi, but they are not discussed or highlighted by the Muslim chroniclers, as they did not involve any cry for jihad. Instead, the chroniclers focus on the 'rebels', for instance, the Bachgoti Rajputs under Sikandar Lodi, who were to be eliminated or subdued, and campaigns against whom were portrayed as jihad involving destruction of temples as well.[16] On the contrary, the chroniclers do not show much enthusiasm in narrating the kings' campaigns against the Muslim administrators in the regions. The Afghan sovereigns reinstated those administrators who

[14] For some such examples recorded in the late-sixteenth century Persian histories, see *Waqi'at-i-Mushtaqi*, fols. 8b, 9a–b; *Tabaqat-i-Akbari*. Also see the previous chapter.

[15] See for instance, K.S. Lal, *Twilight of the Sultanate* (Bombay, 1963), p. 192.

[16] *Tabaqat-i-Akbari*.

did not oppose them and included their name in the khutba and the sikka while those opposing them were to be crushed. We shall further illustrate the Afghan rulers' attitude towards the Rajputs through Sher Shah's campaigns in Rajasthan and Malwa.

With the Mughals driven out of Hindustan and the pretender Mallu Khan, styled as Qadir Shah, made to realize that kingship was not his cup of wine,[17] the politico-military suzerainty of the Afghans under Sher Shah was poised to take on the formidable Rajputs in Rajasthan and Malwa. There were two options open to the Afghan ruler in the matter. One was to force or persuade the chieftains to accept his political supremacy and allow them to run the local administration with his governors supervising the affairs of the region from 'above'. This arrangement could have served several purposes. The acceptance of the ritual status of the king as the sovereign of Hindustan meant expansion in Rajput strongholds without much resistance and violence. The indirect rule initially arranged could gradually become more pervasive, and the local administration may in course of time be centralized. Moreover, acceptance of political subordination ensured the flow of revenue in the form of annual tributes without much care for the revenue extraction machinery in a newly subjugated area. Finally, the chieftains and their retainers once integrated in the imperial army through such measures as the rule of branding,[18] could well be used for subsequent campaigns in other regions such as the Deccan,[19] and later for more ambitious plans to conquer Afghanistan[20] and Coastal Iran.[21]

The other option was to aim at a direct and uniform rule throughout the dominion, involving annihilation of the Rajput chieftaincies with large-scale loss of soldiers on both sides. Even if a capable but reckless Muslim empire-builder took such a step, the problem of legitimacy for ruling the predominantly non-Muslim population would

---

[17] *Waqiʻat-i-Mushtaqi*, fols. 52a–53b; *Tarikh-i-Sher Shahi*, pp. 173–8; *Tarikh-i-Daʼudi*, pp. 140–6; *Tarikh-i-Khan-i-Jahani wa Makhzan-i-Afghani*, Vol. I, pp. 318–20; *Tabaqat-i-Akbari*, fol. 203b.

[18] For the rajas bringing their soldiers for dagh, see *Waqiʻat-i-Mushtaqi*, fols. 51a–b.

[19] *Tarikh-i-Sher Shahi*, p. 194.

[20] *Tarikh-i-Khan-i-Jahani wa Makhzan-i-Afghani*, Vol. I, p. 335.

[21] *Muntakhab-ut-Tawarikh*, Vol. I, pp. 369–70.

continue to haunt him. Sher Shah realized that the first option was much more viable. Thus his policy towards Rajputs was primarily aimed at incorporating them in his imperial network. The significance of the incorporation of the 'loyal' Rajput clans was already brought home to him in his early career as the shiqqdar of his father's iqta in Bihar. He befriended the loyal zamindars and destroyed the belligerent ones. Subsequently, he conferred zamindari rights on the Ujjainiya Rajputs along with the others. The Ujjainiyas, whom Sher Shah favoured in the beginning of his career, sprang into prominence after his rise to power.[22]

As noted in chapter two, Bodhraj refers to the significant role played by Gajpati, styled as Maharaja Gajraj, and his two thosand Ujjainiya Rajputs in Sher Khan's victory in the battle of Surajgarh against the sultan of Bengal. In fact, it is suggested that the leader of the Bengal army, Ibrahim, was killed at the hands of Gajpati while trying to escape from the battlefield. Sher Khan was much pleased with Gajpati for his bravery, and allowed him to retain the spoils of war, comprising elephants, horses and other equipments which had fallen into his hands. At the time of the Maharaja's departure, Sher Khan tied with his own hands the bejeweled sword on his waist, bound his arm with bejeweled armlet, placed a string of pearl around his neck, put a bejeweled *kalangi* on his *sirpech* (head-dress), and gave the territory of Baksar in assignment. Besides, some gifts for the Maharaja's younger brother, Bairisal, were also sent.[23] It may be noted that Gajapati and Bairishal were the sons of Badal with whom Sher Khan had, in his younger days, entered into an alliance of friendship.[24]

[22] Siddiqui, *Afghan Despotism*, p. 96. Also, the Raghuvanshis of Jalhupur and Sheopur in Banaras owed their rise from the days of Sher Shah when Daman Deo, their ancestor received from the Afghan ruler the rent-free grant of the pargana of Katehar. The place he made his headquarters was named Chandrawati after his wife, or daughter. He also built a massive fort there on the steep bank of the Ganges the ruins of which are the reminder of his prowess, *Uttar Pradesh District Gazetteers, Varanasi* (Lucknow, 1965), p. 49.

[23] *Ujjainiya ki Varta*, pp. 25–33. Also see, Syed Hasan Askari, 'The Ujjainiya Ancestors of Babu Kuar Singh', *Journal of the Bihar Research Society* (Hereafter *JBRS*) Vo. XLI, Part I, March 1955, pp. 106–31; Brahmadeva Prasad Ambashthya, 'The Accounts of the Ujjainiyas in Bihar', *JBRS*, Vol. XLVII, Parts 1–4, January–December 1964, pp. 420–40.

[24] *Ujjainiya ki Varta*, pp. 22–4.

During his campaigns in Malwa and Rajasthan after ascending the throne, the rajas were left untouched in their ancestral possessions on usual conditions of obedience and service to the king. Such Rajput bastions as Chittor, which had long tradition of resistance to Muslim rule, were peacefully captured by Sher Shah, with the rajas formally handing over the keys of the forts to his officials. After the formal subjugation, the chieftains were reinstated on their ancestral seats of power (*gaddis*). According to Abbas Sarwani, Sher Shah marched towards Chittor following the campaign against Maldeo in 950/1543. When the fort of Chittor remained only at the distance of twelve *kos*, the raja of the palace sent him its keys. Thus Sher Shah came into the fort, and appointed Shamsher Khan (the younger brother of Khawas Khan), Mian Ahmad Sarwani and Husain Khan Ghilzai as its in-charge.[25] Based on an inscription found on a step-well called Ganesh Baori at Toda Raising, dated V.S. 1604/1547, D.C. Sircar has suggested that Rana Udaysimha offered his allegiance to Sher Shah in 1543 or 1544 and continued to rule as a feudatory of the Surs for some years even after the death of Sher Shah and the accession of Islam Shah to the throne.[26] Even Chanderi for which Babur had to fight a much-trumpeted jihad came in Sher Shah's control without any bloodshed. The fort was soon handed over to a more legitimate Rajput claimant.

Devoid of any war cry for the cause of Islam, these peaceful conquests could not take the pride of place in the late sixteenth century Muslim expansionist discourse, which forms the basis of modern knowledge on Sher Shah. It seems that the popularity of jihad in the Sunni Muslim circles was heightened during the period. Knowing that what sold was the account of 'resistance' and how it was overcome, intellectual labour accordingly emphasized the importance of the role of sword or gun, and as also on the invisible men of God, or the mardan-i-ghayb, who were said to have fought on behalf of Sher Shah. The latter's 'achievements', that is, the destruction of chieftains who had refused to accept the imperial authority, is extolled. For instance,

[25] *Tarikh-i-Sher Shahi*, pp. 198–9.

[26] D.C. Sircar, 'Rana Udayasimha and the Sur Emperors of Delhi', *IHQ*, Vol. 30, No. 1, 1954, pp. 25–30 and 'Rana Udayasimha's Relations with Islam Shah', *IHQ*, Vol. 31, No. 3, 1955, pp. 273–5. For a different opinion, see Arya Ramachandra G. Tiwari, 'Maharana Uday Singh and the Sur Emperors of Delhi', *IHQ*, Vol. 30, No. 4, 1954, pp. 311–26.

Rizqullah Mushtaqi takes pleasure in recording that Sher Shah achieved three grand victories through the blessing of God. One of them was the destruction of Maharath Chero; second, the infidels of Raisin[27] were massacred and, third Maldeo was driven away from his wilayat and Islam and Muslims were again strengthened in the *khitta* of Nagaur.[28] We shall return below to the Muslim chroniclers' perception of Sher Shah's action against certain Rajput warlords and see how they were shaped by the ethnic, political and ideological affiliations of the authors themselves, and the context in which they were producing their works. Besides, we shall take up the writings of some modern scholars to see their treatment of medieval accounts and point out how their conclusions were also influenced by the dominant historiographical trend of their own time.

It will be appropriate here to turn to the Rajputs who dared to offer resistance to Sher Shah, and see what was in store for them. The Afghans continuously bombarded the besieged chieftains. For a change, artillery came to play an important role in Sher Shah's campaigns. Earlier, the highly mobile cavalry gave a death blow to the sultanate of Bengal and to the Mughals led by Humayun. Recollecting the shocking affairs of Chausa and Qannauj, the Mughals however erroneously felt that artillery was the mainstay of Sher Shah's army.[29] It may also be noted that though their increasing presence must have curtailed the mobility of his army, Sher Shah made a judicious use of the elephants in destroying the Rajput death squads attacking the Afghans with *barchhas*, or swords in hands. Returning to the besieged Rajputs, they had at least three options. Firstly, they could still ask for terms, accept a subordinate position, and shift to a different territory assigned to

---

[27] Raisen district of the Bhopal Commissioner's division in Madhya Pradesh lies mostly on the Malwa plateau and partly in the Narmada valley, *Madhya Pradesh District Gazetteers, Raisen* (Bhopal, 1979), p. 1.

[28] *Waqiʿat-i-Mushtaqi*, fol. 56b.

[29] It may be noted that gunpowder had come to India from China before 1351 through varied agencies and channels. It came to Bengal and Calicut through sea, and to Assam by land. In the north-west, it was introduced by the Mongols in the second half of the thirteenth century, Iqtidar Alam Khan, 'The Role of the Mongols in the Introduction of Gunpowder and Firearms in India', *PIHC*, 55th Session, Aligarh, 1994, pp. 194–200; idem, 'Origin and Development of Gunpowder Technology in India: AD 1250–1500', *IHR*, Vol. 4, No. 1, July 1977, pp. 20–9.

them. Secondly, having vacated the fort they could go to any area hitherto not in control of Sher Shah. Finally, pushed to a point from where they could only think in terms of resorting to *jauhar*, and fight to the finish. These three options were available to Puranmal of Malwa, Maldeo of Rajasthan, and to Kirat Singh of Kalinjar.

Puranmal was allowed by Sher Shah, during his Malwa campaign shortly after the victory at Qannauj, to continue to hold the charge of the fort of Raisin and the adjoining region, although he was amongst those guilty of not responding to the farman to attack Agra and Delhi in collaboration with Sher Shah's son Qutb Khan leading to his death at the hands of the Mughals.[30] But the die was cast when Puranmal upheld the cause of some Muslim administrators, who were resisting Sher Shah's expansion in Malwa. Accordingly, the king started his Malwa campaign for the second time and came to besiege the fort of Raisin (1543). After the siege of the fort for six months when the continuous cannon-shots began to breach the wall of the fort on all sides, Puranmal was struck with fear and came out in person to pay his respects to Sher Shah. Soon it was agreed that Puranmal would vacate the fort and hand over its charge to Sher Shah's nobles. Sher Shah's son Adil Khan and the nobleman Qutb Khan Naib gave the assurance of the safety of Purnamal and his family. Puranmal came out of the fort and occupied the place allotted to him by Sher Shah in the middle of his army camp. Surrounded from all sides by the Afghans, the chieftain had no scope for flight in the eventuality of a sudden attack on him. Armed with a *fatwa* (juristical ruling) from the leading Muslim religious leaders, Sher Shah ordered the massacre of the Rajputs. Even before they were attacked, the Rajputs started killing their women and children, and then rushed out to die in honour. Barring a few wounded women and children, they were all put to death.[31]

Sher Shah's attention then turned towards Rajasthan. The decade (1530–40) during which Humayun was preoccupied with his campaigns against Bahadur Shah in Malwa and Gujarat, and Sher Shah in the east, the chieftains in Rajputana were left to fend for themselves.

---

[30] See chapter two.

[31] *Waqi'at-i-Mushtaqi*, fols. 54b–56a; *Tarikh-i-Da'udi*, pp. 151–5; *Tarikh-i-Sher Shahi*, pp. 183–92; *Tarikh-i-Khan-i-Jahani wa Makhzan-i-Afghani*, Vol. I, pp. 323–6; *Tabaqat-i-Akbari*, fols. 203b–204a. Also see, *Tarikh-i-Farishta* (RAS Microfilm), p. 374; *Khulasat-ut-Tawarikh* (RAS Microfilm), pp. 394–5.

Free from any threat of intervention from outside, Maldeo of Jodhpur had emerged as the most powerful raja of the region annihilating all the smaller chieftaincies around, including Nagaur and Ajmer which had sizeable Muslim presence. Nagaur had been captured from the control of a Muslim administrator during the reign of Sultan Ibrahim Lodi.[32] The emergence of Marwar under Maldeo is attributed to his ability to assemble huge forces and to exploit the mobility that the greater use of horses allowed, though at this stage horses were not used by the Rajputs in combat.[33]

The capture of a territory from the control of a Muslim administrator was a sufficient provocation for the Afghan rulers. If the khutba and the sikka had any meaning for the general Muslim population in North India, the ruler was expected to respond to the challenge. More serious from the point of view of the Mughal-Afghan interface was Maldeo's non-cooperation in capturing fugitive Humayun who had sought to use Rajasthan as a base to fight back against Sher Shah.[34] Besides, the small chieftains smarting under the 'highhandedness' of Maldeo were inviting Sher Shah to undertake a campaign in the region against the raja. A Sanskrit work called *Karma Chandra Vansotkirtankam Kavya*, composed in 1593, records that Jet Singh, Rao of Bikaner, being attacked by Maldeo, sent his minister Nag Raj to Sher Shah to seek help against the Rathor prince. The chief of Merta, Biram also reportedly sought his aid against his oppressor.[35] Thus, Sher Shah started his campaign against Maldeo in 950/1543-44. Instead of allowing the Afghans to besiege him in a fort, Maldeo came with a large body of horsemen to the borders of Ajmer and began skirmishes. Sher Shah found himself in danger when he learned that his supply line was cut off by the Rajputs. Maldeo however became suspicious of

[32] *Waqi'at-i-Mushtaqi*, fol. 56b; *Tarikh-i-Sher Shahi*, p. 195. For the rise of Maldeo, see also James Tod, *Annals* and *Antiquities of Rajasthan or the Central and Western Rajput States of India*, ed., William Crooke, Vol. II, reprint (Delhi, 1971), pp. 954–5; Ishwari Prasad, *Life and Times of Humayun*, p. 175.

[33] Cf. Norman P. Ziegler, 'Evolution of the Rathor State of Marwar: Horses, Structural Changes and Warfare', in Karine Schomer, John L. Eradman, and Deryck O. Lodrick, eds, *The Idea of Rajasthan—Explorations in Regional Identity*, Vol. II, *Institutions* (Delhi, 1994), pp. 192–216.

[34] Siddiqui, *Afghan Despotism*, p. 104.

[35] Ishwari Prasad, *Life and Times of Humayun*, p. 176; Siddiqui, *Afghan Despotism*, p. 104.

the loyalty of his nobles, and fled from the place. His nobles decided to offer a fight, and some two thousand Rajput soldiers were massacred.[36]

In the case of Kalinjar that cost Sher Shah his life, Raja Kirat Singh did not ask for peace. In view of the massacre at Raisin, the ruler must have held that any terms of agreement with Sher Shah were meaningless. The Afghan ruler was thus compelled to capture the fort by force. Abbas Sarwani however suggested that the motive behind the capture of the fort was to acquire a dancing girl in Kirat Singh's harem, about whom Sher Shah had heard a lot of praise. If he seized the fort by force, the chieftain would certainly cause jauhar and thus burn that slave girl as well.[37] Be that as it may, the fort was captured by force. The Afghans carried out a general massacre and 'sent all the non-believers to hell'. The raja who had confined himself in a house with his seventy soldiers was killed by the Afghans, after Sher Shah had succumbed to the burns on 10 Rabi I 952/22 May 1545.[38]

The chroniclers' celebration of Sher Shah's reported action against the chieftains in conflict may have stemmed from a search in the late sixteenth and early seventeenth century for an alternative in the wake of emperor Akbar's alleged deviation from Islam. Thus, while the accounts of Sher Shah's conflict with the Bengalis or the Mughals are not entirely free from religious elements, his campaigns against the Rajputs have been portrayed as jihad. The reasons for his action are generally given as aggrandizement of the rajas, denigration of Islam and humiliation of the Muslims at their hands.[39] In the accounts of Mushtaqi and Abdullah (who often copies Mushtaqi), Sher Shah is shown to be approaching the ulama for not only a fatwa to undertake a campaign against the infidels, but also to legalize the unilateral breach of oaths and vows, and chastisement of the infidels at an appropriate

---

[36] *Tarikh-i-Da'udi*, p. 157; *Tarikh-i-Sher Shahi*, pp. 196–8; *Tarikh-i-Khan-i-Jahani wa Makhzan-i-Afghani*, Vol. I, pp. 327–9; *Tabaqat-i-Akbari*, fols. 204a–b. Also see, *Tarikh-i-Farishta* (RAS Microfilm), pp. 374–5.

[37] *Tarikh-i-Sher Shahi*, p. 201.

[38] Ibid., pp. 201–4; *Waqi'at-i-Mushtaqi*, fols. 56b–57a; *Tarikh-i-Da'udi*, pp. 158–9; *Tarikh-i-Khan-i-Jahani wa Makhzan-i-Afghani*, Vol. I, pp. 329–31; *Tabaqat-i-Akbari*, fols. 204b–205a.

[39] Puranmal was said to have kept two thousand Muslim women in his harem as dancing girls, who were supposed to be liberated by Sher Shah, *Tarikh-i-Sher Shahi*, pp. 182–3; *Tarikh-i-Farishta* (RAS Microfilm), p. 374.

moment.[40] The Afghan chronicler Abbas Sarwani seeks to establish that either Sher Shah was compelled by popular pressure to ask for fatwa or he was merely acting in conformity with the 'just' suggestions of the leading ulama and Sufis who accompanied him during the campaigns.[41] Finally, Ni'matullah Harawi blatantly resorted to an alleged tradition of the Prophet, which sanctioned the legal validity of treachery with the enemy (al-harb khud'at).[42]

Significantly our earliest authorities have not been able to offer any tangible pretext for the siege and capture of Kalinjar. Nizam-ud-Din Ahmad notes that when Sher Shah marched towards Kalinjar, which was the strongest fort in Hindustan, the raja of Kalinjar took a hostile attitude, and shut himself up in the fort.[43] Abbas Sarwani suggests that when Sher Shah arrived near Kalinjar, Raja Kirat Singh did not come to receive him. Sher Shah, therefore, surrounded the fort and threw up entrenchment around it.[44] Then the issue of Sher Shah's desire for the slave girl, noted above, is mentioned as the motive behind the capture of the fort. Realizing that it was not a very convincing explanation, recourse has been made to the suggestion of certain leading Sufis to the effect that no prayer can equal the conducting of a campaign against the infidels; if one is killed, he becomes a shahid or martyr; if he is victorious, he is revered as a ghazi. Following the suggestion, Sher Shah gave order for the occupation of the fort by force.[45] Sufis and ulama were indeed present in Sher Shah's camp at this time. Two of them, Shaykh Khalil and Mulla Nizam Danishmand were amongst those who were charred to death along with Sher Shah in the accidental fire during the siege.[46] The fire also showed the limitation of the use of the artillery by the Afghans at this stage.

[40] *Waqi'at-i-Mushtaqi*, fols. 54b–55a; *Tarikh-i-Da'udi*, p. 152.

[41] *Tarikh-i-Sher Shahi*, pp. 190–1.

[42] *Tarikh-i-Khan-i-Jahani wa Makhzan-i-Afghani*, Vol. I, p. 327. For the early Islamic justifications of the killing of captives and the destruction of enemy fortifications, see Majid Khadduri, *The Islamic Law of Nations—Shaybani's Siyar*, Translation with an Introduction, Notes and Appendices (Baltimore, 1966), pp. 95–102.

[43] *Tabaqat-i-Akbari*, fol. 204b.

[44] *Tarikh-i-Sher Shahi*, p. 201.

[45] Ibid., pp. 201–2.

[46] *Tabaqat-i-Akbari*, fol. 204b; *Tarikh-i-Farishta* (RAS Microfilm), p. 376.

Later reports add that certain supernatural beings played a significant role in the capture of the fort of Kalinjar. Badauni writes that he heard a story from a 'most trustworthy source', that on that eventful day of assault, in which the deeds of every individual assailant were conspicuous, and the standards and faces could be easily identified, he saw a fully armed soldier, who had not previously been seen nor was ever after seen, clothed from head to foot in black, wearing a plume of the same colour upon his head, and urging and encouraging men in the battle. Then he entered one of the galleries and made his way into the fort. Badauni's informant searched for him everywhere after the battle, but did not find him. The men in the other trenches also gave the same account, saying they saw several similar looking horsemen who kept advancing until they had entered the fort and vanished. Thus, a report became current that in the battle, certain men from the invisible world had come to the aid of the Muslims.[47]

Modern authorities have taken a strong exception to Sher Shah's 'bigotry' and 'treacherous action' against non-Muslims.[48] Clearly, the condemnation stems from an uncritical acceptance of the accounts given by the chroniclers. The reports of the cold-blooded massacres of the Rajputs at Raisin and Kalinjar are read literally, and generalized to confirm the assumption as true. In doing so, these studies ignore the question whether the alleged treatment of the Rajputs by Sher Shah was unique for the period; that he had particularly singled out the Rajputs for this 'special' treatment; and that his attitude towards them was similar or uniform with all the clans in different regions throughout his career as a ruler in Bihar or as a king of Hindustan. Further, this evaluation also emanates from an understanding that it was Akbar who started the policy of tolerance towards non-Muslims and their incorporation in state service in medieval India. In our opinion this assumption needs reconsideration as it not only neglects the attempts

---

[47] *Muntakhab-ut-Tawarikh*, p. 483.

[48] Sri Ram Sharma, *The Religious Policy of the Mughal Emperors*, first published 1940, reprint (Bombay, 1972), pp. 26–7; Ishwari Prasad, *Life and Times of Humayun*, p. 172 (for 'Jehad' against Raisin); Dirk Kolff, *Naukar, Rajput and Sepoy*, pp. 102–8; Qanungo, *Sher Shah and his Times*, pp. 388–91. Denying the accusations of religious fanaticism levelled against Sher Shah, Siddiqui has suggested that the ruler was actually a forerunner of Akbar in adopting a policy of tolerance towards all irrespective of race or creed, *Afghan Despotism*, pp. 105–6 and 108.

at integration by the earlier sultans, nobles and Sufis but also ignores the complex processes of attraction and repulsion of Muslim and non-Muslim groups/individuals in medieval India.

If the examples given by sixteenth-seventeenth century writers are any indication, Sher Shah was ruthless in chastising his opponents during the course of his conquest. The case of the Gakkar chief Sarang Khan may be cited here. Owing allegiance to the Mughals, the Khan had offered some resistance to the Afghan army campaigning in pursuit of the fugitive Humayun after the battle of Qannauj. When he was compelled to submit before Sher Shah, the emperor ordered him to be executed, had his skin filled with straw and then displayed.[49] In this context, mention may also be made of the powerful Khan-i-Khanan Lodi who enjoyed considerable prestige amongst the Afghans despite his association with the Mughals, and was unceremoniously put to death.[50] The case of the Mughal governor of Bengal, Jahangir Quli Beg, who was killed after being lured into a false treaty is yet another illustration of this.[51] It must be noted that all these victims of Sher Shah were Muslims. In many cases, the justification given for the acts of violence is clear bluff. The topos of the loyalty of the Afghans and their service to the Mughals and the discrimination and humiliation, which they got in return, is also utilized for legitimating the onslaught against Humayun. Also, the treatment meted out to some Rajput chieftains, though not unusual, was explained in terms of the struggle for 'the cause of Islam'. On the other hand, those who collaborated, or even submitted without resistance, were considered to be a party to the project and were rewarded for their service. Thus, the close cooperation with the Ujjainiya Rajputs, and the restoration of the chiefs after the peaceful conquest of Rajputana does not fit with the model of a Muslim ruler out to destroy the infidels, and convert Hindustan into a dar-ul-Islam.

It will be fruitful to consider here some evidence, which further illustrate the ambivalence. As a measure of recognition of the power that they enjoyed and the need for legitimacy from them, Muslim rulers alienated a large chunk of land under their control for revenue

[49] Ishwari Prasad, *Life and Times of Humayun*, p. 162.
[50] *Tarikh-i-Sher Shahi*, p. 146.
[51] Ibid., p. 144; *Riyaz-us-Salatin*, p. 144.

free grants, variously called *suyurghal,* madad-i-ma'ash or *in'am* to religious institutions, holy men, persons of high lineage (for instance, those claiming to be the descendants of Prophet Muhammad), and the needy (including the widows of nobles and saintly persons).[52] To begin with, these grants were revenue assignments of temporary nature, subject to renewal at frequent intervals such as the death of either the ruler who had initially issued the farman (official order) or that of the grantee (in which case the latter's descendants wanted their names to be inserted in the order). By late seventeenth century, the grant-holders came to acquire proprietary rights over the land allotted to them. Even as the land, both cultivated and waste-but-cultivable, earmarked for the purpose was a small fraction of the total area under cultivation, the grantees came to acquire immense political clout. This often led to a clash of interests between the traditional landlords and the newly emerging landed aristocracy. Further, even as temples and places of worship of various non-Muslim religious traditions benefited from these grants, they were particularly significant for the making of small Muslim communities in towns and rural areas and therefore for a slow, but gradual expansion of Islam in various regions controlled by Muslim rulers. The documents pertaining to land grants are important for studying the significant linkage between agrarian expansion and the spread of Islam.[53]

It may also be pointed out that such grants to non-Muslim spiritual power holders such as Brahmans and yogis could be more helpful in diffusion of their authority, realizing this the rulers generously conferred the grants on them as well. Such grants were quite frequent under the Mughals, including under Aurangzeb Alamgir. However, the latter had issued a farman in 1672–3, ordering the resumption of revenue free grants to all non-Muslims. Another ruling of the monarch,

[52] For a recent study of these grants in a later context, see Jigar Mohammed, *Revenue Free Land Grants in Mughal India: Awadh Region in the Seventeenth and Eighteenth Centuries, 1658–1765* (New Delhi, 2002).

[53] For such connections, see Richard Eaton, *The Rise of Islam and the Bengal Frontier, 1204–1760* (Delhi, 1994); Andre Wink, *Al-Hind, Vol. II.* Compare this with C.A. Bayly's interpretation that these grants led to frequent conflicts between the new Muslim landed aristocracy and established Hindu landlords, taking on a communal colour and breaking into religious violence, 'The Pre-History of "Communalism"? Religious Conflict in India, 1700–1860', *MAS,* Vol. 19, No. 2, 1985, pp. 177–203.

released in 1690, recognized the hereditary rights of mainly Muslim madad-i-ma'ash holders, thereby strengthening their position. The above developments clearly show a shift in official policy towards the grantees even though royal orders may not have been strictly implemented.[54]

In any case, the practice was prevalent in the time of the Afghan rulers as well. The *Tawarikh-i-Daulat-i-Sher Shahi* contains a farman of Sher Shah according to which the pious and deserving people amongst the Hindus got land-grants from him for their maintenance. He also granted land as endowment (*waqf*) for the upkeep of the temples.[55] The need to portray him as a devout and orthodox Sunni Muslim ruler may have compelled the Persian authorities to suppress the information concerning the grant to non-Muslim divines. Yet one such grant to a Brahman (*zunnardar*) by Sher Shah has sneaked into the narrative of Abdullah. It is reported that while moving in a boat for the campaign towards Kalinjar, Sher Shah came across a Brahman taking bath on the bank of the river, at pargana Hamirpur in Kalpi. The boatmen were asked to anchor the boat to the bank. The Brahman did not recognize the king and thus remained indifferent. Sher Shah was, however, impressed by his honesty and granted him as in'am the village where he stayed. A cash amount of five hundred rupees was also given to him.[56] This evidence has been neglected by the modern historians of the Mughal period who tend to believe that Akbar's 'inclusion' of non-Muslim grantees as subjects of state largesse was a 'new departure'.[57]

---

[54] Jigar Mohammad insists that 'Aurangzeb made no material change in the system of assignment' and did not 'reverse the earlier policy drastically', *Revenue Free Land Grants in Mughal India*, pp. 37–8.

[55] The extant fragments of the *Tawarikh-i-Daulat-i-Sher Shahi* of Hasan Ali Khan were published along with the English translation of the portion said to be containing the farmans of Sher Shah in *Medieval India Quarterly* (henceforth *MIQ*), Vol. I, No. 1, July 1950. S.A.A. Rizvi and I.H. Siddiqui have, however, condemned it to be a later forgery. Siddiqui specifically dates its 'fabrication' to the reign of Shah Jahan, see Rizvi, *MIQ*, Vol. I, No. 2, October, 1950, pp. 74–80; Siddiqui, 'Examination of the Contents of *Tawarikh-i-Daulat-i-Sher Shahi* of Hasan Ali Khan', in idem, *Mughal Relations with the Indian Ruling Elite* (Delhi, 1983), pp. 178–89.

[56] *Tarikh-i-Da'udi*, pp. 138–9.

[57] Richards, *The Mughal Empire*, p. 92.

The quest for legitimacy may also be seen in Sher Shah's architecture, chiefly his tomb at Sahsaram. Any Hindu visitor to his mausoleum, treated now as a holy shrine, is bound to have a feeling of *déjà vu* as the building is located in the middle of a lake. Though the water of the lake and the allusion to water and greenery of the heaven in the Quranic verses inscribed on the inner walls of the tomb may be viewed as an index of Islamic religiosity,[58] the lake attached to a temple complex symbolizing ritual purity, and also for the actual purpose of bathing, is a common feature at noted *tirthasthans* or centre's of pilgrimage in India. Thus, the layout of the tomb serves the purpose of eliciting the admiration of Muslims and non-Muslims alike. The attempt at integration and the recognition of the need for legitimacy may also be viewed in Sher Shah's coinage. The details inscribed on the coins were both in Arabic and Devnagri scripts.[59]

Thus the sources portray the Afghans, like the Mughals, in conflict with only those who challenged, or refused to acknowledge, their political power. Generally, they showed a liberal and tolerant attitude towards non-Muslims. Their relationship with the Rajputs was clearly marked by an honourable alliance of dominance and subordination, which recognized the status of the latter as the rajas of their territories. In such alliances, the chieftain was expected to give his daughter to the ally as an acknowledgement of the acceptance of his inferior position, and for ensuring the durability of the relationship. Marriage was indeed a significant determinant in the Rajput alliance with the Afghans, as was to be the case with the Mughals later on.[60]

Even in the early medieval period, marriage was an institution explicitly used to build political alliance and open avenues of economic exchange between 'houses'—families as politico-economic units. For the ruling elite of the putative Ksatriya lineage, 'selection' and marriage

---

[58] Catherine Asher highlights Islamic elements in the architecture, and denies any influence of the non-Muslim environment. She also ignores its impact on the local religious milieu, 'Mausoleum of Sher Shah'; Percy Brown, 'The Influence of Sher Shah Sur on the Islamic Architecture of India'. Also see Introduction above.

[59] Wright, *Coinage and metrology of the Sultans*, pp. 263–89; see also Introduction in this book.

[60] Cf. Frances H. Taft, 'Honour and Alliance: Reconsidering Mughal-Rajput Marriages', in Karine Schomer, Joan L. Erdman, et. al., eds, *The Idea of Rajasthan*, Vol. II, pp. 217–41.

was the most important method of sealing political alliances between kings. Wars were often concluded with the defeated house offering women in marriage to the victors. The practice of *kanyadana* (gift of a maiden) tended to establish the superiority of the groom's family over that of the bride.[61] Further, as Norman Ziegler suggests, Rajput loyalties and identifications on a local level may be conceived in terms of both descent, operative within the brotherhood among those related by ties of male blood, and sets of hierarchical, binary relationships based on service and exchange, operative within a kingdom between a ruler and his servants. Each of these institutions or sets of relationships also had a territorial aspect, based on the extent of kin recognition that defined the '*watan*' of a brotherhood, and was based on structural ties between a ruler and his retainers, which defined the territory of the kingdom. Cross-cutting all levels and included within the concept of 'territory' were also affiliations through ties of alliance and marriage.[62] In understanding medieval Rajput cultural conceptions, it is important to note that the Muslim was also treated as a Rajput. The traditions generally represent the Rajput *jati* (caste) as being divided into two categories: Muslim/Turk and Hindu. This category of 'Muslim' within the Rajput jati did not include all Muslims, but only those who were warriors and who possessed sovereignty and power equal to, or greater than, the Hindu Rajput such as the Afghans and the Mughals. The Muslim emperor in particular, held a position of high rank and esteem, and the traditions often equate him with the Ksatriya cultural hero Ram. What basically distinguished the king from the local Rajput rulers was simply his possession of greater sovereignty and power and his greater ability to grant favours and rewards. Service for the Muslim sovereign or one of his subordinates was thus no different from service for a local ruler or *thakur*.[63] Thus, the Rajput support for, or adherence to the Mughal throne rested primarily upon a basic 'fit' between Rajput ideals and aspirations, and Mughal actions in this area, which did not challenge fundamental Rajput tenets regarding order and precedence. Mughal policy of support for local rulers, of alliance through marriage,

[61] Daud Ali, 'Anxieties of Attachment: The Dynamics of Courtship in Medieval India', *MAS*, Vol. 36: 1, 2002, pp. 103–39.

[62] Norman P. Ziegler, 'Some Notes on Rajput Loyalties During the Mughal Period', in J.F. Richards, ed., *Kingship and Authority*, pp. 215–51, especially, p. 230.

[63] Ibid., p. 235.

and of granting lands in return for service and allegiance all found a base of support in local ideology and allowed Rajputs in turn to find fulfillment of their own ideals through subordination and loyalty to the Mughal throne.[64]

Before moving further, we would like to have a general overview of the role of the Rajputs in the Mughal-Afghan conflict. During the early period of Babur's invasion and conquest of Hindustan, the Rajputs fought with the Afghans, and continued to offer resistance through the Afghan pretender Sultan Mahmud. The period of Sher Shah's conflict with Humayun witnessed the Rajputs settling scores with each other and generally resorting to an ambivalent attitude towards the two, though complaints of the capture of the territories previously under the control of the Muslims were not uncommon. Once the issue of badshahat of Hindustan was settled, the Rajputs, barring a few, did not make any delay in acknowledging the suzerainty of the Sur emperor.

In fact non-Muslims in the service of the Afghans could be noticed from an earlier period. A number of Rajput chiefs were in the service of the Lodis.[65] Later, Hemu's elevation to the status of the chief commander of the Sur army, who died fighting against the Mughals after Humayun's return from Persia,[66] speaks volumes on the incorporation of non-Muslims in the Afghan imperial project. The extent to which this incorporation, or alliance, was effective may further be seen in the fact that Akbar's early encounters with the Rajputs during the period of Mughal consolidation in the second half of the sixteenth century was actually a corollary to the latter's support to the Afghans.[67]

Perhaps this alliance continued in, and resistance dragged to, the seventeenth century as well. It is in the context of the recurrent resistance of the Rajputs against the Mughal expansion that Bodhraj's account of the lasting Ujjainiya-Sur alliance can be understood. Apart

---

[64] Ibid., p. 240.

[65] I.H. Siddiqui, 'The Composition of the Nobility under the Lodi Sultans', *MIAM*, Vol. 4, 1977, pp. 10–66.

[66] Referring to Hemu, the 'Hindu' general who had styled himself as Raja Vikramaditya, J.F. Richards suggests that his success in the second battle of Panipat would have been a remarkable reassertion of the Sanskritic/Brahmanical monarchical tradition, long subservient to Muslim rulers, in North India, *The Mughal Empire*, p. 13.

[67] Cf. A.R. Khan's essay, in Irfan Habib, ed., *Akbar and His India*.

from the importance of this backdrop, the memory of Sher Shah's generous help and political support to the Ujjainiyas and the latter's spirit of sacrifice reflected chiefly in the battle against the sultans of Bengal is significant in itself. Finally, though it sounds heretical to suggest that 'Afghans' or 'Rajputs' were synonyms in the military tradition of medieval North India,[68] the extent to which they identified with each other may be seen in the claims of a Rajasthani bardic poem, 'Qaimkhan Raso', that Sher Shah was the son of a Rajput mother. It is suggested that Sher Shah's mother was 'a daughter of the ruling Qaim Khani Rajput family of Fatehpur-Jhunjhun (Shekhawat)' near Narnaul.[69] Mention may be made here of Mian Hasan's early connections with the Rajputs. Abu'l Fazl has noted that Hasan was, for a long time, in the service of Raimal, the grandfather of Raisal, a noble in Akbar's court.[70] The possibility of Hasan picking up a Rajput wife cannot be denied, but the suggestion that Sher Shah was born to her is not only scandalous from the point of view of the Afghans, but also is not supported by any other authority.

However instances of the Afghan rulers, nobles and even Sufis marrying non-Muslim women were not unusual during the period. Sher Shah himself married at least two non-Muslim women. The *Tawarikh-i-Daulat-i-Sher Shahi* relates that the relationship between Farid and his father, Hasan Sur had strained due to the former's love affair with the daughter of a Rajput chief, Jai Singh Rathore. Fascinated by her beauty, Farid fell madly in love with her and lost his mental peace. When Jai Singh came to know of the affair between Farid and his daughter, he decided to run away with her, but in vain. Farid got an inkling of the plan, at once threw Jai Singh into prison and obtained the hand of the girl in marriage. Shortly afterwards Jai Singh was set free as he had outwardly reconciled to Farid, although inwardly he was determined to take revenge. One day Jai Singh turned up and after some conversation took out his dagger and attacked Farid. The author of the *Tawarikh*, Hasan Ali Khan, who claims to be present there quickly jumped up, caught hold of the dagger and put Jai Singh to death. The news of Jai Singh's murder caused severe grief to his daughter. She

---

[68] Dirk Kolff, *Naukar, Rajput and Sepoy*, pp. 57–8; Cf. Ziegler, 'Some Notes on Rajput Loyalties', p. 235.

[69] Qanungo, *Sher Shah and his Times*, p. XI.

[70] *Akbarnama*, fol. 81b.

stopped taking food and passed away after sometime. On her death, Farid also lost interest in worldly affairs. As the grief caused by her death to Farid was too severe to bear, he also decided to follow her in death by committing suicide. The author again claims that he consoled Farid in such a way that he refrained from taking such a drastic step.[71]

The sources of the Afghan period relate several episodes in which the lovers do not hesitate to take the 'drastic step' and sacrifice their lives for their beloved. The tales end with the suggestion that the lovers unite and live together after their departure from this world. The purpose of the narration of these stories was to suggest that the people of the Afghan period were not only 'sincere' in their love, but also as Shaykh Rizqullah Mushtaqi put it: 'The time was good'. Writing in his old age, in the reign of Akbar, the shaykh lamented: 'Today neither love nor time is sincere; such people have passed away'. Though, we shall return again to the Sufi shaykhs' reflections on their contemporary society in chapter six, we may turn to a few anecdotes to have a feel of the 'time'. Two episodes which we shall recount here are useful for the Hindu-Muslim tangle in medieval India and the different ways in which the rulers sought to handle the problem. Also comes in the picture the ubiquitous Sufi with his love for God and the desire for love.

Mushtaqi records that a student reached a place called Bhogaon in the course of his journey. Being thirsty, he went to the well and found a beautiful girl drawing water. He saw her and was captivated by her at the very first sight. Although, the other women offered him water to drink, he insisted on taking it from her hands. Her companions said to the girl: 'He is a traveller. Be kind to him'. On their advice, she agreed to give water to the student who took his hands to his mouth to drink it. The girl poured water upon his hands from her bucket. As he continued to stare at her face, the water fell down and he could not drink. Irritated, the girl drew away the remaining water from her bucket and turned away her face in anger. Again, other girls offered him water but he said: 'I shall take water only from her hands, otherwise not, and I will die'. The girls said to their companion: 'We offer him water but he refuses to accept it; he will accept water from your hands only'. She said: 'If I ask him to jump into the well, will he do it?' No sooner had he heard these words that he leapt into the well, causing an uproar among

---

[71] Siddiqui, 'Tawarikh-i-Daulat-i-Sher Shahi' of Hasan Ali Khan', pp. 180–1.

the girls. They said to her: 'What have you done? You are responsible for his death'. She felt ashamed and also jumped into the well.

The matter was reported to the shiqqdar who reached the spot along with the relatives of the girl and others. The nets were drawn into the well and their dead-bodies were brought out. They were found holding each other by hand. The relatives of the girl wished to cremate her, but the shiqqdar differed from them, saying. 'she has died for the sake of a Musalman. They have been brought out together, therefore, it is not proper for you to cremate her body'. It was ultimately decided that she should be buried near the grave of the student, and the order of the shiqqdar was carried out. At night the relatives of the girl decided to open the grave and take out her body for cremation. When they opened her grave, they did not find her body. They examined the grave and found a passage between the two graves. A candle was also burning and both the boy and the girl were sitting on a cot. When they saw this, they closed the grave and went away.[72] Even as a modern, rational mind will not accept such stories as true, it is clear that the above tale highlights the dominant Sufic adherence to the fundamental unity of mankind, and the notion that the differences between Hindus and Muslims are of a superficial nature, and that the lover unites with his beloved in death.

Another anecdote related by Abdul Haqq Muhaddis Dehlawi refers to a conflict between the Mughal governor Mirza Muhammad Zaman and the Sufi shaykh, Saiyid Sultan Bahraichi over a Hindu woman. The relatives of the woman had sought the Mirza's help in taking away the woman from the shaykh's protection. However, the Mirza had to submit before the shaykh as the latter counterposited his action on the basis of the shari'at. He argued that the Hindu woman whom he loved, and had married, had converted to Islam at his hands; and drew out his sword for a fight with the Mirza on the issue.[73]

The above episode not only points to the Sufis' interest in conversion, but also the occasional tension in their relationship with the rulers. Significantly, the religious divines at times took rigid *shar'i* position and wanted things to be different from what the rulers were comfortable with. Indeed, on several issues the kings are found to be taking a liberal position despite pressure from the 'orthodox party'. We saw

---

[72] *Waqi'at-i-Mushtaqi*, fol. 21b.
[73] *Akhbar-ul-Akhyar* (Urdu trans.), pp. 478–9.

above that there was hardly any serious and systematic attempt on the part of the rulers to implement the shari'at as the law of the land, destroy places of worship of non-Muslims, convert them to Islam, or even collect jizya on a regular basis. Yet the ulama and the Sufis portrayed them as the ideal Muslim rulers, and ignored or legitimized many of their acts of omission and commission.

The conquered people, however, had not fully reconciled themselves to a subordinate position. The Hindu resistance in the period appears to be both overt/open (that is, in the form of armed struggle) and co-vert/'everyday' variety (reflected in an increased religiosity, *bhajan*, *kirtan*, peaceful monotheistic movements, etc.). Sixteenth-century Marathi Bhakti poet Eknath's presentation of a hard-hitting argument between a Hindu and a Muslim in his drama-poem, *Hindu-Turk Samvad*, may be mentioned here. The aggressive Muslim protagonist was made to realize that both Hindus and Muslims were created by God. Their 'goal is one', though 'the ways of worship are different'. Eknath's Hindu character also castigates the Muslim who is supposed to catch a Hindu and convert him to Islam: 'Did God make a mistake in making a Hindu? Is your wisdom greater than His?' The practices and rituals of the Sufi shrines are also questioned: 'You tell us we wor-ship stones. Why do you place blocks of stone over the dead?'... 'You cover the stone with flowers and silk cloth; you burn incense before it!' More punching is the criticism of the popular veneration or 'worship of a *haji* of stone (Ka'ba in Mecca)'. The drama ends on a consensus: 'The argument was about oneness. The argument became agreement'.[74] The consensus does not dissolve the question of identity. It only shows the author's concerns to illustrate the commonality of certain beliefs and rituals, and resist conversion of Hindus to Islam. On the other hand, at times, the Muslims also manifested an extraordinarily mag-nanimous attitude in their treatment of the Hindus. Yet it is clear that the Muslims, at least the elite who have left their works in the Persian language, were conscious of the presence of an 'other' in the person of the Hindu. It is in this context of a perceived overwhelming presence of an, often dangerous, 'other' that the process of formation of com-munity identities of Muslims in India needs to be examined.

[74] Eleanor Zelliot, 'A Medieval Encounter Between Hindu and Muslim: Eknath's Drama-Poem *Hindu-Turk Samvad*', first published 1982, reprinted in Eaton, ed., *India's Islamic Traditions*, pp. 64–82.

It has been suggested recently that the 'development of strict orthodoxy' in Indian Islam in the midst of 'idolatrous and polytheistic population' was diametrically opposed to 'the attempt to find a common denominator for the two civilizations, to establish a mutually acceptable *modus vivendi* for their respective adherents', though conciliatory trend was always weaker than the orthodox one'.[75] The above formulation is fraught with problems. The use of the expression 'two civilizations' presupposes non-Muslims and Muslims as two biologically, racially, even culturally different sets of people. It ignores the vast majority of Indian converts to Islam. It may be kept in mind that conversion did not happen in one day, except in individual cases. Several communities or groups of people underwent a long process of Islamic acculturation. Diffusion of Islam in the regions also unleashed the emergence of a large number of 'syncretistic' cults or communities. Politics determined their classification as 'Islamic' or 'Hindu' and even pushed them to be identified as part of Islam or what is termed as 'Hinduism', or may be as something new (Sikhism for instance, though attempts to appropriate Sikhism into Hinduism continues), as we shall further see in chapter six below.

It does not mean however that politics always created conflict in society. The attitude of Muslim rulers towards their diverse subjects differed, basing on reasons such as personal temperament and political expediency. It could be ambivalent, pragmatic and in a few cases even programmatic. If the juristically inclined ulama wanted an all-out war against the kuffar, the Muslim attitude towards the latter was tempered by the more politically correct position taken by a large number of Sufis of a variety of spiritual lineages. The Sufic approach to some such problems in the context of the Afghan period will be examined in the next section.

[75] Friedmann, 'Islamic Thought', pp. 50–1. Aziz Ahmad also refers to the 'two mutually exclusive religious, cultural and historical attitudes, each confronting the other in aggressive hostility', in his 'Epic and counter-Epic in Medieval India', first published in 1963, reprinted in Eaton, ed., *India's Islamic Traditions*, p. 37. As Eaton has pointed out Ahmad's classification, prepared not long after Partition, of Muslim epic of conquest and a Hindu epic of resistance and of psychological rejection, which grew in mutual ignorance of the other, 'likely reflected the hardened political and ideological positions that had crystallized with the creation of independent India and Pakistan', *India's Islamic Traditions*, p. 35.

PART III

RELIGION, POLITICS, AND SOCIETY

5

The Political and the Sufic Wilayat

GENERALLY REFERRED TO IN PERSIAN literature as sufi, shaykh, *khwaja*, *arif, salik, buzurg, wali, darwesh*, or majzub,[1] the Sufis played an important role in shaping the politics and society of the Afghan dominion. Basing on the contemporary and near-contemporary Sufi texts, including the tazkiras (biographical dictionaries), this chapter seeks to take into account the political role of the Sufis. The question of their interactions in Indian society will be dealt with in a subsequent chapter. Our sources include the *Siyar-ul-Arifin* of Jamali Kamboh, *Waqi'at-i-Mushtaqi* of Rizqullah Mushtaqi, *Akhbar-ul-Akhyar* of Abdul Haqq Muhaddis Dihlawi, and the *Gulzar-i-Abrar* of Ghausi Shattari. The last chapter of the second volume of the *Tarikh-i-Khan-i-Jahani wa Makhzan-i-Afghani* of Khwaja Ni'matullah Harawi also contains valuable material on the lives of the shaykhs who were Afghans by birth, or were identified as Afghans. The references to the involvement of the Sufis in contemporary politics may be found in a large number of anecdotes on their relations with the emperors and the nobles. Several examples of the bestowal of kingship by the Sufis and their participation in the military campaigns have been noted above. All this influenced and shaped the ideals of governance and are crucial for a better appreciation of contemporary politics.

It is important to note here that a discussion on Sufis' relationship with the Afghan rulers is significant, for it brings in valuable details from the careers of a large number of 'smaller' Sufis from the period. Existing historiography on Sufism in medieval India is dominated by

---

[1] For these terms current in the sources see the dictionaries of the period, *Kashf-ul-Lughat wal Istalahat, Mu'aiyyid-ul-Fuzala, Sharfnama-i-Ahmad Maneri, Tuhfat-us-Sa'adat*.

the presence of some 'great' Sufis such as the first five shaykhs or khwajas of the Chishti order. The Chishtis had safeguarded their control over Delhi despite a persistent pressure from the Suhrawardis in the thirteenth and fourteenth centuries. The Suhrawardis were eventually able to enjoy considerable clout in the Afghan regime, including the wilayat of Delhi, where figures like Sama-ud-Din Suhrawardi could flourish without any opposition from the Chishti rank. Other, newer orders like the Shattaris were bringing in new competition for power and prestige within the fold of Islamic mysticism, even as shrines of Sufis like Mu'in-ud-Din Chishti and Qutb-ud-din Bakhtiyar Kaki could be flourishing and gaining in popularity in the period. The chapter thus refers to the specificity of a changing political scenario, even as the account is linked to the grand narrative on Sufism in medieval India. Thus, for a change, we are dealing with fresh biographies and 'lesser' traditions even though comparisons and contrasts with the dominant trends will not be without value.

KINGS' DEVOTION TOWARDS THE SUFIS

The badshah and the courtiers visited the Sufis' hospice (khanqah or jama'atkhana), sought blessings from them and received gifts from the Sufis which were treated as *tabarruk* (sacred relic). Jamali extensively describes the visit of Bahlul Lodi to his pir, Sama-ud-Din. The shaykh, a disciple of Shaykh Sadr-ud-Din Multani alias Raju Qattal (son of the leading fourteenth century Suhrawardi saint Makhdum Jahaniyan Jahangasht), had left his homeland Multan on the eve of Timur's invasion, and went to Jaunpur. The shaykh travelled extensively in central India before settling down in Delhi where he died in 909/1503–4, and was buried near Hauz-i-Shamsi in the vicinity of the Chishti saint Khwaja Qutb-ud-Din Bakhtiyar Kaki's tomb. Pious and learned, Sama-ud-Din was venerated by the prominent Sufis and scholars of the time. His son, Shaykh Nasir-ud-din Dehlawi was the Shaykh-ul-Islam of Delhi during the reigns of the Afghan sultans, Sikandar Lodi and Ibrahim Lodi, and continued under the Mughal emperor Babur. The elder son Shaykh Abdullah Biyabani (d.1529) was also a leading Sufi of the time.[2]

---

[2] A. Halim, 'Mystics and Mystical Movements of the Saiyyid-Lodi Period (AD 1414 to AD 1526)', *Journal of the Asiatic Society of Pakistan*, Vol. VIII, No.2, 1963, pp. 71–108, especially pp. 97–9.

Jamali informs that once Sama-ud-Din's lecture on the type of people, including the rulers, who will be deprived of God's blessing, moved Sultan Bahlul so much that he wept and submitted that despite the sins committed by him his devotion towards the Sufis was gradually increasing. He also hoped that this could lead to his salvation. Seeing that the sultan was crying, other visitors to the hospice also started weeping. Impressed by the honesty and integrity of the sultan, the shaykh gave his own special prayer-carpet to him. The sultan respectfully put the prayer-carpet on his head and left the place (*sultan musalla bar sar nihad wa maraja'at namud*).[3]

The Sufis were asked to stay in the dominion and pray for peace and stability, and the durability of the rule of the sovereign, who in turn prayed to God and thanked Him for the blessed presence of the Sufis in his kingdom. Shaykh Muhammad Mallawa (d. 900/1494–5) had come to Delhi during Sikandar Lodi's reign and was popularly known as Misbah-ul-Ashiqin. Initially a disciple of Shaykh Ahmad Rawati, he was later trained by Shaykh Jalal Gujarati. Among his disciples were Abdul Haqq Muhaddis Dehlawi's paternal grandfather, and his uncles, Shaykh Sa'dullah and Shaykh Rizqullah Mushtaqi, the author of the *Waqi'at-i-Mushtaqi*. Abdul Haqq in an anecdote shows the power of the shaykh's prayer to yield bumper crops. When Sikandar Lodi heard about this miracle of the Sufi, he thanked God for the presence of such saintly persons in his Sultanate.[4] We shall return to Shaykh Mallawa again in the next chapter for an episode in which a Hindu chief was prevented by his companions from falling at the feet of the shaykh and converting to Islam. The shaykh is buried at the famous village of Mallawa near Qannauj.[5]

Cash and land grants were given to the individual Sufis. Rizqullah Mushtaqi has recorded the grants of land and cash to several religious persons including the Sufis. He also gives some anecdotes in this regard. One is particularly funny. He writes that once when Bahlul Lodi had come out from the lavatory and was cleaning himself, a

---

[3] *Siyar-ul-Arifin*, fols. 235a–236b. For the evidence of Bahlul Lodi's devotion for the shaykh, see also *Azkar-i-Abrar*, Urdu translation of *Gulzar-i-Abrar* (Lahore, A.H. 1395), pp. 209–10.

[4] Abdul Haqq Muhaddis Dihlawi, *Akhbar-ul-Akhyar*, Ms. I.O. Islamic 1450, OIOC, British Library, London, fols. 160a–b.

[5] Ibid., fol. 160b.

Mulla named Tughlaq appeared. Oblivious to the sultan's awkward situation, the Mulla demanded of him to fix a stipend for a person whom he thought was deserving and had brought along. Treating it as a religious duty, the sultan at once fixed the stipend for him, allowed the Mulla to depart and then went in for ablution. Concluding the story, Mushtaqi wondered how a ruler of his time would behave.[6]

Mushtaqi was possibly uncomfortable with the treatment meted out to a section of the *aimma* (religious persons who enjoyed maintenance grants) under Akbar during whose rule he wrote the *Waqi'at-i-Mushtaqi*. He is however all praise for Humayun's attitude towards them. He writes that the king so venerated the holy men that one day when Amir Hindu Beg complained about the *waza'if* (stipends) to the men of religion amounting to eighteen crore tankas while the soldiers were dying of starvation, the king warned him not to utter anything against the holy men: 'I have dedicated the revenue of this entire country to the religious persons, and we shall conquer another country for ourselves'. Efforts were also made by the rulers to maintain Sufic institutions such as the tomb. Abdul Haqq records that even the nobles took steps in this direction. Malik Zain-ud-Din and his brother, Shaykh Wazir-ud-Din, belonged to a family which had close links with the rulers of Delhi. Zain-ud-Din was a wakil of Khan-i-Jahan, a cousin of Sikandar Lodi, and had good relations with the latter. He had assumed responsibility of maintaining the tombs and shrines in and around Delhi. He also treated the ulama, Sufis and other saintly persons with respect and devotion, and thus always kept them pleased.[7] Zain-ud-Din's younger brother, Wazir-ud-Din did not serve on any official position, but fought for the Afghans in the first battle of Panipat.[8] Zain-ud-Din was poisoned by a servant of his. Thus, notes Abdul Haqq, both the brothers achieved martyrdom for which they used to pray.[9]

The rulers and the courtiers invited the Sufis to have meals with them. The sources, while referring to Sher Shah's personal routine and welfare measures, mention that the monarch used to take his meal in

---

[6] *Waqi'at-i-Mushtaqi*, fol. 6b.

[7] Abdul Haqq Muhaddis Dihlawi, *Akhbar-ul-Akhyar*, Kutubkhana Rahimiya, Deoband, n.d., (hereafter printed text), pp. 232–3.

[8] Ibid., p. 233. For anecdotes related to the two brothers, also see *Waqi'at-i-Mushtaqi*, fols. 31b–32a.

[9] *Akhbar-ul-Akhyar* (printed text), p. 233.

the company of the Sufis. The same is true of the Lodi sultans and the Mugahl emperor Humayun. Often the emperor visited the hospice of the Sufis to have dinner with them. Rizqullah Mushtaqi refers to an episode concerning a feast in the house of Shaykh Bahlul, which illustrates the great esteem in which Humayun held the saintly persons.[10]

The Sufis not only participated in the campaigns which the rulers conducted in the various regions, but also gave suggestions on how to make the expeditions successful. Certain Sufis were approached in times of crisis such as an attack from outside. Mushtaqi records that Sultan Husain Sharqi of Jaunpur came to invade Delhi twice, but on both the occasions he was defeated and driven away. On the first occasion, as he reached Delhi and laid siege to it, Bahlul Lodi stood bare-headed and prayed at the tomb of Qutb-ud-Din Bakhtiyar Kaki throughout the night. Early in the morning a man (*mard ghayb*) appeared from the heaven and handed over a staff, asking him to hit the invaders. Bahlul Lodi at once made preparations and attacked Sultan Husain Sharqi. In the battle which ensued Sultan Husain's army was defeated and he retreated to Jaunpur.[11]

This event took place in the year 1478, and, as I.H. Siddiqui puts it, was a turning point in the career of Sultan Bahlul. First Bahlul concluded a peace-treaty on the terms set by Sultan Husain Sharqi as his army was much smaller, and then made a surprise attack on the retreating Jaunpur army. He seized their goods and treasures along with forty nobles. Sultan Husain saved himself by fleeing.[12] We shall deal again with the inter-relationship between the Sufis, Afghans and the Sharqis of Jaunpur in the next section. At the time of Babur's invasion of Hindustan, Sultan Ibrahim Lodi went around the city to meet the Sufis and seek their help in repelling the attack, but in vain. He had seemingly antagonized some influential Sufis of the realm who switched over to the Mughals after their success over the Afghans, and, as noted above, the Shaykh-ul-Islam of Delhi survived the capture of the city by the Mughals.

[10] The badshah (Humayun) and the grandees were present. Shaykh Bahlul was seated on the right hand, Bandagi Shaikh Muhammad on the left, and Bandagi Shaykh Ala-ud-Din was sitting in front. In the meantime, Bandagi Shaykh Khalil arrived. The king asked him to sit on his head, pointing to the roof as there was a room upstairs. He was assigned his seat there, *Waqi'at-i-Mushtaqi*, fol. 46a.

[11] *Waqi'at-i-Mushtaqi*, fols. 6b–7a.

[12] Siddiqui, *Afghan Despotism*, pp. 22–3.

The Sufis were also approached for prediction about the fate of a campaign. Shah Mansur prophesied the failure of Humayun's Gujarat expedition. According to a report, Humayun had sent an agent to him to ascertain the viability of the operation. Mansur took out an arrow from the agent's quiver, broke its wings, and then replaced it in the quiver. The badshah, on hearing about this incident, interpreted the Sufi's action to symbolize the failure of the campaign, saying that the army would suffer as the soldiers would scatter, though he (the ruler) would return to his place safely.[13]

High offices were also offered by the sovereign to the noted Sufis in a bid to ally with them. Some Sufis accepted government service and functioned as the *shaykh-ul-Islam* or the *sadr-us-sudur*; others did not. Abdul Haqq claims that his maternal grandfather, Zain-ul-Abidin *alias* Shaykh Adhan Dehlawi (d. 934/1527–8) refused Ibrahim Lodi's offer to appoint him as his patron.[14] Adhan Dehlawi was a disciple of Shaykh Sama-ud-Din, who, as noted above, was much venerated by the Lodi sultans, Bahlul and his son and successor, Sikandar. In view of the kings' devotion, a large number of Sufis and other saintly persons came to settle in the dominion. Abdul Haqq gives several examples. Some of them served as the envoys of the kings. Shah Qamis had come from Bengal to Salora, Khizrabad. He again went to Bengal as an envoy of the monarch and died there. His body was brought to Salora where he was buried.[15]

Other Sufis even entered into matrimonial alliances with the rulers. Shah Abdullah Qureshi was a majzub and a descendant of the fourteenth century Suhrawardi saint of Multan, Shaykh Baha-ud-Din Zakariya. When his family shifted from Multan to Delhi in the reign of Sultan Bahlul, the latter got his daughter married with Abdullah.[16] He subsisted upon a handsome grant from Bahlul Lodi till his death in 903/1497–8. It may be noted here that Abdullah's father Shaykh Yusuf Qureshi was a former ruler of Multan who had managed to

[13] *Akhbar-ul-Akhyar*, fol. 244a. For a different account and other episodes from the life of Shah Mansur, see *Azkar-i-Abrar*, pp. 263–4.

[14] *Akhbar-ul-Akhyar*, fols. 204b–205a. His tomb lies to the west of Hauz-i-Shamsi in Delhi, ibid., fol. 205a. Also see, Halim, 'Mystics of Sayyid-Lodi Period', p. 102.

[15] *Akhbar-ul-Akhyar*, fol. 189a.

[16] Ibid., fols. 195a–b. For a brief biographical sketch, also see *Azkar-i-Abrar*, p. 197.

escape from prison and sought asylum with Bahlul Lodi at Delhi. Bahlul repeatedly failed to restore Yusuf on the throne of Multan. Earlier Yusuf was elected to the throne in 854/1450–1, and was deposed and imprisoned by Rai Sihar, his father-in-law and the chief of the Langah Rajputs, who later on usurped the throne and took the title of Sultan Qutb-ud-Din. Reports of such marriages and conversion to Islam, involving non-Muslim chiefs and the Sufi saints are not uncommon in the period. Abdullah's son Rukn-ud-Din Qureshi was a pious man who was appointed Shaykh-ul-Islam of Delhi in the reign of Sikandar Lodi. A younger son of Abdullah, Shaykh Hasan, was a disciple of Shaykh Burhan Chishti of Kalpi and was a scholar of Persian poetry and well-versed in other sciences as well.[17]

Yet other Sufis impressed the badshah so much that he became devoted to them. A close associate of Shah Abdullah Qureshi, Shaykh Haji Abdul Wahhab Bukhari had also left Multan and came to Delhi. Disciple of Maulawi Sadr-ud-Din Bukhari and descendant of Saiyid Jalal-ud-Din Bukhari who was the grandfather of Makhdum Jahaniyan Jahangasht, Abdul Wahhab was much venerated by Sultan Sikandar Lodi. Later, as we shall see below, their relationship had deteriorated over an argument on the sultan's not keeping beard. The shaykh died in Delhi in 932/1525–6. The chronogram 'Shaykh Haji' gives the date of his death. It is related that during his second visit to the Haramain Sharifain, Mecca and Medina (which he undertook after coming to Delhi), he saw in his dream the Prophet directing him to return to Delhi.[18] Probably he was contemplating to stay on in the Hijaz. Abdul Wahhab had written a commentary, or *tafsir*, on the Quran in 915/1509–10. Abdul Haqq Muhaddis Dihlawi has discussed some points from this tafsir, which was probably written when the shaykh was in an ecstatic state.[19] We shall return to this commentary in the next chapter. Shah Jalal Shirazi had also come to Delhi from Hijaz in the reign of Sikandar Lodi. The langar was run at his house continuously. Apart from other things, the visitors were also served with bread and *firni*

---

[17] Halim, 'Mystics of Sayyid-Lodi Period', pp. 96–7.

[18] *Akhbar-ul-Akhyar*, fols. 195b–196a. Ghausi Shattari incorrectly notes that Abdul Wahhab fought along with Sultan Sikandar Lodi in a battle against Babur, and was killed with the sultan and his soldier, *Azkar-i-Abrar*, p. 230.

[19] *Akhbar-ul-Akhyar*, fols. 196b–201b.

(a dish made of ground rice, milk and sugar). Jalal Shirazi was a disciple of Shaykh Muhammad Nur Bakhsh, and had his daughter married with Shaikh Mudassir, son of Shaykh Haji Abdul Wahhab Bukhari who is referred to above. Shirazi died in 944/1537–8, and was buried near the grave of Abdul Wahhab.[20]

Some other Sufis, though they decided to settle in Delhi or Agra, avoided getting directly involved in the whirlpool of politics. They led austere lives and engaged themselves in mystical affairs. Shaykh Muhammad Maudud Lari came to Agra in 900/1494–5, and developed close relationship with Shaykh Aman Panipati (d. 957/1550–1). On account of this association, he shifted to Panipat after a prolonged stay at Agra.[21] Maulana Darwesh Muhammad Wa'iz was originally from the Mawara-un-Nahr or Transoxania. He spent several years in Haramain Sharifain in Arabia before coming to Hindustan during the Afghan rule. He led an austere life and died in Delhi.[22] Mir Saiyid Ibrahim, son of Mu'in Abdul Qadir al-Hasani of Iraj, came to Delhi in the reign of Sikandar Lodi. Disciple of Shaykh Baha-ud-Din Qadiri Shattari, Saiyid Ibrahim was an eminent saint and scholar in Delhi during the period. He died in 953/1546–7 and was buried in the Nizam-ud-Din shrine complex.[23]

LEGITIMACY AND INVOLVEMENT IN POLITICS

The Sufis who either belonged to the established families of the dominion or came not long before, and were able to cultivate friendly relations with the kings—a relationship which recognized the equal status of the Sufis and the rulers if not the superiority of the former though claims to this effect were often made—served as legitimizers of the political authorities. They prayed for the continuation of the 'just' rule of the sovereign. In their assemblies and in their writings, they praised the monarchs for their piety, justice, devotion towards the men of religion and for their welfare measures. Though ideally the

[20] Ibid., fols. 201b–202a.

[21] Ibid., fol. 210b. For Shaykh Aman Panipati, see also, ibid., fols. 216b–218a; Noting that Maudud Lari died in A.H.937, Ghausi Shattari suggests that the shaykh had come to India in the reign of Babur, *Azkar-i-Abrar*, p. 233.

[22] *Akhbar-ul-Akhyar*, fol. 239b.

[23] Ibid., fols. 236a–237a.

Sufis were expected to keep some distance from politics, they tended to get entangled in it. Their involvement in politics began with the belief that they had the power to bestow kingship on someone whom they thought deserving. References to the bestowal of kingship to Sher Shah have been cited above. Several examples of the conferring of the crown to the early Turkish sultans of Delhi are also to be found in the sources.[24]

Significantly, the sources refer to an episode in which the founder of the Lodi kingdom purchased the badshahat of Delhi from a Sufi of Samana. According to Mushtaqi, once three men came to Hindustan in connection with their trade. On their way back, they halted in the town of Samana. All the three men Ballu (Bahlul), Firuz Khan and Qutb Khan paid a visit to Saiyid Abban, who was absorbed in the thought of God, and possessed spiritual power and was known for his saintliness. As they sat down, the shaykh said: 'I sell the throne of Delhi for two thousand tankas. Is anybody willing to purchase it?' Ballu enquired whether the shaykh would accept one thousand and six hundred tankas as he had only that sum with him. When the shaykh gave his assent, he placed the amount before him. Keeping the money with him, the shaykh said: 'you may go now. The badshahat of Delhi has now been bestowed on you. These persons will serve you'. As they turned away, Bahlul's companions remarked: 'What did you do? You did not have anything except that amount'. Bahlul responded: 'I have done well. This sum was not sufficient for my entire life. I would have spent it within a short time. If he is a saintly man and his prophesy proves true, I would have entered into a profitable deal; and if it does not turn out to be true, to do a service to a Saiyid is an act of piety. In no way have I committed a mistake'.[25] While recording this episode, Nizam-ud-Din Ahmad has also noted that the suggestion in some histories about Malik Bahlul's involvement in trade had no foundation whatsoever. Probably his paternal ancestors were traders and used to come to Hindustan.[26] Ni'matullah has also narrated the story and followed Nizam-ud-Din Ahmad in suggesting that Bahlul was not engaged in trade, though his ancestors may have been.[27] The majzub's

---

[24] Aquil, 'Miracles, Authority and Benevolence'.

[25] *Waqi'at-i-Mushtaqi*, fol. 3b.

[26] *Tabaqat-i-Akbari*, fol. 132a.

[27] *Tarikh-i-Khan-i-Jahani wa Makzan-i-Afghani*, Vol. I, pp. 130–2.

prophecy encouraged Bahlul in later years to dream of acquiring the Sultanate.[28]

The princes also rushed to the Sufis for their blessings and prayers during the succession crises. Even though the nobles had supported the candidature of Nizam Khan after the death of Bahlul, the prince went to the foremost Sufi of Delhi before his enthronement and indirectly sought his support and blessings. Mushtaqi records that the prince went to meet Shaykh Sama-ud-Din Suhrawardi with a work on prosody with him. He did not inform the shaykh about the real purpose of his visit, and after the salutation he respectfully sat down and requested the shaykh to teach him the first lesson from the book. The shaykh read out an invocation from the chapter and explained its meaning as, 'may God render you fortunate in both the worlds'. Mian Nizam requested him to repeat it thrice. The shaykh did so. Thereafter, the prince asked for leave, informing him about the nobles' invitation for his enthronement. Then he kissed the ground and departed. Appreciating the prince's move, Mushtaqi attributed this to his 'remarkable wisdom and intelligence'.[29] Nizam-ud-Din Ahmad has also recorded that before leaving for enthronement, prince Nizam went to pay his homage to Shaykh Sama-ud-Din and asked him to pray on his behalf. He also requested him to teach the book of *Mizan Sarf* (a treatise on Arabic grammar). When the shaykh read in it *as'adakallah t'ala fi darain*, that is, 'may the most high God make (you) fortunate in both worlds', the sultan made him repeat it thrice, and then kissing the hand of the holy man, and taking that prayer to be a good omen, commenced his journey.[30] Ni'matullah has not only drawn on the account of Nizam-ud-Din Ahmad, but also added that the shaykh prayed for the success of the rule of the new sultan so that he would be known as the Sikandar (Alexander) of his time.[31] Thus, it is hinted that the title Sikandar was actually given by the shaykh himself.

In a divergent account of prince Nizam Khan's visit to Sama-ud-Din Kamboh, Badauni has noted the prince's fear that the shaykh might support the claims of his brothers.[32] Though the leading nobles had

---

[28] Ibid., Vol. I, p. 132. See also *Tabaqat-i-Akbari*, fol. 132a.
[29] *Waqi'at-i-Mushtaqi*, fol. 13b.
[30] *Tabaqat-i-Akbari*, fol. 149b.
[31] *Tarikh-i-Khan-i-Jahani Wa Makhzan-i-Afghani*, Vol. I, pp. 218–19.
[32] *Muntakhab-ut-Tawarikh*, Vol. I, p. 313.

supported Nizam's claim to the throne, his enthronement was not without controversy. His candidature was objected to by Isa Khan, Bahlul Lodi's cousin who remarked that 'the son of a gold worker's daughter is not fit to be the king'.[33] Badauni adds that Sama-ud-Din indirectly offered his blessings and best wishes to Nizam, obliging him by repeating thrice at his request the meaning of as'adakallah.[34]

Nizam's ascendance to the throne as Sultan Sikandar Lodi was disliked by his brother Barbak Shah. Abdul Haqq Muhaddis Dihlawi has not mentioned his name, but has recorded that the rebellious brother of Sikandar Lodi was a disciple of Shaykh Hasan Tahir (d. 909/1503–4), disciple of Raji Hamid Shah and khalifa of his son Raji Saiyid Nur. One day, the rebel approached the shaykh and requested him to pray that the kingdom of Delhi be conferred upon him. Instead of praying for him, the shaykh advised him to obey the command of his brother and forget the idea of overthrowing him as kingship was bestowed upon him by God. When Sikandar Lodi came to know of this he was impressed by the shaykh's integrity and spiritual attainments, and this further increased the sultan's urge to visit the Sufi shaykhs.[35] Shaykh Hasan Tahir's family had come from Multan to Bihar. After the downfall of the Sharqis, Tahir moved to Agra and later to Delhi where he stayed in Vijaymandal palace, which had been abandoned by the royalty.[36] His preceptor Raji Sayyid Nur was known for his miracles, and reportedly used to dress like a woman to hide his identity. He died in Manikpur. Sayyid Nur's father, Raji Hamid Shah was a disciple of Shaikh Hisam-ud-Din Minikpuri, himself a disciple of the fourteenth century Chishti Sufi Shaikh Nasir-ud-Din Chiragh-i-Dehli.[37]

Earlier a darwesh had prophesied prince Nizam's victory over his brother Barbak Shah. The young prince however told the mystic not to utter such words so openly. Mushtaqi has recorded that Nizam in his youth had fought a battle against Barbak Shah at Qannauj. As he was mounting on the horse, the Sufi came and requested him to place his hand in his, and then predicted his victory. The prince withdrew

[33] *Farishta.*

[34] *Muntakhab-ut-Tawarikh*, Vol. I, pp. 313–14.

[35] *Akhbar-ul-Akhyar* (printed text), p. 201.

[36] Ibid., pp. 201–2.

[37] For brief biographical notices of Raji Hamid Shah and Raji Saiyid Nur, see also, *Akhbar-ul-Akhyar* (printed text), pp. 200–1.

his hand and said that in a fight between two Muslims, one ought not to side with anyone, but say that those whose success was in the interest of Islam should emerge victorious.[38] Later, this story was recounted again by Nizam-ud-Din Ahmad[39] and Ni'matullah Harawi.[40]

The above episodes are examples of the ruler's concern for legitimization of his action by the Sufi shaykh. Whether a Sufi actually prophesied or prayed on behalf of a sultan or not, the repeated mentioning of these episodes in the various contemporary accounts is an indicator of the importance attached to these acts, the importance of the Sufi in the society and how crucial it was for the sultan to be perceived to be having the backing of a religious person of the stature of a well known Sufi, and thereby gaining legitimacy and respect from the subjects. The psychological gains were immense to the king or the aspirer who could justify his ambition to acquire the kingdom by stating that he was blessed by a certain wali, or friend of God.

The Sufis not only bestowed kingship but also lamented the death of a 'just' ruler. There was also a lurking danger that their power and prestige might be threatened in a new dispensation, especially when they were openly associated with the earlier rule. Jamali's uncomfortable position after the death of Sikandar Lodi is a case in point. He had written a marsiya on the death of the sultan. A particular couplet had become very popular already in the lifetime of Jamali:

Aye sulaiman zaman ah kujai akhir
Ta-kunam pesh tu az fitna-i-diwan faryad

(O Solomon of the times, alas! Where are you now?
(Tell me) so that I may place before you an appeal against the intrigues of the *diwan*.)

Jamali has complained that the new sultan, Ibrahim Lodi's teacher, Farid, was a despicable person. He presented the couplet to the king and told him that Jamali has referred to him and his other Afghan associates as demons (*devan*, a corruption of the word diwan used in the verse). Thus the ruler and the other Afghans had become distrustful of Jamali. He himself has written that though nobody had the courage to harm him, his anxiety was natural. Then he saw in a dream that Shaykh Sadr-ud-Din had sent a piece of cloth for him from Multan

---

[38] *Waqi'at-i-Mushtaqi*, fol. 11b.
[39] *Tabaqat-i-Akbari*, fol. 149a.
[40] *Tarikh-i-Khan-i-Jahani wa Makhzan-i-Afghani*, Vol. I, pp. 215–16.

with the instruction to wrap himself in it. He did so and performed the prayer of thanksgiving. When he woke up, whatever little anxiety he had earlier was gone. Also, Sultan Ibrahim's resentment was replaced by affection for Jamali.[41] Yet Jamali has lamented Ibrahim Lodi's hostile attitude towards Sikandar Lodi's close associates who were removed from their position. He added that some unworthy and seditious creatures had occupied important positions at the court and became the close confidantes of Sultan Ibrahim.[42]

The Sufis' attitude towards politics is best reflected in their stand and role in the case of a conflict between rival protagonists. We have seen above that they supported and even participated in Sher Shah's campaign against the rajas. They also supported Sikandar Lodi's action against them and condemned their occupation of the territories previously under the control of the Muslims. We shall return to this problem in a section on the Sufis' attitude towards non-Muslims in the next chapter. Here we shall restrict ourselves firstly to a discussion on their role in the attempts at empire-building by the Sharqis of Jaunpur and the Afghans led by Bahlul Lodi, and then in the conflict between the Afghans and the Mughals in the first half of the sixteenth century. The Sharqi monarchy emerged in 796/1393–4. The Sharqis exercised their sway over much of North India and their kingdom extended from Rapri to Kahalgaon. Qannauj, Koil, Sambhal, Bahraich, Badaun and Bulandshahar acknowledged their supremacy. Bayana offered its allegiance to them and the Rajputs of Gwalior also once paid tribute. Tirhut and Orissa were invaded more than once and paid tribute. Even Delhi, was more than once almost within their grasp. The last of the Sharqis was overthrown by Sultan Bahlul in 886/1481–2. Jaunpur was once more occupied by Sultan Husain in 1486. But before his death, two years later, Bahlul had installed his son Barbak as the ruler of Jaunpur, and left Husain in possession of the territories from Chunar to Bihar. A rare inscription of Husain from Bihar is dated 892/1486–7. The last of his coins was struck, perhaps at Kahalgaon, in 910/1504–5. Bahlul issued his own coins in 888/1483–4 and 894/1488–9 from Jaunpur.[43]

[41] *Siyar-ul-Arifin*, fols. 126a–127a.

[42] Ibid., fols. 126a–b.

[43] S.H. Askari, 'Discursive Notes on the Sharqi Monarchy of Jaunpur', *PIHC*, 23rd Session, Aligarh, 1960, pp. 152–3.

There are several references to the Sufis' support to the Afghans against the Sharqis of Jaunpur in our sources. We have earlier noticed Mushtaqi's account of the first siege of Delhi by the Sharqis and the miraculous staff which Bahlul Lodi had received at the shrine of Qutb-ud-Din Bakhtiyar Kaki in Delhi. Mushtaqi has also noted that earlier the Sharqi king had sought blessings from Shaykh Badi-ul-Haqq before his march to Delhi, which the shaykh denied as he said that he was praying for Sultan Bahlul with whom he identified the cause of Islam.[44] In the encounter which took place, the Sharqis had suffered a serious setback and agreed for peace.

On expiry of the period of peace which had been agreed upon Sultan Husain again proceeded towards Delhi with a huge army,[45] supported by the rebel governor of Bayana, Ahmad Khan, son of Yusuf Khan Jalwani, who had the public prayer read in the name of Sultan Husain.[46] Jamali has recorded that his pir Sama-ud-Din was staying in Bayana at this time. Sultan Ahmad Jalwani came to him, along with Saiyid Khunda Mir Rasuldar styled as Murtaza Khan, and asked him to pray for the success of the Sharqi king's campaign for the conquest of Delhi. Hearing this the shaykh was much perplexed and immediately reminded Ahmad Khan of Sultan Bahlul's favours to him and his family. The shaykh also added that his betrayal of the sultan could only lead to his degradation. Further, referring to the Sharqi ruler, Sultan Husain, he said that he could not pray for that unjust and oppressive tyrant. On the contrary, 'that dear one', Sultan Bahlul, was deeply religious.[47] Jamali has added that Ahmad was ashamed to hear the shaykh's response. Although he was extremely short-tempered, and his utterances could even border on infidelity, he kept quiet that day fearing the shaykh's wrath, and later gradually reconciled himself to serve Bahlul.[48] It may be that he could not muster enough resources in favour of the Sharqis who were eventually destroyed. The Shaykh's suggestion gave him an honourable explanation for reconciliation with Bahlul Lodi. Also, Shaykh Abdul Ghani Jaunpuri, the spiritual guide of Sultan

[44] *Waqi'at-i-Mushtaqi*, fol. 7a.

[45] *Muntakhab-ut-Tawarikh*, Vol. I, p. 308.

[46] Ibid.; *Tabaqat-i-Akbari*, fols. 137a-b; *Tarikh-i-Khan-i-Jahani wa Makhzan-i-Afghani*, Vol. I, p. 156.

[47] *Siyar-ul-Arifin*, fols. 234a-b.

[48] Ibid., fols. 234b–235a.

Husain, had disapproved the Sharqi king's attack on Bahlul Lodi. Though residing at Jaunpur after the fall of the Sharqi dynasty, Abdul Ghani used to pay occasional visits to Sikandar Lodi at Agra.[49] The Sufis' support to the Lodis seems to stem from the need which a section of the Muslims recognized for a powerful centralized Delhi Sultanate where their interests could be safeguarded. Writing about the early compromises of Bahlul Lodi in entering into peace-treaties with the Sharqi ruler, Badauni is amused by the presence of two kings at the distance of just 'seven days' journey', and gives a couplet on how two kings cannot rule from one place:[50]

Jaye do shamshir niyami ke did
Takht do jamshid maqami ke did

(Who has ever seen a scabbard which can contain two swords
who has ever seen the thrones of two Jamshids in one place)

In case of the Mughal-Afghan encounter, the Sufis generally adopted the policy of wait and watch, though we have already referred to a Sufi praying for Ibrahim Lodi without success. Also, the 'martyrdom' of a few saintly persons in the battle of Panipat and the condemnation that a large-scale massacre by the Mughals evoked in the wake of the conquest have been noted above. Once it was established that the Mughals have come to stay and could not be wished away, the Sufis took diverse positions. Some of them sided either with the Mughals or the Afghans, some others kept aloof, and still others kept changing their position with the fluctuating fortunes of the two parties. The cases of Jamali and his two sons, Abdul Hai 'Hayati' and Shaykh Gadai illustrate the position taken by the Sufis in the changing trajectory of politics at this stage.

Several examples of Jamali's views on the Lodi rulers have been given above. We shall briefly recapitulate the nature of his relations with them and then go on to discuss his attitude towards the Mughals. Jamali must have been too young to develop a close personal relationship with Bahlul Lodi. The sultan was a devotee of Jamali's uncle,

---

[49] Halim, 'Mystics of Sayyid-Lodi Period', pp. 90–1. Another Sufi Khwaja Muhammad Isa had prophesied victory for Sultan Husain Sharqi in his fight against Bahlul Lodi which however did not come true according to him due to the Sharqi ruler opening the war aggressively. Ibid., p. 86.

[50] *Muntakhab-ut-Tawarikh*, Text, Vol. I, p. 308/ Eng. trans., Vol. I, p. 405.

father-in-law and pir, Sama-ud-Din, and used to visit the shaykh and seek his blessings and benediction. Jamali's reference to one such visit of the king to the shaykh's hospice and the impact of the latter's exhortation on him has been noted before. The devotion of Bahlul's son, Sikandar Lodi towards Sama-ud-Din has also been mentioned. The monarch would frequently visit the shaykh. Jamali must have seen him during those meetings. In course of time, there developed a close relationship between the two, and the king held him in great esteem and treated him as his friend. Later authorities too have highlighted the friendship between the two. As noted above, Jamali also wrote a qasida in praise of the emperor and heart-tormenting marsiya on his death. One particular couplet of the marsiya led to an estrangement with Sikandar's son and successor, Ibrahim Lodi. Though Shaykh Sadr-ud-Din's intercession had diffused the tension between them, Jamali did not write any qasida for Ibrahim Lodi, nor there is any marsiya by him on his death. On the contrary, he celebrated the victory of Babur over Ibrahim Lodi in the battle of Panipat; he commanded respect of the Mughal emperor. Abdul Haqq mentions a verse of the qasida which Jamali wrote in praise of Babur:[51]

Shah dushman kush zahir-ud-din muhammad babur an-ke
Kishwar-i-bangala ra az alghar kabul ba-shikand

(Such is the slayer of enemies king Zahir-ud-Din Muhammad Babur
He subdues the ruler of Bengal by sacking Kabul)

After Babur's death, Humayun became the emperor and Jamali wrote a qasida for him as well.[52] As noted above, he also acknowledged him on the completion of his *Siyar-ul-Arifin*. Jamali must have become a close companion of the emperor as he participated in his Gujarat campaign, in 942/1535–6. According to Abdul Haqq, Jamali died in Gujarat during the campaign on 10 Zil Qa'd 942/12 May 1536.[53] The chronogram *khusrau hind budah* (He was Khusrau of Hind) gives the date of his death.[54]

---

[51] *Akhbar-ul-Akhyar*, fol. 206b.

[52] Ibid.

[53] Abdul Haqq also notes that his body was brought to Delhi and was buried at a place at 'Qutb Sahib' which he had selected in his lifetime, *Akhbar-ul-Akhyar*, fol. 206b.

[54] *Muntakhab-ut-Tawarikh*.

Jamali's two sons, Shaykh Abdul Hai 'Hayati' (d. 959/1551–2) and Shaykh Gadai (d. 976/1568–9) were noted saints of their time. In the conflict which ensued between Humayun and Sher Shah, Hayati seems to have sided with the Afghans or perhaps joined them after the defeat of the Mughals in two successive battles at Chausa and Qannauj. For he is found to have accompanied Sher Shah in his Malwa campaign, and is particularly referred to in connection with Mallu Khan's escape.[55] Like his father, he was also a poet and was especially known for his extempore composition of the verses.[56] Though he died at the young age of 36, he was already a leading shaykh under the Surs. Abdul Haqq has recorded that the scholars, poets and *qalandars* who came from the direction of Afghanistan during the period stayed at the shaykh's house. The latter ensured that they were treated well.[57] His power and prestige had particularly increased under Islam Shah Sur. The king who enjoyed the company of the saints and scholars treated Hayati as a boon companion. The shaykh had also written a history of the period and dedicated it to Islam Shah. The work, however, was non-extant already by the late sixteenth century. The Mughals had by then returned with a vengeance.

Unlike Hayati, his elder brother Shaykh Gada'i followed Jamali in throwing his lot with the Mughals. After Sher Shah's victory over Humayun, Gada'i left for Gujarat and stayed there for a few years before leaving for Hijaz. During his stay in Gujarat he treated the fugitive Bairam Khan very well and ensured that the Khan reached Humayun's camp in Sindh safely. Earlier the Khan was captured by the Afghans, but Sher Shah did not order his execution as he was told that at the time of his arrest the Mughal noble was staying in the house of Shaykh Mulhi Qattal. For according to the contemporary belief of the Afghans, those seeking protection at Mulhi Qattal's house should be granted amnesty. Later Bairam Khan fled from Sher Shah's custody and reached Gujarat, and from there as noted above went over to Humayun in Sindh.[58]

---

[55] *Waqi'at-i-Mushtaqi*, fol. 53b.

[56] *Akhbar-ul-Akhyar* (printed text), p. 234.

[57] Ibid., pp. 234–5.

[58] *Tarikh-i-Sher Shahi*, pp. 159–62. See also, Sukumar Ray, *Bairam Khan*, ed., M.H.A. Beg (Karachi, 1992), pp. 58–61.

Gada'i, on the other hand, left for Haramain Sharifain, and came back to Delhi in the first year of Akbar's reign. Expressing his deep sense of gratitude for the shaykh's help in Gujarat, Bairam Khan appointed him on the post of *Sadarat*.[59] Serving on the post during the period of regency (1556–60), Gada'i enjoyed unprecedented power and antagonized not only a number of Sufis and ulama, but also the emperor.[60] His arrogant attitude and arbitrary style of functioning proved to be an important factor leading to the differences between Akbar and Bairam Khan and the fall of the latter's regency. When Bairam Khan left for Gujarat in 1560 with the intention of going for Hajj, Shaykh Gada'i also accompanied him. However, Bairam Khan was attacked and killed by the Afghans at Patan in January 1561,[61] and the shaykh took shelter in Jaisalmer.[62] After staying there for some-time, Gadai returned to Delhi. Akbar treated him well this time and fixed a grant for him. However, due to opposition from the courtiers and other influential persons, he could not be reinstated in the court. Leading a retired life on pension, the shaykh enjoyed the company of beautiful women.[63] His relationship with the ulama and some of the other Sufis continued to be bitter. The bitterness is reflected, among other things, in the composition of the chronogram on the news of his death in 976/1568–9: [64] *murda khok kalan* (the great hog is dead).

Indeed, too much dabbling in politics could be a matter of disgrace for the Sufis and made them vulnerable to attacks from the antago-nists. We have already noted the execution of Shaykh Bahlul at the hands of Mirza Hindal. Badauni has written that Mirza Hindal put to death Shaykh Bahlul, the elder brother of Shaykh Muhammad Ghaus Gwaliori, at the instigation of certain 'evil minded' advisors, in 945/1538–9. The shaykh enjoyed the full confidence and friendship of

---

[59] *Akhbar-ul-Akhyar* (printed text), p. 235. Nizam-ud-Din has mentioned that Gadai was appointed as Sadr in the third year of Akbar's reign, *Tabaqat-i-Akbari*, fol. 22b.

[60] For the shaykh's power and prestige during the period, see also I.H. Siddiqui, 'Shaikh Gada'i Kambo: The Representative of the Indian Elite at the Mughal Court (1556–60)', in his *Mughal Relations with the Indian Ruling Elite*, Delhi: Munshiram Manoharlal, pp. 90–105.

[61] Ray, *Bairam* Khan, pp. 218–19.

[62] *Akhbar-ul-Akhyar* (printed text), p. 235.

[63] Ibid.

[64] *Muntakhab-ut-Tawarikh*.

Humayun.[65] As mentioned above, other authorities have suggested that the shaykh was executed on the charge of being in league with Sher Shah, and of supplying arms to him. Sufic memory, however, considered Shaykh Bahlul as a martyr and his execution was commemorated by the chronogram:[66] *faqad mat shahida*. Referring to Shaykh Bahlul's execution, Abdul Haqq has noted that his brother Muhammad Ghaus Gwaliori was also favoured by Humayun. The Mughal ruler was a devotee of his preceptor Shaykh Haji Hamid (d. 967/1559–60) too.[67] Muhammad Ghaus stayed at Kalinjar fort for several years and prospered there. After the advent of Sher Shah, Ghaus, like Gada'i, had to migrate to Gujarat, and returned again in the reign of Akbar. He however could not influence the emperor, his differences with Gada'i being one of the factors. Humiliated, he left for Gwalior.[68]

Also, the tragic case of Saiyid Shah Muhammad Firuzabadi, illustrates the popular veneration of the Saiyids and Sufis, and the expectation of a certain degree of integrity in their character. According to Abdul Haqq, the shaykh had come from Deccan to settle in Delhi. He claimed that he was the last shaykh of the chain of Shaykh Abdul Qadir Jilani, founder of the Qadiri order of Sufism, and was soon very popular in Delhi. This was the time when Ibrahim Lodi was faced with the danger of Babur's invasion of Hindustan. The king used to visit the Sufi shaykhs for their intercession. He was, however, defeated in the battle. Saiyid Shah Muhammad stayed for a long time at the fort of Firuzabad during the reign of Babur. His prestige and following remained intact under Humayun. The Afghan ruler Islam Shah was extremely devoted to him. When the nobles and the public saw the king's devotion towards the shaykh, they became his disciples in large numbers. Even some darwesh offered their allegiance to him and became his khalifas.

Two saintly persons, both Saiyids, happened to visit Delhi at this time. One was called Mir Shams-ud-Din Muhammad. A bachelor, who

[65] Ibid., Vol. I, p. 350. Also see, *Azkar-i-Abrar*, pp. 234–5.

[66] *Muntakhab-ut-Tawarikh*, Vol. I, p. 350.

[67] Haji Hamid was a disciple of Shah Qazin, a disciple of Shaykh Abdullah Shattari but had received *khilafat* from Qazin's son, Abul Fateh, *Akhbar-ul-Akhyar*, fols. 228a–b.

[68] For useful information on the life and mystic teachings of Ghaus Gwaliori, see *Azkar-i-Abrar*, pp. 290–302.

was said to have travelled all over the Muslim world, Shams-ud-Din was a scholar of wide ranging interests. He kept some books and a couple of servants during his journey. He had stayed for a while at Kabul where he was much venerated by Humayun. The second, Saiyid Abu Talib, was a handsome young man who had fled from Baghdad under unavoidable circumstances. Shams-ud-Din and Abu Talib happened to meet each other during the journey, and decided to travel together to Hindustan.

When Saiyid Shah Muhammad Firuzabadi heard of their arrival in Delhi, he tried to attract them towards him. Shah Muhammad had several daughters and was unable to find suitable matches for them. Even before the arrival of the two Saiyids, Shah Muhammad used to say that he was an Arab with relatives in Arabia, and that the marriage of his daughters would not be a problem if some of them came over to Hindustan. The arrival of the Saiyids kindled his hopes. He offered them his hospitality. The Saiyids stayed with him, and were very well served. After several days had passed, Shah Muhammad sent a proposal to Saiyid Abu Talib for marriage with his daughter. Abu Talib politely refused the offer explaining that he was a traveller and intended to remain a bachelor. Incidentally, soon after the two Saiyids were found murdered in the house of Shah Muhammad. The news of the twin murder created a flutter in the city. The people were shocked and their mourning was reminiscent of the scene of Karbala. The biers of the two saints were taken out in a procession with black flags. The young and the old, men and women who participated in the procession were crying like mad persons. Their bodies were transported to Medina where they were buried.

Shah Muhammad was accused of the murder. His disciples and followers turned hostile and wanted action taken against him. The leading nobles Taj Khan and Shaykh Farid went to question him. He denied responsibility for their death, and suggested that some thieves might have broken into the house, and killed them. The king, Abdul Haqq identified him as 'Sher Shah Lodi', referred the case to the ulama who were supposed to give their judgement in the light of the shari'at. The leading ulama from Lahore, Delhi, Jaunpur and other places gathered together. Shah Muhammad was questioned again. He again denied any involvement in the matter, and remarked that they may punish him in whatever way they wanted to, but like a true Saiyid, he would endure everything. The ulama struggled hard to gather evidence of his involvement on the basis of which they could give their judgement. While the case was going on he was kept in custody and had to bear torture.

Shaykh Aman Panipati was repeatedly requested by the ulama who were already hearing the case to join them and help resolve the matter. Panipati refused to come saying that grieved as he was to hear of the assassination, he could not believe that Shah Muhammad, a Saiyid, could resort to such dastardly act. Further, his participation in a case in which a Saiyid was being insulted would tantamount to his own disgrace on the day of judgement. Finally, as he was already shattered by the news of the death of the two Saiyids, the execution of the third would disintegrate him completely. Shah Muhammad thus, remained in jail, and died there. The anger of the public had not yet subsided. They tied his feet with ropes and dragged the body through the streets of the bazaars, and later buried him outside the fort of Delhi. The shaykh was earlier suspected of using malevolent jinns (demons) to get things done for himself.[69]

Further, in the wake of competition between the rival Sufis for the territorial authority in the wilayat and influential position in political circles, they used political power to subdue each other, often leading to acrimonious conflicts. The example of Shaykh Jamali's conflict with Saiyid Husain Pai' Minari (d. 942/1535–6) may be given here. Saiyid Husain had come to Delhi in the reign of Sikandar Lodi, but did not like the king and stayed away from his court. Some noble women had become his followers so he had no need to worry about his maintenance.[70] He had some differences with Shaykh Jamali who used to ridicule him and accuse him of debauchery. One day, Saiyid Husain could not control his anger, and cut-off his private parts and sent them to Jamali. Abdul Haqq has noted that there were conflicting reports regarding this incident. Some persons denied that this had happened. The truth, according to the author, was that Saiyid Husain was suffering from dropsy, and was operated on the advice of the doctors.[71]

---

[69] *Akhbar-ul-Akhyar*, fols. 188a–191b.

[70] Ibid., fol. 206b.

[71] *Akhbar-ul-Akhyar* (printed text), pp. 235–6. Sir Syed Ahmad Khan identifies him as Imam Zamin and gives the date of his death in 944/1537–8. He had got his little tomb constructed, adjacent to Qutb Minar in Delhi in his own lifetime, *Asar-us-Sanadid*.

The Sufis' conflict with each other stemmed from their claims to wilayat which fused religious and political categories of authority in the territory controlled by a Sufi. A reference to the notion of the boundary of the wilayat is to be found in the *Akhbar-ul-Akhyar*. Shaykh Bakhtiyar, a disciple of Shaykh Ahmad Abdul Haqq, had sought his permission for a long journey in connection with his trade. The shaykh gave his consent with the warning that he should not cross the river as his wilayat stretched up to this side of the river only.[72] Though the Sufis generally respected each other's area of control, their desire for power and prestige in the wilayat brought them in conflict with the rulers.

TENSION BETWEEN THE SUFIS AND THE RULERS

The wilayat of the shaykh practically encroached on the king's territorial authority. In fact, wilayat or spiritual rule over a territory ran parallel to the king's jurisdiction, administered through his officials. It was below the shaykh's dignity to be seen as being under the king's patronage, indicated through such gestures as accepting royal grants or attending his court, or even to extending permission to the monarch to visit his hospice, with the shaykh receiving the sovereign with the same politeness as was the lot of other visitors. The shaykh's authority over a wilayat had an obvious bearing on the course of political events and material fortunes of the area. The belief in the shaykh's power to bestow kingship, his role as the protector of the people in times of crisis and as the healer of the sick legitimated and enhanced his authority in his wilayat. The shaykh's indifference towards court rituals, his occasional refusal to allow the reigning badshah to visit his hospice and his encroachment into the power base of the king, that is, the courtiers and the ordinary soldiers, were a potential threat to the king's power.[73]

Thus, in their quest for an authoritative position in the society some Sufis refrained from getting directly involved in political matters. This

---

[72] *Akhbar-ul-Akhyar* (printed text), p. 197.

[73] For a study of the connotation of authority of the shaykh's wilayat, leading to conflict with the rulers in the Delhi Sultanate, see Digby, 'The Sufi Shaikh and the Sultan'; Aquil, 'Miracles, Authority and Benevolence'.

could however be construed by the rulers as an insulting indifference towards them. Shaykh Ahmad Dharsuwi (d. 957/1550–1), a descendant of the thirteenth century Suhrawardi Sufi, Shaykh Baha-ud-Din Zakariya, led a long life and saw the reigns of several kings from Bahlul Lodi to Islam Shah Sur. In his early life, he was in the service of one of the sultans. One night, while guarding the palace, it is recounted, his heart was transformed. He thought that he should serve the one who protects him, and not the one whom he himself protects. Renouncing the world, he went to the shrine of Mu'in-ud-Din Chishti at Ajmer. In the company of a 'lover of God', Mu'in-ud-Din, and, Shaykh Ahmad Mujid Shaibani, who were staying there, the shaykh was blessed with 'divine bounty'.[74] Abdul Haqq adds that the shaykh later settled at Dharsu, near Narnaul, and strove to reform the Saiyids there who were increasingly getting 'de-Islamized'.[75] We shall refer in the next chapter to the question of cultural appropriations on the one hand and the felt need for reform on the other.

Returning to the relation between the Sufis and the rulers, even where the latter were devoted to a particular Sufi he was concerned whether they adhered to the shari'at, at least outwardly, or blatantly violated it. The example of Shaykh Ali Bin Husam-ud-Din may be cited here. During the shaykh's visit to Gujarat, Sultan Bahadur desired to have an audience with him to offer cash and land grants. He refused to have any connection with the ruler as his deportment betrayed his 'un-Islamic' disposition. Qazi Abdullah Sindhi, however, persuaded the shaykh to let the sultan visit him. The following day, the king sent one crore Gujarati (tanka) to the shaykh. The latter handed over the entire amount to the Qazi, saying that the amount belonged to him as he was the mediator between him and the ruler.[76] Sultan Mahmud of Gujarat, too, often visited the shaykh who generally remained indifferent towards him on account of his so-called unlawful dress.[77] Abdul Haqq gives another anecdote which shows that though the shaykh visited the house of a wazir, his indifference towards the wishes of the host bordered on the humiliation of the latter.[78]

---

[74] *Akhbar-ul-Akhyar* (printed text), pp. 192–3.
[75] Ibid., p. 193.
[76] Ibid., p. 266.
[77] Ibid., pp. 269–70.
[78] Ibid., p. 268.

Also, Khwaja Husain Nagauri (a descendant of Sufi Hamid-ud-Din Nagauri and disciple of Shaykh Kabir who was also a descendant of the former) refused the invitation of the sultan of Mandu, Ghiyas-ud-Din Khalji, to visit him. The shaykh however went when he was informed that the sultan was in possession of a sacred hair (*mu'-i-mubarak*) of the Prophet. During his visit to Mandu, the shaykh prayed at the grave of the sultan's father. The shaykh himself refused to accept the gifts offered by the ruler, but let his son receive them on the condition that he would spend the amount on the construction of the tombs of his grandfather and that of Hamid-ud-Din Nagauri, as his preceptor had prophesied that he would receive some wealth which he should thus utilize.[79] The Sufi memory has it that Husain Nagauri's son did not get any wealth subsequently.[80]

Some other Sufis and their sons could not be lured into accepting the grants. Mian Khan Zafarabadi (d. 970/1562–3) was a disciple and khalifa of Shaykh Hasan Tahir, who had declined to pray for the rebellious brother of Sikandar Lodi. Zafarabadi maintained distance from the rulers and rejected cash and land grants from them. Even his sons refused to accept the grants. Once Humayun put all the seals, concerning the imperial farman on grants, on a plain paper and sent it to the shaykh in the hope that he himself wrote the number of villages and the amount of cash which he wished to take as the grant from the ruler. The shaykh turned down the offer saying that he does not need them and that it was unlawful to deprive the Muslims of their right. The king then suggested that the shaykh should let his sons accept the grant, as they might need it. The shaykh responded that he had no right to dictate them to accept, or reject, the grants. It was up to them to decide. Subsequently, the farman was sent to his eldest son, Shaykh Abdullah who also, begged to be excused and remarked that only that person who strictly followed on the foot-steps of his father should be called a son.[81] Makhdum Shaykh Abdul Qadir (d. 940/1533–4),

---

[79] Abdul Haqq has also noted that the tomb of Husain Nagauri was constructed by Ghiyas-ud-Din Khalji, though its gate was built by some other kings of Mandu. Also, the building of the tomb of Hamid-ud-Din Nagauri and its gate was constructed by Muhammad Bin Tughluq who had fortified the town of Nagaur as well, *Akhbar-ul-Akhyar*, fols. 168b–169a.

[80] *Akhbar-ul-Akhyar*, fol. 169a.

[81] Ibid., fols. 209b–210a.

popularly known as Abdul Qadir Sani or Makhdum Sani, of Uchch, also refused to accept the largess from the ruler, though his two brothers, Saiyid Abdullah and Saiyid Mubarak, were in the service of the king, and his father Makhdum Shaykh Muhammad Husaini Jilani had accepted the royal gift of land. After Makhdum Jilani's death, the ruler not only wanted to renew the endowment in favour of the successor, Makhdum Sani, but also increase it. Makhdum Sani, however, turned it down saying that this may be granted to the needy or the seeker.[82]

Thus, some Sufis were ashamed of taking the grants from the public treasury, and at times could take the issue to its extreme. Shaykh Husam-ud-Din Muttaqi Multani was known to be a rigid follower of the shari'at. He would not stand in the shade of the tomb of the Suhrawardi Sufi, Shaykh Baha-ud-Din Zakariya at Multan, as he explained that money from the public treasury was used for its construction.[83] Further, Shaykh Ahmad Abdul Haqq of Rudauli, disciple of Shaykh Jalal-ud-Din Panipati and the spiritual teacher of Shaykh Abdul Quddus Gangohi,[84] condemned the ruling elite as dogs. Abdul Haqq Muhaddis Dihlawi relates that during the shaykh's stay in Awadh, he had kept a female dog as pet. The shaykh invited the notables of the place for a feast organized to celebrate the birth of her pups. Next day, when Shaykh Jamal Gujari, a disciple of Shaykh Salah Darwesh who was based at Rudauli, complained on not being invited, Shaykh Ahmad Abdul Haqq responded that only the dogs of the city were called for the feast held by his dog (*mezbani sag bud sagan ra talbidim*). The shaykh added that according to the tradition of the Prophet, the world is like a carcass and its seekers are dogs. He further said that since he

[82] For this and other episodes in the lives of Makhdum Sani and his father, Makhdum Jilani, see *Akhbar-ul-Akhyar*, fols. 183b–186b.

[83] *Akhbar-ul-Akhyar*, fol. 195a.

[84] Shaykh Abdul Quddus Gangohi (1453–1537) was the disciple, brother-in-law and khalifa of Shaykh Ahmad Abdul Haqq of Ruduali. He spent thirty-five years of his life at Rudauli and when circumstances did not favour his stay there, he migrated to Shahabad in 896/1491, early in the reign of Sikandar Lodi at the suggestion of his disciple, Umar Khan Kasi, one of the sultan's nobles. He remained there for another thirty-five years. After the battle of Panipat, Babur sacked the town of Shahabad and Abdul Quddus went to Gangoh and died there in 1537 at the age of eighty-four, M. Zameer Uddin Siddiqui, 'Shaikh Abdul Quddus of Gangoh and Contemporary Rulers', *PIHC*, 31st Session, Varanasi, 1969, pp. 305–11. For more on Abdul Quddus, see chapter six.

considered Jamal Gujari as a human being, he did not call him. In fact, the shaykh used to complain that during his long journey from Sindh to Bengal he did not come across a single Muslim anywhere, except Jamal Gujari of Awadh.[85]

Together with such provocative remarks and actions, the use of royal symbols by certain Sufis could also lead to a misunderstanding. Abdul Haqq has referred to the frightening demeanour of Shaykh Abdullah Shattari who was a descendant of Shaykh Shahab-ud-Din Suhrawardi, and his use of drums to attract the people for training in his Shattari branch of Sufism.[86] The shaykh would dress like a sultan and his disciples who accompanied during his long journey wore the costumes of soldiers.[87] Shattari would also sit on a chair on an elevated platform resembling a throne, and kept security guards posted outside the house where he would stay during the course of his tour. Abdul Haqq says that when the shaykh was staying at Sarharpur, the leading Chishti shaykh of the place, Shah Da'ud, who wanted to meet the Shattari shaykh, forcibly broke into the house. Shah Da'ud kicked the gate-keeper who had tried to stop him and entered the premises trampling on the gate-keeper's chest as he lay on the floor.[88] The episode points to the assertion of power by the incumbent Sufi in his wilayat, which was subsequently recognized by the visiting shaykh.[89] Returning to the use of royal symbols, another Sufi, Saiyid Ali (d. 905/1499–1500), would occasionally wear the uniform of a soldier. A Saiyid from Sawana, who had gone to Jaunpur and had become a disciple of Shaykh Baha-ud-Din Jaunpuri, he too used to get the drum beaten outside his house. One day, he saw the Prophet in his dream who inquired as to why he got the drum beaten. The shaykh replied that the drum was beaten to announce the arrival of the Prophet himself.[90]

In the eventuality of a conflict with the rulers the Sufi had the option of migrating to some other territory where his status was recognized.

---

[85] *Akhbar-ul-Akhyar*, fol. 175a. For a biographical note of Shaykh Ahmad Abdul Haqq, see also ibid., fols. 173a–174b.

[86] *Akhbar-ul-Akhyar*, fol. 162b.

[87] *Azkar-i-Abrar*, pp. 161–6. Also see Haqq, 'The Shattari Order of Sufism in India', pp. 167–75.

[88] *Akhbar-ul-Akhyar*, fol. 176a.

[89] Ibid.

[90] Ibid., fols. 208b–209a.

This is illustrated from the case of Shaykh Abdullah Biyabani, son of Shaykh Sama-ud-Din Suhrawardi (the leading Sufi in the Lodi Sultanate). Biyabani was based in Delhi, that is, when he was not roaming in the forest or the desert which earned him the sobriquet Biyabani (from *biyaban*, lit.: wild, savage, desert). He had once interceded on behalf of some Saiyids who were imprisoned by the ruler. On the king's refusal to oblige him, the shaykh left the place remarking that it was haram (unlawful) to stay in the dominion and settled in Mandu, where he was welcomed by the ruler. He did not accept any gift from the king, but wanted the assurance that his officials would not disturb him. He died in Mandu and was buried there.[91] Some cases of the migration of the pro-Mughal Sufis to the territory outside the control of Sher Shah have been noticed earlier. Generally, they left for Gujarat and from there to Hijaz. Shaykh Salim Chishti, a descendant of Shaykh Farid-ud-Din Ganj-i-Shakar, also left for Haramain in 962/1554–5, after his conflict with Hemu. This was his second visit, first being in 931/1524–5. He came back in 976/1568–9 in the reign of Akbar and cultivated good relation with him. The birth of Akbar's son, Salim (later Jahangir), and his upbringing at the shaykh's house is well-known. The shaykh was born in 897/1491–2, and died in 979/1571–2.[92]

Another option for a Sufi locked in conflict with the ruler was to stay in the territory and perform miracles to establish his supremacy and authoritative position in the wilayat. The case of Shaykh Haji Abdul Wahhab's encounter with Sikandar Lodi over the sultan not keeping beard may be cited here. Though the ruler had agreed that as a Muslim king he was supposed to keep beard, he said that he would do so only if his pir insisted on it. After the shaykh left the place, the sultan commented: 'The shaykh thinks that the people who come to visit him (the shaykh) and kiss his feet, do it owing to his own spiritual power. He does not understand that were I to cause any of my slaves to sit on a litter, and order all my nobles to carry it on their shoulders, they would do so'. When Abdul Wahhab came to know of this remark, he cursed the sultan saying: 'His (sultan's) comment will stick in his throat'. Mushtaqi concludes that the disease of the throat from which the king suffered was caused by the shaykh's curse.[93] Nizam-ud-Din

---

[91] *Akhbar-ul-Akhyar* (printed text), pp. 218–19. See also *Azkar-i-Abrar*, p. 225.

[92] *Akhbar-ul-Akhyar* (printed text), pp. 289–90.

[93] *Waqi'at-i-Mushtaqi*, fols. 27b–28a.

Ahmad has not mentioned the curse, but referred to Sultan Sikandar's throat-disease. According to him, the sultan contracted an illness, not letting him eat anything or even drink water (*luqma wa ab dar galu namiraft*). Although he carried on his duties normally, gradually the infection became serious, leading to his death in this condition.[94]

The mutual inter-dependence of the Sufis and the kings and the occasional tension in their relationship has perhaps compelled some modern scholars to suggest that the Afghan period witnessed a 'spiritual anarchy' wherein the Sufis of various silsilas were hankering for power and wealth. Presumably, this hypothesis is also based on the premise that the Sufis of the earlier period, that is, the thirteenth and fourteenth centuries, kept themselves aloof from the politics of their time. The assumption has already been questioned in some recent researches, and the role of the Sufis in politics, including that of the Chishtis who were considered to be far removed from the quagmire of court intrigue, is no longer viewed as a scandal.[95] We have shown elsewhere that a number of Sufis visited the reigning sultans. Others avoided visiting the sultan's court and following its rituals. A section of them may have also felt that a tactical 'on stage' distance from the rulers was in order for the reconciliation of a hostile non-Muslim population of the loosely conquered territories. Thus, the Sufis came to settle in centres of political influence or in areas already made sacred by the non-Muslim religious traditions. Other strategic places where they chose to stay were the much-trodden trade routes. Certainly Sufi orders were against the idea of settling in a forest or at lonely places. There is also no evidence of noted Sufis deliberately staying in the localities of low-caste Hindus only.

It has also been pointed out that some Sufis did accept land and cash grants from the rulers. They prayed for their victory over the kuffar. Often during the campaign, the soldiers made a detour to visit a hospice or a shrine and sought blessings. Also the shaykhs were approached

---

[94] *Tabaqat-i-Akbari*, fol. 148b.

[95] A great deal of evidence has been marshalled in support of the suggestion that the Sufis were involved in politics, see Digby, 'The Sufi Shaikh as a Source of Authority in Medieval India'; idem, 'The Sufi Shaikh and the Sultan'; Eaton, *Sufis of Bijapur*; Zilli, 'Early Chishtis and the State'; Aquil, 'Miracles, Authority and Benevolence'. For the later phase, see also, Muzaffar Alam, 'Assimilation from a Distance'.

to inquire about the fate of the Muslim army campaigning away from Delhi. Some Sufis even contributed in striking the roots of Muslim control in newly conquered territories by sending khalifas along with the army. Others allowed their sons to join the sultan's army and fight jihad against the infidels. Yet others went to report the events of the campaign. Most of the sultans, members of the royal family and the court officials were actually *murid*s of the shaykhs, who bestowed kingship on a person of their choice and snatched it away when dissatisfied with his performance. Occasionally matrimonial alliances between the families of the Sufis and the sultans also took place. The *tabarrukat* of the shaykhs, including the saliva-infused food leavings, were much valued, among others, by the members of the royal family. So the langar was an attraction not only for the hungry paupers, but was also cherished by the royal family and rich officials.[96] All this is also reminiscent of our illustrations from the lives of the Sufis of the Afghan period which we have given above. Thus there does not appear to be any decisive break in the Sufic approach towards politics and government in the period. So also was the case with society's belief in the paranormal power of the Sufi shaykh. Indeed, miracle continued to be the source of the shaykh's authoritative position in the wilayat. It was believed that the provocation of the *jalal* or wrath of the shaykh could be disastrous, and his miracle could be a source of benevolence as well. We shall discuss these issues in the next chapter.

---

[96] The above discussion on the Sufis' interaction with the ruling elite in the thirteenth and fourteenth centuries' Delhi Sultanate is based on Aquil, 'Sufi Cults, Politics and Conversion'.

6

Sufi Traditions and Hindu-Muslim Interactions

THE SUFIS PLAYED AN IMPORTANT role in the politics of the Afghan dominion of the late fifteenth and early sixteenth century, as we saw in the previous chapter. These Sufi shaykhs mainly belonged to the various branches of the Chishti and Suhrawardi orders (silsilas), even as the Qadiris and Shattaris were also making their presence felt.[1] It may however be noted here that the distinctions between the Sufis of the diverse spiritual traditions often tended to get blurred. Many of these Sufis were reported to have attained higher stages (maqamat) in the mystic path (tariqat). Karamat constituted an important aspect of the beliefs and practices of the Sufis and was a significant source of their authority. The word karamat denotes the marvels displayed by the 'friends of Gods' or auliya (sing. wali). The saints are supposed to get the power to perform miracles on account of their devotion to God.[2] The sources distinguish between the miracles attributed to the prophets, Sufis, yogis or Hindu mystics, and the street charmers.[3] Even as the Sufi tradition notes the impeccability of the prophets and the fallibility of the saints, the legitimacy for karamat is derived from the mu'jizat or miracles of the Prophet. In his Kashf-ul-Mahjub, said to be the earliest known mystical treatise in Persian, Shaykh Ali Hujwiri 'Data

[1] Halim, 'Mystics of the Sayyid-Lodi Period'; Haq, 'The Shuttari Order of Sufism in India'.

[2] L. Gardet, 'Karama', in Encyclopaedia of Islam, New Edition, Vol. 4 (Leiden, 1973).

[3] Fawa'id-ul-Fu'ad, conversations of Shaykh Nizam-ud-Din Auliya compiled by Amir Hasan Sijzi. Persian text with an Urdu translation by Khwaja Hasan Sani Nizami (Delhi, 1990), Vol. II: 23rd meeting.

Ganj Bakhsh', in fact, identifies the karamat of the Sufis with the mu'jizat of the Prophet.[4]

The Islamic 'fundamentalists' aspire to revive the 'golden period' under the Prophet and the *khulafa-i-rashidin* or the rightly-guided caliphs of the seventh century Arabiya. The term fundamentalist is being used here for the Muslim religious scholars or ulama who believed in the Quran and the Traditions (hadis) of Prophet Muhammad as the ultimate sources of law and minimized the importance of later interpretations and practices of Islam.[5] They discriminate in their recognition of the paranormal power of the saints and the prophets. While the claims of the supernatural abilities of the Sufis are refuted by them, the prophets' ability to perform miracles is recognized. On the other hand, while seeking to understand Sufic beliefs and practices from a 'scientific perspective', some 'liberal' scholars of the history of Islam in India not only dismiss popular religion as unimportant but also strive to reform it. They wish to reform the 'superstitious' past from their own 'modern', 'scientific' or 'rational' standpoint. This is well reflected in their approach towards the miracles of the Sufi shaykhs. These scholars generally dismiss miracle stories in the medieval sources, particularly Sufi literature, as later concoctions designed to make the gullible believe in the blessed power of the Sufis.[6] It is only recently that some scholars have turned their attention to the tales of miracles in Sufi literature and highlighted the significance of miraculous combats between the Sufis and their opponents.[7]

We shall draw attention below to the significance of miracles in Sufi fraternities of the Afghan period. The discussion will primarily be based on an authoritative collection of the biographies of the Sufis, *Akhbar-ul-Akhyar* of Abdul Haqq Muhaddis Dihlawi, himself a saint of considerable reputation, eminent Traditionist or scholar of the traditions of the Prophet, and prolific writer. There is a possibility that

[4] A.J. Wensinck, 'Mu'djiza', in *Encyclopaedia of Islam*, New Edition, Vol. 7 (Leiden, 1990).

[5] For fundamentalism in Indian Sunni Islam, see Ahmad, *Intellectual History of Islam*, pp. 8–11.

[6] Mujeeb, *Indian Muslims*, pp. 118–21, Rizvi, *History of Sufism*, Vol. I, pp. 4–5; Siddiqui, 'The Early Chishti Dargahs', p. 12.

[7] For this see Alam, 'Competition and Coexistence'; Digby, 'Hawk and Dove in Sufi Combat'; Aquil, 'Conversion in Chishti Sufi Literature'.

the stories of miracles may have sprung up among the beleaguered Afghans under the Mughals when Abdul Haqq recorded them in his work. However, the acceptance of such a proposition is tantamount to questioning the credentials of Abdul Haqq as a biographer. Modern scholars admire his insistence on the use of reliable contemporary documents as evidence. He is also said to have checked the authenticity of his material by using the same tools with which the hadis or prophetic reports were examined.[8] Still, in order to corroborate the reliability of Abdul Haqq's account we shall consult the sources dating back to the Afghan period itself. For this purpose we shall take up the *Siyar-ul-Arifin* of Suhrawardi Sufi, Shaykh Jamali.[9] The *Waqi'at-i-Mushtaqi* of Rizqullah Mushtaqi, a paternal uncle of Abdul Haqq, who saw the reigns of Lodi and Sur Afghans, will also be consulted. Further, to check whether these miracle stories might have suddenly emerged in the Afghan period only, we shall compare the various motifs in miracles related by Jamali, Mushtaqi and Abdul Haqq with those found in the Chishti malfuzat (conversations of a saint recorded by one of his disciples) and tazkiras (biographical dictionaries) of the fourteenth century. We shall mainly illustrate from the discourses of Nizam-ud-Din Auliya in *Fawa'id-ul-Fu'ad*, of Nasir-ud-Din Chiragh-i-Dehli in *Khayr-ul-Majalis* and the voluminous collection of the biographies of the Chishti shaykhs, Amir Khwurd's *Siyar-ul-Auliya*. We shall also draw on a set of malfuzat, rejected by historians as spurious and useless.[10]

The anecdotes of marvellous feats either narrated by a leading shaykh before his disciples in the hospice (khanqah or jama'atkhana), or recorded by a biographer, claim that they were performed by the Sufis both in the wake of encounters with opponents and as acts of benevolence. In both cases, miracles served to establish the Sufis' authoritative position in society. It is not our concern here to establish the authenticity or historicity of wondrous stories recorded in Sufi literature, but to show that miracles were very much an integral part of the Sufi discipline, as has been the case with diverse religious traditions. Yet, there was an emphasis on the need for the Sufi shaykh to hide his

---

[8] K.A. Nizami, *Hayat-i-Shaykh Abdul Haqq Muhaddis* (Delhi, 1953).

[9] For Jamali's career, see previous chapter. See also M.Z. Huda, 'Jamali, The Poet of Ludis and Mughals', *Journal of the Asiatic Society of Pakistan*, 1968–9, Vol. 13, No. 3, pp. 253–89 and Vol. 14, No. 1, pp. 21–49.

[10] For a discussion of the value of these works, see 'Introduction'.

supernatural capabilities, just as the prophets were expected to display them.[11] Despite the suggestions for restraint, sources are replete with stories of a wide range of miracles performed by the Sufis cutting across the different silsilas, and time and space. Perhaps the context facilitated the reported occurrence of a particular type of miracle. However, generally the themes were of a universal nature. Besides drawing attention to the various types of miracles and how they served to establish the authority of the Sufi shaykh in society, we shall focus below on stories of miraculous conversion of non-Muslims to Islam. The sources record a large number of accounts of individual and group conversion at the hands of various Sufi shaykhs. Here we shall illustrate anecdotes concerning the Sufis of our period (late fifteenth and early sixteenth century) only. However, occasional digression into the lives of those of the earlier period, mainly the thirteenth and fourteenth centuries, for the purpose of comparison and contrast will be a useful exercise.

The word conversion is being used here to connote the incidents of non-Muslims reading the kalima (profession of faith in Islam), embracing Islam, and becoming disciples of the Sufis.[12] Many Sufis who mingled freely with people adhering to diverse formal/informal religious traditions largely considered it unadvisable to use political power for spreading Islam by forcibly bringing non-Muslims to its fold. Some of them would refrain from converting people without a proper 'introduction' to Islam, through personal interaction over a long period of time. The most powerful and articulate argument on the question came from the influential Chishti saint Nizam-ud-Din Auliya, who asserted that no amount of force could change the heart of these people. In this context, the words 'Hindu' and 'qaum' are used already in the early decades of the fourteenth century. They should spend time in the company of good Muslims to be transformed into good Muslims themselves.[13] Conversion then will become a matter of formality. Thus, it is through a long-term association with Sufi centres like hospices and shrines, facilitated by a number of attractions, that many individuals

---

[11] Gardet, 'Karama'; Wensinck, 'Mu'djiza'.

[12] For a detailed discussion of the diverse views on the Sufis' role in conversion and Islamization, see Aquil, 'Sufi Cults, Politics and Conversion'.

[13] *Fawa'id-ul-Fu'ad*, Vol. IV, 40th Meeting.

and groups of people embraced Islam. Colonial enumeration may have played a role in sharpening of categories such as Muslim or Hindu. This does not mean that they did not exist altogether in medieval times. To deny this is to ignore the views of medieval Muslim intellectuals like Ziya-ud-Din Barani, who clearly identified himself with one political and, shall we say, cultural group as against many others. Barani has shown that contestations were involved in what constituted a community or *umma* of Islam in relation to the kafirs. It is also clear that the self-righteous, privileged group amongst Muslims wanted to utilize all the tools of dominance to subdue those who belonged to a different group within a socially-stratified and sectarian-conflict ridden society referred to by the generic term Islamic. Barani wanted the kafirs to be sent to hell, even as he condemned the rise of Islam's internal 'others' such as the converted Indian Muslims in the Delhi Sultanate as a complete perversion. Though Barani himself belonged to the influential Chishti tradition, the dominant voice within this Sufi order tended to be cautious and inclusive.[14]

Sufi literature also refers to instances when the performance of miracles did not lead to the conversion of the adversary to Islam. There were reports when the non-Muslim opponents or spectators were amazed by the miraculous ability of the Sufi shaykhs, but did not convert. In such cases the Sufis had to be content with the recognition of their spiritual power only. The sources also show that at times the Sufis could adopt a very hostile attitude towards non-Muslims, generally condemned as kafirs or infidels. Some of them participated in the campaigns against the non-Muslim chieftains, which were projected as holy war or jihad. We shall illustrate below, through the letters written by Chishti Sufi, Shaykh Abdul Quddus Gangohi to the Afghan and Mughal rulers, that some Sufis were not averse to occasionally using political power to subdue non-Muslims even as they flaunted their credentials as belonging to a liberal Chishti tradition. In some cases, their approach could be as uncompromising as of any orthodox alim (plural: ulama/religious scholars) of medieval India. (The terms orthodox and orthodoxy are being used here for the group of ulama, referred to as *ulama-i-su* or 'wicked divines' in Aziz Ahmad's words,

---

[14] For a more detailed discussion of the above issues with reference to Barani's writings, see Aquil, 'On Islam and *Kufr* in the Delhi Sultanate'.

who insisted on a strict conformity, *taqlid*, to the Hanafi school of jurisprudence, fiqh, and condemned any deviation from it as heresy).[15] On the other hand, we shall also see the Sufis' valuable contribution to what is traditionally referred to as syncretism and synthesis in the field of religion and culture. Among other things, we shall try to come to terms with Abdul Quddus' seemingly contradictory role in this regard. Finally, an attempt will also be made to understand the ulama's efforts to establish their own interpretation of the shari'at or Islamic law as a way of life in the realm. Yet hardly any alim of the Delhi Sultanate questioned the general belief in the miraculous ability of the Sufis. In fact, the major shaykhs who have either narrated or recorded miracle stories were leading scholars of their times. As noted above, Abdul Haqq Muhaddis Dihlawi was counted amongst the noted authorities on the traditions of the Prophet. Nizam-ud-Din Auliya was a qualified alim in his own right, and was in his early years looking for a government job in Delhi. He could have ended up becoming a qazi (judge), but Shaykh Najib-ud-Din Mutawakkil, younger brother of the leading Chishti Shaykh Farid-ud-Din Ganj-i-Shakar, drew him to the mystic path.[16] Thus, even though miracle stories recounted by them seem to be of folkloric nature, the narrators themselves belonged to a literate culture. Moreover, the tales, which we shall refer to below, were recorded in the Sufi sources in Persian, itself a language of the elite. We shall therefore refrain from using such terms as 'popular belief' and 'popular culture' for describing the rituals and practices of the saint-cults in the period. They were as much part of the elite cosmology as of the ignorant, illiterate and depressed masses.

MOTIFS IN MIRACLE STORIES

Miracle stories recorded by Abdul Haqq mainly relate to the production of gold, walking on water, sitting on fire, levitation, curing various diseases, revival of the dead, prayer for rain causing downpour, production of bumper crops, controlling demons, and presence of Sufi shaykhs at more than one place simultaneously. These motifs cannot be said to

---

[15] For the dominance of the Hanafite ulama in the subcontinent, see Ahmad, *Intellectual History of Islam*, pp. 1–3.

[16] *Akhbar-ul-Akhyar*, fol. 58a.

have appeared suddenly in the reign of Akbar, or in the Afghan period for that matter. They could be found as central to many religious sects and cults across time and space. We shall illustrate below, in some detail, only those motifs of which some explanations are to be found in the sources, or whose occurrence can be understood in the context of the Delhi Sultanate. Highlighting the achievements of Shah Abul Ghayb Bukhari, son of Shaykh Haji Abdul Wahhab Bukhari, as a mystic, Abdul Haqq notes that the majzub once stood on a lighted stove for a long time and emerged from it unscathed.[17] Such claims were not at all scandalous in Sufi circles or even in the larger ambit of the followers. In fact, earlier Rizqullah Mushtaqi had recounted an episode in which Shaykh Hasan Majzub, the lover of Prince Nizam later known as Sultan Sikandar Lodi, was not hurt by fire. Mushtaqi asserted that neither fire burnt the saints, nor water harmed them.[18] In the case of Abul Ghayb he was not only a majzub, but also a Saiyid or a descendant of Prophet Muhammad.[19] Medieval Muslim cosmology, still persisting in some measure, has it that a pure Saiyid is not burnt in fire at all. A biographical dictionary of the Mughal nobles records that Saiyid Muhammad Khan Barah, a noble of Jalal-ud-Din Muhammad Akbar, was provoked by some critics questioning his genealogy to walk into knee-deep fire which barefooted faqirs (itinerant monks) kept burning at night. The Barah Saiyid had claimed that as a pure Saiyid the fire would not have any effect on him. He stood in the fire for about an hour, and was not burnt. Satisfied with his claim, the people persuaded him to come out.[20]

Clearly such episodes were not peculiar to the reign of Akbar. Earlier too Shaykh Jamali had recorded in the early sixteenth century the account of the feat performed by Chishti Sufi, Khwaja Usman Harwani, pir (preceptor) of Mu'in-ud-Din Chishti, in a village of fire-worshippers. Harwani sat unscathed inside the fire-chamber of the local temple. Beholding the miracle, the villagers embraced Islam at the hands of the shaykh.[21] This story was narrated earlier by Nizam-ud-Din Auliya's disciple and khalifa or spiritual successor, Nasir-ud-Din Chiragh-i-Dehli, in mid-fourteenth century. According to him, after

---

[17] Ibid., fol. 240a.
[18] *Waqi'at-i-Mushtaqi*, fols. 13a–b; *Tarikh-i-Da'udi*, pp. 27–9.
[19] *Akhbar-ul-Akhyar*, fol. 240a.
[20] *Ma'asir-ul-Umara*, p. 38.
[21] *Siyar-ul-Arifin*, fols. 9a–10b.

his arrival at the village, Harwani addressed the inhabitants and suggested that since they had been worshipping the fire for a long time, it should not burn anyone who jumped into it. Frightened, none of the fire-worshippers (*atish prastan*) volunteered to do so. The shaykh then asked whether they would be convinced of the truth of Islam if he entered the fire-chamber, sat there awhile and came out unhurt. When they agreed to the proposal, the shaykh immediately took a Hindu child (*hindu bachcha*) in his arms and plunged into the fire. The Hindus and the fire-worshippers gathered there recited the kalima and embraced Islam when the shaykh came out of the fire-chamber with the boy in tow. When the people asked the child how he felt inside, he announced that it seemed as if he was sitting in a garden.[22]

Jamali has added that Usman Harwani was actually provoked by the head-priest of the mammoth fire temple to resort to this marvelous exploit. Elaborating further, Jamali has recorded that after the conversion of several thousand villagers to Islam, the shaykh accepted the priest, Mukhtiya, as a disciple. He was trained in mystic discipline, joined the rank of the saints and became renowned as Shaykh Abdullah. The child, renamed Ibrahim, also grew up to be a saint. The fire temple was demolished by the people and in course of time a big shrine-complex emerged on the site which also housed the tombs of Abdullah and Ibrahim. Jamali has sought to provide an element of authenticity to his account by adding that he had actually visited the site during his long sojourn to the holy places of Islam, stayed there for about a fortnight and received blessings. The locals informed Jamali that Usman Harwani had resided there for two and a half years. His hospice (khanqah), including the inner chamber (*hujra*), was intact at the time of Jamali's visit.[23] Writing in the early seventeenth century, the Mughal princess Jahan Ara Begam gave a more detailed version of Harwani's encounter with the fire-worshippers (*mughan*), and their conversion to Islam.[24]

Such 'devilish practices' as entering fire or riding lions are generally said to be borrowed by the Sufis from the Mongolian shamans after

[22] *Khayr-ul-Majalis*, 11th Meeting.

[23] *Siyar-ul-Arifin*, fols. 9b–11a.

[24] Jahan Ara Begam, *Mu'nis-ul-Arwah*, in Qamar Jahan Begum, *Princess Jahan Ara Begam: Her Life and Works* (Karachi, 1992), pp. 14–17. Also see, *Jawahir-i-Faridi*, pp. 236–7.

the rise of the Mongols. However, the motif of trial by fire, and specifically of being tossed into an oven, is of ancient origin.[25] Moreover, the legitimacy for the transformation of fire into a garden comes from the Quran. Abdul Wahhab Bukhari, father of Abul Ghayb, the majzub who was not hurt by fire, had written a tafsir or commentary of the Quran. According to Abdul Haqq, Abdul Wahhab has noted that if ever Prophet Muhammad paid a visit to hell, it would be transformed into a garden during the period of his stay there.[26] It is common belief that the spirit of Muhammad was transferred to his descendants from one generation to another. This legitimized the claims of Abul Ghayb and the Barah Saiyid emerging unscathed from the fire. The Saiyids, therefore, are supposed to be venerated by other Muslims who are placed lower in hierarchy, notwithstanding the claims of egalitarianism in Islam. Though the superiority of the Saiyids has been questioned and disputed from time to time, the critics were eventually made to recognize the established view.

Returning to the themes in miracle stories, several episodes relate to the production of gold by the Sufis. Alchemy was said to be practiced by certain mystics, particularly the yogis as a device to produce gold. Though some Sufis believed that the production of gold was possible through this method, they were generally skeptical about it. Abdul Haqq has recorded that Saiyid Jalal-ud-Din Quraishi, a peripatetic darwesh, was once provoked by a reference to alchemy made in his presence. He said that he spat on alchemy. Abdul Haqq noted that as he said it, his spittle fell on a copper utensil, which was immediately transformed into gold.[27] Abdul Haqq had also heard that there were 'showers of gold' in the house of Shaykh Abul Fath Jaunpuri (d. 1454), grandson of Qazi Abdul Muqtadir. The author has written that this tale was quite well known but he could not find it in the shaykh's malfuzat recorded by his khalifas. However, one of his descendants, Abdul Wahhab, himself a noted saint, drew the attention of the author to a collection of the malfuzat of Qazi Abdul Muqtadir compiled by his grandson, Abul Fateh Jaunpuri, in which such an occurrence is

---

[25] Reuven Amitai-Preiss, 'Sufis and Shamans: Some Remarks on the Islamization of the Mongols in the Ilkhanate', *Journal of the Economic and Social History of the Orient*, Vol. 42, No. 1, 1990, pp. 27–46.

[26] *Akhbar-ul-Akhyar*, fols. 196b, 198a.

[27] Ibid., fols. 225b–226a.

recorded. Abdul Haqq found out that this miracle was actually attributed to Qazi Abdul Muqtadir. Qazi Shah who was a khalifa of Abdul
Muqtadir had told the Chishti shaykh, Nasir-ud-Din Chiragh-i-Dehli
that about fifteen to twenty coins had fallen from above in front of
him just outside the house of his pir. He collected the coins and went
inside to hand them over to Abdul Muqtadir. The latter refused to accept the amount despite the fact that his household had been starving
for three days. The more Qazi Shah urged the shaykh to accept the
amount, the greater was the shaykh's anger.[28]

Qazi Shah's narration of the miracle would hardly have surprised
Chiragh-i-Dehli as in the Chishti sources of the Delhi Sultanate there
are several similar episodes.[29] In a story narrated by Nizam-ud-Din
Auliya it is said that Khwaja Fuzail Ayaz had been a bandit before he
turned to the mystic path. Repentant for his misdeeds, he called all
those whom he had robbed, sought their forgiveness and returned
their belongings. Among them was a Jew who refused to forgive the
shaykh saying that he would be convinced of his sincerity only if the
shaykh produced gold from the ground underneath his feet. The
shaykh promptly performed the feat to the satisfaction of the Jew, who
thereafter converted to Islam. He then informed the shaykh that it was
mentioned in the Jewish scriptures that those whose contrition was
accepted by God were blessed with the power of converting soil into
gold. He added that by asking the shaykh to do so he only wanted the
confirmation that his repentance had been accepted.[30] Earlier versions
of this anecdote were recorded by Sadid-ud-Din Muhammad Awfi
in his *Jawami-ul-Hikayat*[31] and Farid-ud-Din Attar in his *Tazkirat-ul-
Auliya*.[32]

[28] Ibid., fols. 161b–162a.

[29] *Fawa'id-us-Salikin*, conversations of Shaykh Qutb-ud-Din Bakhtiyar Kaki,
compilation attributed to Shaykh Farid-ud-Din Ganj-i-Shakar, Urdu trans. (Delhi,
n.d.), p. 15; *Rahat-ul-Qulub*, p. 82; *Afzal-ul-Fawa'id*, conversations of Shaykh
Nizam-ud-Din Auliya, compilation attributed to Amir Khusrau, Urdu trans.
(Delhi, n.d), pp. 32–3, 102, 126; *Asrar-ul-Auliya*, conversations of Shaykh Farid-
ud-Din Ganj-i-Shakar, compilation attributed to Shaykh Badr-ud-Din Ishaq, Urdu
trans. Muinuddin Durdai (Karachi, 1978), p. 202.

[30] *Afzal-ul-Fawa'id*, p. 13.

[31] Siddiqui, *Perso-Arabic Sources of Information*, pp. 13–14.

[32] *Tazkirat-ul-Auliya*, Farid-ud-din Attar. ed. R.A. Nicholson, 2 Parts (London/
Leiden, 1905 and 1907): Part I, p. 76.

The recurrence of the production of gold theme in miracle stories recorded in the Sufi sources of the Delhi Sultanate can be understood in the light of the fact that India was known to be a veritable storehouse of gold, the balance of payment in International trade being then loaded in India's favour. The rulers were frequently found to be campaigning in various regions in quest of booty as also for more regular tributes. We have also seen in the first two chapters how large amounts of gold were exchanged as payment for protection and as gift or bribe. That such and such Mughal nobles were purchased by the Afghan empire builder Sher Shah is a common refrain in sixteenth century accounts of political conquests. The lust for gold was said to be common to rulers, nobles, and the general populace. This explains the apathy of the public towards Muhammad Bin Tughluq's (ruled 1325–51) experiment with token currency in the early fourteenth century. The sultan had to abandon the project amidst utter confusion owing to lack of support from the people and the circulation of fake coins in the dominion. The end result was the condemnation of the sultan as 'gold-hungry'.[33] On the other hand, Qutb-ud-Din Aibak (ruled 1205–10) was highly respected for his generosity, which earned him the title of 'lak-bakhsh' or the giver of lakhs.[34] Particularly venerated by the people were the Sufis who were believed to have the power to produce gold at will, but did not turn their hospice into a place of hoarding. The Sufis distributed in charity whatever they received. They resorted at times to miracles to help the needy, and only rarely for their own maintenance as in the case of the thirteenth century Chishti Sufi, Qutb-ud-Din Bakhtiyar Kaki, who according to his early biographers could also miraculously produce bread (kak) for his family's sustenance which earned him the sobriquet 'Kaki'; reports about his producing a gold coin everyday for the same purpose are also recorded in the sources.[35] Generally, the performance was reserved for subduing an antagonist or for creating an aura around himself in the situation of an 'arrogant' ruler or nobleman sending gifts, which

---

[33] For Muhammad Bin Tughluq's eventful reign, see Husain, *Tughluq Dynasty*.

[34] *Tabaqat-i-Nasiri*. Minhaj-us-Siraj. ed. Abdul Hayy Habibi, Vol. 1 (Kabul, 1963–4), pp. 415–16.

[35] *Siyar-ul-Auliya*.

included some gold coins as well, and thus proclaiming that he did not need the charity of kings.

Going by the accounts in the biographical dictionaries, miracles were indeed used as weapons by Sufi shaykhs to overawe and terrorize their opponents, and establish their authoritative position in society. Several episodes of the provocation of the jalal (wrath) of the shaykh are to be found in the sources. Particularly instructive is Shaykh Abdul Wahhab's curse which was believed to be the cause of Sikandar Lodi's illness before his death.[36] The Chishti sources of the Delhi Sultanate contain, in fact, instances which demonstrate the immediate and sudden death of opponents caused by the curse of Sufi shaykh Farid-ud-Din Ganj-i-Shakar. The Sufi memory particularly celebrates the 'elimination' of the two Delhi sultans—Qutb-ud-Din Mubarak Shah Khalji (ruled 1316–20) and Ghiyas-ud-Din Tughluq (ruled 1320–5)—in the wake of their conflict with Nizam-ud-Din Auliya.[37] As mentioned in the previous chapter, the source of this rivalry lay in the wilayat of the shaykh which encroached for all practical purposes, the territorial authority of the ruler. If a major shaykh laid claims to wilayat or spiritual rule over a territory which the king ruled by the force of his arms, then it was below the dignity of the shaykh to be seen under the monarch's patronage, as indicated by such gestures as accepting grants or attending his court (darbar). The rituals of the court were designed to emphasize the supremacy of the sovereign over those who attended. The emperor, in turn, was expected to avoid visiting the hospice of the shaykh, with the latter receiving him with the same politeness as was the lot of ordinary disciples and followers.

Thus, the shaykh's indifference towards the rituals of the court, his occasional refusal to allow the ruler to visit his hospice, his encroachment into the power base of the king, that is the nobles and the soldiers, and his perceived ability to bestow kingship on a favourite prince or nobleman constituted a threat to the political authority. In the tussle over the royal and Sufi claims to authority, the official ulama sided with the king and in their bid to support their master raised the question of the violation of the shari'at by the shaykh. The Sufi is shown to

---

[36] *Waqi'at-i-Mushtaqi*, fols 27b–28a. For the conflict between Abdul Wahhab and Sultan Sikandar Lodi, also see the previous chapter.

[37] Aquil, 'Miracles, Authority and Benevolence'.

come out victorious in the ensuing encounter, sometimes by establishing his superior knowledge of the shari'at, and on other occasions by resorting to miracle. The message that came out from the mystic circle was loud and clear: the person who provokes a shaykh is uprooted. Often the provocation of the jalal of a shaykh affected even the populace as it could cause famine and epidemic in the realm.

If a Sufi shaykh's curse caused destruction, his prayers could protect the people in times of crisis. Several anecdotes of rulers frantically rushing to the Sufis for intercession in the face of invasion from outside are to be found in the sources. As mentioned in the previous chapter, Sultan Bahlul Lodi was said to have received a spiritually treated stick at the shrine of Qutb-ud-Din Bakhtiyar Kaki, which was used to disperse the Sharqis of Jaunpur who had laid siege of Delhi. Similar references are to be found in the sources of the earlier period which was marked by the Mongol attacks, shaking the Muslim world for over a hundred years from the early thirteenth to the mid fourteenth century. In the case of a siege of Multan by the Mongols, Nasir-ud-Din Qubacha visited Bakhtiyar Kaki, among other saints, and sought his help. The shaykh gave him an arrow and asked him to throw it in the direction of the invaders from the terrace of his palace at night. Qubacha took the arrow and performed the 'ritual' as advised by the shaykh. No invaders were to be found in the neighbourhood next morning. The magical arrow was believed to have created havoc in the enemy camp, and compelled the invaders to take to their heels,[38] even as the Sufi circle will not own it as a *jadu* or magic; it was considered to be a legitimate karamat or marvel of the saint. It may be noted here that whereas Qubacha invoked the blessings of Bakhtiyar Kaki directly in Multan, over two centuries later Bahlul Lodi sought the intercession of his *dargah* (shrine) in Delhi. Such episodes actually point to the limitations of the military power of the political authorities, which made the people turn to the Sufi saints for protection. The belief that the shaykh had the power to influence the destiny of his spiritual territory was given further impetus by the persistent Sufic claim that the towns and cities would be destroyed if the *barkat* (blessings) of the shaykh were withdrawn.

The Sufi shaykh was much sought after for his thaumaturgic role as well. Apart from the 'manufactured' *ta'wiz* (amulets), tombs, waters

---

[38] *Rahat-ul-Qulub*, p. 34; *Siyar-ul-Auliya*, p. 60; *Siyar-ul-Arifin*, fols. 59a–b.

of tanks and relics which were generally known for their healing power, other methods in alternative medicine included what may be termed 'divine touch', 'blowing', or 'breathing'. Makhdum Shaykh Abdul Qadir, also known as Shaykh Abdul Qadir Sani, of Uchch used to claim that he could cure all kinds of illness by just touching the patient. He explained that he got this power on account of his spiritual association with Shaykh Abdul Qadir Jilani, founder of the Qadiri order of Sufis, who was also known for his ability to cure blindness and leprosy. It is reported that Makhdum Shaykh Abdul Qadir used a bamboo stick for curing the widespread epidemic of 'ache in the ribs,' in the region of Uchch. The pain was found to be incurable and a lot of people had already perished. As directed by the Prophet in his dream, the shaykh would touch the ribs of the patient with the stick, and the pain would disappear for good. It is further related that once Multan was under the grip of a fatal plague (ta'un). The people rushed to Abdul Qadir Sani for the grass which grew at the place where he used to perform his ablutions. The grass was said to be very effective for curing the disease.[39] Another report suggested that the mere mention of the name of Shaykh Taqi, a weaver, of Kara-Manikpur, and said to be the preceptor of the saint-poet Kabir,[40] served as an antidote to poisoning, for instance, due to snake-bite.[41]

Needless to mention, such incidents are not unique for the Afghan period. A large number of anecdotes can be found in the sources concerning the Sufi's role as a healer in the thirteenth and fourteenth centuries. Implicit in it was perhaps the belief that the sickness of a person was caused by one or other kind of demon (jinn). The Sufi shaykh owing to his spiritual knowledge and power was capable of dealing with demons and providing relief to the sick. In fact, some of the Sufis were venerated for their ability to destroy the demons. An inquiry into the history of the medical practices and health services provided by the government in the period can help us to explain better the Sufi's popularity as a healer. However, to suggest that such healers flourished only in the medieval period because of the widespread credulity of the people and lack of medical facilities is not entirely convincing. *Pir babas*

[39] *Akhbar-ul-Akhyar*, fols. 186a–b.

[40] For Kabir, see Charlotte Vaudeville, *A Weaver Named Kabir—Selected Verses with a Detailed Biographical and Historical Introduction* (Delhi, 1993).

[41] *Akhbar-ul-Akhyar*, fol. 162a.

continue to be much sought after in the Indian subcontinent even in this so-called enlightened age. In fact, modern psychiatrists draw striking similarities between the diagnoses of the seemingly contradictory frameworks of western psychiatry and Islamic demonology.[42]

Sources also record a large number of references to the Sufis being approached by people for providing relief from such natural calamities as drought and famine.[43] Existing knowledge on the history of the Delhi Sultanate does point to a constant problem of drought in the period. Quoting a tradition of the Prophet, Sufi sources suggest that drought was actually a sign of divine scourge.[44] Accordingly, the rulers and their subjects rushed to the Sufi shaykh for his intercession. Chiragh-i-Dehli relates that disturbed by drought, the sultan (Shams-ud-Din Iltutmish) had sent messengers to the saints informing them that his job was to fight battles and it was their duty to pray for the fulfillment of the needs of the masses. They were asked to pray for rain. Qazi Hamid-ud-Din Nagauri, a Suhrawardi Sufi, suggested that a *mahfil-i-sama* (music assembly) be organized. The proceedings of the *sama* coincided with a downpour, so heavy that the people were heard saying that they had enough of it.[45]

The belief that drought and famine were actually a punishment from God for the sins committed by the people explained away the ruler's failure to tackle these problems. The suggestion that the king's job was to fight battles and it was the Sufis' duty to ensure the well being of the people shows that the Sufi shaykh was not expected to remain indifferent at times of crisis. The Sufi's active participation in such situations created further bases for his claim to authority in society. Miracle-working, coupled with humility, made the public venerate the shaykh. The relations between the shaykh and followers were seen in terms of mutual fidelity and aid. The people's veneration of the shaykh bordered on worship, and in turn they were blessed with his patronage

---

[42] Sudhir Kakar, *Shamans, Mystics and Doctors—A Psychological Inquiry into India and its Healing Traditions* (Delhi, 1982).

[43] *Siyar-ul-Arifin*, fols. 69b–71a; *Akhbar-ul-Akhyar*, fols. 245a–b.

[44] *Asrar-ul-Auliya*, pp. 219–21.

[45] *Khayr-ul-Majalis*, 8th meeting. For the popularity of music or *qawwali* in Sufi circles, see Bruce B. Lawrence, 'The Early Chishti Approach to *Sama*', in M. Israel and N.K. Wagle, eds, *Islamic Society and Culture: Essays in Honour of Professor Aziz Ahmad* (Delhi, 1983).

and his protection. The departure of a shaykh from a particular area was considered as a bad omen—the forerunner of disastrous times to follow. Thus, people 'appropriated' a miracle-working shaykh, expected him to stay in their neighborhood, and perform miracles for them. Particularly cherished by the disciples were reports of the victory of Sufi shaykhs in miraculous encounters with non-Muslim religious leaders, leading to conversion in some cases.

MIRACLE AND CONVERSION/RECOGNITION OF SPIRITUAL POWER

Abdul Haqq Muhaddis Dihlawi highlights the Sufi shaykh's role as the propagator of Islam in the Afghan period. The author's references to miraculous healing by Abdul Qadir Sani of Uchch have been noted in the previous section. He has also recorded that a number of infidels and sinners accepted Islam just by having a glimpse of Abdul Qadir Sani's spiritual accomplishments.[46] The Sufi sources also narrate cases when non-Muslim visitors or antagonists resist the temptation to convert to Islam, even as the paranormal powers of the shaykhs are appreciated. In this connection, a particular incident recorded by Abdul Haqq is both significant and interesting. Listening to qawwali at his house, Shaykh Muhammad of Mallawa, near Qannauj, went into a trance. The Hindu chief of the area, who happened to be passing that way with a friend, heard the sound of the music and the raptures. He peeped through the window and from what he saw inside, he went into a trance. When he regained his consciousness, he told his friends and companions that he saw the Musalman dancing with his God in his lap, and if he were not pulled out he would have gone to him, fallen at his feet and accepted his religion.[47] However, according to Abdul Haqq, nobody had the power to resist Saiyid Kabir-ud-Din Hasan's invitation to convert. A peripatetic Sufi, later settled at Uchch, Hasan was well known for his miraculous abilities. He converted a large number of infidels to Islam.[48]

It would be erroneous to assume that such anecdotes of miraculous conversion emerged suddenly in the Afghan period. The Sufi literature

[46] *Akhbar-ul-Akhyar*, fol. 184b.
[47] Ibid., fol. 160b.
[48] Ibid., fol. 194a.

from the Delhi Sultanate records a large number of cases of miraculous encounters between the Sufi shaykhs and the non-Muslim miracle-workers or mystic power-holders such as yogis, *sanyasis,* gurus or brahamans. The arrival of a Sufi shaykh in a non-Muslim environment and his decision to settle there was considered in certain cases to be an encroachment on the authority of the incumbent priest, or the ruler of that territory. The shaykh's authority in such instances was established only after his victory in a combat. While due recognition was given to the supernatural power of the non-Muslim religious leaders, the shaykh's victory in the duel against his opponents proved his superior spiritual stature and thus convinced the local challengers, the yogi, or the ruler of the finality of his faith. The yogi became a *waliullah* (friend of God), and the ruler a pious badshah. The conversion of the yogi and the ruler was also sometimes followed by mass conversion in the territory. In the event of the refusal of the adversary to convert to Islam even after defeat in the contest, there were two possibilities depending upon whether the former recognized the superior miraculous ability of the shaykh. Either he was allowed to leave the place and settle elsewhere, or eliminated by a curse.

One comes across a number of anecdotes of the arrival of yogis and brahamans in the shaykh's hospice as well. Some of them came with the specific purpose of testing the abilities of the shaykh; and seeing him display his powers, were often overawed. The shaykh's superiority having been established as asserted by the biographers or the compilers of Sufi 'discourses', the visiting non-Muslim religious leader would either embrace Islam and become a disciple to rise to the high status of a wali in his own right or, feeling humiliated, take to his heels. Sometimes yogis came from distant hill-forests to inform the shaykh that the knowledge of his sainthood was revealed to them while meditating in desolate caves, and duly accepted it by prostrating before him. In some cases, levitatory contests were held between visiting yogis and the incumbent shaykh in which the former was shown to have been defeated. Contrary to the general belief that the early mystic records did not refer to a single case of conversion, some fantastic stories of conversion at the hands of miracle-working shaykhs are to be found in the sources.[49] Apart from the public display of miracles as recorded

---

[49] Aquil, 'Conversion in Chishti Sufi Literature'.

in the Sufi literature, the narration of the accounts of miraculous conversions by the Sufi shaykhs to their audience in their hospices with the appended laudatory comments helped in their further perpetuation among their followers and the general populace. In highlighting the 'achievements' of Sufi shaykhs in a non-Muslim environment, or in relation to a visiting yogi in their wilayat, the sources chiefly aim at projecting their image as disseminators of Islam.

Though the Sufi shaykh himself was sure about his righteousness and recognition of his spiritual power being established in the wake of an encounter with a yogi, he was often concerned about the yogi's 'bad' influence on his disciples. Farid-ud-Din Ganj-i-Shakar is reported to have asked young Nizam-ud-Din Auliya not to take interest in the yogi's knowledge of matters of worldly interest. Further, in an anecdote recorded in the *Lata'if-i-Quddusi*, Shaykh Abdul Quddus Gangohi appeared in the dream of a disciple, Dattu Sarwani, an Afghan soldier, asking him to avoid the company of a sanyasi, called Anant Guru.[50] Apparently, Dattu was being haunted by his conscience which manifested itself in his dreams. The soldier was aware that in spite of the fact that the sanyasi spoke about the unity of God, he was not a Muslim. The senior Afghan nobles had also not paid any heed to the sanyasi's preaching and his offer to pray for their victory against the Mughals. Further, Dattu must have been conscious of his loyalty towards his pir Abdul Quddus Gangohi, and aware of the latter's attitude towards yogis. The Hindu mystics are condemned by Abdul Quddus in the course of a discussion of wahdat-ul-wujud (monism as a reality) recorded in the main part of the *Lata'if-i-Quddusi*.[51] Abdul Quddus' letters to the Afghan and Mughal rulers also bring to the fore his hostile attitude towards non-Muslims in general. In his letter to Babur, it is suggested that the kafirs be excluded from high offices, particularly those of the revenue department. He further added that important revenue posts in the provinces be given only to the pious Muslims, who assess and realize the tax in strict conformity with the tenets of the shari'at. The Hindus were to be forced to accept their inferior status as compared

---

[50] Quddusi, *Shaykh Abdul Quddus aur un ki Ta'limat*, pp. 257–9; Simon Digby, 'Dreams and Reminiscences of Dattu Sarwani'.

[51] Simon Digby, 'Shaikh Abd al-Quddus Gangohi (A.D. 1456–1537): The Personality and Attitude of a Medieval Indian Sufi', *MIAM*, Vol. 3, 1975, pp. 1–66.

to Muslims and prevented from wearing the same kind of dress as was worn by the latter.[52] These demands remind us of the normative, orthodox Islamic rules referred to in chapter four.

The significance of this outrageous letter, from the point of view of the majority non-Muslims of the realm, lies in the fact that it was written by a noted Chishti Sufi of the period, Abdul Quddus Gangohi, whose own mystical practices and beliefs seemed to be heavily coloured by Hindu spiritual traditions, as we shall see in the next section. The letter shows that it is not entirely accurate to say that unlike the other Sufi orders such as the Suhrawardis, and later the Naqshbandis, the Chishtis were always tolerant and accommodative, and cared little or not at all about the conversion of Hindus because they believed in wahdat-ul-wujud.[53] It would be more appropriate to locate the fluctuating attitude of the Sufis towards Hindus in the political context of the period. In fact the attitude of the Muslims, whether kings, courtiers or Sufis, kept varying with the ever-changing fortunes of their political power throughout the medieval period. Both the court-chronicles and the Sufi sources testify that the campaigns of the Muslim army, called the lashkar-i-Islam, for the conquest of areas hitherto controlled by non-Muslim chieftains, or to suppress their rebellions, were portrayed as jihad. Large numbers of Sufis are shown to be participating in such campaigns either as sword-wielding warriors, or for providing moral support and legitimacy. Also, probably the barkat of the presence of Sufis in the army camp encouraged the soldiers to fight with greater zeal.

Once the conquest was over Muslims felt that they were secure and safe. The earlier manifestations of fanaticism gradually gave way to a more open-minded attitude towards non-Muslims. They were willing to appreciate and absorb from diverse sources of tradition. The appropriation was not limited to the field of politics only, but was equally strong

[52] Quddusi, *Shaykh Abdul Quddus aur un ki Ta'limat*, pp. 453–6; Digby, 'Shaikh Abd al-Quddus Gangohi'; Iqtidar Alam Khan, 'Shaikh Abdul Quddus Gangohi's Relation with Political Authorities: A Reappraisal', *MIAM*, Vol. 4, 1977, pp. 73–90.

[53] For a discussion of different views on the Sufi attitude towards the non-Muslims and more specifically the question of their role in conversion, see Aquil, 'Sufi Cults, Politics and Conversion'. Cf. Nizami, *Some Aspects of Religion and Politics in India*, pp. 177–8; Rizvi, *A History of Sufism in India*, Vol. I, pp. 215–26; Mujeeb, *Indian Muslims*, pp. 297–8.

in language, religion and culture which we shall elaborate further in the next section. This liberal mindedness of the Muslims stemmed from the sense of power that they enjoyed in the dominion. Rather than aspiring to wipe off the Hindus and eradicate infidelity, at the height of their power Muslims could be found to be very accommodative. As long as the Hindu 'other' was politically submissive, there was no harm in borrowing from non-Islamic sources. It was also pragmatic not to alienate the subjects, the majority of who remained outside the fold of Islam throughout the medieval period. The need for integrating the chieftains for a more lasting control of the various regions has also been noted in chapter four. The rulers were, however, frequently advised by the Muslim elite, as by Abdul Quddus in the above letter and earlier by Ziya-ud-Din Barani in his *Fatawa-i-Jahandari*, not to appoint the Hindus to high positions, as there was a lurking danger that their rebellion might cost dearly. Instances of their revolts were, indeed, neither few nor far between.

Thus, while the rulers exploited the symbols of Islam to legitimize their campaigns, the ulama and occasionally even the Sufis in search of revenue-free land grants and authoritative position in the society betrayed their reactionary attitude. The ulama dreamt of the establishment of a strong Muslim dominion where their interpretation of the shari'at would be the law of the land. The Sufis also felt secure in a territory controlled by a Muslim governor. Keeping this in view, as mentioned above, they supported Muslim rulers even if the latter flouted the dictates of shari'at in their personal lives and in matters of governance. Also, though they were confident of their righteousness and ability to perform miracles in the case of conflict with non-Muslim rulers or religious leaders, the sources refer to several cases in which Sufis had to migrate from a place where a non-Muslim chieftain had rebelled and was persecuting Muslims. For such episodes in the lives of the Sufis of the Afghan period, we shall again turn to Abdul Haqq's *Akhbar-ul-Akhyar*. The author notes the capture of the fort of Ajmer by the Rajput chief Rana Sanga, who allegedly martyred a large number of Muslims there. Following a vision of Khwaja Mu'in-ud-Din Chishti, in which he warned of the impending calamity, Shaykh Ahmad Mujid Shaibani had left the place with a small party of Muslims, seven days before the Rana captured Ajmer.[54] Abdul Haqq also records that during

---

[54] *Akhbar-ul-Akhyar*, fol. 171a.

this period the kuffar had converted the tomb of Mu'in-ud-Din Chishti into a temple, and had placed an idol inside. Sultan Bahadur of Gujarat had visited Ajmer as a disgruntled prince at this time. The prince had prayed that if he were blessed with the crown he would wreak vengeance on the infidels of the place for desecrating the Chishti shrine. On hearing this, Bayin Majzub, who was said to be present there, indirectly announced the bestowal of kingship on the prince. Later, having assumed sovereignty, Sultan Bahadur marched to Ajmer and fulfilled his vow.[55]

Threat to life and desecration of religious places in the wake of rebellions compelled Muslims to support the clamour for a strong Muslim Sultanate. Evidently, Muslim memory was haunted by reports of persecution in a hostile Hindu environment. One particularly ghastly incident narrated by Abdul Haqq was the cold-blooded massacre of Muslims engaged in a congregational Id-prayer at Narnaul.[56] There were however also instances of Hindu-Muslim coordination and reconciliation in the medieval period. We shall see in the next section that attempts were made, at various levels, and consciously or otherwise, to learn from each other and create an environment of peaceful coexistence.

SYNCRETISM AND SYNTHESIS

Islam's interaction with other religio-intellectual traditions in India has paved the way for what is generally referred to as syncretism and synthesis in the field of religion and culture, since at least the thirteenth century. The role played by the Sufis in this connection is particularly highlighted by the scholars. The propagation of the belief in Sufi circles that an individual soul could achieve union with God, formalized in the doctrine of wahdat-ul-wujud, brought the Sufis very close to certain streams of non-Muslim mystical traditions such as the Natha Yogis. Amongst the votaries of the doctrine was the leading Chishti Sufi of the Afghan period, Abdul Quddus Gangohi.[57] Despite the fact that in political matters the shaykh's approach could be similar to the

---

[55] Ibid., fol. 243a.
[56] Ibid., fol. 46a.
[57] Quddusi, *Shaykh Abdul Quddus aur un ki Ta'limat*, pp. 234–42.

shari'a-minded ulama of the period, he not only defended his belief in wahdat-ul-wujud in his *Rushdnama* but also attempted to establish the mutual compatibility of Natha Yogi and Sufi ideologies. In view of the ulama and the rivals of the Chishtis denouncing the practice of drawing inspiration from the teachings of non-Muslim mystics, Abdul Quddus explained that his discussion of the theory of wahdat-ul-wujud and other Sufic principles was based on the teachings of the fifteenth century Chishti Sufi, Shaykh Ahmad Abdul Haqq of Rudauli, and that he had learned of them by mystical intuition. His son, Shaykh Rukn-ud-Din also suggested in his notes on the margins of the work that his father's attitude towards the Natha Yogis was based on the Quran and the traditions of the Prophet. Abdul Quddus, however, was less apologetic. He asserted that spiritual truths were common to all religions.

The *Rushdnama* is written in mixed prose and poetry. It draws upon those verses of the Quran and the traditions of the Prophet which provide the base for Sufi beliefs and practices, and quotes Persian verses from the leading Sufi poets. What gives the *Rushdnama* a distinctive character is the profuse use of Hindi verses composed by Abdul Quddus himself and his teachers. Some verses by Natha Yogis and Siddhas have also been quoted. There are six references to either 'Gorakhnath', 'Shri Gorakh', 'Natha' or 'O! Natha' in the *Rushdnama*. As in many Natha texts, these words at five different places in the work imply Ultimate Reality and Absolute Truth, while in the sixth place, the word refers to the Perfect Siddha or Perfect Man.[58] Abdul Quddus used 'Alakh Das' as his Hindi nom de plume.[59] The Natha described the supreme Creator as Alakh-Nath (the Incomprehensible or Invisible one) or as Niranjan. The shaykh also used the name Alakh Niranjan in the same sense. He identified Niranjan with Khuda and called him the Creator of the different worlds.[60] Modern authorities have studied, in detail, the influence of yogic elements in the religious teachings and practices of Abdul Quddus.[61] Though the Natha influence on Abdul Quddus' understanding of wahdat-ul-wujud is somewhat over-emphasized, there were indeed some significant parallels in the thought of the shaikh

[58] Rizvi, *A History of Sufism in India,* Vol. I, p. 336.
[59] Quddusi, *Shaykh Abdul Quddus aur un ki Ta'limat,* p. 415.
[60] Rizvi, *A History of Sufism in India,* Vol. I, p. 337.
[61] Digby, 'Shaikh Abd al-Quddus Gangohi'; Rizvi, *A History of Sufism in India,* Vol. I.

and that of Gorakhnath. At least, the Hindi verses of the shaykh in support of *wajudi* doctrine clearly reveal that he used Natha idioms and metaphors to express his thought, even as it was rooted in Islamic tradition. Further, in accord with his more general tendency to elevate the Sufi tradition which he had inherited, the yogic concepts are allegorized and refined in Abdul Quddus' references to them. His treatment of yogic ideas and techniques of ecstasy, probably passed on to him in the khanqah at Rudauli, may be seen as an attempt to adapt an unorthodox, non-Muslim tradition within the confines of a learned, though profoundly Indianized Islam. Muslim religious scholars, patronized by the rulers and high officers of late-fifteenth and early-sixteenth century Hindustan, may not have appreciated an uncritical borrowing of yogic ideas.[62] Indeed, the ulama may have been scandalized by the shaykh's emphasis upon two favourite aspects of the mystical discipline, *salat-i-ma'kus* and *sultan-i-zikr,* which reflect the influence of Natha practices. For years after the evening prayers, the shaykh would perform the salat-i-ma'kus, also referred to as *namaz-i-ma'kus,* or *chilla-i-ma'kus* when probably performed for forty days/nights.[63] This was generally carried out by hanging upside-down in a well with the legs tied to a branch of a tree. According to traditional Chishti explanation, the antecedents of the practice can be traced to Shaykh Farid-ud-Din Ganj-i-Shakar who was said to have performed it in the thirteenth century, and even earlier to Shaykh Abu Sayid bin Abi'l Khair, and before him, to Prophet Muhammad himself.

Abdul Quddus and other Sufis of the Chishti silsila were not exceptional in their willingness to learn from the Indian spiritual traditions. Saiyid Muhammad Ghaus Gwaliari, a leading shaykh of the Shattari order,[64] popularized Hindu mystical practices through his translation of the *Amritkund,* and drew attention to the similarities in the mystical terminology of Muslims and Hindus. In fact, several versions of the *Amritkund* in Persian and Arabic known as *Hauz-ul-Hayat* or *Bahar-ul-Hayat* were already in circulation in the Sufi circle of the period. Abdul Quddus had extensive knowledge of this yogic treatise and imparted its essence to his disciples.[65] Originally in Sankrit,

[62] Digby, 'Shaikh Abd al-Quddus Gangohi'.
[63] Quddusi, *Shaykh Abdul Quddus aur un ki Ta'limat,* pp. 196–8.
[64] *Azkar-i-Abrar,* pp. 290–302.
[65] Rizvi, *A History of Sufism in India,* Vol. I, p. 335.

Amritkund had earlier been translated into Arabic by Qazi Rukn-ud-Din Samarqandi, the author of the *Kitab-ul-Irshad* who visited Lakhnauti in the early thirteenth century and was introduced to Hatha-yogic principles by a Siddha called Bhojar Brahman. The work was later translated into Persian. A further Arabic version was again prepared by a brahman from Kamrup, apparently in collaboration with a Muslim scholar. This version was re-translated into Persian by Muhammad Ghaus.[66]

Unlike Abdul Quddus, Muhammad Ghaus' interest in the Hindu religious traditions was not restricted merely to understanding and borrowing mystical practices from them. The fanaticism noticed in Abdul Quddus' approach towards the Hindus is hardly to be found in Muhammad Ghaus. In fact, Abdul Qadir Badauni has noted that the shaykh treated everybody, including the kuffar (sing. kafir) with great honour and respectfully stood before them.[67] This was a cause of discomfiture for the orthodox Muslims and even some fellow shaykhs criticized him and denied him the status of a true ascetic. Badauni too was defensive on this issue. He wrote that God alone knows what the shaykh's motives were in venerating the infidels.[68]

Indeed, unsure of its own yardstick to judge the standard norms of behavior, Islamic orthodoxy occasionally refrained from passing judgment on certain objectionable acts of saintly persons. In fact, examples of 'covering up' such cases abound. The case of Kabir illustrates the point further. Though the later Sufi tradition has appropriated Kabir as a disciple of Shah Taqi of Kara-Manikpur, hardly any discussion on his life and ideas are to be found in early Sufi circles. Though Kabir probably lived in the period immediately preceding the Afghan rule,[69] he left an enduring impact on the religious attitude and culture of the subsequent period. His case is particularly relevant for an understanding of Islamic interaction with non-Muslim religious traditions at the popular level. The non-Islamic traditions were already powerfully influenced by the principles of Islam as conveyed to them by the Sufis.

[66] Ibid. For the popularity of *Amritkund* in the Sufi circles, also see Husain, *Glimpses of Medieval Indian Culture*; Abdul Latif, *The Muslim Mystic Movement in Bengal, 1301–1550* (Calcutta, 1993); Eaton, *The Rise of Islam.*

[67] *Muntakhab-ut-Tawarikh*, Vol. III, p. 5.

[68] Ibid., Vol. III, pp. 5–6.

[69] Vaudeville, *A Weaver Named Kabir.*

Kabir's trenchant criticism of idol worship and the caste system of the Hindus, and his emphasis on monotheism clearly influenced religious leaders like Guru Nanak who lived in the Afghan period. The role played by Kabir and Nanak in syncretism and synthesis has been much emphasized by modern scholars.

However, the influence of Islam or for that matter of any other system of ideas, on Nanak's teachings has been denied by a Sikh historian. For, it is suggested that the Guru's ideas had 'a sure degree of originality' as they were a product of 'illumination' upon him.[70] On the other hand, while noting that in its initial inspiration the Sikh movement showed a genuine monotheistic eclecticism in which Islamic influence was clearly discernible, another scholar doubts that the 'syncretic appeal' of the medieval religious leaders had any lasting influence. It is also pointed out that the transformation of Sikhism from an eclectic faith into a rabid anti-Muslim militant group is perhaps the most tragic instance of the failure of syncretism in India.[71] Indeed, the Sikh accounts both lament and extol a prolonged episode of 'struggle' and 'sacrifice' of the Gurus against the alleged oppression of Mughal rule under the successors of Akbar. The religio-political community of the Sikhs, comprising prosperous Khatri traders and upwardly mobile Jat peasants, was gradually emerging as an alternative political culture in medieval India. Ironically, the evolution of the separatist, as against the syncretistic, community or *panth* of the Sikhs with its distinct cultural boundary marker, was taking place in the reign of Akbar—of all emperors! It was only a matter of time before the Mughal administrative machinery geared up to keep the Gurus and their *masands* (revenue agents) in check. The sympathetic Sikh narrative claims that Akbar's catholicity could protect the Gurus and their followers against open violence but it could not obviate the nefarious designs of their enemies. The removal of a protecting umbrella could increase the heat of hostility. With the death of Akbar, withdrawal of imperial protection came rather suddenly and in a violent form.[72]

Sikhism's transformation from syncretism to hostility towards Islam, or for that matter the division of the followers of Kabir into the Hindu

[70] J.S. Grewal, *Sikh Ideology, Polity and Social Order* (Delhi, 1996), pp. 1–6.

[71] Aziz Ahmad, *Studies in Islamic Culture in the Indian Environment* (Oxford, 1964), pp. 152–5.

[72] J.S. Grewal, *The Sikhs of the Punjab* (Cambridge, 1990), pp. 60–1.

and Muslim Kabirpanthis, did not stop the process of syncretistic borrowings from diverse religious traditions. Despite assaults from Hindu and Muslim reformist and revivalist movements, syncretism in popular beliefs has survived in India. A common feature in most of the existing syncretistic cults is the worship of a galaxy of saints— legendary or otherwise. The lasting appeal of the saints who actually lived in the medieval period can be attributed to their willingness to mix with 'all kinds of men'—often criticized by the ulama as in the case of Muhammad Ghaus.

The popularity of the Sufi saints was also, in a measure, due to their willingness to adopt the vernaculars as their language of communication with the masses, and, in fact, at times for the expression of their own mystical experiences. Most early references in Indian Islam to the use of Hindvi, or regional languages, come from Sufi circles. Already in the thirteenth and fourteenth centuries, Hindvi couplets sung in the musical assemblies of the Sufis were quite popular. For some Sufis, Persian poetry no longer created the same level of ecstasy as in Hindvi. The popularity of the vernacular poetry was more conspicuous in the Sufic fraternities of the period of our study.[73] The period is marked as an important stage in the growth and development of Hindi literature.[74] As mentioned above, Abdul Quddus and his mystic teachers at Rudauli composed verses in Hindi. His *Rushdnama* has a large number of *dohas* and *chaupais* in the language. Significantly, in a particular couplet, the first line is in Persian and the second in Hindi:[75]

Sidq rahbar sabr tosha dost manzil dil rafiq
Satta nagri dharma raja joga marga nirmala

---

[73] Cf. Abdul Haq, *Urdu ki Ibtadai Nasho-numa mein Sufiya-i-Karam ka Kaam* (Karachi, 1953); Alam, 'The Pursuit of Persian: Language in Mughal Politics'; Annemarie Schimmel, 'The Vernacular Tradition in Persianate Sufi Poetry in Mughal India', in Leonard Lewishon and David Morgan, eds, *The Heritage of Sufism: Late Classical Persianate Sufism (1501–1750)*, Vol. 3 (Oxford, 1999).

[74] A. Halim, 'Growth and Development of Hindi Literature During the Sayyid-Lodi Period', *Journal of the Asiatic Society of Pakistan*, Vol. II, 1957, pp. 85–6.; also see, Stuart McGregor, 'On the Evolution of Hindi as a Language of Literature', *South Asia Research*, Vol. 21, No. 2, 2001, pp. 203–17.

[75] Quddusi, *Shaykh Abdul Quddus aur un ki Ta'limat*, pp. 419; Simon Digby, 'Shaikh Abd al-Quddus Gangohi', p. 66.

(Sincerity is the guide; patience the provision for the journey; the friend our destination; the heart our companion;
Truth is the city; righteousness its king; yoga the pure road.)

As stated earlier, in many of the Hindi verses the influence of Hindu mystical traditions particularly that of the Nathas, is clearly visible.

Of particular significance is the contribution to what is referred to as the *prem-gatha* literature of the period by such Sufi poets as Shaykh Qutb Ali alias Qutban, Mir Saiyid Manjhan, and Malik Muhammad Jai'si. A disciple of the Shattari Shaykh Burhan of Kalpi, Qutban (c.1500) wrote his love story entitled *Mrigavati* in Awadhi dialect, and dedicated it to 'Sahu Husain', probably Ala-ud-Din Husain Shah (ruled 1493–1518) of Bengal.[76] Qutban might even be referring to Husain Shah Sharqi of Jaunpur, who having lost his last stronghold, Bihar, to Sikandar Lodi in c.1494–5 was cooling his heels as a guest of Ala-ud-Din Husain Shah, in Bengal. In this verse romance of Hindu origin and background, Qutban compared his patron with the heroes of Hindu mythology and not with, say, the Perso-Islamic Rustam, Nausherwan, or Hatim. It is suggested the tragic end of Mrigavati symbolized the union of the seeker with the divine soul.[77] Further, *Mrigavati's* plot repeats the pattern of the Sita legend, a fair princess in the clutches of a demon. It ends with the self-immolation of the two queens on the pyre of the dying king. The plot of Manjhan's *Madhumalti* follows the same pattern.[78] Manjhan, author of *Mugdhavati* and *Madhumalti*, was a protégé of the Sur Afghans. The love story of Madhumalti and prince Manohar differs from Qutban's work in being longer and having additional characters. Again, writing in pure Awadhi, Manjhan's description of nature is located in its Indian setting.[79] The Sufi poetry of love in Hindi reached its culmination under Malik Muhammad Jai'si.[80] As noted in chapter three, Jai'si was not averse

[76] Halim, 'Growth and Development of Hindi Literature', pp. 85–6.

[77] Ibid., p. 86.

[78] Ahmad, *Studies in Islamic Culture*, p. 241.

[79] Halim, 'Growth and Development of Hindi Literature', pp. 86–7. Cf. Simon Weightman, 'Symbolism and Symmetry: Shaykh Manjhan's Madhumalati Revisited', in Lewishon and Morgan, eds, *The Heritage of Sufism*, Vol. 3.

[80] Halim, 'Growth and Development of Hindi Literature', pp. 87–8; S.H. Askari, 'A Newly Discovered Volume of Awadhi Works Including *Padmavat* and *Akhravat* of Malik Muhammad Jaisi', *JBRS*, Vol. 39, Parts 1–2, 1953, pp. 10–40.

to draw on the social and political ideals from diverse contexts even if to celebrate Sher Shah's excellence as a ruler. Written in purest Awadhi in Persian script, Jai'si's *Padmavat* is a significant example of cultural cross-referencing in medieval India. From the perspective of a purist, it symbolizes the secession of a Muslim mind from its own culture and choosing self-expression in the rival Hindu culture.[81]

With the realization that Aziz Ahmad considers the theme of Jai'si's poem as 'alien' to the Indian Muslim tradition, and which does not fit well with his model of Hindu-Muslim interactions in medieval India, we quote below the author's brief remark on the work: 'The Chishti Sufi heritage which reached him through his heterodox, rural preceptor Bodle Shah seems to have been submerged in his knowledge and assimilation of Hindu mystical literature; and although he shows no direct impress of Rama or Krishna cults, he seems to have been under the influence not only of Kabir but of popular Hindu lore and yoga. The cosmography of the poem is Hindu, though the poem conforms to the tradition of Persian *mathnawis* in devoting a section to the praise of the Prophet. In the eulogy of Sher Shah Suri, the imagery is drawn from Hindu mythology. As a love-poem it follows not the Persian tradition but that of Hindu love-romances like *Premaval* and *Madhumalti*. In the legend of the banishment of Raghava Chetan's magic there might be a faint echo of the story of the disgrace of Satan; but if so, it is oblique. Chetan's magic is steeped in Hindu astronomy and the ethical verdict on his magical practices is one of Hindu ortho-doxy: "Those who do not walk in the way of the vedas lose themselves in the forest"'.[82]

Islamic orthodoxy did not always remain indifferent to such cultural appropriations in Islam. Though at times found to be 'covering up' some heterodox behaviour and practices, as noted above, or dismissing them as aberrations, the orthodoxy could gear up against any statement or action which might be viewed by it as a source of fitna (sedition) in society. In such a situation, the need to check the degeneration of Islam was also strongly felt. Indeed, several reformist/revivalist movements emerged in medieval Islam in India, from time to time. The leaders of

---

[81] Ahmad, *Studies in Islamic Culture*, p. 241; also see Shantanu Phukan, '"None Mad as a Hindu Woman": Contesting Communal Readings of Padmavat', *Comparative Studies of South Asia, Africa and the Middle East*, Vol. 16, No. 1, 1996.

[82] Ahmad, *Studies in Islamic Culture*, pp. 241–2.

such movements wanted to reform or purify Islam by reviving the model of Islamic society that existed at the time of the Prophet and during the reigns of the four rightly guided caliphs. They all tried therefore, to bring contemporary Islamic practices in line with the Quran and the Tradition of the Prophet. In doing so, they generally opposed, or neglected, the authority of the four schools of jurisprudence in Sunni Islam. Even when they accepted the authority of the schools, known as the mazahib, they generally rejected the exclusive authority of any one school such as Hanafism in North India. Instead, they claimed the right of *ijtihad* or the exercise of individual reasoning in the interpretation of the Quran and the Tradition, as against the orthodoxy's command for taqlid or blind following of the authority of the founder of one of the mazahib.

Further, these movements were generally led by charismatic leaders, who, besides being Saiyids were already quite well known for their piety and learning. Such leaders felt and claimed that God had given them the mission to rejuvenate Islam. Many of them emerged in the sixteenth century, when the first thousand years or millennium of Islam came to an end. Many Islamic traditions believe that a *mahdi* or a new Muslim leader or *mujaddid*, the renovator of Islam would emerge at this time. Since the leaders of these movements wanted to reform or purify Islam, they were generally hostile to heterodox currents within Sunni Islam such as the Sufis who borrowed from non-Muslim religious traditions, and to the non-Sunni Muslims such as the Shi'is. The impact of these movements was therefore anti-syncretic.

One such messianic movement was launched by Saiyid Muhammad of Jaunpur to reform society in the late fifteenth and early sixteenth centuries.[83] The emphasis on decline and decay during this period as against the perceived order and prosperity in the reign of Akbar has compelled some modern scholars to ignore the millennarian hypothesis for the rise of Saiyid Muhammad's Mahdawi movement. The Muslim world was under the grip of severe apocalyptic worries during the period. In India, however, Saiyid Muhammad's movement evoked a limited response as it called for a high degree of asceticism.

---

[83] For the Mahdawi movement, see Rizvi, *Muslim Revivalist Movements*; Qamaruddin, *The Mahdawi Movement* (Delhi, 1985); Ahmad, *Intellectual History of Islam*, pp. 27–9.

The institutionalization of the movement in the *hijarat* (jihad by way of migration) and the *da'ira* (temporary or semi-permanent camps often consisting of hutments made of mud walls and thatched roofs outside a town) was a further check against the spread of the movement. Moreover, criticism against the existing political system meant incurring the wrath of the rulers in various regions. Further, though Saiyid Muhammad himself commanded some respect from the Sunni elite, the movement was generally described as *gumrah*, or deviating from the path of Islam.[84] Hunted by Islamic orthodoxy throughout his wanderings, the self-proclaimed Mahdi died at Farah in the North West in 1504. Two of his close disciples, Abdullah Niyazi and Shaykh Alai were persecuted by the narrow-minded theologian Makhdum-ul-Mulk, who was the shaykh-ul-Islam under Islam Shah Sur, and under Akbar. Aziz Ahmad writes, 'Niyazi renounced his faith under the lash, and Alai died under it'.[85]

More important from the perspective of Afghan history was the emergence of the Raushaniya movement led by Bayazid bin Abdullah Ansari (1525–72).[86] Himself an Afghan, Bayazid was associated with Muslim mystics and Hindu yogis in his early life. His emphasis on the *pir-i-kamil* (the perfect preceptor), the use of *ta'wil* (metaphorical interpretation in explaining the five pillars of Islam), and the injunctions of ritual purity can be traced to the doctrines of the Ismailis. Also, he must have learnt the doctrine of transmigration of souls from the yogis. Bayazid also claimed to be a Mahdi and was called '*Pir-i-Raushan*' (illumined preceptor) by his followers, while his opponents condemned him as '*Pir-i-Tarik*' (saint of darkness). Like other movements, the Raushaniyas were also condemned by Islamic orthodoxy as heretics, but the movement flourished among certain Afghan tribes in the North West. This resurgence of the Afghans was viewed by the Mughals as a political threat.

---

[84] *Akhbar-ul-Akhyar* (Urdu trans), p. 439.

[85] Ahmad, *Intellectual History of Islam*, p. 28.

[86] Bayazid Ansari's major works included *Sirat-ul-Tauhid, Khair-ul-Bayan, Halnama, Maqsud-ul-Muminin* and *Khair-ul-Talibin* of which the last is not extant now, see Rizvi, 'Available Works of Bayazid Raushanai', *PIHC*, 24th Session, Delhi, 1961, pp. 181–7. For the Raushaniya movement, also see Rizvi, *Raushaniyya Movement*; Ahmad, *Intellectual History of Islam*, pp. 30–1.

Athar Abbas Rizvi has briefly discussed the contents of Bayazid Ansari's extant works which are found to be similar to the ideas and beliefs of the pantheistic Sufis. The main cause of the opposition to the Raushaniya movement, according to Rizvi, 'lay in the great success Bayazid had ultimately obtained in working up the Afghan national feelings to a pitch that might successfully meet the Mughal invasion of their homeland'. Also, the ulama and the Sufis whom Bayazid had 've-hemently attacked for their wordly-mindedness did not fail to exploit the situation to their advantage and joined the Mughals in branding Bayazid and his followers as heretics engrossed in darkness'.[87] Thus, despite his trumpeted profession of respect for the leaders of diverse religious traditions, Akbar ensured that the movement was crushed to the hilt. The persecution of the Raushaniyas in the North West coincided with Akbar's relentless campaign against the Afghan strongholds in the region of Bihar and Bengal in eastern India.

With the consolidation of Mughal power by the end of the sixteenth century, the hapless Afghans could only rue the change in their fortune and hope or pray for the emergence of another Sher Shah. Nor were the Mughals secure about their success. A detailed examination of the continued Afghan threat to Mughal rule under Akbar and his successors is out of the purview of the present research. It may however be noted that Mughal history is haunted by the threat of the phenomenal rise of the Afghans who could suddenly emerge like ants and locusts, or like the proverbial phoenix, rise from the ashes.

---

[87] Rizvi, 'Available Works of Bayazid Raushanai'.

Conclusion

IT WOULD BE WORTHWHILE TO recapitulate and summarize below some of the main points of the preceding chapters. We examined the view that the period of the Afghan rule witnessed the disintegration of the 'centralized' political structure of the Delhi Sultanate resulting in a general crisis. We also took note of the suggestion that this disintegration was caused by the 'tribal' or 'centrifugal' character of Afghan polity. Contrary to the notion that Afghan polity was tribal in nature, and that a decentralized-tribal polity is incompatible with peace and stability, we found that rather than merely depending upon tribal lineages and customs, the Afghan rulers drew on the universal tropes of kingship for the articulation of their power. Further, though we refrained from ascribing any distinct model to the Afghan polity, the details of governance recorded by the medieval authorities point to a kind of 'welfare monarchy' in the period. Sixteenth century accounts have portrayed the Afghan kings as ideal rulers, whose welfare mechanism, personal piety and madad-i-ma'ash grants to holy-men were much celebrated. These accounts cannot be dismissed as mere imaginations of the Afghan historians, for the non-Afghan writers have also presented largely the same picture of the period. It may be said that they were influenced by the progress made under the Mughal emperor Akbar, but were yet in search of an ideal ruler. These historians may then have projected backward in time some of the later developments.

However, Malik Muhammad Jai'si's eulogy for the rule of Sher Shah, particularly for his munificence, generosity and concern for justice militates against such an assumption. We noticed that public weal was an important feature of the Afghan political discourse. The rulers were sensitive to the aspirations of the people and kept in touch with the general social conditions through charitable endeavours, in particular in times of drought and scarcity. In this connection, reference may be made to the arrangement of public kitchen (langar) by the king—a social service which was particularly associated with the Sufi establishments. Significantly, the Sufis of the period attribute supernatural power to their contemporary monarchs. We noticed several anecdotes bearing on the miraculous power of the Afghan rulers. Needless to say that they were also seen as the shadow of God on earth. Further, reports of bestowal of kingship to rulers by Sufi shaykhs abound in our sources. In a curious inversion of roles, a leading Sufi of the period chose to address the king as 'shaykh'. Thus the badshah or sultan combined in himself the qualities of a philanthropic ruler and a thaumaturgic Sufi. In fact he was supposed to possess some of the divine attributes as well.

Many of these issues which are very important for a more informed understanding of the historical processes tend to recede into background when we exaggerate Akbar's achievement beyond a point. Though some scholars have highlighted the significance of the earlier processes, the study of medieval Indian history continues to suffer from what has recently been termed as the 'play of light and shade'. While there is an over-emphasis on Akbar and Aurangzeb, other phases in Mughal history remain largely neglected, apart from indifference to the pre-Mughal period, particularly the fifteenth century regional sultanates. In highlighting the Mughal non-sectarian policies, it is assumed, for instance, that it was Akbar who first encouraged the Rajputs and other non-Muslim groups to join the imperial service. Clearly such an approach amounted to disregarding the earlier liberal attempts at broadening the base of the state apparatus. Indeed the Mughal liberal policy formed part of a process to which their predecessors, the Afghan rulers, had made significant contributions.

The Rajput question offered two options to the Afghans. The first was to aim at a direct and uniform rule throughout Hindustan. This would call for the extirpation of the indigenous chieftains which in turn implied large-scale loss of soldiers. The other option was to make these 'zamindars' accept their suzerainty and allow them to run the local administration on the condition that it would be closely supervised by the governors appointed by the Afghan king. This arrangement was useful on several counts. Acceptance of the Afghan paramountcy meant expansion of Afghan power in Rajput strongholds without much resistance as well as a kind of undisturbed flow of revenues from the countryside. Further, the military support of the Rajput allies could also enhance the prospects of conquest and control of new or hostile regions. The Afghan rulers found this more viable. Their policy towards the Rajputs was thus aimed primarily at incorporating them in their imperial projects. The refusal to cooperate in the matter could lead to a large-scale bloodbath, generally characterized as jihad. Sher Shah fought several of them and so did Sikandar Lodi, at least insofar as the late sixteenth century Afghan memory is concerned. The general Muslim opinion on the reports of such encounters was no different, unless one was a Mughal ideologue like Abu'l Fazl, who by contrast completely vulgarized the celebrations.

However, such matters of opinion apart, the Afghan kings were in conflict only with those who challenged, or refused to acknowledge, their power. Generally, they showed a liberal and reconciliatory attitude towards the non-Muslims. Their relationship with the Rajputs was marked by an honourable alliance of dominance and subordination, recognizing duly the status of the latter as rulers of their respective territories. This alliance was often cemented through a wedlock between an Afghan king/prince and a Rajput princess. A logical sequel of this alliance was that a number of the Rajput chiefs fought against Babur along with the Afghans during the early phase of his invasion and conquest of Hindustan. They continued to offer resistance to the Mughals later through the Afghan 'pretender' Sultan Mahmud Lodi, a brother of Ibrahim Lodi who died fighting Babur's Mughal army to save his kingdom of Hindustan. The period of Sher Shah's conflict with Humayun witnessed the Rajputs settling scores with each other and generally resorting to an ambivalent attitude towards the two. However, complaints of their capturing territories previously under the control of Muslims were also not uncommon. Once the issue of the badshahat of Hindustan was settled, the Rajputs, barring a few, acknowledged the suzerainty of the Sur ruler. In fact, non-Muslims in the service of the Afghans could be noticed from a very early period, under Sultan Bahlul Lodi. A century later, Hemu's elevation to the status of chief commander of the Sur army speaks volumes of the extent and nature of the integration of non-Muslims in the Afghan imperial project.

The extent to which this alliance was effective may further be seen in the report that Akbar's early encounter with the Rajputs was due to the latter's support to the Afghans. Also, the degree to which they identified with the Afghans may be seen in their claim that Sher Shah was the son of a Rajput mother. Indeed, instances of marriage between Afghan nobles and non-Muslim women were not unusual. On the other hand, large numbers of Muslim women could also be found in the harems of the non-Muslim warlords. A major Muslim grudge against the Rajput ruler of Raisin was precisely on this count.

Alongside all this, conditions for appropriations and borrowings were also created. The Sufis of the period played a prominent role in this process. In fact a number of scholars of Sufism have shown that the Sufis of the earlier period, that is, the thirteenth and fourteenth centuries, had laid a firm ground for a tolerant attitude towards the non-Muslims. The Sufis had also influenced state policy in a bid to ensure that it was at least not in total contravention of the shari'at. Ideally, though the need to implement the shari'at as the state law was expressed on and off, its limitations were appreciated as well. We have referred above to a large number of anecdotes of the Sufis' conflict and collaboration with the kings and the nobles. They point to the different ways in which the Sufis intervened in contemporary politics. Many of them are said to have settled in centres of political influence under the Afghan kings. They accepted land and cash grants from the rulers, and prayed for their victory over their foes, kafirs or Muslims. Some of the Sufis contributed to the consolidation of Afghan power in the newly conquered territories, some others participated even in the military campaigns. Most of the kings, members of the royal family and courtiers were actually disciples of one or the other Sufi shaykhs. A number of Sufis also had matrimonial alliances with the royal families.

There were, however, the cases of fight between the Sufis and the kings, which emanated generally from the Sufis' assertion of authority over a given wilayat. The ruler took such assertion as an encroachment upon his power and territorial jurisdiction. The belief in the shaykh's ability to grant kingship, his image of a healer of the sick and protector of the people furnished him with enormous power in his spiritual territory. The shaykh's indifference towards court rituals, his occasional refusal to allow the ruler to visit his hospice, and his influence over the nobles and soldiers who constituted the power base of the monarch, was a threat to the political power. In cases of conflict between royal and Sufic claims to authority, the ulama sided with the king and raised the question of violation of the shari'at by the shaykh in such matters as listening to music, and refusing to attend the congregational prayers. The shaykh, in turn, condemned the ulama on occasion even as the 'inhabitants of hell'. In most of the cases of such encounters, the shaykh is shown to have come out victorious, either by establishing his superior knowledge of the shari'at, or by resorting to the performance of miracles.

Our sources also record a large number of tales of miraculous combats between the Sufi shaykhs and their opponents, including the non-Muslim religious leaders. The shaykh's authority was established only after he scored victory in these contests. While due recognition is given to the wondrous powers of such non-Muslim mystics as the yogis, the shaykh's triumph over his rivals proved his superior spiritual stature and often led to the conversion of his opponent to Islam. Reports of conversion by a Sufi shaykh brought him immense prestige and authority in his wilayat. Images of the Sufis as disseminators of Islam were thus built and propagated. These portrayals were, however, not uncontested. The ulama were least impressed with the achievements of Sufic Islam, finding its 'quality' a bit too questionable, and seeking to purge it of all the innovations that did not conform to the foundational categories of the orthodox, Sunni Hanafite Islam. They tried continuously to establish their own reading of the shari'at as the sole legitimate way of life. The movement of Saiyid Muhammad of Jaunpur, which we have briefly alluded to, was one such attempt. Though the movement itself drifted towards a perceived heresy and was crushed by the rulers, it did contribute its own share to the religious setting of the period.

Much before the emergence of the Afghans in northern India, Islam's interaction with the local religio-cultural traditions had prepared the ground for religious syncretism and cultural synthesis. Though religious identities tended to get exclusive and standardized under political compulsions, mutual borrowings continued unabated. The process of appropriations was accelerated considerably in the period of our study. The doctrine of wahdat-ul-wajud brought the Sufis close to certain streams of non-Muslim thought. Amongst the votaries of the doctrine was the leading early sixteenth century Chishti Sufi, Shaykh Abdul Quddus Gangohi. Some of the Sufis also found much to learn from the Indian mystic traditions. Saiyid Muhammad Ghaus Gwaliori, a noted Shattari Sufi of the Afghan period, popularized yogic practices in Muslim mystic circles. Mastering versions of the Indic treatise, *Amritkund*, Ghaus Gwaliori also drew attention to the similarities in the spiritual terminologies of Muslims and Hindus. Conversely, non-Muslim religious traditions also began to be shaped by the principles of Islam as represented by the Sufis. This is clearly visible in Kabir's and Nanak's preachings, in particular in their emphasis on mono-theism. The contribution of the Sufis of the period to the growth and development of vernacular literature and devotional music is also equally noteworthy. The growth of vernacular literature may have been retarded with the advent of the Mughals who patronized Persian as the language of the empire.[1] However, the view that the process of integration of Hindu and Muslim cultures was destroyed by Akbar's interference in religious matters is untenable.[2] Yet, as noted above, the degree to which the Rajputs and the Afghans had come closer in up-holding their 'common' cause is very well reflected in the fact that the Rajputs often sided with the Afghans in their fight against the Mughals.

There are more than one explanation of Humayun's defeat at the hands of the Afghans in the two battles fought successively in Chausa and Qannauj, and the subsequent flight of the Mughals to Persia. The contemporary chroniclers, as they were unable to explain the defeat of the powerful Mughals, generally attribute Sher Shah's success to the hand of God. Another favourite explanation of the Mughal defeat, found in the sixteenth century Mughal chronicles, is the 'treachery' of the 'wretched' Afghans. Some modern scholars also have accepted this explanation rather uncritically. Yet another reading of the period traces Humayun's problems to the Mongol theory of kingship, which envis-aged the division of the kingdom amongst the sons of the deceased king. It is further suggested that Humayun's position was weakened by the rebellions of his brothers. All these explanations ignore the bril-liant qualities of Sher Shah as a military commander. The Afghan em-pire builder comes out as an unmatched mobilizer of the available

---

[1] Alam, 'The Pursuit of Persian: Language in Mughal Politics'.
[2] For such a hypothesis, see Siddiqui, *Afghan Despotism*, p. 109.

resources. He recruited not simply the professional Afghan soldiers, but organized for his purpose the entire 'qaum' of the Afghans settled in Hindustan. For these Afghans the establishment of the Mughal rule had meant redundancy and migration. Besides, there was widespread hostility against the Mughal invaders who had not only defeated the Afghan and Rajput armies, but also had indulged in large-scale plunder. A great many Afghans of the North West were willing to march down the country of Hindustan either as mercenaries or as warriors for the cause of Afghan honour. Sher Shah exploited all these factors in leading the riposte against the Mughals. We have illustrated in detail how his rivals, contending for the mantle of leader of the Afghans, and on a larger scale, for organizing a campaign against Mughal rule were eliminated from the scene. Unfortunately for the Afghans, Sher Shah died in an accident before re-establishing the Afghan kingdom on a firm footing. The Mughals returned with a vengeance to condemn the Afghans as the dangerous 'other'. Though by the end of Akbar's reign the Afghans had reconciled to the Mughal rule, their marginalization continued throughout the Mughal period, and consequently in the historiography of medieval India as well.

Select Bibliography

Abel, A. 1991a. 'Dar al-harb', *Encyclopaedia of Islam* (New Edition), Vol. 2, Leiden: Brill, 126.

———. 1991b. 'Dar al-Islam', *Encyclopaedia of Islam* (New Edition), Vol. 2, Leiden: Brill, 127–8.

Afsana-i-Shahan, Muhammad Kabir bin Shaikh Ismail. British Museum, Ms. Add. 24,409, OIOC, British Library. London.

Afzal-ul-Fawa'id, conversations of Shaykh Nizam-ud-Din Auliya, compilation attributed to Amir Khusrau, Delhi, 1305 A.H. Urdu trans. Delhi: Maktaba Jam-i-Noor, n.d.

Ahmad, Aziz. 1964. *Studies in Islamic Culture in the Indian Environment.* Oxford: Clarendon Press.

———. 1969. *An Intellectual History of Islam in India.* Edinburgh: University Press.

Ahmad, Qeyamuddin. 1973. *Corpus of Arabic and Persian Inscriptions of Bihar, A.H. 640–1200.* Patna: K.P. Jayaswal Research Institute.

Akbarnama, Abu'l Fazl. Mss. I.O. Islamic 4, OIOC, British Library, London. Eng. tr.: H. Beveridge, 3 Vols. Asiatic Society, Calcutta, 1879–1921.

Akhbar-ul-Akhyar, Shaykh Abdul Haqq Muhaddis Dihlawi. Ms., IO Islamic 1450, OIOC, British Library, London. Edition: Kutubkhana Rahimiya, Deoband, n.d. Urdu tr: Subhan Mahmud and Muhammad Fazil (Delhi, 1990).

Alam, Muzaffar. 1989. 'Competition and Coexistence: Indo-Muslim Interaction in Medieval North India.' *Itinerario* 13(1): 37–59.

———. 1996. 'Assimilation from a Distance: Confrontation and Sufi Accommodation in Awadh Society', in R. Champakalakshmi and S. Gopal, eds. *Tradition, Dissent and Ideology, Essays in Honour of Romila Thapar.* Delhi: Oxford University Press, pp. 164–91.

———. 1998. 'The Pursuit of Persian: Language in Mughal Politics.' *Modern Asian Studies* 32(2): 317–49.

———. 2000. '*Akhlaqi* Norms and Mughal Governance', in Muzaffar Alam, Francois 'Nalini' Delvoye, and Marc Gaborieau, eds. *The Making of the Indo-Persian Culture: Indian and French Studies*. Delhi: Manohar, pp. 67–95.

————. 2002. '*Shari'a* and Governance in the Indo-Muslim Context', in David Gilmartin and Bruce B. Lawrence, eds. *Beyond Turk and Hindu: Rethinking Religious Identities in Islamicate South Asia*. Delhi: India Research Press, pp. 216–45.

————. 2004. *The Languages of Political Islam in India, 1200–1800*. Delhi: Permanent Black.

Alam, Muzaffar and Sanjay Subrahmanyam, eds. 1998. *The Mughal State, 1526–1750*. Delhi: Oxford University Press.

Alavi, Seema. ed. 2002. *The Eighteenth Century in India*. Delhi: Oxford University Press.

Ali, Daud. 2002. 'Anxieties of Attachment: The Dynamics of Courtship in Medieval India', *Modern Asian Studies* 36(1): 103–39.

Ali, M. Athar. 1986–7. 'Recent Theories of Eighteenth Century India', *Indian Historical Review* 13(1–2): 102–10.

————. 1993. 'The Mughal Polity—A Critique of Revisionist Appraoches', *Modern Asian Studies* 27(4): 699–710.

————. 1997. *The Nobility under Aurangzeb*, reprint. Delhi: Oxford University Press.

Ambashthya, Bramadeva Prasad. 1957. 'Some Farmans, Sanads, Nishans and Inscriptions in Bihar', *Journal of Bihar Research Society* 43(3–4): 215–39.

————. 1961a. 'Tradition and Genealogy of the Ujjainiyas in Bihar', *Proceedings of the Indian History Congress*, 24th Session, Delhi, pp. 122–7.

————. 1961b. 'The account of the Ujjainiyas in Bihar', *Journal of Bihar Research Society* 47(1–4): 420–40 and plate.

————. 1977. *Decisive Battles of Ser Sah*. Patna: Janaki Prakashan.

————. 1984. *Non-Persian Sources of Indian Medieval History*. Delhi: Idarah-i-Adabiyat-i-Delli.

Amin, Shahid. 2002. 'On Retelling the Muslim Conquest of North India', in Partha Chatterjee and Anjan Ghosh, eds. *History and the Present*. Delhi: Permanent Black, pp. 24–43.

Amitai-Preiss, Reuven. 1990. 'Sufis and Shamans: Some Remarks on the Islamization of the Mongols in the Ilkhanate.' *Journal of the Economic and Social History of the Orient* (henceforth *JESHO*), 42(1): 27–46.

Andreyev, Sergei. 1999. 'The Rawshaniyya: A Sufi Movement on the Mughal Tribal Periphery', in Leonard Lewishon and David Morgan, eds. *The Heritage of Sufism: Late Classical Persianate Sufism (1501–1750)*, Vol. 3. Oxford: Oneworld.

Ansari, Zoe and Abul Faiz Sahar, eds. 1989. *Khusro Shanasi*. Delhi: Taraqqi Urdu Bureau.

Anwar, Firdos. 2001. *Nobility under the Mughals, 1628–1658,* New Delhi: Manohar.

Aquil, Raziuddin. 1995–6. 'Sufi Cults, Politics and Conversion: The Chishtis of the Sultanate Period', *Indian Historical Review* 22(1–2): 190–7.

———. 1997–8. 'Conversion in Chishti Sufi Literature (13th–14th Centuries)', *Indian Historical Review* 24(1–2): 70–94.

———. 2003a. 'Miracles, Authority and Benevolence: Stories of *Karamat* in Sufi Literature of the Delhi Sultanate', in Anup Taneja, ed. *Sufi Cults and the Evolution of Medieval Indian Culture,* Delhi: ICHR and Northern Book Centre, pp. 109–38.

———. 2003b. 'Episodes from the Life of Shaikh Farid-ud-Din Ganj-i-Shakar', *International Journal of Punjab Studies* 10(1–2): 25–46.

———. 2004a. 'Scholars, Saints and Sultans: Some Aspects of Religion and Politics in the Delhi Sultanate', *Indian Historical Review* 31(1–2): 210–20.

———. 2004b. 'On Islam and Kufr in the Delhi Sultanate: Towards a Reinterpretation of Ziya-ud-Din Barani's *Fatawa-i-Jahandari*', presented in 'Rethinking a Millennium: International Seminar in Honour of Prof. Harbans Mukhia', Delhi.

Arjomand, Saïd Amir. 2001. 'Perso-Indian Statecraft, Greek Political Science and the Muslim Idea of Government.' *International Sociology* 16(3): 455–73.

Asher, Catherine. 1977. 'The Mausoleum of Sher Shah Suri', *Artibus Asiae* 39: 273–98.

———. 1988. 'Legacy and Sher Shah's Patronage of Imperial Mausolea', in Katherine P. Ewing, ed. *Shari'at and Ambiguity in South Asian Islam.* Berkeley: University of California Press.

———. 1992. *Architecture of Mughal India.* Cambridge: Cambridge University Press.

Ashraf, K.M. 1959. *Life and Conditions of the People of Hindustan.* Delhi: Jiwan Prakashan.

Askari, S.H. 1953a. 'A Newly Discovered Volume of Awadhi Works Including *Padmavat* and *Akhravat* of Malik Muhammad Jaisi', *Journal of Bihar Research Society* 39(1–2): 10–40.

———. 1953b. '*Mirat-ul-Muluk*: A Contemporary Work Containing Reflections on Later Mughal Administration', *Indica*, The Indian Historical Research Institute Silver Jubilee Commemoration Volume, Bombay, pp. 27–37.

———. 1955a. 'Bihar in the Time of the Last Two Lodi Sultans of Delhi', *Proceedings of the Indian History Congress,* 18th Session, Calcutta, pp. 48–57.

———. 1955b. 'The Ujjainiya Ancestors of Babu Kuwar Singh', *Journal of Bihar Research Society* 41(1): 106–31.

————. 1960. 'Discursive Notes on the Sharqi Monarchy of Jaunpur', *Proceedings of the Indian History Congress*, 23rd Session, Aligarh, pp. 152–63.

Askari, S.H. and Qeyamuddin Ahmad, eds. 1983/1987. *The Comprehensive History of Bihar*, Vol. II, Parts I & II. Patna: K.P. Jayaswal Research Institute.

Asrar-ul-Auliya, conversations of Shaikh Farid-ud-Din Ganj-i-Shakar, compilation atrributed to Shaikh Badr-ud-Din Ishaq. Urdu trans. Muinuddin Durdai. Karachi: Nafis Academy, 1978.

Athar, Ali. 1995. 'The role of the *Piyadah* in the Sultanate of Delhi', *Journal of the Asiatic Society* 37(2): 24–8.

Avasthy, Rama Shankar. 1938. 'Sher Shah, his Accession and Coronation', *Proceedings of the Indian History Congress*, 2nd Session, Allahabad, pp. 368–75.

————. 1967. *The Mughal Emperor Humayun*. Allahabad: University of Allahabad.

Al-Azmeh, Aziz. 1997. *Muslim Kingship—Power and the Sacred in Muslim, Christian, and Pagan Polities*. London/New York: I.B. Tauris.

Azkar-i-Abrar, Urdu translation by Fazal Ahmad of the Persian text *Gulzar-i-Abrar* by Muhammad Ghausi Shattari. Lahore, AH 1395.

Bagley, F.R.C. 1964. *Ghazali's Book of Counsel for Kings*. London: Oxford University Press.

Banerji, S.K. 1935. 'Humayun's Succession to the Throne, December 1530', *Indian Historical Quarterly* 11(3): 537–46.

————. 1938. *Humayun Badshah*, 2 Vols. Bombay: Oxford University Press.

Barnett, Richard B. ed. 2002. Rethinking Early Modern India. Delhi, Manohar.

Bayly, C.A. 1996. *Empire and Information: Intelligence Gathering and Social Communication in India, 1780–1870*. Cambridge: Cambridge University Press.

Beames' Contribution to the Political Geography of the Subas of Awadh, Bihar, Bengal and Orissa in the Age of Akbar, B.P. Ambashthya, ed., 1976. Patna: Janaki Prakashan.

Bhattasali, N.K. 1936. 'The Date of Sher Shah's Accession', *Islamic Culture* 10: 127–30.

Bjorkman, W. 1973. 'Kafir', *Encyclopaedia of Islam* (New Edition), Vol. 4, Leiden: E.J. Brill.

Brittlebank, Kate. 1997. *Tipu Sultan's Search for Legitimacy: Islam and Kingship in a Hindu Domain*. Delhi: Oxford University Press.

Brown, Percy. 1939. 'Influence of Sher Shah on the Islamic Architecture of India', *Proceedings of the Indian History Congress*, 3rd Session, Calcutta, pp. 636–46.

Buchanan, Francis. 1986. An Account of the District of Shahabad in 1812–13 (first published 1934). Delhi: Usha Publications.

Chattopadhyaya, B.D. 1998. *Representing the Other? Sanskrit Sources and the Muslims (Eighth to Fourteenth Century)*. Delhi: Manohar.

Currie, P.M. 1989. *The Shrine and Cult of Muin al-Din Chishti of Ajmer*. Delhi: Oxford University Press.

Darke, Hubert. trans. 1960. *The Book of Government or Rules for Kings, The Siyasat-nama or Siyar al-Muluk of Nizam-ul Mulk*. London: Routledge & Kegan Paul.

Darling, Linda T. 2002. '"Do Justice, Do Justice, For That is Paradise": Middle Eastern Advice for Indian Muslim Rulers', *Comparative Studies of South Asia, Africa and the Middle East* 22(1–2): 3–19.

Day, Upendra Nath. 1965. *Medieval Malwa—A Political and Cultural History 1401–1562*. Delhi: Munshiram Manoharlal.

Deyell, John S. 1987. 'The Development of Akbar's Currency System and Monetary Integration of the Conquered Kingdoms', in John F. Richards, ed. *The Imperial Monetary System of Mughal India*. Delhi: Oxford University Press, pp. 13–67.

Digby, Simon. 1965. 'Dreams and Reminiscences of Dattu Sarwani', *Indian Economic and Social History Review* 2(1): 52–80 and 2(2): 178–94.

———. 1975. 'Shaikh Abd al-Quddus Gangohi (AD 1456–1537): The Personality and Attitude of a Medieval Indian Sufi.' *Medieval India: A Miscellany* 3: 1–66.

———. 1982. 'The Currency System', in Tapan Raychaudhuri and Irfan Habib, eds. *The Cambridge Economic History of India, Vol. I: c. 1200–c. 1750*. Hyderabad: Orient Longman.

———. 1986. 'The Sufi Shaykh as a Source of Authority in Medieval India.' *Purushartha* 9: 55–77.

———. 1990a. 'Hawk and Dove in Sufi Combat', *Pembroke Papers I*: 7–25.

———. 1990b. 'The Sufi Shaikh and the Sultan: A Conflict of Claims to Authority in Medieval India', *Iran* 28: 71–81.

———. 1994. 'To Ride a Tiger or a Wall? Strategies of Prestige in Indian Sufi Legend', in Winand M. Callewaert and Rupert Snell, eds. *According to Tradition: Hagiographical Writing in India*. Wiesbaden: Otto Harrassowitz.

Dwivedi, S.D. 1968. 'Rajput Resistance in Medieval India', *Proceedings of the Indian History Congress* 30th Session, Bhagalpur, pp. 163–65.

Eaton, Richard M. 1978. *Sufis of Bijapur, 1300–1700, Social Roles of Sufis in Medieval India*. Princeton: Princeton University Press.

———. 1984. 'The Political and Religious Authority of the Shrine of Baba Farid in Pakpattan, Punjab', in Barbara D. Metcalf, ed. *Moral Conduct and Authority: The Place of Adab in South Asian Islam*. Berkeley: University of California Press.

————. 1994. *The Rise of Islam and the Bengal Frontier*. New Delhi: Oxford University Press.

————. 2002. *Essays on Islam and Indian History*. New Delhi: Oxford University Press.

————. ed. 2003. *India's Islamic Traditions, 711–1750*. Delhi: Oxford University Press.

Elias, Jamal J. ed. 2000. *Sufi Saints and Shrines in Muslim Society*, in *Muslim World* (Special Issue), 90(3–4).

Ernst, Carl W. 1992. *Eternal Garden: Mysticism, History and Politics at a South Asian Sufi Centre*. Albany: State University of New York Press.

Ernst, Carl W. and Bruce B. Lawrence. 2002. *Sufi Martyrs of Love: The Chishti Order in South Asia and Beyond*. New York: Palgrave Macmillan.

Erskine, Williams. 1973. *History of India under the two Sovereigns of the House of Taimur*, 2 Vols, reprint. Delhi: Idarah-i Adabiyat-i Delli.

Faruqi, Ihsanul Haq. 1963. *Sultan-ut-Tarikin*. Karachi: Dairah Mu'inul Ma'arif.

Fatawa-i-Jahandari, Ziya-ud-Din Barani. ed., Afsar Salim Khan, Lahore, 1972.

Fawa'id-ul-Fu'ad, conversations of Shaikh Nizam-ud-Din Auliya' compiled by Amir Hasan Sijzi. Persian text with an Urdu translation by Khwaja Hasan Sani Nizami. Delhi: Urdu Academy, 1990.

Fawa'id-us-Salikin, conversations of Shaikh Qutb-ud-Din Bakhtiyar Kaki, compilation attributed to Shaikh Farid-ud-Din Ganj-i-Shakar. Urdu trans. New Delhi: Maktaba Jam-i-Noor, nd.

Gardet, L. 1973. 'Karama', *Encyclopaedia of Islam* (New Edition), Vol. 4, Leiden: E.J. Brill.

Gommans, Jose J.L. 1995. *The Rise of the Indo-Afghan Empire, c. 1710–1780*. Leiden: Brill.

Gordon, Stewart. 1994. *Marathas, Marauders and State Formation in Eighteenth Century India*. Delhi: Oxford University Press.

————. ed. 2001. *Robes and Honor: The Medieval World of Investiture*. New York: Palgrave.

Grewal, J.S. 1990. *The Sikhs of the Punjab*. Cambridge: Cambridge University Press.

————. 1996. *Sikh Ideology, Polity and Social Order*. Delhi: Manohar.

Habib, Irfan. 1963. 'Evidence for Sixteenth Century Agrarian Conditions in the Guru Granth Sahib', *Proceedings of the Indian History Congress*, 25th Session, Poona, pp. 186–94.

————. 1978. 'Economic History of Delhi Sultanate—An Essay in Interpretation', *Indian Historical Review* 4(2): 287–303.

————. 1982. *An Atlas of the Mughal Empire*. Delhi: Oxford University Press.

————. 1988–9. 'Slavery in the Delhi Sultanate, Thirteenth and Fourteenth Centuries: Evidence from Sufic Literature', *Indian Historical Review* 15(1–2): 248–56.

————. ed. 1997. *Akbar and His India*. Delhi: Oxford University Press.

————. 1999. *The Agrarian System of Mughal India, 1556–1707*, new edition. Delhi: Oxford University Press.

Habib, Mohammad. 1974/1981. *Politics and Society During the Early Medieval Period, Collected Works of Mohammad Habib*, 2 Vols. K.A. Nizami, eds., Delhi: People's Publishing House.

Habib, Mohammad and K.A. Nizami, eds. 1992. *A Comprehensive History of India, Vol. V, Part One, The Delhi Sultanate* (AD 1206–1526), first published 1970, second ed. Delhi: People's Publishing House.

Habibullah, A.B.M. 1961. *The Foundation of the Muslim Rule in India*, 2nd edn. Allahabad: Central Book Depot.

Haidar, Mansura, ed. 2004. *Sufis, Sultans and Feudal Orders: Professor Nurul Hasan Commemoration Volume*. Delhi: Manohar.

Haider, Najaf. 1989–90. 'The Lodi Coinage—Some Questions', *Proceedings of the Indian History Congress,* Golden Jubilee Session, Gorakhpur, pp. 229–35.

————. 1999. 'Mughal and Mahmudis: The incorporation of Gujarat into the Imperial Monetary System', *Proceedings of the Indian History Congress,* Diamond Jubilee (60th) Session, Calicut, 1999, pp. 270–86.

Halim, Abdul. 1938. 'Sultan Bahlul Lodi: The Place of his Death and Duration of his Reign', *Journal of Indian History* 17(3): 325–31.

————. 1947. 'Muslim Kings of the Fifteenth Century and the Bhakti revival', *Proceedings of the Indian History Congress,* 10th Session, Bombay, pp. 305–10.

————. 1957. 'Growth and Development of Hindi Literature During the Sayyid-Lodi Period', *Journal of the Asiatic Society of Pakistan* 2: 69–89.

————. 1958. 'Growth of Urdu Language and Literature During the Sayyid-Lodi Period', *Journal of the Asiatic Society of Pakistan* 3: 43–66.

————. 1962. 'Religious Movements in Northern India (1414–1526)', *Journal of the Asiatic Society of Pakistan* 7: 47–87.

————. 1963. 'Mystics and Mystical Movements of the Sayyid-Lodi Period (1414–1526)', *Journal of the Asiatic Society of Pakistan* 8: 71–108.

————. 1974. *History of Lodi Sultans of Delhi and Agra*, reprint. Delhi: Idarah-i Adabiyat-i Delli.

Hameed-ud-Din. 1961. 'The Lodi Sultans and the Rajput States', *Journal of Indian History* 39(2): 313–26.

Haq, Abdul. 1953. *Urdu ki Ibtadai Nasho-numa mein Sufiya-i-Karam ka Kaam*. Karachi: Anjuman Taraqqi Urdu.

Haq, M.M. 1971. 'The Shuttari Order of Sufism in India and its Exponents in Bengal and Bihar', *Journal of the Asiatic Society of Pakistan* 16(2): 167–75.

Haqq, M. Enamul. 1975. *A History of Sufism in Bengal*. Dacca: Asiatic Society of Bangladesh.

Hardy, Peter. 1978. 'The Growth of Authority over a Conquered Political Elite: The Early Delhi Sultanate as a Possible Case Study', in J.F. Richards, ed. *Kingship and Authority in South Asia*. University of Wisconsin—Madison, pp. 192–214.

Hasan, Muhibbul. ed. 1968. *Historians of Medieval India*. Meerut: Meenakshi Prakashan.

———. 1985. *Babur: Founder of Mughal Empire in India*. Delhi: Manohar.

Hashimi, Abdul Quddus. 1987 (1965). *Taqwim-i-Tarikhi (Qamus-i-Tarikhi)*. Islamabad: Idarah-i Tahqiqat-i Islami.

Huda, M.Z. 1968–9. 'Jamali, The Poet of Ludis and Mughals', *Journal of the Asiatic Society of Pakistan* 13(3): 253–89 and 14(1): 21–49.

———. 1969. 'Sultan Sikandar Ludi—A Poet and Patron of Letters', *Journal of the Asiatic Society of Pakistan* 14(3): 289–304.

Hughes, Patrick Thomas. 1995. *Dictionary of Islam*, reprint. Delhi: Munshiram Manoharlal.

Humayun-Nama, Gulbadan Begum. A.S. Beveridge, ed. and trans. *Humayun-Nama of Gulbadan Begam*, first published 1902, reprint. Delhi: Oriental Reprint, 1983.

Husain, Afzal. 1999. *The Nobility under Akbar and Jahangir: A Study of Family Group*. New Delhi: Manohar.

Husain, Agha Mahdi. 1976. *Tughluq Dynasty*. Delhi: S. Chand.

Husain, Yusuf. 1957. *Glimpses of Medieval Indian Culture*. Bombay: Asia Publishing House.

Hussain, Syed Ejaz. 2003. *The Bengal Sultanate: Politics, Economy and Coins (AD 1205–1576)*. New Delhi: Manohar.

Ibn Hasan, 1970 (1936). *The Central Structure of the Mughal Empire and its Practical Working upto the year 1657*. Delhi: Munshiram Manoharlal.

Imamuddin, S.M. 1958. 'The Nature of Afghan Monarchy in India', *Islamic Culture* 32: 268–75.

———. 1959. 'Some Persian Literacy Sources of the Afghan History of India', *Islamic Culture* 33: 39–49.

———. 1961. 'A Study of the Jagir System in Afghan India', *Islamic Culture* 35: 259–65.

Jackson, Paul. 1985. 'Khair-ul-Majalis: An Examination', in C.W. Troll, ed. *Islam in India*, Vol. II. Delhi: Vikas.

Jackson, Peter. 1999. *The Delhi Sultanate: A Political and Military History*. Cambridge: Cambridge University Press.

Jawahir-i-Faridi. 1884. Ali Asghar. Lahore: Victoria Press.

Jawami-ul-Kalim, conversations of Syed Muhammad Gesu-Daraz compiled by Syed Muhammad Akbar Husaini. Urdu tr.: Muinuddin Dardai, Delhi: Adabi Duniya, 1994.

Joshi, Rita. 1985. *The Afghan Nobility and the Mughals, 1526–1707*. Delhi: Vikas.

Juneja, Monica. ed. 2001. *Architecture in Medieval India: Forms, Contexts, Histories*. Delhi: Permanent Black.

Juneja, M.M. 1989. *History of Hisar from Inception to Independence, 1354–1947*. Hisar: Modern Book.

Kakar, Sudhir. 1982. *Shamans, Mystics and Doctors—A Psychological Inquiry into India and its Healing Traditions*. Delhi: Oxford University Press.

Karim, A. 1960. 'Date and Place of Sher Shah's Accession', *Journal of the Asiatic Society of Pakistan* 5: 63–71.

Kashf-ul-Lughat wal Istalahat, Abdur Rahim Bin Ahmad Sur. British Museum Ms., Add. 5611, OIOC, British Library, London.

Kashf-ul-Mahjub, Shaikh Ali Hujwiri. 1976. Eng. trans. R.A. Nicholson. London: Luzac.

Khadduri, Majid. 1966. *The Islamic Law of Nations—Shaybani's Siyar*, Translation with an Introduction, Notes and Appendices. Baltimore: Johns Hopkins Press.

Khair-ul-Majalis, conversations of Shaikh Nasir-ud-Din Chiragh-i-Dehli. 1959. compiled by Hamid Qalandar, ed. K.A. Nizami, Aligarh.

Khalidi, Tarif. ed. and trans. 2001. *The Muslim Jesus: Sayings and Stories in Islamic Literature*. Cambridge and London: Harvard University Press.

Khan, Ahsan Raza. 1977. *Chieftains of the Mughal Empire During the Reign of Akbar*. Simla: IIAS.

Khan, Hasan Ali. 1950. '*Tawarikh-i-Daulat-i-Sher Shahi*', *Medieval Indian Quarterly* 1(1): 57–65.

Khan, Hussain. 1970. 'The Genesis of Roh (The Medieval Homeland of the Afghans)', *Journal of the Asiatic Society of Pakistan* 15(3): 191–7.

———. 1971. 'The Political and Economic Conditions of Roh', *Journal of the Asiatic Society of Pakistan* 16(2): 177–82.

Khan, Iqtidar Alam. 1961. 'Mughal-Afghan Relations, 1559–74', *Proceedings of the Indian History Congress*, 24th session, Delhi, 120–2.

———. 1972. 'Turko-Mongol Theory of Kingship', *Medieval India: A Miscellany* 2: 8–18.

———. 1977. 'Shaikh Abdul Quddus Gangohi's Relation with Political Authorities: A Reappraisal', *Medieval India: A Miscellany* 4: 73–90.

———. 1987–8. 'The Karwansarays of Mughal India: A Study of Surviving Structures', *Indian Historical Review* 14(1–2): 111–37.

————. 1999a. 'Re-examining the Origin and Group Identity of the So-called Purabias, 1500–1800', *Proceedings of the Indian History Congress*, Diamond Jubilee (60th) Session, Calicut, pp. 363–71.

————. ed. 1999b. *Akbar and his Age*. Delhi: Northern Book Centre.

Khan, Kunwar Refaqat Ali. 1976. *The Kachhwahas under Akbar and Jahangir*. Delhi: Kitab Publishing House.

Khan, M. Anwar. 1977. 'Modern Afghan Researches on Lodis and Surs', *Islamic Studies* 16: 363–6.

Khan, M. Ifzal-ur-Rahman. 1995. 'The Attitude of the Delhi Sultans Towards Non-Muslims: Some Observations.' *Islamic Culture* 69(2): 41–56.

Khan, Sir Sayed Ahmad. *Asar-us-Sanadid*, ed., Khaleeq Anjum. Delhi, 1990.

Khan, Yar Muhammad. 1961. 'The Use of Artillery During the Sultanate Period', *Islamic Culture* 35: 198–203.

Khazinat-ul-Asfiya, Maulwi Ghulam Sarwar, Vol. I. Kanpur: Newal Kishore, n.d.

Khulasat-ut-Tawarikh, Sujan Rai. Royal Asiatic Society, Persian Mss. No. 53 (Microfilm).

Kolff, Dirk H.A. 1990. *Naukar, Rajput and Sepoy: The Ethnohistory of the Military Labour Markets in Hindustan, 1450–1850*. Cambridge: Cambridge University Press.

Kulke, H. ed. 1995. *The State in India, 1000–1700*. Delhi: Oxford University Press.

Kumar, Sunil. 1985. 'The Value of the *Adab al-Muluk* as a Historical Source: An Insight into the Ideals and Expectations of Islamic Society in the Middle Period (AD 945–1500)', *Indian Economic and Social History Review* 22(3): 307–27.

Lal, K.S. 1980. *Twilight of the Sultanate*, reprint. Delhi: Munshiram Manoharlal.

————. 1992. *The Legacy of Muslim Rule in India*. *Delhi*: Aditya Prakashan.

Lamb, Harold. 1978. *The Emperor of All Men*. Lahore: Oriental Publishers.

Lambton, A.K.S. 1981. *State and Government in Medieval Islam*. Oxford: Oxford University Press.

Lapidus, Ira M. 1996. 'State and Religion in Islamic Societies', *Past and Present* 151: 3–27.

Latif, Sk. Abdul. 1993. *The Muslim Mystic Movement in Bengal, 1301–1550*. Calcutta: K.P. Bagchi.

Lawrence, Bruce B. 1983. 'The Early Chishti Approach to *Sama*', in M. Israel and N.K. Wagle, eds. *Islamic Society and Culture: Essays in Honour of Professor Aziz Ahmad*. Delhi: Manohar.

————. 1984. 'Early Indo-Muslim Saints and Conversion', in Y. Friedmann, ed., *Islam in Asia, Vol. I, South Asia*. Jerusalem: Max Schloessinger Memorial Foundation.

Ma'asir-ul-Umara, Nawwab Samsam-ud-Daula Shah Nawaz Khan and his son Abdul Hayy. Ms. I.O. Islamic 2443, OIOC, British Library, London. 1979. Eng. trans., H. Beveridge, revised, annotated and completed by Baini Prasad, 3 Vols. Patna: Janaki Prakashan.

Mahmood, Tahir. 2003. 'The Dargah of Salar Mas'ud Ghazi in Bahraich: Legend, Tradition and Reality', in Christian W. Troll, ed., *Muslim Shrines in India: Their Character, History and Significance*, reprint Delhi: Oxford University Press.

Makhdoomee, M. Akram. 1936. 'Mechanical Artillery in Medieval India', *Journal of Indian History* 15(2): 189–95.

Malhotra, Yog. 1995. 'Bubur's Jovial Parties', *Journal of the Asiatic Society* 37(2): 18–23.

Marlow, Louise. 1997. *Hierarchy and Egalitarianism in Islamic Thought*. Cambridge: Cambridge University Press.

Marshall, P.J. ed. 2003. *The Eighteenth Century in Indian History, Evolution or Revolution?*. Delhi: Oxford University Press.

Martin, Marie H. 1987. 'The Reforms of the Sixteenth Century and Akbar's Administration: Metrological and Monetary Considerations', in John F. Richards, ed. *The Imperial Monetary System of Mughal India*. Delhi: Oxford University Press, pp. 68–99.

Mcgregor, Stuart. 2001. 'On the Evolution of Hindi as a language of Literature.' *South Asia Research* 21(2): 203–17.

Mirza, M. Wahid. 1986. *Amir Khusrau*. Delhi: National Amir Khusrau Society.

Misra, Satish Chandra. 1952. 'Revenue System of Sher Shah', *Proceedings of the Indian History Congress*, 15th Session, pp. 232–9.

———. 1957. 'Administrative System of the Surs (Sher Shah and His Successors)', *Islamic Culture* 31: 322–39.

———. 1969. 'The *Sikka* and the *Khutba*: A Sher Shahi Experiment', *MIAM*, Vol. I.

Mohammed, Jigar. 2002. *Revenue Free Land Grants in Mughal India: Awadh Region in the Seventeenth and Eighteenth Centuries (1658–1765)*. Delhi: Manohar.

Moreland, W.H. 1926. 'Sher Shah's Revenue System', *Journal of the Royal Asiatic Society*, pp. 447–59.

———. 1929. *Agrarian System of Moslem India*. London.

Mu'aiyyid-ul-Fuzala, Muhammad bin Lad. British Museum Ms., Or. 261, OIOC, British Library, London.

Mujeeb, M. 1972. *Islamic Influence on Indian Society*. Meerut: Meenakshi Prakashan.

———. 1985. *Indian Muslims*. Delhi: Munshiram Manoharlal.

Mukhia, Harbans. 1976. *Historians and Historiography During the Reign of Akbar*. Delhi: Vikas.

————. 2004. *The Mughals of India*. Oxford: Blackwell.

Muntakhab-ut-Tawarikh, Mulla Abdul Qadir Badauni. ed. Ahmad Ali, Kabir al-Din Ahmad, and W. Nassau Lees, 3 Vols. Calcutta: Bibliotheca Indica, pp. 1864–9.

Mu'nis-ul-Arwah, Jahan Ara Begam. 1992. In Qamar Jahan Begum, *Princess Jahan Ara Begam: Her Life and Works*. Karachi.

Nasr, S.H. 1972. *Sufi Essays*. London: Allen and Unwin.

Nath, Ram. 1985. *History of Mughal Architecture*, 2 Vols. Delhi: Abhinav.

————. 1994. *History of Mughal Architecture*. Delhi: Abhinav.

Nicholson, R.A. 1975. *The Mystics of Islam*. London: Routledge and Kegan Paul.

Nizami, K.A. 1953. *Hayat-i-Shaikh Abdul Haqq Muhaddis*. Delhi.

————. 1955. *The Life and Times of Shaikh Fariduddin Ganj-i-Shakar*. Aligarh: Muslim University.

————. 1961. *Some Aspects of Religion and Politics in India During the 13th Century*. Aligarh: Muslim University.

————. 1989. *Akbar and Religion*. Delhi: Idarah-i-Adabiyat-i Delli.

————. 1991a. *The Life and Times of Shaikh Nizamuddin Auliya*. Delhi: Idarah-i-Adabiyat-i Delli.

————. 1991b. *The Life and Times of Shaikh Nasiruddin Chiragh*. Delhi: Idarah-i-Adabiyat-i Delli.

————. 1992. 'The Lodis (1451–1526)', in M. Habib and K.A. Nizami, eds. *A Comprehensive History of India, Vol. V, part one, The Delhi Sultanate (AD 1206–1526)*, first published 1970, 2nd edn. (Delhi: Peoples Publishing House, pp. 664–709.

Nizamu'ddin, Muhammad. 1929. *Introduction to the Jawami'u'l-Hikayat wa Lawami'u'r-Riwayat of Sadidu'd-Din Muhammad Al-'Awfi*. London: Luzac.

Nurul Hasan, S. 1964. 'Revenue Administration of the *Jagir* of Sahsaram by Farid (Sher Shah)', *Proceedings of the Indian History Congress*, Ranchi, 1964, pp. 102–7.

Padmavat, Malik Muhammad Jaisi. 1935. In *Jaisi Granthawali*, ed., Ramchandra Shukla, Varanasi: Nagri Pracharini Sabha.

Pandey, A.B. 1964. *The First Afghan Empire in India*, 2nd edn. Calcutta: Bookland.

Perlin, Frank. 1985. 'State Formation Reconsidered', *Modern Asian Studies* 19(3): 415–80.

Phogat, S.R. 1978. *Inscriptions of Haryana*. Kurukshetra: Vishal Publication.

Phukan, Shantanu. 1996. 'None Mad as a Hindu Woman': Contesting Communal Readings of Padmavat', *Comparative Studies of South Asia, Africa and the Middle East* 16(1).

Platts, John T. 1993. *A Dictionary of Urdu, Classical Hindi and English*, reprint. Delhi: Munshiram Manoharlal.

Prasad, Ishwari. n.d. *The Life and Times of Humayun*. Allahabad: Central Book Depot.

Prasad, Pushpa. 1990. *Sanskrit Inscriptions of Delhi Sultanate*. Delhi: Oxford University Press.

Prasad, Rajiva Nain. 1968. 'The Role of Ujjainia Rajputs in the Political History of Bihar (AD 1500–AD 1605)', *Proceedings of the Indian History Congress*, 30th Session, Bhagalpur, pp. 167–77.

Prawdin, Michael. 1961. *The Mongol Empire—Its Rise and Legacy*. Eng. trans. Edan and Cedar Paul. London: George Allen and Unwin.

Qadiri, Muhammad Ayyub. 1963. *Makhdum Jahaniyan Jahangasht*. Karachi: Idarah Tahqiq wa Tasnif.

Qamaruddin. 1985. *The Mahdawi Movement in India*. Delhi: Idarah-i-Adabiyat-i Delli.

Qanungo, Kalika Rajan. 1921. 'A Critical Study of Abbas Sarwani's History of Shershah', *Journal of Bihar and Orissa Research Society* 7: 90–5.

———. 1965. *Sher Shah and his Times*. Bombay: Orient Longmans.

Qiwam-ul-Aqa'id, Muhammad Jamal Qiwam, ed., Nisar Ahamd Faruqui. In *Qand-i-Parsi*, VII (1994). Urdu trans., Nisar Ahamd Faruqui, Rampur, 1994.

Quddusi, Aijazul Haq. 1961. *Shaykh Abdul Quddus aur un ki Ta'limat*. Karachi: All Pakistan Educational Conference.

Qureshi, I.H. 1971. *The Administration of the Sultanate of Delhi*, fifth revised edn. Delhi: Oriental Reprint.

———. 1985a. *Ulema in Politics*. Delhi: Renaissance Publication House.

———. 1985b. *The Muslim Community of the Indo-Pak Subcontinent, 610–1947*. Delhi: Renaissance Publication House.

Rahat-ul-Muhibbin, conversations of Shaikh Nizam-ud-Din Auliya compilation attributed to Amir Khusrau. Urdu trans. New Delhi: Maktaba Jami-Noor, n.d.

Rahim, M.A. 1956a. 'The Origin of the Afghans and their Rise to the Sultanate of Delhi', *Journal of the Pakistan Historical Society* 4: 64–70.

———. 1956b. 'The Nature of the Afghan Monarchy and the Position of the Afghan Chiefs', *Journal of the Pakistan Historical Society* 4: 116–32.

———. 1956c. 'Islam Shah Sur', *Journal of the Pakistan Historical Society* 4: 247–77.

———. 1961. *History of Afghans in India, AD 1545–1631, with Special Reference to their Relations with the Mughals*. Karachi: Pakistan Publication House.

Rahman, S.S. Abdur. 1966. *Hindustan Amir Khusrau ki Nazr Mein*. Azamgarh: Darul Musannefin.

————. 1979. *Amir Khusrau Dehlawi*. Azamgarh: Darul Musannefin.

————. 1980. *Sufi Amir Khusrau*. Azamgarh: Darul Musannefin.

Rashid, A. 1964. 'Famine in the Turco-Afghan Period', *Proceedings of the Indian History Congress*, Ranchi Session, pp. 84–9.

Ray, Sukumar. 1992. *Bairam Khan*, ed., M.H.A. Beg. Karachi: Institute of Central and West Asian Studies.

Reddy, C. Srinivasan. 1991. 'Approaches to the Mughal State', *Social Scientist* 19(10–11): 90–6.

Riazul Islam. 1970. *Indo-Persian Relations: A Study of the Political and Diplomatic Relations Between the Mughal Empire and Iran*. Teheran: Iranian Culture Foundation.

Richards, J.F. 1965. 'The Economic History of the Lodi Period: 1451–1526', *JESHO* 8(1): 47–67; reprinted in Sanjay Subrahmanyam, ed. 1994. *Money and the Market in India 1100–1700*. Delhi: Oxford University Press, pp. 137–55.

————. 1978. 'The Formulation of Imperial Authority under Akbar and Jahangir', in J.F. Richards, ed. *Kingship and Authority in South Asia*. University of Wisconsin—Madison, pp. 252–85.

————. 1991. *The Mughal Empire*. Cambridge: Cambridge University Press.

Riyaz-us-Salatin, Ghulam Husain Salim. Eng. trans., Abdus Salam, first published 1903, reprint. Delhi, 1975.

Rizvi, S.A.A. 1950. 'The Authenticity of the Title Page and the Colophon of *Tawarikh Daulat-i-Sher Shahi*', *Medieval India Quarterly* 1(2): 74–8.

————. 1961. 'Available Works of Bayazid Raushanai', *Proceedings of the Indian History Congress*, 24th Session, Delhi, pp. 181–7.

————. 1965 (1993). *Muslim Revivalist Movements in Northern India in the Sixteenth and Seventeenth Centuries*, reprint. Delhi: Munshiram Manoharlal.

————. 1967–8. *Rawshaniyya Movement*, in Abr-Nahrain, edited by J. Bowman Leiden, reprint. Delhi: Munshiram Manoharlal, n.d.

————. 1975. *Religious and Intellectual History of the Muslims in Akbar's reign with Special Reference to Abul Fazl*. Delhi; Munshiram Manoharlal.

————. 1978. *A History of Sufism in India, Vol. I, Early Sufism and its History in India to AD 1600*. Delhi: Munshiram Manoharlal.

Rose, H.A. 1909. 'The Legend of Khan Khawas and Sher Shah the Chaugatta (Mughal) at Delhi', *Indian Antiquary* 38: 113–18.

Rosen, Stephen Peter. 1996. *Societies and Military Power: India and its Armies*. Delhi: Oxford University Press.

Ross, E.D. 1926–8. 'Fresh Light on Khawass Khan', *Bulletin of the School of Oriental and African Studies* 4: 717–20.

Roy, Nirode Bhushan. 1954. 'Some Interesting Anecdotes of Sher Shah from the Rare Persian Ms. of *Tazkirat-ul-Muluk*', *Journal of the Asiatic Society, Letters*, 20(2): 219–26.

———. 1958. 'Anecdotes of Sher Shah (from the Manuscript of *Tarikh-i-Da'udi*)', *Islamic Culture* 32: 250–61.

Roy, Nishith Ranjan. 1939. 'Humayun and Maldeo', *Proceedings of the Indian History Congress*, 3rd Session, Calcutta, pp. 124–32.

Rushdnama or *Alakhbani*, Shaikh Abdul Quddus Gangohi. Introduction, translation into Hindi, and annotation by Saiyid Athar Abbas Rizvi and Shailesh Zaidi, Aligarh: Bharat Prakashan, 1971.

Saksena, Banarsi Prasad. 1925. 'Baizid Biyat and his Work-"Mukhtasar"', *Journal of Indian History* 4(3): 43–60.

———. 1966. 'General Presidential Address', *Proceedings of the Indian History Congress*, 28th Session, Mysore, I–XXXIV.

Saran, Parmatma. 1952. *Studies in Medieval Indian History*. Delhi, 1952.

———. 1941 (1973). *The Provincial Government of the Mughals 1526–1658*, second Edition (first Asia edition). Bombay: Asia Publishing House.

Sarkar, Jadu Nath. 1969. *Military History of India*. Delhi: Munshiram Manoharlal.

Sarkar, Jagadish N. 1970. *The Art of War in Medieval India*. Bombay: Orient Longman.

Schimmel, Annemarie. 1975. *The Mystical Dimensions of Islam*. Chapel Hill: University of North Carolina Press.

———. 1980. *Islam in the Indian Subcontinent*. Leiden: E.J. Brill.

———. 1999. 'The Vernacular Tradition in Persianate Sufi Poetry in Mughal India', in Leonard Lewishon and David Morgan, eds. *The Heritage of Sufism: Late Classical Persianate Sufism (1501–1750)*, Vol. 3. Oxford: Oneworld.

Sharfnama-i-Ahmad Maneri, Ibrahim Qiwam Faruqi. British Museum Ms., Add. 7678, OIOC, British Library, London.

Sen, S.N. 1941. 'A Note on the Purana Qila of Delhi', *Journal of Indian History* 20: 35–37.

Sensarma, Major P. 1976. *The Military Profile of Sher Shah Sur*. Calcutta.

Sharma, Sri Ram. 1926. 'Sher Shah and Maldev', *Journal of Indian History* 5(1): 66–71.

———. 1932. 'Humayun and Maldev', *Journal of Indian History* 11(2): 192–202.

———. 1936. 'Administrative System of Sher Shah', *Indian Historical Quarterly* 12(4): 581–606.

———. 1940 (1972). *The Religious Policy of the Mughal Emperors*, reprint. Bombay.

Siddiqi, M. Shakil Ahmad. 1979. *Amir Hasan Sijzi Dehlawi: Hayat aur Adabi Khidmat*. Lucknow: Nami Press.

Siddiqui, Iqtidar Husain. 1966. 'Position of *Shiqqdar* Under the Sultans of Delhi', *Proceedings of the Indian History Congress*, 28th Session, Mysore, 202–8.

———. 1969. *Some Aspects of Afghan Despotism in India*. Aligarh: Three Men.

———. 1971. *A History of Sher Shah Sur*. Aligarh: P.C. Dwadesh Shreni & Co.

———. 1977. 'The Composition of the Nobility Under the Lodi Sultans', *MIAM* 4: 10–66.

———. 1982. 'The Afghans and their Emergence in India as Ruling Elite During the Delhi Sultanate Period', *Central Asiatic Journal* 26: 241–61.

———. 1983. Mughal Relations with the Indian Ruling Elite. Delhi: Munshiram Manoharlal.

———. 1989. 'The Early Chishti Dargahs', in Christian W. Troll, ed., *Muslim Shrines in India—Their Character, History and Significance*. Delhi: Oxford University Press.

———. 1992. *Perso-Arabic Sources of Information on the Life and Conditions in the Sultanate of Delhi*. Delhi: Munshiram Manoharlal.

———. n.d. *Sher Shah Sur and his Dynasty*. Jaipur: Publication Scheme.

———. ed. 2003. *Medieval India: Essays in Intellectual Thought and Culture*, Volume I. Delhi: Manohar.

Siddiqui, M. Zamiruddin. 1969. 'Shaikh Abdul Quddus of Gangoh and Contemporary Rulers.' *Proceedings of Indian History Congress*, 31st Session, Varanasi, pp. 305–11.

———. 1972. 'The Intelligence Services Under the Mughals', *Medieval India: A Miscellany* 2: 53–60.

Sinha, H.N. 1940. 'Sher Shah's Parganahs and their Administrative Officials: Miscellany', *Indian Historical Quarterly* 16(1): 166–9.

———. 1962. 'The Mughals and the Afghans', *Journal of Indian History* 40(3): 677–711.

Sircar, Dinesh Chandra. 1954. 'Rana Udayasimha and the Sur Emperors of Delhi', *Indian Historical Quarterly* 30(1): 25–30.

———. 1955. 'Rana Udayasimha's Relation with Islam Shah', *Indian Historical Quarterly* 31(3): 273–5.

Siyar-ul-Arifin, Shaikh Jamali. British Museum Ms. Or. 5853, OIOC, British Library, London. Urdu tr.: Ayub Qadiri, Lahore 1976.

Siyar ul-Auliya, Amir Khwurd. Lahore, 1978. Urdu tr.: Abdul Latif, Delhi, 1994.

Steingass, F. 1996. *A Comprehensive Persian-English Dictionary*, reprint. Delhi: Munshiram Manoharlal.

Strausand, Douglas. 1990. *The Formation of the Mughal Empire*. Delhi: Oxford University Press.

Subrahmanyam, Sanjay. 1992. 'The Mughal State—Structure or Process? Reflections on Recent Western Historiography', *Indian Economic and Social History Review* 29(3): 291–321.

———. 2001. *Penumbral Visions: Making Polities in Early Modern South India*. Delhi: Oxford University Press.

Tabaqat-i-Akbari, Nizam-ud-Din Ahmad. Ms. I.O. Islamic 3320, OIOC, British Library, London. Edition: B. De, ed. Calcutta: Bib. Indica, 1913–31.

Tabaqat-i-Nasiri, Minhaj-us-Siraj. ed. Abdul Hayy Habibi, Vol. 1. Kabul: Historical Society of Afghanistan, 1963–4.

Talbot, Cynthia. 1995. 'Inscribing the Other, Inscribing the Self: Hindu-Muslim Identities in Pre-colonial India.' *Comparative Studies in Society and History* 37(4): 692–722.

Talib, G.S. ed. 1973. *Baba Shaikh Farid—Life and Teaching*. Patiala: Farid Memorial Society.

Tarikh-i-Da'udi, Abdullah. ed. S.A. Rashid, Aligarh: Aligarh Muslim University, 1954.

Tarikh-i-Farishta or *Gulshan-i-Ibrahimi*. M. Qasim Hindu Shah Astrabadi known as Farishta, Ms. I.O. Islamic 1251, OIOC, British Library, London; Royal Asiatic Society, Persian Mss. No. 61 (Microfilm).

Tarikh-i-Firuz-Shahi, Ziya-ud-Din Barani. British Museum Ms. 6376, OIOC, British Library, London.

Tarikh-i-Haqqi, Shaykh Abdul Haqq Muhaddis Dehlawi. Royal Asiatic Society, Persian Mss. No. 47 (Microfilm).

Tarikh-i-Khan Jahani wa Makhzan-i-Afghani, Khwaja Ni'matullah. ed. S.M. Imamuddin, 2 Vols, Dacca, 1960–2.

Tarikh-i-Rashidi, Mirza Muhammad Haider Dughlat. 1972. Eng. tr.: N. Elias and E.D. Ross, London.

Tarikh-i-Salatin-i-Afaghina, Ahmad Yadgar. ed. M. Hidayat Husain, Calcutta, 1939.

Tarikh-i-Sher-i-Shahi, Abbas Khan Sarwani. ed. and trans. S.M. Imamuddin, Dacca, 1964.

Tazkirah-i-Humayun wa Akbar. Bayazid. ed. M. Hidayat Husain, Asiatic Society, Calcutta, 1941.

Tazkirat-ul-Auliya, Farid-ud-din Attar. ed. R.A. Nicholson, 2 Parts. London/Leiden, 1905 and 1907.

Tazkirat-ul-Waqi'at, Jauhar Aftabchi. British Museum Ms. Add. 16711, OIOC, British Library, London. Eng. tr.: Charles Stewart, reprint. Delhi, 1972.

Thapar, Romila. 2004. *Somanatha: The Many Voices of a History*. Delhi: Penguin.

Tiwari, Ramachandra G. 1954. 'Maharana Udai Singh and the Sur Emperors of Delhi', *Indian Historical Quarterly* 30(4): 311–26.

Trimingham, J.S. 1973. *The Sufi Orders in Islam*. Oxford: Oxford University Press.

Tripathi, Ram Prasad. 1921–2. 'The Administration of Sher Shah', *Journal of Indian History* 1(1): 126–46.

———. 1972. *Some Aspects of Muslim Administration*, reprint. Allahabad: Central Book Depot.

———. n.d. *Rise and Fall of the Mughal Empire*. Allahabad: Central Book Depot, nd.

Tuft, Frances H. 1994. 'Honour and Alliance: Reconsidering Mughal-Rajput Marriages', in Karine Schomer and Joan L. Erdman, et. al., eds. *The Idea of Rajasthan, Exploration in Regional Identity, Vol.II, Institutions*. Delhi: Manohar, pp. 217–41.

Tuhfat-us-Sa'adat, Shaikh Muhammad Ibn Ziya. British Museum Ms. Add. 7683, OIOC, British Library, London.

Uttar Pradesh District Gazetteers (Post-Independence Series, in progress).

Vaudeville, Charlotte. 1993. *A Weaver Named Kabir—Selected Verses with a Detailed Biographical and Historical Introduction*. Delhi: Oxford University Press.

Waqi'at-i-Mushtaqi, Rizqullah Mushtaqi. British Museum Ms., Or. 1929, OIOC, British Library, London. Ed. & tr.: I.H. Siddiqui. Delhi, 1993.

Weightman, Simon. 1999. 'Symbolism and Symmetry: Shaykh Manjhan's Madhumalati Revisited', in Leonard Lewishon and David Morgan, eds. *The Heritage of Sufism: Late Classical Persianate Sufism (1501–1750)*, Vol. 3. Oxford: Oneworld.

Wensinck, A.J. 1990. 'Mu'djiza', *Encyclopaedia of Islam* (New Edition), Vol. 7. Leiden: E.J. Brill.

Wilson, H.H. 1997. *A Glossary of Judicial and Revenue Terms*, reprint. Delhi: Munshiram Manoharlal.

Wink, Andre. 1997. *Al-Hind: The Making of the Indo-Islamic World, Vol. II, The Slave Kings and the Islamic Conquest, 11th–13th Centuries*. Leiden: Brill.

Wright, H. Nelson. 1974. *The Coinage and Metrology of the Sultans of Delhi*, reprint. Delhi: Oriental Reprint.

Yamamoto, Kumiko. 2003. *The Oral Background of Persian Epics: Storytelling and Poetry*. Leiden and Boston: Brill.

Zakhirat-ul-Khawanin, Farid Bhakkari. 1993. A Biographical dictionary of the Mughal nobles. Eng. tr.: Z.A. Desai. Delhi.

Zaki, M. 1996. *Muslim Society in Northern India During the Fifteenth and First Half of the Sixteenth Centuries*. Calcutta: K.P. Bagchi.

Zeigler, N.P. 1978. 'Some Notes on Rajput Loyalties During the Mughal Period', in J.F. Richards, ed. *Kingship and Authority in South Asia*. University of Wisconsin—Madison, pp. 215–51.

————. 1994. 'Evolution of the Rathor State of Marwar: Horses, Structural Change and Warfare', in Karine Schomer and Joan L.Erdman, et. al., eds. *The Idea of Rajasthan, Exploration in Regional Identity, Vol. II, Institutions.* Delhi: Manohar, pp. 192–216.

Zilli, I.A. 2003. 'Early Chishtis and the State', in Anup Taneja, ed. *Sufi Cults and the Evolution of Medieval Indian Culture,* Delhi: ICHR and Northern Book Centre, pp. 54–108.

Index